The Classic Citroëns, 1935–1975

The Classic Citroëns, 1935–1975

John Reynolds

McFarland & Company, Inc., Publishers
Jefferson, North Carolina, and London

The present work is a reprint of the illustrated case bound edition of The Classic Citroëns, 1935–1975, *first published in 2006 by McFarland.*

The majority of the pictures that illustrate this book are contemporary press photographs originally issued by Automobiles Citroën and obtained from Citroën Communication France, or from the Ludvigsen Library, the Neill Bruce/Peter Roberts Collection, and the Motor Racing Publications Collection. Other material was kindly provided by the Michelin archives at Clermont Ferrand and by the following private collectors and enthusiasts: Malcolm Bobbitt, Stephen Cooper, Antoine Demetz, Stephen Loft-Simson, Wouter Jansen, Olivier de Serres and Ken Smith.

LIBRARY OF CONGRESS CATALOGUING-IN-PUBLICATION DATA

Reynolds, John, 1941 May 31–
The classic Citroëns, 1935–1975 / John Reynolds.
p. cm.
Includes bibliographical references and index.

ISBN 978-0-7864-7171-3
softcover : acid free paper ♾

1. Citroën automobile — History.
2. Automobile industry and trade — France — History.
I. Title.

TL215.C56R49 2012 629.222'2 — dc22 2005024679

BRITISH LIBRARY CATALOGUING DATA ARE AVAILABLE

On the cover: 1973 Citroën DS23 (*Automobiles Citroën*); sky background © 2012 PhotoSpin.

Manufactured in the United States of America

McFarland & Company, Inc., Publishers
Box 611, Jefferson, North Carolina 28640
www.mcfarlandpub.com

Contents

Acknowledgments

Few motoring writers working in the English language have ever attempted to explore the mysterious territory of the Michelin Tire company or to examine the connections between Automobiles Citroën and its erstwhile parent company, the Société Michelin. Fewer still have done so with any success. The great exception was the late Jan P. Norbye, whose small volume *Michelin Magic*, published in 1982, was the first — and perhaps only — book to penetrate the walls of secrecy surrounding the subject and to explain the processes that led to the invention of the revolutionary steel belted radial tire by Michelin, and the effect that this discovery had on the equally revolutionary automobile designs subsequently produced by Citroën.

The author is therefore thankful indeed that before his untimely death in March 2003, Jan Norbye was kind enough to enter into a long correspondence on the subject, and to make available much of his archive of technical and commercial information gathered while writing *Michelin Magic* some twenty years previously. It is doubtful that, without Jan Norbye's generous help and encouragement, this book could ever have been produced.

The author was also fortunate enough to receive considerable support and assistance from John Blunsden of Motor Racing Publications Ltd who presented his collection of Citroën press and publicity photos, obtained during the 1960s and 1970s when the vehicles described in this book were new.

Also, special acknowledgments are due to the following individuals who offered information or illustrations: Leonardo Bertoni, Malcolm Bobbitt, Roger Bradford, Neill Bruce, George Burton, Bernard Citroën, Robert Delpire, Antoine Demetz, Wouter Jansen, Stephen Loft-Simson, Julian Marsh, Yann Martin, Geoffrey Mathews, Rob Moss, Jon Pressnell, Andre de Saint-Sauveur, Oliver de Serres, Ken Smith, Tony Stokoe, and Jacques Wolgensinger.

Finally, grateful thanks are owed to Paul Niblett of Michelin U.K., Stoke on Trent; Didier Derbal of Michelin France; Julian Leyton of Citroën U.K.; plus, as ever, Gro Hoeg, Anne-Marie Michel and Annick Rouaud of Automobiles Citroën, Paris.

Introduction: The Cars That Monsieur Bibendum Built

When the final shortlist for the recent Car of the Century Competition was published, in November 1999, it was revealed that no fewer than three of the final 26 cars—selected by a panel of motoring journalists from the 700 candidates initially proposed by the public—carried the Citroën Double Chevron badge. The trio in question were, of course, the Traction Avant of 1934–1957, the 2CV of 1948–1990 and the DS19 of 1955–1975.

It was a unique achievement. Although a few others among the many automobile constructors nominated for this prestigious international award could claim responsibility for producing more than just one single short-listed car, only Citroën could claim to have designed and built three semi-finalists.

When the final result of the competition was announced on the eve of the Millennium, on December 31, 1999, the DS19 was placed third in the poll, behind the Model T Ford and the Austin/Morris Mini, but ahead of the Volkswagen Beetle. Moreover, in a similar competition held just a few weeks previously, the DS19 had been voted Industrial Product of the Century by a panel of experts drawn from the automotive and industrial design community.

Citroën enthusiasts around the world were elated. It seemed to them that the reputation of the Double Chevron marque had been revived and revitalized at long last. These results recalled the good old days in the 1950s, 1960s and 1970s when, despite the frequent accusations of eccentricity, quirkiness and general unorthodoxy made by conservative critics, Automobiles Citroën was acknowledged universally to be the undisputed leader of the avant-garde.

Throughout this period, the heyday of the DS, 2CV and Traction Avant, the Citroën company was held to be the fountainhead of progressive design and creative engineering, with an unrivalled reputation for individuality and imagination. By consistently producing innovative products that set new standards of technical excellence, almost regardless of effort and expense, it had achieved a position of pre-eminence and prestige not just within the international automotive community but also among the general motoring public. Yet despite all the rejoicing at the Car of the Century results, few people paused to enquire exactly how and why this remarkable situation had ever come about, and many questions went unanswered.

Why, for example, were all three of these classic Citroëns launched within a comparatively short space of time—a mere 20 years? Why were all of them not only radically different from the rival, conventional cars of their time, but also widely different from each other in their design and construction? Why were all three created by the same pair of individuals, the engineer André Lefèbvre and the stylist Flaminio Bertoni? Why did neither member of this hugely influential team become well known during his lifetime? Why are they still comparatively unknown and unrecognized today, to the extent that neither of them was ranked among the top fifty names listed in yet another millennium poll, "The Hundred Most Influential Persons ... in the European Automobile Industry," published by *Automotive News Europe* in September 1999? And, lastly, what about the role played by Citroën's owners and masters during the hey-days of these three great cars, the Michelin tire company? Did the Michelin men stand back complacently and allow Citroën its head, managing their subsidiary remotely from their base at Clermont-Ferrand and acting as uncommitted and

The unique and incomparable DS19, introduced in 1955, was the offspring of a remarkable parentage. It was conceived, born and nurtured to maturity during the 40-year marriage of France's two foremost automobile engineering companies of that era, Citroën and Michelin.

disinterested observers, as has often been suggested? Or, on the contrary, were they actively involved in encouraging, directing and financing Citroën's creativity, which paralleled their own achievements in a different sphere of automobile design and manufacture?

This book attempts to answer these questions, and to pose a few more. But before commencing these inquiries, it is essential to remember and restate an obvious but frequently overlooked fact: the corporate history of the Citroën company (which is now approaching its centenary year) has never consisted of an unbroken thread of events or an uninterrupted line of progress. On the contrary, having passed through the hands of three quite different owners in the space of 97 years, its lifespan can be divided into four distinct phases, each with a special individual character or culture, representing a coalescence of different products, methods, attitudes, aims and business philosophies.

The first of these epochs, lasting from its foundation by André Citroën in 1905 until 1924, does not really count, for it was only during the last five of these 14 years, from 1919 onwards, that the company became involved in the manufacture of automobiles. Previously, when registered as the specialist engineering business André Citroën et Cie, a private company, and its offshoot the Société des Engrenages Citroën, its activities were concerned solely with the manufacture of gear-wheels and, during World War I, of munitions.

The second phase dates from the formation of the Société Anonyme André Citroën, a publicly-quoted joint-stock company, on July 28, 1924, until the SAAC entered a period of judicial administration in December 1934. This, of course, was the brief but amazingly productive 10-year period when the company assembled automobiles under the unfettered ownership and control of its charismatic founder, André Citroën.

Although when it commenced car production in 1919, the Citroën firm lay 20 years behind its greatest rivals, the old-established French marques Peugeot and Renault, by 1929 André Citroën's flair, energy and enterprise had propelled it into first position, as the largest automobile manufacturer outside the USA and the fourth largest in the world. His factory at the Quai de Javel in Paris was the first in Europe to employ a moving production line and other American sequential-assembly methods; and in pioneering the mass-production, mass-marketing and mass-ownership of the automobile, André Citroën brought about a technological and sociological revolution simultaneously, altering forever the urban and rural landscape of the continent. Indeed, the history of the Citroën company — more so than any other European industrial organization — is also the history of the twentieth century, simply because the creativity he inspired and fostered spilled over from automobile engineering to encompass many other spheres of popular culture, including advertising, graphic art, photography, cinema, architecture and even geographical exploration.

The third epoch, which lasted from 1935 until 1976, was the 42-year-long period when the Michelin tire firm reigned supreme at the Quai de Javel, having acquired control of the Société Anonyme André Citroën on January 15,

André Lefèbvre (1894–1964), the unsung genius of automobile design who created four of the most revolutionary vehicles ever put into large-scale series production. The protégé of both Gabriel Voisin and André Citroën, he was numbered among the leading champions of front-wheel-drive. During his career at Citroën between 1933 and 1958 he was primarily responsible for the Traction Avant, the 2CV, the Type H van and the DS19. However, his influence extended well beyond his death until the late 1970s, so that the GS and CX were also designed in accordance with his ideas.

André Citroën (1878–1935), the founder of the Double Chevron marque and the builder of its Quai de Javel factory in Paris. His career as an industrialist began with the manufacture of precision gearwheels and, later, during World War I, munitions. He did not start making cars until 1919.

The Citroën factory at the Quai de Javel in Paris, on the left bank of the Seine not far from the Eiffel Tower, as it appeared circa 1936. Established by André Citroën in 1915 and reconstructed in 1933, it finally ceased production in 1974 and was later demolished. Exactly 3,227,105 vehicles had been built there, from the Type A to the DS23. Today it is the site of the Parc André Citroën.

1935. After rescuing the Traction Avant and restoring Citroën to financial viability, the new Michelin management embarked on a further period of invention and innovation, in synergy with its own research activities, which ultimately produced the Michelin steel-belted radial-ply tire, a truly revolutionary advance in transport technology. Indeed, a count of the major milestones of popular motoring since 1920 shows that many of the most significant steps forward were marked by the presence of either the Citroën Double Chevron badge or by the rotund pneumatic figure of the Michelin Man, Monsieur Bibendum.

By 1960, after enjoying a period of spectacular regrowth throughout the 1950s, Citroën had overcome the problems caused by the economic depression of the 1930s and the depredations of World War II and was once again the leading automobile manufacturer in France. In 1968, the entire firm was reorganized and its vehicle manufacturing operations were devolved into a subsidiary company, the Société Anonyme Automobiles Citroën, controlled by a parent holding company known as Citroën SA.

The fourth and present epoch has lasted from 1976 until the present day, a period during which Automobiles Citroën has operated as a subsidiary of the PSA Group, owned and controlled by its former rival Automobiles Peugeot. In theory it remains an autonomous, independent partner in the Group with its own identity and image, but, in practice, pooled design resources and common manufacturing and administrative facilities mean otherwise. Engines, transmissions, major body platforms and much other componentry are shared. So with the single exception of the hydro-pneumatic suspension system which remains a unique Citroën feature (though currently

Robert Puiseux (1892–1991), the industrialist of vision who led Citroën and Michelin simultaneously, from 1950 to 1958. It was he who gave the go-ahead for the manufacture of the Citroën DS19 and the Michelin X radial tire, generally acknowledged to be two of the most significant advances in the history of the automobile.

fitted to the C5 model only), the Citroën cars of today can no longer claim any appreciable technical advantages or qualitative superiority over their Peugeot counterparts. Such differences as exist are entirely superficial, reflecting image and external appearance only. In other words, Citroën's status has been demoted from an independent thoroughbred marque into a brand-name that provides an alternative means of marketing the hybrid products originated by the PSA Group's facilities and technologies.

From these dates it can easily be calculated that the dominant chapters in the Citroën story were written during the four decades when the Michelin family had custody of its destiny. Its tenure lasted nearly twice as long as that of the current owners, Peugeot, and more than three times that of André Citroën, himself. Indeed it was under the Michelin regime that the company produced not merely the Traction Avant, the 2CV and the DS/ID series, but also all the other cult cars so highly regarded today, including the Type H panel van, the Citroën-Maserati SM and, lastly, the GS/GSA and CX ranges.

Yet throughout this period, the official message consistently handed out to the press by Citroën's public relations staff was that the company's owners were merely creditors whose sole interest was to safeguard their investment. As a tire-maker first and foremost, Michelin was not really concerned with the intimate details of motor car production; on the contrary, it was merely acting as the reluctant custodian of the proud heritage of France's largest and foremost automobile maker, keeping it alive until another more suitable owner could come along to take the responsibility off its hands.

In fact, this denial was merely a smokescreen concealing a profound involvement in automobile design and manufacturing, an enthusiasm which, in reality, acted as an accelerator on the pace of change in the industry rather than a brake. Far from remaining indifferent to, or critical of, Citroën's idiosyncratic and extravagant inventiveness, its new owners or god-fathers actively endorsed and encouraged this creativity.

As we shall see, the classic Citroëns examined in this book could never have been designed and constructed without the unstinting technological and financial contribution made by the Michelin men, who had a motive for ensuring the continued survival of their ward or chargeling that went much further than merely the financial interest natural to any parent or guardian company. In truth, these vehicles could surely be called the cars that Monsieur Bibendum built!

1
André Citroën

On the 4th of June, 1919, the very first Citroën. car, No. 00001, a Type A torpedo or open-bodied tourer, was delivered to its proud owner, a certain Monsieur Testemolle of Beaulieu sur Dordogne. Just 15 years later, on the 21st of December, 1934, the Commercial Court of Paris declared the insolvency of the Citroën company, placing it in a state of judicial administration, and committing its affairs to the custody of its largest creditor, the Michelin tire company. Less than 200 days later, its founder, André Citroën, was dead, a ruined man.

The events that unfolded at such a rapid — some said reckless— pace throughout the 180 months that separated these two events amounted to one of the most exciting and significant chapters in the history of the motor car. A story of contrasting achievement and failure on the grandest possible scale, it reads today like an adventure novel and shows without doubt that André Citroën was truly one of the founders of the modern world. No man did more to mobilize and motorize the population of France, or, indeed, to advance the development of the automobile industry in Europe as a whole.

But although he was often called the Henry Ford of France, André Citroën was much more than a motor-magnate. In creating his Double Chevron marque, he pioneered not only the manufacturing technology that made the mass-produced popular car a reality in France, England, Italy, Germany and the rest of Europe following the Great War, but he also created the mass-marketing culture of car buying and ownership that has surrounded this ultimate consumer product ever since. In doing so, his mastery of salesmanship and publicity made him an international celebrity, renowned for his flamboyant behavior and free-spending lifestyle, which consistently caused headline news around the world throughout the 1920s and early 1930s.

Although the automobile and the internal combustion engine were not actually invented in France, it was certainly the French who first discovered popular motoring as we know it today. Unlike their Anglo-Saxon neighbors, the people of France embraced the promise of the horseless carriage with enthusiasm from the very start. By 1900, they were already turning out more examples of this new contraption than the Americans, Germans and British put together, and Paris was well established as the capital of the automotive world. After the First World War this early interest was redoubled, and in 1919 France was still the second largest car market in the world after the USA. Consequently, it fell to the infant French motor industry to pioneer not just the technical configuration of the popular European automobile but also many of the techniques employed in its mass production and marketing. By 1924, three great volume-production automobile companies had been established in France — Peugeot, Renault and Citroën — of which the Société Anonyme André Citroën ranked as the youngest, though by no means the most junior.

In fact, the Citroën company was already in existence well before the 1914–1918 war, having been founded by André Citroën in 1905, not as a car-making concern but as an engineering business, specializing in the making of gearwheels. Yet even though his famous Double Chevron badge did not appear on the radiator cowling of a motor car until 1919, he can justly be numbered among those early pioneers who devised and established the technical configuration of the cars we drive today.

André Gustave Citroën was born on February 5, 1878, at 44 rue Lafitte in the 9th arrondissement of Paris, the youngest child of Levie Citroën, a Dutch-Jewish diamond merchant from Amsterdam who, with his Polish-Jewish wife, had settled in France, adopted French nationality and established his family as wealthy and much respected members of the Parisian jewelry and goldsmith community. The Citroën family could trace their Dutch origins back at least a hundred years to Napoleonic times, when an ancestor, who worked as a costermonger selling fruit from a barrow in the streets of Amsterdam, adopted the patronymic Limoenman or Lemon Man. Long after the migration of the family to France, this name eventually mutated into its Gallic form, Citroën, citron being the French word for lemon.

Unfortunately, in 1884, when André was only six, his father committed suicide having lost his fortune after speculating unwisely in a South African diamond mining venture, leaving the five Citroën children to be raised and tutored by their mother and supported by their grandfather. At the age of seven he was enrolled at the fashionable Lycée Condorcet in Paris, moving later to the Lycée Louis le Grand where he excelled in his academic studies; for his Baccalaureate exams he achieved the highest marks of any candidate in France for that academic year. Eventually, in 1898, at the age of 20, he entered the celebrated École Polytechnique in Paris, the technical and engineering academy of the French Military and Civil Services, which since its foundation in 1794 has provided the French army with its engineering and gunnery officers. By virtue of its rigorous academic standards (its curriculum is devoted principally to the study of advanced mathematics) "l'X" remains a *corps d'elite*, the springboard for ambitious high-flyers seeking a career path that would take them straight to the commanding heights of French public life. Today, Polytechniciens continue to dominate France's industrial, commercial and political affairs; the current Chairman of the Peugeot-Citroën group, Jean-Martin Folz, is among their number.

Graduating two years later, in 1900, André Citroën was commissioned as a lieutenant and posted to the 2nd Regiment of Heavy Artillery stationed at le Mans, to begin the two-year period of national service that until recently was obligatory for all young Frenchmen. That same year, while on leave from his unit, he made a trip to Poland to visit his sister Jeanne who had married a Polish-Jewish banker living in Warsaw. During this visit, he was introduced to a distant relation who managed a foundry near Lodsz that specialized in casting gearwheels and other mechanical components using the traditional sand-box method — that is to say, with molds that contained, pressed in sand, the impressions left by patterns that had previously been carved in wood. Here he noticed a set of reduction gears of a most unusual design; instead of having simple straight cross-cut teeth, these had a complicated arrangement of V-shaped teeth, shaped like corporal stripes, set around the circumference of both wheels, which were beveled so that they meshed together with precision at a right angle. In theory, this made them ideally suited for transmitting heavy power loads through 90 degrees while at the same time increasing or decreasing the turning speed of the output shaft.

As Citroën recognized immediately, these double helical gears were much more efficient than conventional straight-cut gears and therefore capable of withstanding far greater loads. Silent running, they generated no axial thrust, which meant that more power could be transmitted through them with minimal loss of efficiency due to friction. However, in practice, it had so far proved impossible to realize the advantages promised by this design. As his Polish hosts explained, the difficulty lay in producing the gearwheels to the very high standard of dimensional accuracy essential to ensure a perfect mesh. This precision could simply not be achieved by their normal process of casting and fettling; the only answer was to cut the teeth from a solid blank of high-quality cast or forged steel by removing the metal from the grooves, a machining operation that currently was well beyond the capabilities and skills, not just of this small Polish factory, but also of most of the major mechanical engineering companies in Europe. In fact, the very high degree of precision required had eluded every other engineering company that had attempted the task. Without the very high manufacturing tolerances upon which accurate engagement between wheel and bevel depended, all advantages over conventional gears were lost. When simply cast or molded, helical gears could never achieve this essential accuracy of interplay. Only if they were machined from high-quality cast or forged steel could the necessary precision and durability be achieved.

But Citroën was not discouraged. As an engineering student he was already well aware of the exciting new developments in metallurgy and machine-tool design that were then taking place in the USA and which were already transforming the capacity of heavy industry to produce complex high-precision metal components for industrial machinery and military equipment. This new metalworking technology from America would solve the problem and provide him with a highly profitable business, he anticipated. So with characteristic speed and decisiveness, he purchased the patents and licensing rights on the spot, with finance provided by his brother-in-law, Bronislaus Goldfeder.

Opposite: **The very first Citroën, no. 00001, a Type A torpedo or open tourer, photographed in front of the Quai de Javel factory in 1933 with its owner, Monsieur Testemolle of Beaulieu-sur-Dordogne, who had purchased it in 1919. Fourteen years and 300,000 kilometers later, the car was repurchased and restored, to be exhibited in the company's showrooms at the Place d'Europe in Paris.**

Two years later, his military service completed, André Citroën, now age 24, began his career as an *ingeneur-constructeur* by opening a small engineering business located in the rue Saint-Denis near the Gare du Nord in Paris, in partnership with two friends from his school days at the Lycée Condorcet, André Boas and Jacques Hinstin, with the express intention of perfecting a technique for manufacturing these double helical gears. Fortunately for Citroën, his mastery of gear-cutting technology was well timed, as it coincided with the almost universal adoption of electric motors as the preferred power-source throughout industry and commerce. All over Europe and the USA, the traditional motive-power method, in which a factory's machines were collectively propelled by a system of belts and chains coupled to one large central stationary steam or gas engine, gave way to the concept of individual power sources, supplied by electricity. But for this to take place, the existence of highly-efficient, quiet-running gear-systems was also required, so as to reduce the high rotational speed of electric motors to fit the requirements of industrial machinery.

Undoubtedly, Citroën rode to fame and fortune on the back of this revolution; his first recorded patent application covering an innovation of his own devising, taken out in Paris in October 1910, was for a speed-reduction gearbox. But although it represented the state-of-the-art in motive power technology at the turn of the century, unlike his later manufacturing activities, this gear-cutting business always remained a small-scale, highly specialized enterprise. The precision machining of these large, complex gears was a slow and expensive process and there was no mass-production for stock. Normally each item was custom-built to order, to fit a specific machine or purpose, and therefore the greater part of Citroën's work involved finding potential customers and persuading them of the advantages of his products, a task that called on his talents as a publicist and marketing man. Moreover, since his two partners in the venture had other interests and employment, at first he was obliged to do almost everything himself, acting as chief engineer, production manager, office manager and sales manager, visiting customers to demonstrate his wares.

The business prospered. By 1905 it had been consolidated as a registered private company, trading as Citroën, Hinstin et Compagnie. By 1907 sales offices had been opened in Moscow, Brussels and London, and by 1910 it had expanded sufficiently for its activities to have been moved to bigger and better premises located at the Quai de Grenelle, a new industrial development area on the left bank of the Seine. Eventually, in 1913, it was incorporated as a limited liability public company, the Société des Engrenages Citroën, the directors and principal shareholders being André Citroën, his brother Hugues Citroën, André Boas and Jacques Schwob de Hericourt, a friend of Jacques Hinstin. Hinstin was by then fully occupied elsewhere, running the Sizaire and Naudin car firm. Indeed, the successor of the Société des Engrenages Citroën still exists today as a subsidiary of the Peugeot-Citroën industrial group, specializing in the manufacture of large industrial gearwheels weighing as much as 180 tons. This long tradition of gear-making is celebrated symbolically in the famous Citroën Double Chevron company logo and trademark. Devised by André Citroën himself, this badge is derived directly from the V-shaped pattern of his double helical gears.

Clearly, right from the start, the engineering challenge that really interested André Citroën was solving the technical problems of large-scale industrial production. Rather than inventing new products or processes himself, his life's work was to be concerned with devising ever more brilliant ways of manufacturing and marketing the ideas spawned by the many other gifted engineers he employed and supported. From the start also, André Citroën's skills and expertise were based not in the field of light industry such as bicycle-making or agricultural engineering (as was the case with the majority of pioneer motor manufacturers) but in the far more substantial terrain of heavy engineering, a fact that was to be of great importance when the time came to start making cars. First, it gave him the resources to begin manufacturing on a grand scale, so that the output of Citroën vehicles quickly overtook that of his already well-established rivals, propelling him to first place in the league of French car manufacturers within a relatively short time. Second, and more significantly, his skills also gave him a great measure of technological independence. Thus, when he eventually decided to abandon the manufacture of conventionally engineered motor cars in favor of a series of radically innovative and advanced new products, his company was able to realize these ambitions largely from within its own technical resources, without being held back by limitations posed by a lack of skill and imagination on the part of outside suppliers, a factor which so often led to the failure of less self-sufficient would-be innovators in the automotive world. Finding the financial resources to mount such a revolution was to be another problem altogether!

As we have already noted, Citroën preferred to style himself as an *ingeneur-constructeur* (engineer-manufacturer) in acknowledgement of the fact that he was more a specialist in manufacturing technology and organization than an automobile engineer and designer per se. Just like Henry Ford, he was a disciple of that guru of modern industrial methodology, the American metallurgist Frederick Winslow Taylor of the Bethlehem Steel Works in Pennsylvania, whose experimental fast-cutting lathe, equipped with chrome tungsten tools that could rapidly cut through case-hardened steel, he had first seen demonstrated at an industrial trade fair held in Paris in 1900. Indeed it was this technology that had made the machining of his helical gears a possibility. As the father of time and motion studies, Taylor had set out in his book *Shop Management*, first published in 1903, the principles and philosophy governing the scientific organization of work, the division of labor and the adoption of sequential assembly methods. This was followed in 1911 by the hugely influential manual *Principles of Scientific Management*, the bible of Taylorism.

André Citroën's first personal involvement in the making and marketing of cars occurred as early as 1908, when he was appointed as a technical and management consultant to the old, established Mors company, with which he had family connections. The Mors firm was then experiencing severe difficulties, due in part to the defection its chief designer, Henri Brasier. By advising on the complete reorganization of all aspects of its business, including the improvement of its products, the modernization of its machinery and the provision of fresh working capital, Citroën was able to transform the company's affairs. Within five years, sales and production had increased ten-fold, from 120 cars a year to 1200.

In 1912, in connection with his work for the Mors company, Citroën made his first visit to the United States, a trip that was to have a profound impact on his thinking. Here, at the Ford factory in Detroit, he saw the advanced machine tools and moving production-line assembly methods that Henry Ford had developed in order to increase output and bring down the prices of his cars, by adopting the principles of Taylorism. Impressed by the energy and enterprise of Ford's operations, Citroën realized immediately that if, like their American counterparts, European motorists of all classes and incomes were also to enjoy, in the future, the personal freedom and social mobility already provided by automobile ownership in the USA, there was no alternative but to carry these techniques of mass-production back to France. Only the liberty of movement afforded by the car could bring true social democracy and economic progress to Europe, André Citroën avowed. And so by revolutionizing the means of motor-car production, he aimed to bring about a technological and sociological revolution simultaneously. "L'auto n'est pas un instrument de luxe, mais essentiellement un instrument de travail," he said later, in 1933, pointing out that the car was no longer a luxury item, the exclusive plaything of the rich, but had become an indispensable tool of economic activity, essential for carrying the nation's goods and raw materials, transporting its citizens and providing recreation for its entire population.

On the outbreak of the First World War in 1914, as a captain in the reserves, Citroën was recalled to military service with his former regiment which, in common with other artillery units in the French Army, was experiencing a severe shortage of ammunition. Realizing that his personal contribution to the war effort would be far better directed at manufacturing shells than firing them at the enemy, he quickly drew up far-reaching proposals for mass-production of ammunition, which were accepted with alacrity by the military authorities. With the active backing of the Armaments Ministry, and in partnership with the key associates and investors in his gear-cutting business, he then acquired 30 acres of market gardens at the Quai de Javel in Paris, adjacent to the Quai de Grenelle premises, and there he quickly established a vast ordnance factory capable of producing 55,000 shells per day. Employing more than 12,000 workers and utilizing the latest machinery from the United States, this factory was the harbinger of things to come. By the end of the war, more than 28 million shrapnel shells had been manufactured there, all of them produced specifically for the 75mm breech-loading field gun which was the pride of the French artillery. Thanks to its sophisticated hydraulically operated recoil mechanism, the first of its kind, this weapon did not require relaying after every shot and could therefore keep up an unprecedented rate of highly accurate fire; more than 12 shells per minute could be shot by a well-drilled gun crew.

But with the ending of hostilities in 1918, demand for the products of Citroën's munitions factory ceased as abruptly as it had begun. Clearly, with so many jobs at risk and so great an investment in the balance, there could be no return to vegetable growing at the Quai de Javel. With characteristic determination, Citroën made a swift decision; the plant would be converted to an automobile factory and he would enter the motor car business as soon as possible. Moreover, he would do so not, as his advisors recommended, as a specialist constructor of elaborately engineered luxury cars intended mainly for the amusement of the aristocracy and plutocracy, but as the mass-producer of simple, robust and practical light cars, inexpensively priced to suit the purposes and pockets of the bourgeoisie.

In May 1919 the first Citroën car — the 1327cc 10hp Type A, designed by Jules Salomon — rolled off the assembly line that he had installed at the Quai de Javel. Priced at 11,000 francs, it was not only much cheaper than anything offered by Citroën's competitors, but it also offered far better value for the money. Because the Type A was the first European car to be built using American mass production techniques, it came to its buyer ready for the road. Unlike most other cars available at the time, normally supplied as a rolling chassis plus engine for completion by

Launched in the spring of 1919, initially in torpedo or open tourer form, the 10HP Type A was the first mass-produced European car. Unlike any other Continental or British car of its time, it came ready for the road, fully equipped with not only a body and wheels plus tires but also electric headlights and a self-starter. Eventually it was made available in a wide variety of body styles all sharing the same chasis, engine and transission.

a specialist coachbuilder, it left the factory fully finished and fitted out. There was nothing else to buy; the car came complete with bodywork, hood, wheels, tires, electric lights, horn, tools and even a self-starter as standard equipment. Within a fortnight of the first appearance of the advertisements announcing its arrival, created and placed in the press by Citroën personally, more than 16,000 advance orders were taken for the car!

At first, 30 vehicles left the factory daily, but by the end of 1920 this output had risen to 100 cars a day. In 1921 the Type A was replaced by the Type B2 equipped with a 1452cc engine, while in 1922 came the little 5hp Type C2, popularly known as the *petite citron* because of its customary yellow paintwork. The two new models were as well received by the public as the first, so that by 1924 Citroën output of all types had reached 250 cars a day, an astonishing rate of production for the time.

Sustaining this rate of production called for more than organizational genius, of course. And so, to expand the market for his products, André Citroën brought another of his remarkable talents to bear — his flair for marketing, publicity and promotion. A network of franchised dealerships was established throughout France, Western Europe and North Africa, the first example of this now universal method of selling cars; Citroën finance and insurance schemes were introduced, making it possible for customers to buy their cars on payments for the first time in Europe; full-page advertising campaigns were mounted; a fleet of brand-new Citroën taxis was set up in Paris; Citroën road signs were erected at every crossroads in France; endurance trials and record-breaking marathon runs were staged; all manner of novel marketing initiatives were employed to establish the Citroën marque and foster brand loyalty. Later, André Citroën was to have the

Opposite top: **At the end of World War I André Citroën converted his munitions factory at the Quai de Javel into a car assembly plant, the first in Europe to employ a moving production line. Each vehicle was put together sequentially using identical, interchangeable components, following the system pioneered by Henry Ford in the USA.** ***Opposite bottom:*** **André Citroën shows off his first product, the Type A, to his wife and family. Note that his wife is in the driver's seat. Strangely, for a man who was such an enthusiastic champion and promoter of the automobile, he was a reluctant driver and relied on a chauffeur.**

ultimate bright advertising idea. For 10 years, between 1924 and 1934, every night his name was flashed before the public in letters 100 feet high, by 250,000 electric light bulbs wired to the Eiffel Tower—a spectacle visible for 60 miles in all directions.

In 1920 Citroën acquired the sole rights to a novel lightweight caterpillar track system, designed to replace the rear wheels of a car with an endless flexible rubber band rather than the heavy hinged plates of a crawler tractor. To exploit this device he formed a special company, the Société Citroën-Kegresse-Hinstin, to provide its inventor, Adolphe Kegresse, with the finances and facilities required to manufacture and market a range of Autochenilles or caterpillar tracked vehicles, built at a factory located at Levallois on the northern outskirts of Paris. Employing the engine and chassis of Citroën's B2 car, these caterpillar cars or light tractors proved an immediate success, thanks to the famous series of endurance expeditions that the master publicist staged to demonstrate their remarkable cross-country abilities. The first of these expeditions, led by André Citroën's associates Georges-Marie Haardt and Louis Audouin-Dubreuil, took place in the winter of 1922-1923. Accomplished in 22 days, this 2,000-mile journey, from Algiers to Timbuktu by a convoy of five Citroën-Kegresse half-tracked vehicles, was the first complete crossing of the Sahara Desert by motor vehicle.

A master of marketing and publicity as well as of manufacturing, André Citroën pioneered many of the techniques still commonly used to sell cars today, including the extensive use of press and poster advertising.

This *Raid Sahara* attracted so much favorable newsreel and newspaper coverage that Citroën immediately decided to embark upon an even more remarkable trail-blazing adventure—a full-scale 12,500-mile Trans-African crossing from Algiers to Mombassa (and then on by sea to Madagascar) by way of the Sahara, Niger and the Sudan, again by a convoy of P2 half-tracks. Undertaken in 18 months, between October 1922 and March 1924, this expedition, known as the *Croisiere Noire*, was a journey of research and exploration over unpaved paths and tracks, traversing deserts, savannahs, swamps and tropical rain forests and venturing into uncharted territory; yet all 8 vehicles and 16 crew (which included a zoologist, a geologist an artist and a cinematographer

Opposite top: **In 1921, the Type A was replaced by the B2, equipped with a more powerful 1452cc engine. By now, output of the Quai de Javel factory was exceeding 100 cars a day, so that there were already more than 13,000 Citroëns on the roads of France.** ***Opposite bottom:*** **The car that made André Citroën's reputation was the 5HP Type C2, originally introduced in 1922 in a boat-tailed two-seater form, but later, in 1924 as the three seater Type C3, known as the Trefle or Cloverleaf, seen here. Costing less than half the price of most other popular cars of the 1920s, a total of over 80,000 examples of the 5CV were sold. Despite a huge demand, production was discontinued in 1926 when Citroën realized that he could build bigger and better cars, in greater numbers, for the same cost and thus make larger profits.**

For ten years, between 1924 and 1934, the sides of the Eiffel Tower were illuminated every night by the word Citroën, spelled out in giant radiant letters by 250,000 light-bulbs, visible for sixty miles. When the American aviator Charles Lindbergh arrived in France after making the first non-stop solo crossing of the Atlantic by air, in May 1926, these spectacular illuminations acted as a beacon to guide him to a safe landing in Paris.

as well as 10 driver/mechanics) came through unscathed. During the journey, the expedition shot about 90,000 feet of film and 8,000 photographs, produced more than 300 botanical drawings and 15 books of sketches, and collected samples of more than 300 mammals, 800 birds and 1,500 insects, some of which were unknown to science at that time.

Later, during 1931 and 1932, a second *Raid* took place—the Citroën Trans-Asiatic expedition or *Croisiere Jaune,* led once more by the redoubtable Haardt and Audouin-Dubreuil. A genuine scientific, geographical and archaeological expedition sponsored by the French and British governments and also the National Geographic Society of the USA, this mission covered the 8,000 miles from Beirut to Peking in less than nine months, traversing the Himalayas and the Ghobi Desert, a journey so difficult and dangerous that it has never been attempted again.

The spring of 1925 saw the introduction of the B10 model, which brought a further important technical innovation from the Quai de Javel—the first use in Europe of closed, pressed-steel bodies spray-painted with synthetic lacquer, a technology licensed from the Budd Manufacturing Company of Philadelphia, USA, and the outcome of André Citroën's second visit to America, made early in 1924. The Budd firm, founded by Edward Gowan Budd in 1912, had already become the leading manufacturer of all-steel automobile bodies, supplying Willys Overland, Dodge and the Buick division of General Motors amongst other U.S. clients. Budd also pioneered the adoption of all-steel railway carriages and railcars and was later responsible for designing and constructing the first diesel-powered all-stainless-steel trains which appeared on U.S. tracks in the mid 1930s, most notably the Zephyr, the Silver Meteor and the Super Chief.

The career of the B10 was short-lived, however, for at the Paris motor show later that year it was replaced by the B12 which featured a strengthened chassis and improved suspension arrangements. At the following year's show, the B12 (which had used the 1452cc engine of the old B2) was in turn replaced by the B14, an entirely new and improved all-steel bodied vehicle which had a larger

In the spring of 1925 André Citroën introduced the B10 model which represented the first use in Europe of all-steel closed sedan bodywork, produced under license from the U.S. Budd company.

Top: At the October 1925 Paris motor show, however, the B10 was superseded by the B12. Although it closely resembled its predecessor in external details, the B12 featured an improved chassis and suspension. ***Bottom:*** For the following season, the B12 was replaced by the B14, powered by a new 1538 cc engine.

In 1926, André Citroën opened the first of his overseas factories, at Slough on the outskirts of London, to produce right-hand-drive vehicles for the British market. Here he is seen at the inauguration of the Slough Works, in February that year.

1538cc engine and also drum brakes on all four wheels, another Citroën innovation. Yet despite its continuing popularity, in September 1926 the little 5CV (by then in its ultimate C3 Cloverleaf three-seater form) was deleted from the range, as Citroën decided that its continued construction was uneconomical because the car was technically outdated. By switching to all-steel bodies throughout his range, he could build bigger, better, stronger cars for the same cost and, by selling them at deservedly higher prices, make bigger profits. Later, he claimed that his adoption of Budd methods had permitted an increase in production from around 30 to 50 cars a day to between 400 and 500.

Thanks to the positive reception given to the B14 and its successors, the B14F of 1927 and B14G of 1927/8, Citroën's wealth and confidence grew in equal measure. The next leap forward, he decided, would be to replace his existing products entirely, and at the October 1928 Paris Salon he introduced two new models, the four-cylinder AC4 and the six-cylinder AC6, each available in up to 16 different standard body styles, plus seven utility versions of the AC4 and four of the AC6. The new cars created a sensation. Together, they marked the seventh change in the line begun less than a decade earlier, and both were part of a move upmarket, offering greater technical refinement and a higher degree of performance and comfort than their predecessors. The AC4—which duly became the first European car to exceed 200,000 units—was derived directly from the earlier B14, but featured an all-new, high-revving 1628cc engine designed by Arthur-Leon Michelat, the former chief engineer of Delage; while the 2442 cc AC6—Citroën's first six-cylinder engined car—was entirely new in every respect. Completely American in style and concept, this long, spacious, opulent and stylish vehicle lay somewhere between a popular mass-produced model and a coach-built lux-

At the October 1928 Paris Salon, André Citroën introduced two new models, both offering greater technical refinement and higher standards of comfort. They were the four-cylinder AC4 and the six-cylinder AC6 (the first six from Citroën), each available in up to 16 different standard body styles, plus seven utility versions of the AC4 and four of the AC6. The AC4 sedan, seen here, was an immediate best-seller and soon became the first European car to exceed 200,000 units.

ury car, and consequently it offered the middle-class customer extraordinary value for the money. As ever, Citroën's aim was to consolidate his position as an international supplier of robust, reliable, well-engineered cars and utility vehicles, conventionally designed in the Ford and Chrysler manner, and to give his European customers cars that were the equal of anything that could be bought in the USA. The success of the AC4 and AC6 only served to reinforce his reputation as the Henry Ford of France.

By the end of the decade, just ten years after starting up his automobile business, André Citroën had achieved his initial objectives with spectacular success. With annual production now topping 100,000 vehicles, and with almost half a million Citroën cars and vans having been made and sold, his company had by now overtaken all its older, established rivals to become the largest and most successful motor manufacturer in Europe—indeed, the fourth largest car manufacturer in the world, topped only by the American giants, Ford, Chrysler and General Motors. Employing 30,000 workers and capable of turning out 400 cars and light commercial vehicles every day, the Citroën company had created a service and distribution network of 5,000 agents in France, plus ten subsidiary sales companies and four independent factories abroad.

In the autumn of 1931, when at the height of his fame and fortune, Citroën made another trip to the United States (his third and last) to fulfill a number of engagements, including attending the Congress of American Major Industries held at Columbia University in New York, on October 21, at which he delivered an important address before a large audience of U.S. industrialists, including such leading figures as Walter Chrysler. Henry Ford was not present on this occasion, but a few days later Citroën journeyed to Detroit to meet him, on the 24th and 25th of October. Here, at Ford's great Rouge plant,

In the autumn of 1931, André Citroën (aka the Henry Ford of France) made his third and final visit to the USA, where he addressed the Eighth Congress of American Heavy Industries at Columbia University, New York. Next he traveled to Dearborn, Michigan, to meet Henry Ford and tour the River Rouge plant, where this historic photograph of, perhaps, the two most important and influential men in the history of the mass-produced automobile was taken.

in a ceremonial display of friendship and accord, the two motor-magnates exchanged not only ritual handshakes but examples of their latest products. André presented Henry with a splendid C6 G sedan — looking as American as any U.S.–made car — and received a Model A open tourer in return. Altogether over the two-day visit, Citroën spent six hours alone with Ford, touring the factory and inspecting the innermost secrets of the Dearborn design offices and research laboratories including, most probably, the new V-8 engine that Ford was about to reveal to the world only five months later, at the end of March of the following year. Doubtless, the pair also toured the Greenfield Museum and Model Village that Ford had created a couple of miles from his factory two years previously, in association with his mentor Thomas Edison. Opened by President Hoover in 1929, this, the world's first theme park, was already regarded as a national monument, a permanent recreation of the rural, craft-based way-of-life of eighteenth and nineteenth century America that Ford's industrial and transport revolution was already sweeping away forever.

The historic official pictures of them shaking hands showed the contrast between these two tycoons, the greatest industrial personalities of their era; on one hand, the short, rotund, genial Frenchman, bald and bespectacled; and, on the other, the somberly-dressed, silver-haired American patriarch, tall, gaunt and austere. Just like Ford, Citroën lived solely for his business. His principal interest lay in constantly improving and enlarging his factories, but there the similarities ended. The forefather of the twentieth century, but somehow not quite a member of it, Henry Ford was a curiously erratic and capricious character for so successful an industrialist and businessman. An enigmatic personality, full of contradictions and given to unpredictable swings of enthusiasm, he ruled his empire with intrigue and intimidation rather than by intellect. As a homespun, rocking-chair philosopher and philanthropist, he believed in pacifism, teetotalism and re-incarnation. For his own recreation, Ford enjoyed nothing more than to make expeditions into the forests with friends such as Thomas Edison, Harvey Firestone and the naturalist John Burroughs, sleeping out in a fleet of elaborately equipped, chauffeur-driven camping cars. In this rural idyll these "vagabonds" would whittle hickory walking sticks, chop logs, do a little bird-watching, sing folk songs around a campfire like boy scouts, and join with local farmers in old-time country dancing. It is impossible to imagine a lifestyle less like that of the sophisticated, cosmopolitan André Citroën, whose customary haunts were casinos, race-courses and five-star hotels, and whose only interest in ornithology was observing feathers adorning the high-kicking showgirls at the Folies-Bergere.

Unlike Henry Ford and his own great French rival, Louis Renault, André Citroën was not the conventional kind of industrialist. Although a forceful, dynamic entrepreneur, he was far from being the kind of ruthless, hard-nosed businessman who thinks only of profits and losses on a balance sheet. On the contrary, his attitude about money and toward the accountants and bankers who controlled it was cavalier in the extreme. A progressive, socially responsible employer who paid generous wages and provided model working conditions for his employees, he was at the same time a gregarious socialite who enjoyed, to the full, the extravagant pleasure-seeking lifestyle pursued by the *beau monde* in France between the wars. His ten years in the motor industry had made him a very rich man (though not quite on the monumental scale of Henry Ford) but he had no great interest in acquiring property or possessions; he owned no town mansion or country estate, much less the yachts, race horses and art treasures that other millionaires collected. A devoted family man, his sole passion was his love for gambling at the racetrack and the casino, where on one memorable occasion (at Deauville in 1924) he won the equivalent of almost two million pounds in today's money in a single sitting. Unquestionably, this love of gambling spilled over into his business affairs. His famous saying, "Des l'instant ou une idée est bonne, le prix n'a pas d'importance"—the moment an idea proves desirable, its price becomes of no importance—was characteristic of his brave but less than cautious response to commercial challenges and risks. Yet for a man who loved to take a chance, his business philosophy was remarkably untainted by the get-rich-quick casino culture mentality which prizes short-term gains above long-term returns. As he often remarked, had he not been a gambler, ready to take risks that others avoided, and to follow a long-term strategy, he would never have realized his spectacular industrial and commercial achievements.

In truth, during his final years, Citroën became a victim of his own rebounding publicity and propaganda. Portrayed in the popular French press as a frivolous, feckless charlatan, he was condemned in certain quarters as being merely a showman and socialite interested only in self-promotion, an accusation (not entirely devoid of anti–Semitism) that his gambling exploits served only to exacerbate. But for all his flamboyant showmanship he was certainly no dilettante, content to dabble in motor-car manufacture for the wealth and celebrity it brought him. Although the urge to impress rivals and outdo enemies was always a powerful motivating force behind the relentless expansion of his activities, more important still was his desire to achieve genuine technological and social progress. Dissatisfied with compromise, he knew that the fight for market leadership could never be won simply by undercutting his rivals in price. To overtake his competitors in sales he would need to outdistance them in technology. Ultimately, he would have to throw convention to the wind and offer his customers an exciting new model of radical, indeed revolutionary, design.

By the early 1930s this ambition had become an obsession for André Citroën. Paris was still the capital of the avant-garde world, the focal-point of progress in art, music, literature, photography and fashion, as it had been throughout the 1920s. As a leading member of fashionable society, he was determined that the city should also remain at the center of creativity in automobile design and technology. On paper, despite of the Wall Street crash and the onset of the Great Depression, his company was doing well. With sales fast approaching 100,000 units per year (95,000 in 1929), the marque was well established alongside Renault and Peugeot in the French "Big Three." But on the road, its products were beginning to look old hat, decidedly dated and old-fashioned compared with the exciting new ideas coming from the more adventurous minor European manufacturers. Standing high off the ground, they appeared boxy and clumsy in contrast with the long, lean, low look then in fashion among the leading designers and coachbuilders of *voitures de luxe*. Something altogether more stylish and sophisticated was called for, Citroën avowed. Until now, his success had been founded on an astute exploitation of the principles of mass production, so as to reduce prices to the minimum while at the same time maximizing sales by an outstanding flexibility in manufacturing and assembly methods—a system which also allowed for a wide variety of body-style options to be offered. The time had now come to add another factor to his formula, by introducing highly advanced engineering ideas and greater originality in design. This would permit an even more ruthless exploitation of the laws of economics, by making it possible to carry out very long production runs of each new model. What he needed was a car so far ahead of his competitors that it wouldn't matter to his customers if it had been in production for two years or for 20. That car, of course, was to be the Traction Avant, the world's first mass-produced front-wheel-drive passenger vehicle. In the course of its quarter-century-long production life, it would come to represent not only the embodiment of the avant-garde nature of the Citroën firm itself, but also a symbol of originality and individuality in automobile engineering generally—in other words, a French cultural icon.

But before this adventurous new product could be introduced, a further stop-gap range of conventional rear-wheel-drive cars would be required. Consequently three new models, the four-cylinder 8CV (1452cc) and 10CV

(1767cc) plus the six-cylinder 15CV (2650cc) sedans, were duly introduced at the October 1932 Paris Motor Show. These cars were simply re-engineered versions of the old C4 and C6 designs, fitted with new high-strength all-steel bodies but mounted on a traditional ladder-type under chassis. Constructed using the latest technology supplied by Budd Manufacturing Company, these Monopiece bodies were formed by joining together five large pre-formed sections rather than by welding numerous smaller pressed-steel stampings and panels as before, in the C4/C6 cars. These vehicles were the first Citroëns to carry the Double Chevron emblem on their radiator grilles, emblazoned like a heraldic motif on a shield (from January 1933 onwards; previously the Citroën insignia had been confined to a small blue and yellow enameled badge mounted on the top of the radiator shell). All three vehicles also featured an innovative vibration-damping engine mounting system, acquired by Citroën under license from Chrysler in the USA, and imaginatively marketed as the Systeme Moteur Flottant or Floating Power system.

Citroën's conventional rear-wheel-drive cars of the 1930s were rugged and robust vehicles, designed and built in the American manner. This is the splendid six-cylinder C6G Roadster introduced in October 1931.

The following year the range was augmented by two more cars, the 10 Legere and the 15 Legere, using existing bodies and engines in a new combination. The former was produced by fitting the 1767cc four-cylinder engine from the 10CV into the body of the 8CV, while the latter was a sports edition of the 15CV, realized by fitting the 2650cc six-cylinder engine in a long wheelbase version of the body and chassis of the 10CV. This new range was well received by the public. Over 95,000 examples were sold by the end of 1935, reversing the fall in sales experienced in 1931 and 1932 and enabling Citroën to recover a 45 percent share of the French volume market during 1933. Eventually, this new collection became known as the Rosalie series, in honor of the 8CV example nicknamed Petite Rosalie which, driven by racing driver Cesar Marchand on the Montlhery test track between March 15, and July 27, 1933, clocked 300,000 kilometers (close to 186,500 miles) in 134 days at an average speed of 57.8 mph during a non-stop endurance trial organized by the Yacco Oil Company. In doing so, it broke 132 international and 78 world endurance records, to establish standards that remained unbeaten for 30 years. In due course, between October 1931 and May 1936, a succession of no fewer than nine of these Citroën-built, Yacco-sponsored Rosalie cars took to the track. Petite Rosalie, the most famous of them, was actually the third.

In January 1934, the Rosalie range was revised yet again by the introduction of a number of styling changes, including a raked-back radiator shell and streamlined semi-enclosed front fenders. This new look was referred to as the Nouvel Habillage. Last, early in April 1934, a modified final series of Rosalie cars was introduced — the 8B, 10B and 15B, available in various body styles and all featuring independent front suspension by torsion bars, in line with the arrangements adopted for the revolutionary new Traction Avant front-wheel-drive model, the existence of which was soon to be announced, and which would shortly enter series production alongside the Rosalie on the adjacent, second assembly line at the Quai de Javel factory.

Evidently, it was intended that the Rosalie models would be permanently withdrawn in September 1934; certainly none were exhibited at the October 1934 Paris Motor Show for, as we shall see in the following chapter, the Citroën stand was devoted exclusively to the Traction Avant. However, in order to cater to those conservative, traditionally minded customers who hesitated to order the front-wheel-drive car, the Rosalies were re-introduced

The last conventional cars from the Quai de Javel were the three so-called Rosalie models, the 8CV, the 10CV and the 15CV, which also appeared in a variety of body styles. This is the roadster / cabriolet version of the four-cylinder 8CV, built in 1933.

Pictured in this superb study by Citroën's talented house photographer Pierre Louys is the 15CV Legere or light sedan of 1934.

A Citroen-Kegresse caterpillar car of the Citroën Central Asian expedition, seen crossing the Burzil Pass in the Himalayas during July 1931.

in January 1935 in two versions, the 7UA and 11UA, powered by either the 1628cc 7CV or the 1911cc 11CV engines from the Traction Avant, installed in a reversed direction to drive the rear wheels and, in consequence, modified so that the water-pump, fan and radiator were located at the opposite end of the engine block, now at the front. In addition to several light commercial vehicle variants, various passenger body styles were offered; two for the 7UA, a standard wheelbase four-light sedan and a commerciale with opening rear doors, and three for 11UA, a long wheelbase six-light sedan, limousine and commerciale. These products remained in the catalog until the spring of 1938 when the Citroën company finally abandoned rear-wheel-drive forever on its passenger cars and light commercial vehicles, as its founder had originally intended five years earlier.

The Mastery of the Double Chevron Gearwheel

The mechanical principle of double helical gears had first been set down on paper more than 200 years earlier by the English scientist, astronomer, architect and mathematician Robert Hooke (1635–1703), who demonstrated, in theory at least, their advantages over ordinary straight-cut gears. By virtue of the way they ran in constant mesh with no free play between the driving and driven wheels, they eliminated both backlash and side-thrust and thus avoided the shock-loads, stress, vibration, friction and noise inevitably encountered in conventional gears. Silent-running, they were especially suited to all those applications where high-speed running and reversing were required, and particularly where large velocity ra-

Opposite top: **In January 1934 the three Rosalie series models were relaunched with face-lifted, semi-streamlined bodywork known as the Nouvel Habillage, or New Look, recognizable by the raked-back radiator grille and other changes. These cars also featured torsion bar independent front suspension. This is the seven-seater 15CV NH Grand Luxe familiale.** ***Opposite bottom:*** **The Rosalie series were also produced in a number of special Grand-Luxe coach-built versions, with bodies constructed by specialist** ***carrossiers.*** **This is the 15CV-NH Grand Luxe Coach, built by Manessius. Its price was 40,500 FF, substantially more than the 19,000 FF asked for the cheapest car in the series, the 8CV-NH sedan.**

The Citroën Double Chevron emblem, devised by André Citroën personally, was derived from the teeth of his double-helical gear wheels, which were employed in a wide variety of heavy industrial applications such as water pumping stations.

tios, either in the reduction or stepping up of operating speeds, were involved. Such applications included fast-running power-transmission work in factories and generating stations, heavy-duty power-transmission duties in the milling, mining and metal-working industries and in other situations where great exactitude of operation was essential, for instance in printing and textile machinery or in steering and winding gear.

However, up to that point in time, no manufacturer anywhere in the world had succeeded in solving the technical problems involved in cutting a run of true V-shaped helical gear teeth from a block of solid steel with one continuous, uninterrupted stroke of the cutting tool. All previous attempts had involved two cutting strokes per tooth, which left a groove running up the center of the V pattern, thus seriously compromising the strength and accuracy of the mesh. But as Citroën had shrewdly foreseen in Poland two years earlier, recent developments in American machine tool technology had indeed brought this complex machining task within the bounds of possibility. Within a few months he had developed an end-milling machine to his own specification.

In typical Citroën fashion, the adoption of Tout Acier all-steel bodies was promoted by a fanfare of publicity, such as this advertisement published in 1931 and designed by Pierre Louys. No other contemporary European car manufacturer spent so much on advertising as André Citroën.

Using special revolving cutting tools supplied from the USA, this machine was capable of achieving the required dimensional accuracy, forming the teeth by cutting out a series of perfectly profiled grooves in the blank, each groove being fashioned in one single uninterrupted pass of the tool. The publicity material that he produced to market this capacity rightly proclaimed that Citroën helical and double helical gears were "the first genuine machine-cut helical gears, having continuous teeth automatically cut with one tool in one single operation in the solid," a state-of-affairs that continued for many years. So accurately were they made that an efficiency of 98 percent was guaranteed.

2

Development of the Traction Avant, 1931–1934

For a man who was to make such a major contribution to the history of motoring, André Citroën was a surprisingly reluctant motorist. He rarely drove a car, preferring to rely on his chauffeur or even his wife, who was a keen motorist and vice-president of the Automobile Club Feminin de France. Certainly, he was never to be seen in overalls, putting his products through their paces in person on the test track or the racing circuit, nor was he inclined to tinker beneath the hood, mending or improving some faulty component, as other automobile pioneers such as Henry Ford, Louis Renault, William Morris and Herbert Austin loved to do. Citroën was a technologist rather than a practical mechanic and an entrepreneur rather than a practicing engineer, although his engineering training and aptitude were of the highest calibre.

But far from rendering him unsuitable as a car constructor, his personal aversion to the act of driving (poor eyesight may well have been the cause) had important beneficial consequences for other motorists, in that it made him anxious to ease the task of operating a car. He had little interest in motor sport and racing, which he considered dangerous, and he rejected the notion that driving should be confined to hairy-chested men of athletic build and adventurous disposition. On the contrary, he positively promoted and encouraged the use of cars by the female population; in those days, relatively few women were qualified drivers. In all the vehicles he produced, his aim was always to simplify the controls and to reduce the physical and mental effort required in piloting them to the very minimum, in the interests of both safety and enjoyment.

Therefore, when planning his next car, to replace the 8CV and 10CV Rosalie series vehicles, he planned to take the process further by abandoning the traditional Systeme Panhard layout of a front-mounted engine driving the rear wheels, which dated back to 1891, and to adopt instead a radically new and different structural architecture. The *Petite Voiture,* as the concept was designated, was to be a small medium class sedan which would be made in very large numbers and offered at a very low price, so as to re-occupy the position vacated by the demise of the 5CV Type C3 Trefle. It was also Citroën's intention that the *Petite Voiture* would set new standards of speed, economy and security, achieved by a combination of innovative technology and unconventional design. The simple commercial necessity of making the new product accessible to the vast majority of potential customers who had never owned a vehicle before, and who were unaccustomed to possessing or maintaining machinery of any kind, demanded that top priority should be given to improving standards of braking, steering and handling, as well as to making gear-changing an easier matter for the novice driver. Ideally, it would incorporate an audaciously ambitious combination of innovative features, such as front-wheel-drive, hydraulic brakes and even automatic transmission — and the huge investment required to produce it would be recouped by the long production run made possible by its very novelty!

The exact moment at which André Citroën conceived this revolutionary "new concept in motoring," and set its design and construction cannot be pinpointed exactly. However, it is known that in 1932 he was given the opportunity to manufacture under license a small, inexpensive front-wheel-drive design which had just appeared in Germany, the Adler Trumpf, designed by Gustav Rohr. But jealous of Rohr's reputation for innovation and independence, he chose instead to press ahead with producing a FWD car of his own, details of which must already have been forming in his mind. Subsequently, the Adler appeared in France, at the 1933 Paris Salon, marketed as the Rosengart Supertraction.

Earlier, when visiting America in October 1931, he had renewed his contacts with Edward G. Budd of the Budd Manufacturing Company of Philadelphia, the supplier of the presses and tooling employed in constructing the all-steel bodies of his current C4 and C6 cars. During this meeting he was shown a prototype front-wheel-drive car designed by Budd's chief engineer, Joseph Ledwinka, in partnership with the former racing mechanic, William J. Muller. Evidently, this vehicle car was a further development of the FWD concept-car (powered by a six-cylinder Studebaker engine) that the Budd firm had first produced in 1928, and which had already led to the two most notable contemporary American FWD cars, the Ruxton and the Cord. But whereas the original Budd prototype had employed a conventional all-steel body mounted on a ladder-type chassis, the new vehicle featured a novel chassis-less body-shell, intended to demonstrate the advantages of the new unitary construction system which Budd had recently patented. Until now, cars had been constructed by bolting the coachwork onto a separate chassis frame, in a way derived from the age of the horse and cart. Budd's innovation rendered this heavy chassis platform unnecessary. By bracing the outer, visible skin of the body with a minimal internal skeleton of reinforcing pressed steel panels, it was possible to produce a pre-stressed structure made of only five or six major elements, and which provided sufficient strength and stiffness to carry the loads imposed by the engine and transmission, as well as the weight of the driver, passengers and cargo.

When inspecting the Budd prototype, André Citroën realized that this revolutionary monocoque concept provided the way to make the mass-production of a front wheel drive car a practical proposition. Because the bodyshell itself would be capable of holding engine, transmission and suspension together, so that no underlying supporting structure would be required, at last it would be possible to bring the car's weight, ride-height and center of gravity down to the levels he desired. Better still, the large savings in steel made possible by this novel form of construction would result in great economies of scale, providing that the car could be produced and sold in sufficient quantities to absorb the additional production costs resulting from the expensive presses and tooling required. An output of 1,000 cars a day would be required, Citroën estimated.

Determined to break the mold of tradition, André Citroën had sailed back across the Atlantic with the blueprints of the Budd design, to begin the work of adapting this American concept into a much smaller vehicle, more suited to European conditions, but using the same advanced welding technology. Even at this early stage, he realized that whereas all of his previous replacement products were related closely to their predecessors, this new car would be unique, having virtually nothing in common with any existing Citroën model. There could be little inheritance of design, construction or component parts; almost every single item would have to be new and different. At a stroke, it would make all other cars—Citroëns included—out of date.

The car that he envisaged—and which appeared four years later—was of course the Traction Avant, the world's first mass-produced monocoque front-wheel-drive car. Intended to give him a five year lead over his rivals, it remained in production for almost 25 years. Even when its production ceased in 1957, it was still thought by many experts to be technically superior to most other popular cars currently available. Indeed, Citroën's "new concept in motoring" proved to be so innovative and conceptually advanced that it is still recognized today as being the one design that, above all others, set the pattern and standards of the modern family car.

For the very first time on a mass-produced vehicle, such advanced features as front wheel drive, independent front suspension by torsion bars, hydraulic brakes and (later) rack and pinion steering were combined in a long, low-slung all-steel monocoque body shell, embodying the latest notions of graceful, streamlined styling. Rapid and responsive to drive, safe, spacious and comfortable to ride in and affordable to own and run, it was also intended to be an outstandingly reliable and economical vehicle, priced well within the means of the typical business or professional motorist.

The *cahier de charges*, or design specification, that André Citroën issued for his PV project stipulated that it should be a four-seater car constructed on the monocoque principle, weighing no more than 800kg (1,762 lbs.), selling at 15,000 FF and capable of a top-speed of 100 km/h (62 mph) and an average fuel consumption of 7 liters per 100km (33.6 mpg). Its engine was to be a four-cylinder unit rated at 7CV and it was to employ both front-wheel-drive and fully automatic transmission by means of an hydraulic torque converter. His current success, the C4F sedan of 1930–31, cost 19,400 FF, weighed 1,200 kg (2,643 lbs.) and was capable of 90 km/h (56 mph).

Although no other mainstream manufacturer had as yet been interested in marketing a mass-produced front-wheel-drive vehicle, there was, of course, nothing new in the idea; already a number of different designs had been commercialized in limited numbers by various small specialist firms. These predecessors included the Cord and Ruxton in the USA (1928), the DKW and Adler in Germany (1931 & 1932), the Alvis in Great Britain (1928) and, of course, the Tracta in France (1927), designed and built by J.A. Gregoire. What distinguished André Citroën's courage and audacity in adopting the principle was that although its use was ultimately adopted universally by all the major volume car makers, so that it became standard practice in the design of family cars, back in the 1930s when the Traction Avant was launched, he stood alone in his intention to abandon rear-wheel-drive entirely throughout his range. As we shall see, even by the time that the 2CV and DS19 appeared in 1948 and 1955, the Citroën firm was still unique in making only front-wheel-drive cars and, indeed, it continued to be so for many years beyond that point.

Despite the fact that both Renault and Peugeot considered front-wheel-drive to be not just technically unfeasible but actually undesirable, André Citroën understood that the principle offered drivers a far higher standard of stability and safety. First, from the handling and road holding point of view, it obviously made more sense for the engine to pull the car through a bend, as a horse pulls a cart, instead of pushing it from behind, provided of course that the problem of transmitting power to the front wheels—which had to remain steerable—could be solved. But second, by eliminating the drive-shaft tunnel to the rear and lowering both the floor line and the center of gravity, a much more spacious, stable and aerodynamically efficient body shape could also be achieved. Moreover, by lowering the ride-height to the minimum, it would also be possible to increase the stability of the vehicle.

André Citroën also understood that when cornering in a front wheel drive vehicle, the driving force of the car is exerted in the direction of the turn, to maintain the correct trajectory through a curve. In a rear wheel drive car, however, the force is exerted along the fore and aft axis of the vehicle, in the general direction being followed at the time, rather than into the curve. In other words, the driving force imparted by the rear wheels is exerted crosswise to the required direction being followed by the front or steered axle. It therefore follows that, for the same vehicle speed and for the same degree of grip provided by the tires, a front wheel drive car can withstand a greater centrifugal force without loss of tire adhesion and directional stability. This means that it can go into a turn at a higher speed without risk of skidding, or corner safely on more slippery surfaces.

To complicate matters, these centrifugal forces are magnified by factors such as the camber of the road and side winds, so that the vehicle tends to drift sideways in a turn, without necessarily losing grip and skidding. To counteract this drift, the driver must make constant steering corrections to preserve balance and maintain the set course.

Moreover, as this drifting effect is greatest on the driven wheels, in a rear wheel drive car the back axle tends to break contact with the road first, before the front or steering axle, and the driver can only correct this slide by harsh or violent movements of the steering wheel, turning it from lock to lock, a maneuver that calls for great expertise. On a front wheel drive car, however, the driver can correct drift easily and gently by constant slight adjustments of the steering wheel, a technique requiring much less experience and skill. The end result is that, all things being equal, the front wheel drive car is far easier to control and thus inherently safer than its rear wheel drive counterpart, allowing even the most clumsy novice driver to drive at speed with confidence.

Although the head of Citroën's vehicle road-testing evaluation department, Pierre Prevost, was enthusiastic about the idea of adopting front wheel drive, having tested both the Tracta and the Adler Trumpf, not all among André Citroën's senior staff were convinced; however, and many doubted both the technical feasibility and commercial wisdom of his plans. Among the doubters were Louis Guillot, his technical supremo and designer of the C4/C6 series cars, and also Maurice Broglie, who took over from Guillot as the chief of his Bureau d'Etudes or research department in February 1933, following Guillot's death after a long illness.

Consequently, by the end of 1932 it had become clear to *le Patron* that insufficient progress was being made, and that the PV project was well behind schedule. If the new car was ever to emerge, ready for launching at the October 1934 Paris Motor Show as he had always intended, then fresh ideas and energies would be required to make a breakthrough. He therefore began a head-hunt for new talent and consulted his friend, the extravagant and idiosyncratic French aircraft and automobile engineer Gabriel Voisin, whose own activities as a constructor of expensive luxury cars had recently ceased as a consequence of the Depression. As luck would have it, Voisin knew of the right man for the job, but who was currently employed by Citroën's great rival, Louis Renault. Indeed, this individual had previously worked as his assistant, and together the pair had collaborated on a front-wheel-drive project, some three years previously.

So it was that, on Voisin's recommendation, André Citroën appointed the brilliant 39-year-old engineer André Lefèbvre as overall manager of his *Petite Voiture* project, giving him carte blanche to get the car ready on time. André Lefèbvre was then—and, indeed, remains today—a unique figure in motoring history, among the very few persons ever to succeed at the highest level as both a race car driver and race car designer simultaneously. In 1923 he had finished fifth in the Grand Prix de l'Automobile Club de France held at Tours, at the wheel of a two-liter, six-cylinder Voisin of revolutionary conception which he had helped to design. Lightweight and of high aerodynamic efficiency, this car featured a streamlined monocoque body built almost entirely of aluminum, using constructional techniques borrowed from the aircraft industry. Later, in 1929, he had taken part in a famous series of high-speed, long-distance, non-stop endurance runs staged by Gabriel Voisin at the Montlhery circuit near Paris, at which many long-lasting world records were set.

Born on August 19, 1894, at Louvres in the Val-d'Oise department, Lefèbvre had originally trained to be an aircraft designer at the École Superieure d'Aeronautique in Paris, before beginning his career with Voisin in 1915, constructing bombers for the French air force. After the war, when Voisin transferred his attention from aviation to the automobile business, as a manufacturer of luxury cars, Lefèbvre continued in his employment, working as his joint chief assistant designer and chief test driver for a total of 15 years. In the wake of the Wall Street crash of 1929, the market for Voisin's expensive products collapsed and Lefèbvre was obliged to leave and join Automobiles Renault, as deputy to the chief engineer of its *Bureau d'Etudes* or research and design department. Not surprisingly in view of Louis Renault's conservatism, he found the position unsatisfying and uncongenial; indeed, he may well have had frequent arguments with his boss about technical matters.

Due to his aeronautical background, Lefèbvre viewed automobile design from a different perspective to that adopted by most other leading engineers of his day. Obsessed with the idea of adapting the principles and techniques of aircraft construction to the automobile, he believed that the best way to raise a car's performance was not simply to boost the power-output of its engine, but to improve the dynamics of its chassis and the aerodynamic efficiency of its bodywork. Careful attention to such vital considerations as the reduction of drag and the correct positioning of the centers of gravity and aerodynamic pressure would not only produce higher average speeds and lower fuel consumption, but it would also result in better handling and road-holding qualities, resulting in greater comfort and safety, an added bonus. Unlike the majority of the over-powered, under-controlled luxury cars built in the 1920s, the big Voisin cars that he had designed were powerful, high-speed vehicles that could be driven safely right up to the limit of their performance. Because the characteristics and capabilities of engine and chassis had been carefully matched, at 90 mph they could be driven with a degree of assurance and control that was noticeably missing at a mere 60 mph in most of their contemporaries.

Frequently during his two-year stint with Renault, Lefèbvre he tried to persuade Louis Renault to allow him to develop his theories by producing a prototype front-wheel-drive car. But Renault refused, saying that he thought the concept was ridiculous. So when offered the job of masterminding André Citroën's Traction Avant project, he jumped at the chance to put his ideas about FWD into practice and moved to the Quai de Javel without delay, to begin the task of rescuing the project, working virtually non-stop around the clock. He was to remain with the Citroën firm for the next 25 years, as the de facto chief engineer and designer of the *Bureau d'Etudes,* though never as its official leader. Throughout his entire service he held no proper rank or title in the company's hierarchy, yet he was always regarded as the supreme authority and source of policy on all technical matters; routine management and organizational matters did not interest him at all; such trivial details were left to other titular chiefs, such as Broglie, who were little more than administrators.

In fact, André Lefèbvre joined Citroën's Bureau d'Etudes on 12th March 1933, the date that is generally held to mark the point of conception of the Traction Avant. Indeed, it has been claimed elsewhere that the entire car was designed and constructed from scratch within a year of this point, but given the relatively unsophisticated design-engineering, prototyping, manufacturing and communications technologies of that era this is most unlikely to have been the case. Even in modern times, with the benefit of time-saving computer-aided design and production-engineering techniques, the process of bringing out a new car, developed from scratch, takes at least three years from start to finish, and more normally five.

It must therefore be concluded that by March 1933 a substantial amount of work would have already been achieved to define the design and construction of the Traction Avant, either by the Citroën Bureau d'Etudes or by Lefèbvre himself during his previous employment. But exactly how much new thinking he brought with him, or how much of the previous work, undertaken by the Citroën firm before his arrival, were combined and preserved in the final design is difficult to assess. Quite possibly, Lefèbvre brought with him detailed drawings for a front-wheel-drive car that he had designed earlier, but which he had been unable to persuade Louis Renault to produce. But even if this was indeed the case, and the design of the Traction Avant was based on this pre-existing scheme, it is still doubtful that the car could ever have been designed and produced in its entirety and brought to the series production stage from start to finish within twelve months, even if the engineers responsible had taken no sleep at all within that time. Undoubtedly, certain elements of the *Petite Voiture* scheme must already have been established, if not actually realized, by André Citroën and his staff well before Lefèbvre's arrival on the scene, borrowing from the Budd blueprints that Citroën brought back from the USA in 1931.

Clearly, work on the new four-cylinder overhead-valve engine intended specifically for the Traction Avant must have been well advanced by March 1933; indeed, this engine is believed to have already undergone road-tests at Montlhery earlier that year, mounted in a RWD Rosalie model. It had been designed by another newcomer to the Quai de Javel, Maurice Sainturat. Considered to be one of France's greatest automobile engineers of the inter-war years, Sainturat had arrived chez Citroën early in 1932 after a long career that embraced periods at Hotchkiss, Delage and Chenard & Walcker. His first task had been to create an entirely new family of OHV engines intended for Citroën's new range of commercial vehicles, not only much lighter and more powerful than the existing C4/C6 series side-valve engines that they were intended to replaced, but also far cheaper to produce. The first example of the series, a 4580cc six-cylinder unit, was introduced on Citroën's Type 45 lorry in December 1933, closely followed by a 3056cc four-cylinder version, which appeared on the smaller Type 32 lorry October in 1934. The 1303 cc engine of the earliest Traction Avant models was derived directly from this design and shared numerous common features including replaceable wet-liner cylinder barrels, another Citroën innovation. These new engines were also designed in such a way that they could easily be adapted for either RWD or FWD applications.

It is also likely that a considerable effort would already have been applied to establish the underlying structure of the Traction Avant. Well before any thought could be given to the car's external appearance and styling, it would have been necessary for the *service carrosserie* or bodywork department to determine the nature and relationship of the five principal structural elements making up the monocoque. These were the floor-pan, the scuttle (including the two large frontal box sections supporting the engine and front suspension), the two side members (having apertures for the doors), and the rear closing panel (at this stage in its development, the roof of the Traction was to be closed by a fabric panel). Similarly, the transmission arrangements would by then have been well-defined, at least in prototype form.

As we have already seen, to realize his audacious project André Citroën had already recruited an impressive design and development team, employing the very best talents from within the Quai de Javel as well as leading experts from beyond its walls. Working in conditions of absolute secrecy, nominally under the supervision of his chief engineer, Charles Brull, and his directors of product research, testing and quality control, Maurice Broglie, Pierre Prevost and Maurice Norroy, the team was actually led quite independently by Lefèbvre who reported to *le patron* directly. The group included the following individuals; Roger Prudhomme, the foreman of the Bureau d'Etudes; Maurice Sainturat, the engine specialist; Maurice Julien, responsible for suspension design; Jouffret and Alphonse Forceau, both transmission experts; and Raoul Cuinet, who was in charge of bodywork matters, assisted by Maurice Franchiset and Jean Daninos (who later became famous as the founder of the Facel-Vega marque).

Last, but by no means least, among the team was Flaminio Bertoni, a young Italian designer and sculptor then only 30 years of age, who had joined the Citroën design office in July 1932. Ostensibly responsible only for making full-scale plaster models or *maquettes*, he had become directly involved in styling matters in December 1932 when he designed the famous Double Chevron grille for Citroën's current conventional rear-wheel-drive range of cars, the 8CV, 10CV and 15CV Rosalie series, which since their introduction three months earlier, in October 1932, had sported merely a plain grille. Later he was responsible for the styling of a revised and improved range of Rosalie models, the so-called NH or Nouvel Habillage series, which (as detailed in the previous chapter) entered production in January 1934. These cars featured a number of styling improvements contributed by Bertoni, including a new raked-back pattern of radiator grille emblazoned with the same instantly recognisable heraldic Double Chevron emblem that was such a noticeable visual feature of the Traction Avant. Born in 1903 at Varese, near Lake Como just north of Milan, Bertoni — who remained with the Citroën firm until his premature death in 1964 — went on to create, with Lefèbvre, three more of the Double Chevron firm's greatest successes, the 2CV, the DS19 and the Ami-6.

Several independent consultants from outside the Citroën organization were also deeply involved in the creation of the Traction Avant. Among them was Jean-Albert Gregoire, the front-wheel-drive pioneer who had been responsible for the aforementioned Tracta, which had been produced in small numbers between 1927 and 1932. Gregoire's interest and expertise were in the articulated drive shafts required to link the gearbox to the road-wheels in all FWD cars, to transmit the power "around the corner" when the steering was turned. Merely employing a simple Hooke-type universal joint to link the two separate parts of the shaft, as on the driveshaft of a rear-wheel-drive car, would be insufficient, since without the use of a homocinetic or constant velocity coupling at the outer end, it is impossible for the wheels to revolve at a constant speed when cornering. If power is to be transmitted smoothly and progressively from the gearbox to the front wheels under all circumstances, the more complicated CV type of couplings are essential. Without them a FWD vehicle will not corner satisfactorily when its front wheels are set sideways at an extreme angle, with its steering turned to full lock, and the two parts of the shaft are out of alignment. On the Tracta, the problem had been solved by using a new design of constant-velocity drive shafts invented by Gregoire's partner, Pierre Fenaille, and manufactured by Bendix. It was therefore decided that these would be the type to be fitted on the Traction Avant, though in a modified form.

Another consultant on the project was the production-engineering specialist Dennis Kendall, who worked with Cuinet's team and acted as liaison with the suppliers of the new body dies and tooling for the car, the Budd Manufacturing Company of Philadelphia. An English expatriate who had joined the Budd firm in the USA in 1924, Kendall subsequently became director of production at the Quai de Javel for a brief period, before returning to the U.K., where at the outbreak of World War II he was engaged by the British government to set up an armaments factory at Grantham, manufacturing Hispano-Suiza cannons and ammunition for the RAF's Hurricane and Spitfire fighter aircraft in a venture that echoed André Citroën's own beginnings as an industrialist. After the war, Kendall attempted, unsuccessfully, to enter the British motor industry by building at the Grantham plant his own People's Car, based on a design by Gregoire!

Although it is not possible to determine the exact state of progress that had been reached on the PV project by March 1933, it is known that by the end of June, just three months after André Lefèbvre's arrival *chez* Citroën, definitive final plans for the *Petite Voiture* had been drafted and agreed — and that within another two months these specifications and drawings had been translated into a pair of hand-built working prototypes which were shown to André Citroën and his wife for approval in August 1933. The styling of these prototypes had been undertaken by Flaminio Bertoni, of course. It seems that his suggestions had been made with some trepidation in the absence of more convincing proposals from elsewhere. Three previous *maquettes* that he had hand-crafted to demonstrate other designs by other persons had been turned down by *le patron*, so he decided to have a go himself. Years later, he recalled that, accompanied by Cuinet, he presented his designs (in the form of a 1/5 scale plasticine model) to André Citroën and his wife at their apartment at 8 rue Octave-Feuillet, Paris, at some point during the spring of 1933, the exact date of which he had unfortunately forgotten. His ideas were received with both admiration and relief, so much so that he was immediately given a substantial raise in salary by his grateful employer, as well as the go-ahead to develop his ideas further by producing a full-size *maquette*. This task was accomplished in 53 hours of non-stop work, so that the full-scale drawings required for the construction of the two hand-built prototypes could be prepared without further delay.

But then, in September 1933, just as all seemed to have been resolved, André Citroën had a change of mind that threw the design into the melting pot once again. In place of the conventional gearbox and clutch used in the first two running prototypes, he revived his plan to use a novel, infinitely variable fully-automatic transmission system, employing an hydraulic torque converter and epicyclic gears, the creation of a Spanish-Brazilian inventor residing in Switzerland, Dimitri Sensaud de Lavaud. In effect, this *turbine* (as it was referred to at the Bureau d'Etudes) relieved the car's driver of the work of changing gears by constantly synchronizing the speed of its wheels with the speed of its engine, entirely without human intervention. Whatever the resistance encountered by the vehicle's transmission as it moved from a standing start or travelled up a hill, the fluid flywheel of the turbine ensured that the engine's power output would be taken up smoothly and seamlessly — that, at least, was the theory.

It seems that Citroën had first been attracted to the device when he saw it demonstrated at the 1929 Paris Motor Show and had subsequently been approached by Sensaud de Lavaud on the subject early in 1932. Shortly after this meeting he drove an example of his C6 six-cylinder model on which the device had been mounted experimentally. No problems were experienced in these tests, nor indeed were any serious difficulties found by other manufacturers who had previously tried it out, such as Bucciali and Voisin, as early as 1925. The advantages of the system impressed Citroën greatly; as we have already seen, he disliked the physical effort of driving, and so the notion of eliminating the gearshift and clutch pedal altogether was a highly attractive proposition, since so many of his potential customers would be inexperienced drivers, new to motoring.

The next known point in the gestation of the Traction Avant occurred just three months after the August 1933 meeting when the hand-built prototypes had been presented. In mid November 1933, a mission led by Cuinet departed for the Budd plant at Philadelphia on board the luxury liner Ile de France bearing the full-scale drawings required to produce the tooling for the presses that would stamp out the exterior body panels of the series production version of the car. Only the Budd firm possessed the technology necessary to supply these dies, required in conjunction with the Federal flash-welding machines that

André Citroën had purchased earlier from the USA, to fabricate the monopiece steel bodies he had introduced on the Rosalie models. The function of this Federal machine was to unite in one operation the numerous pressings that formed the car's external *cocque* or body-shell. In all other respects, including the construction of the car's internal body structure or *caisse*, the Citroën firm was self-sufficient, having already invested in the necessary American-made plant in order to produce the C4/C6 series vehicles, back in 1928. Even so, as virtually all of the machinery required to produce the Traction's body-shell was supplied by firms in the USA, accessible only by telex-printer or a ten-day sea voyage, the difficulty of communicating with these suppliers would doubtless have led to many difficulties and delays in the process of working-up the design from the prototype to the volume production stage, not merely due to language barriers but also because of the need to translate metric dimensions set out in the French drawings into the measurements used by Americans.

It seems that André Citroën's intention at this point in time, January 1934, was that series production of the car would commence as soon as Cuinet and his team returned from the USA with the tooling, so that a trial pre-production run of some 300 cars would be ready for testing, demonstration and marketing purposes during the spring. Ever overly optimistic, he had planned to launch his New Concept in Motoring at the October 1934 Paris Motor Show, as was customary when introducing all new vehicles in France at that time. But with only nine months remaining, certain vital technical teething troubles had still not been overcome.

Most notable of these *ennuis* was the problem presented by Gregoire's constant velocity drive shafts. In their original form, as used on the Tracta, the Adler Trumpf, the DKW and indeed, the first two hand-built prototypes of the Traction Avant, these shafts had performed without problems. But then Gregoire decided to redesign them in such a way that the retaining housing of their outer universal joints, located within the swivelling hub, actually rotated with the shaft so that the whole assembly formed a single unity. His idea was that, to simplify assembly operations, this sub-assembly could be built up elsewhere before being finally mounted on the vehicle on the production line. Unfortunately Gregoire's second *joint tournant* version proved unsatisfactory and wore out rapidly, within 5,000 to 10,000 kilometers (3,100 to 6,200 miles). According to Gregoire's account of the story, the fault lay in the fact that the Citroën factory was unable to machine them with sufficient precision. As it was not possible to revert to the first *joint non-tournant* version, after the first thousand series production vehicles had been completed the Tracta shafts were replaced by another pattern of CV joint, the Rzeppa, an American design which operated on the ball and socket principle. This design also created problems, at least when applied to the current 7A Traction-Avant, as the ball-cages had a tendency to break, jamming the balls in their housing.

Eventually, in April 1935, it was decided to abandon attempts to employ a true homocinetic drive shaft and to resort to a third arrangement for the outer universal joints, by obtaining a license to manufacture yet another patented American design, known variously as the Glaenzer-Spicer or Hardy-Spicer joint. These couplings took the form of two simple Hooke-type universal joints mounted back to back and linked by a yoke. Another universal joint of the same type formed the coupling at the inboard end of the driveshaft, linking it with the output shaft of the gearbox. Unfortunately, the Glaenzer-Spicer units did not allow the outboard, output part of the drive shaft to revolve at a constant velocity when operating at the sharp angles caused when the swivelling front wheels were steered sharply to the left or right, which greatly restricted the Traction Avant's permitted turning circle. They also required frequent greasing, at 1,000 km (622 mile) intervals.

Solving these complex engineering problems would have been enough of a challenge for most car companies of that era, yet for the Traction Avant design-team there were other equally pressing difficulties to be dealt with, especially concerning manufacturing and production matters. The previous year, after having visited Renault's new establishment located on the Ile de Seguin further down the Seine, André Citroën decided that if he was to produce his new car efficiently and profitably, at the rate of a thousand units a day, he too would have to build a brand new factory, even bigger and better than his arch rival's. Accordingly, between March and July 1933, in a truly amazing burst of building activity, a third of the entire Quai de Javel site was torn down and reconstructed to provide a vast modern press shop and assembly hall, equipped with the very latest tools and machinery from America. Three years of normal work was telescoped into five months of frantic round-the-clock activity. Twelve thousand, five hundred tons of steel work was erected (more than contained in the Eiffel Tower), 1800 concrete piles were sunk and 323,000 sq. ft. of floor space laid down. Even more remarkably, this huge reconstruction program took place without disrupting routine production; the assembly line continued unceasingly throughout, turning out cars at the rate of 400 vehicles per day. The rebuilt factory was inaugurated by a gargantuan banquet held in its vast vehicle delivery hall, on the 8th of October, 1933, to which no fewer than 6,333 guests were invited.

To the assembled revellers, it seemed as if André Citroën had reached the absolute summit of his power, wealth and prestige, and that his position was unassailably secure. But beneath all the bonhomie and merrymaking of these celebrations, the situation was grim. The huge financial burden imposed on his company's resources by the development of the Traction Avant had been made quite insupportable by the extra weight of debt incurred by this massive rebuilding program. So much so that by the end of 1933 the Citroën firm had begun to experience severe financial difficulties that were exacerbated by a sudden fall in sales, caused when customers all over France, hearing rumors about a sensational new car due to be launched at the Paris Motor Show in the autumn, began delaying or cancelling their orders for the old range, depriving the firm of vital sales revenue. During the coming year, production would nose-dive to 56,123 units in contrast to the 71,472 units recorded in 1933; in 1935 it would plummet to 30,759. Between 1931 and 1933, the output of the French automobile industry fell by 20 percent (Citroën's own by 33 percent) and the number of car producers in France dropped from 90 to 28. No less than 118 banks went bust. In the midst of this economic crisis of unprecedented severity, André Citroën had spent more freely than ever before.

The result was that at the end of February 1934 the company experienced a severe cash-flow crisis and André Citroën was unable to honour, from his own resources, the payment of interest due on the loan of 150 million francs he had obtained to finance his ambitious expansion plans. When the bankers refused further short-term credit to cover the 15 million francs he needed to meet his commitments and avoid default, he was forced to appeal to the generosity of his dealers and concessionaires who rallied round to put up the necessary funds, by agreeing to pay for deliveries of stock in advance. All would be well when the Traction Avant was ready for sale, of that he was certain. The new car was bound to be a huge success and would soon restore his fortunes. Not only would his latest gamble get him out of his present difficulties, but it would also keep him in funds for years to come. No other manufacturer had anything like it. It was so advanced that it would take his rivals ages to produce a vehicle that could compete with it.

In truth, by now *le patron* was under severe pressure from all directions, like a veritable *Citron Pressé,* for to add to his financial difficulties further serious problems were occurring simultaneously on the technical side. During the closing days of 1933 he received a report from his chief scientist, Charles Brull, criticizing the choice of Sensaud de Levaud's *convertisseur* and recommending that it be replaced by a conventional gearbox forthwith. Tests on the prototype cars had revealed that, installed on the Traction Avant at least, the device was unreliable due to a tendency to overheat when placed under a heavy load. It seems that its performance was satisfactory when the car was traveling along flat roads or around test tracks and even up gentle slopes, but as soon as the driver attempted to climb a steep hill, the oil in the torque converter inevitably reached boiling point and traction was lost completely until it had cooled down sufficiently for progress to be resumed. But in spite of the evidence provided by Brull, Citroën refused to compromise, which led to a stand-up argument between the pair. It was then that Brull shouted at Citroën, "De Levaud's transmission won't help you. Ditch it before you get yourself ditched because of it." André Lefèbvre was also opposed to the device. "An excellent device for frying chips but useless as a gearbox," was his sardonic comment.

Already, a race against time had begun to get the new car onto the market as soon as possible, in order to revive sales and restore the flow of cash. This meant that staff of the Bureau d'Etudes were working flat out from dawn to dusk seven days a week. At one point its foreman, Roger Prudhomme felt obliged to remind *le patron* that his men were exhausted and needed a weekend off to rest. "My dear Prudhomme," André Citroën replied, "it's no longer a matter of days, but of hours." "In that case, m'sieu, we shall be here on Sunday as usual," came the reply.

There could scarcely have been a more eloquent testament to Citroën's powers of leadership. Charming, affable and considerate, he rarely gave orders but preferred instead to make suggestions which his subordinates could latch onto as if they had thought of the idea themselves. His ability to motivate others was almost magical; merely by walking casually among his employees of every level and ability, recognizing all by name and greeting them with a cheerful smile and warm handshake, he was able to communicate his own enthusiasm for the job and to inspire all around him with his confidence in the future. In doing so he created the unique Citroën *esprit de corps*—a mystical quasi-religion, the temple of which was the Quai de Javel.

As we have already noted, to provide a stock of cars for testing, demonstration, display and publicity purposes, the manufacture of a pre-production series of cars had commenced the moment that Cuinet and his team returned from America with the tooling for the bodyshell, in February 1934. Yet none of these vehicles were actually fitted with transmissions, due to the reservations held by Brull, Lefèbvre and the other senior engineers regarding the viability of Sensaud de Lavaud's *turbine.* The matter was finally resolved when, on the 10th of February, André Citroën demonstrated the first few examples of the Traction Avant to be fitted with the device at a secret preview held before a gathering of his technical and commercial staff. This was the first time that the *Petite Voiture* had been viewed beyond the confines of the *Bureau d'Etudes* or the Montlhery proving circuit. But far from being a triumph, the event was an embarrassing disaster due to repeated problems with the Sensaud de Lavaud transmission. Another test run staged one week later on a circular route over public roads through Suresne and Saint-Cloud confirmed the problem beyond doubt. Of the five cars that set out to cover the course, which included several steep ascents, only one returned without breaking down.

Early in March Citroën finally admitted defeat, ordering that the idea should be abandoned and replaced by a conventional clutch and mechanical gearbox, to be designed and produced by the end of the month, and using the casing of the gearbox from the 8CV Rosalie model. This feat was achieved, reputedly within a couple of weeks, by Jouffret and Forceau. Indeed, it may well be that the *Bureau d'Etudes* had foreseen the inevitability of this volte-face and had begun the work long before André Citroën reversed his decision to use the Sensaud de Lavaud device. The small, compact dimensions of the casing dictated that a three-speed synchromesh arrangement involving a secondary shaft relaying the drive back to the differential was adopted. In fact, to reduce the overall length of the engine and gearbox unit, so that the *bloc moteur* fit within the dimensions already established for the body-shell, the gearbox casing was split around the differential bearings and joined at this point with the clutch bell-housing to form an integral unit. To operate the three-speed gearbox, an unusual rod-and-tower selector mechanism was designed by Lefèbvre, incorporating the "mustard spoon" dashboard-mounted lever that was one of the Traction's idiosyncratic features.

So it happened that on the March 24, 1934, almost exactly one year after the arrival of André Lefèbvre at the Quai de Javel, the top-secret Traction Avant was at last considered ready for unveiling by its creators, at a gathering of forty leading concessionaires held at the Quai de Javel.

Assisted by Lefèbvre, Citroën proudly explained the technical features and styling details of the Citroën *Sept* or 7CV as it was to be called, drawing attention to its low-slung lines and minimal ground clearance. From now on Citroën owners would step down into their vehicles rather than climb up into them, like passengers clambering aboard the horse drawn carriages of yesteryear, André Citroën remarked. By all accounts, dealers were astounded at their first glimpse of the car and particularly by the absence of running boards. But none were permitted to drive the car; the display was static.

Three weeks later, on the 18th of April, the *Sept* was revealed to the world at large at a reception and banquet held at the Magasin d'Europe (the huge showrooms and quasi-museum that André Citroën had opened in 1931, near the Gare Saint-Lazare) where it received a rapturous reception. Among the guests were members of the motoring press and more than 350 representatives drawn from Citroën's network of concessionaires throughout France, all of them eager to get their first glimpse of the new Traction Avant. Each dealer drove home again in an example of the car, for use as a showroom or demonstration vehicle.

Evidently, by this time the car had reached full working order, as many of the journalists present were also allowed to take a test drive, though a good number among them experienced break-downs. Even at this late stage, the car exhibited a catalog of faults including knocking drive-shafts, sticking brakes, snapping torsion bars and even splitting body seams. Nevertheless, the reports that appeared in the French motoring press the following day extolled Citroën's latest achievement to the point of ecstasy. For example, the influential French magazine *l'Auto Journal* proclaimed that "The front-wheel-drive Citroën 7 is so up-to-the-minute, so audacious, so rich in original technical solutions, so different from all that has gone before that it truly deserves to be described as sensational." The journal then went on to commend its creator for having introduced, in the midst of a period of unprecedented crisis, "a car so truly French in the elegance of its engineering and its finesse of styling and design. If France is ever to recapture its pre-eminence as a car producer in overseas markets, it requires the existence of such an advanced vehicle, truly sensational in the way that it combines a high technical specification with a modest price," the journal patriotically concluded.

To recapitulate, as introduced as the Citroën Sept in April 1934, the Traction Avant was a four-seater light sedan powered by a 1303 cc four-cylinder water cooled engine, with bore and stroke dimensions of 72mm × 80mm, and rated as a 7CV under the French *puissance fiscale* system of road taxation. This was the first version of the classic long-stroke power-plant designed by Maurice Sainturat for the Traction Avant, and which was destined to remain in production for more than 40 years in a succession of various different Citroën models. An outstandingly robust and reliable design, it boasted several advanced features normally associated with much more expensive cars. One was the use of overhead valves, driven by pushrods actuated by a camshaft located low down in the block and turned by a timing chain, the first time that Citroën had employed such an arrangement, all previous passenger car engines being of the side-valve type. Another was the use of interchangeable wet-liner cylinder barrels which could be removed and replaced when worn out, with the engine in situ. This innovation, not seen

The first official publicity photograph of the Citroën *Sept* Traction Avant, taken in March 1934. The vehicle depicted was a prototype, differing in certain minor details from the definitive version of the 7CV that actually entered production. Note, for example, that there is only one windshield wiper.

previously on any mass-produced car, avoided the necessity of the re-bore which was more or less inevitable with most other engines of that era, given the current state of metallurgical and manufacturing know-how. The life expectancy of the engine was therefore doubled to more than 100,000 km (62,000 miles) and, more often than not, considerably more than that.

In a radical departure from established practice, the Traction's engine, together with its associated gearbox, transmission and front suspension elements (including torsion bars, suspension links, drive-shafts, swivelling hubs and steering gear) had been designed to form one complete, self-contained unit, the *bloc moteur.* In effect, these various mechanical elements were unified into a single sub-assembly by their connection to a massive u-shaped structural member known as the *berceau*, or cradle, which was in turn attached to the body by silent-bloc mountings that bolted onto four horn-like extensions protruding forward from the body-shell. Thus, the engine pulled the car along as if it were harnessed between two shafts, just as a horse draws a carriage. The arrangement also permitted the entire motive power unit to be assembled and tested separately, away from the car, or withdrawn *en bloc* at a later stage to facilitate maintenance and repair. Similarly, the rear axle and suspension unit was a self-contained sub-assembly, connected to the body-shell by only four bolts on each side.

Indeed, production of the Traction Avant involved a complete re-organization of assembly line procedures at the Quai de Javel, because it was put together in reverse order from that followed in the manufacture of Citroën's previous, conventional, cars. In other words the bodywork was constructed first and the engine and drive train added later to form an integrated structure, instead of the bodywork being mounted on a completely independent chassis to which the mechanical elements had already been fitted. The structure of the Traction Avant involved two separate architectural elements, the infrastructure or *cocque* and the superstructure or *caisse* which were fabricated independently and then united to form the body-shell proper, the panels that formed the exterior surfaces of the *caisse* having previously been seam-welded together by an electrical flash-welding process, in the Federal machine referred to earlier.

The infrastructure comprised the two front box members or *caissons,* left and right, which formed the engine bay, the scuttle or firewall bulkhead, and the floor pan, which was strengthened by two substantial box-section side-rails; while the superstructure comprised the visible exterior pressings, including the two large single-piece side panels which incorporated the door and windshield pillars and the frontal, rear and roof closing panels. To this body-shell were later fastened the detachable elements, including the doors, fenders, hood and radiator grille. In its earliest version, the *Sept*, the Traction Avant had a roof closing panel made of fabric rather than metal, as was the case in most conventional steel-bodied cars of that era, including Citroën's own Rosalie models. It also lacked an opening trunk, so access to the luggage space behind the rear seat was through the rear passenger doors. The *Sept* weighed 2255 pounds, about 300 pounds lighter than its predecessor, the 10CV Rosalie. This weight was distributed so that 56 percent was concentrated at the front and 44 percent at the rear, in contrast to the Rosalie which had 48 percent of its weight resting on its front axle and 52 percent on the rear.

Although its appearance seems hardly sleek to modern-day eyes (at least in comparison to other streamlined car designs of the 1930s such as the Chrysler Airflow), the Traction Avant was actually one of the very first cars to benefit from systematic aerodynamic research in a wind tunnel. The improvements resulting from these studies were such that whereas all previous comparable Citroën models required an engine power output of approximately 75 hp to travel at a constant 110 km/h (68 mph), the Traction Avant required only 56 hp to maintain the same speed.

The visible measures adopted included reducing the frontal area by 20 percent, sloping the windshield and eliminating the running boards. Yet, the most important improvement by far could not be seen. This detail was the smooth, flat underside made possible by the Traction Avant's front-wheel-drive configuration and its torsion bar suspension. With no driveshaft, transmission tunnel, rear differential unit and semi-elliptic leaf springs to be accommodated under the car, the under surface of its floor panel was entirely flat and uninterrupted by recesses and cavities. It was also set much closer to the ground, which permitted a smaller and relatively undisturbed airflow to pass under it, thus eliminating the source of under-body turbulence that so adversely affected the handling and road-holding of contemporary conventional cars.

The other two notable innovations introduced on the Traction Avant were, of course, torsion bar suspension and hydraulically operated drum brakes, using the Bendix system. Neither feature had been seen before on a mass-produced European car. The choice of horizontal torsion bars, mounted longitudinally at the front and transversally at the rear, was particularly interesting in that they allowed the ride-height (or ground clearance) of the car to be reduced to the very minimum consistent with an adequate margin of vertical wheel movement. They also had the advantage of being entirely maintenance-free.

The first series production examples of Traction Avant went on sale in France at the beginning of May 1934. The price quoted for the 1303cc sedan was 17,700 FF, 2,700 FF more than the figure that had been fixed at the outset, but not much more than the price of the by now obsolete Rosalie 10CV model, which it superseded. It seems that the purchasers of the very first car to be sold, on May 4 (chassis no. 00001), were none other than the makers of its tires, Michelin et Cie, a fact that was soon to have enormous significance for the Double Chevron firm.

There now began the stage in the introduction of the new car that André Citroën relished most of all — marketing, advertising and promotional activities. Already, with innumerable astounding stunts or *coups de publicitee* to his credit, he had proved himself to be as much a master of mass-marketing as of mass-production. A pioneer of modern mass-media communications, he took a personal interest in the techniques of publicity design and production, and he invented, or was the first to introduce from the USA, many of the advertising and promotional methods still used in the automobile industry today, such as direct-mail marketing and the use of toys and models to capture the interest of the youngsters who would one day become his future customers. By these and other means he developed a strong sense of loyalty among his clientele. The very high quantity and quality of the printed literature produced by Citroën's advertising department seemed to indicate that he was first and foremost a publisher or impresario rather than an engineer-industrialist!

His interest in graphic design was such that he even opened an in-house publicity outfit (complete with photographic studio and printing works) at the Quai de Javel. This was headed by Pierre Louys, an extremely talented photographer, graphic designer and illustrator who had originally joined his company as a car stylist. Between 1920 and 1935, Louys produced many superb pictorial advertisements, posters and calendars, plus the delightful illustrations that adorned the covers of the company's brochures and other publications, such as its famous house magazine, the *Bulletin Citroën*. As a photographer, he was also among the first to portray cars in realistic, natural, outdoor scenic locations, usually enhanced by attractive female models and, sometimes, their pets as well. In June 1934, therefore, Pierre Louys set off from Paris on a tour of France to undertake a series of publicity shots of the Traction Avant, displayed against no less than 65 widely different backgrounds. Intended for a giant calendar dedicated to the car, his photos were adorned by the presence of a beautiful blonde model who just happened to be English.

In the summer of 1934, Citroën's talented house photographer, Pierre Louys, set off to the south of France with a 7CV sedan and a pretty model who just happened to be English. He brought back a magnificent set of pictures showing the car on location in the Midi, of which this atmospheric shot is just one example.

On the 8th of June, 1934, André Citroën staged a Concours d'Elegance in the Bois de Boulogne, an event that he was particularly fond of holding, since it provided an opportunity to combine automobile glitz with feminine glamour. Seven immaculately groomed Traction Avant cars took part in the parade, each driven by a notable society beauty; four sedans, two cabriolet/roadsters and one faux-cabriolet or fixed-head coupe. By now Lefèbvre and Bertoni had begun to compose variations on a theme intended to widen the Traction Avant range by encompassing several different types and styles of vehicle. But when, after the prize giving, it was time for the cars to move off, none could do so. The brakes on all of them had overheated and locked solid. While his mechanics worked unobtrusively to free the cars, André Citroën stepped forward to distract the attention of the crowd by making an amusing impromptu speech. A few days later, another concours took place at Deauville, the seaside hol-

In June 1934 a 7CV driven by the rally driver Francois Lecot was entered in the Tour of France and Belgium, covering 5,000 km in 77 hrs non-stop, without problems. Here, in one of the very few photographs showing André Citroën with his creation, Lecot (wearing a beret) is greeted at the finish line on June 30, by *le Patron* (wearing a trilby hat).

iday resort favored by the Citroën family, at which his daughter Jacqueline, then age 19, showed off another example of the cabriolet/roadster which he had recently given to her as a birthday present. This car was also taken from a small series of vehicles produced specifically for display at Concours d'Elegance events, and which boasted certain special features.

Despite the ostensibly cheerful tone of these festivities, by now rumours of an impending disaster were spreading fast throughout the motor industry and beyond; André Citroën was in trouble. With the dire shortage of money at the Quai de Javel common knowledge, all his skills in advertising and public relations were called upon to persuade his creditors to hold off in their demand for payment. Exhausted by the physical and mental effort of keeping his business afloat, he grew paler and thinner by the day; to those who saw him in his few public appearances at that time, he seemed but a shadow of his former self. Once a noted bon vivant, Citroën had lost his appetite long ago, but now found that he could not eat at all and complained to his doctor that he was experiencing severe stomach pains. But to anxious enquiries from his colleagues he always gave the same reply, "It is nothing, just a little tummy trouble."

On the wider political and economic scene, a parallel crisis continued to mount. On the February 6 of that year, street-fighting had broken out in Paris when 40,000 demonstrators from the various fascist Leagues marched on the Chamber of Deputies in an attempt to overthrow the Republic. A second French revolution was averted only when police opened fire on the crowd in the Place de la Concorde. A week later, Communists staged a counter-demonstration and called a token general strike. Although the Third Republic was saved, the government headed by Edouard Daladier fell, to be replaced by an equally short-lived administration led by Gaston Domergue. In the current bleak political and economic climate in France there was no likelihood of government support for André Citroën; furthermore, in view of his previously uncooperative, indeed hostile, attitude towards his bankers, they also proved unwilling to mount a rescue bid. To their conventional way of thinking, Citroën's adventurous, enterprising unorthodoxy was profoundly upsetting; having dared to set up his own finance and insurance subsidiaries in competition with them, he had now to pay the price for offending and opposing these powerful financial institutions.

By July 1934 André Citroën had put together his own proposals for the refinancing of his company and the consolidation of its debts. The scheme involved a further injection of capital totalling 180 million francs—a third to be provided by the banks, a third by his dealers and concessionaires and a third by the French government, from public funds. But after much deliberation, both the banks and the government, under its new premiere, Pierre-Etienne Flandin, turned down the scheme and refused to participate. The Socialist opposition led by Leon Blum and Jules Moch demanded nationalization of the Citroën firm, claiming that the matter was one of the most painful crises of modern capitalism. Yet despite the ever-rising tide of unemployment and industrial unrest in France, there were no New Deal–style state rescue schemes on offer. Aware that Flandin was a man of the Right, and, moreover, a friend and frequent social guest of Louis Renault, many political observers detected in the decision a sinister undercurrent of hostility and anti-Semitism towards André Citroën personally. Undoubtedly, old scores were being settled by those with influence and authority whom he had offended in the past. Even among newspaper comment and public gossip, more than a trace of *schadenfreude* was evident. What had happened to all his personal wealth? Why had he no savings or financial reserves of his own to throw into the balance? Had he not gambled it all away at Deauville or lost it on the horses? Had he not admitted that he never really cared how much the croupiers raked off him? Too bad. He should have been more prudent, more cautious and have put something away for a rainy day. The fact of the matter was that André Citroën's flamboyant, free-spending style of business, so in tune with the spirit of the 1920s, now seemed to strike an uncomfortable, discordant note in the austere atmosphere of the 1930s.

Playing out his own personal drama against a backdrop of social instability, political chaos, financial scandal and economic slump, André Citroën was forced to the conclusion that, if the Double Chevron marque was to remain in French ownership, there was only one viable course of action remaining to him. To save his firm and put the Traction Avant on the road, he had no alternative but to appeal for help from old Edouard Michelin, patriarch of the Michelin tire firm which now ranked as his largest trade creditor. He had known the Michelin family for almost 30 years, since his days at Mors, and Edouard, now age 75, had visited the Quai de Javel as recently as 1928, together with his son-in-law Pierre Bourdon (who later had accompanied André Citroën on his 1931 visit to the USA, to meet President Hoover and Henry Ford). Frequently, in the past, the Michelin men had promised him money should he ever need it "Even if we take a majority shareholding and relieve you of all these tiresome financial and administrative worries, you will always have a place as President-General and Technical Director" they had assured him.

Located at Clermont-Ferrand in the Auvergne, the family-owned Michelin firm was the largest manufacturer of tires and wheels in France. As the sole suppliers of this equipment to Citroën from the outset, it had benefited greatly from the success of the Type A, introduced in 1919, which was fitted with Michelin tires, including a spare, as standard. The Type A also did much to popularize the

André Michelin (1859–1931) and his brother Edouard (1859–1940), the joint patrons of the Michelin firm, established at Clermont-Ferrand in 1889, and which had been the sole suppliers of tires and wheels to Citroën since 1919. Edouard was the inventor (in 1891) of the detachable pneumatic car and cycle tires on which the company's fortunes were founded.

removable pressed-steel disc wheels which the Auvergnats had invented earlier, in 1913. As a result, they had prospered in parallel with the rapid expansion of André Citroën's business, though by now they were owed a very large sum indeed — reputedly more than sixty million francs— for goods delivered but not yet paid for. In 1929, at the height of his success, Citroën had negotiated an agreement with the Michelins, giving him a discount of 10 percent on all wheels and tires supplied, providing that his output continued to exceed 80,000 vehicles a year. The following year, production had fallen below this figure and continued to remain there, but the discount was offered and taken nonetheless in the expectancy that sales would shortly revive, allowing the shortfall to be made up according to the terms of the deal. Thus Citroën's debt to the Michelin family mounted inexorably throughout the early 1930s.

Formally established as a sociéte commandite or private family-owned company, Michelin et Cie in 1889, the Michelin rubber firm had flourished with the coming of the automobile, thanks to the remarkable partnership formed between Edouard Michelin and his elder brother André. As the creators of Michelin's famous mascot and trademark, Monsieur Bibendum, the Michelin Man, the pair had become no less famous than André Citroën himself in pioneering the motorization of France. Actually, the brothers were the grandsons of a certain Aristide Barbier, who with his friend Edouard Daubree had founded the firm some 50 years earlier, by opening a factory at Clermont-Ferrand in 1830, to make rubber parts for agricultural machinery and equipment.

André had died in 1931, leaving Edouard in charge — at an age when most other men would have long since retired — assisted by two deputies, his youngest and only surviving son Pierre, and by his *homme de confiance*, or right-hand-man, a certain Pierre-Jules Boulanger. Unlike most of the Michelin management hierarchy, P-J. Boulanger was not actually a member of the family, either by birth or marriage. In response to Citroën's appeal, Edouard promptly sent these two lieutenants to Paris accompanied by engineers from Michelin's own Bureau d'Etudes to inspect the factories and examine the Traction Avant. Their visit, which marked a turning point in the affairs of the Citroën firm and its founder took place on July 25, 1934.

Although the fact was not common knowledge (and, indeed, remains generally unknown in France even to this day), André Citroën must have been well aware that he and Pierre Michelin shared a common Dutch-Jewish heritage. Both Edouard and André Michelin had chosen their wives from among the daughters of a certain Auguste Desirée Wolf, who had been their music teacher when as young men they had studied (architecture and painting respectively) at the École des Beaux Arts in Paris during the 1870s. A professor of music at the Paris Conservatoire and a director of the Pleyel piano-making firm, Wolf could trace his descent back to an ancestor who had traded as a diamond merchant in the Netherlands during the mid eighteenth century — Abraham Bernard Wolf, who was born in Amsterdam in 1737.

Fortunately, unlike the bankers, financiers and politicians who had refused to help Citroën, the Michelin men could grasp the finer points of automobile engineering and were able to recognize the great potential of the Traction Avant. In fact, they were deeply impressed by the vehicle and soon gave their thumbs-up to the rescue scheme. The outcome was that Edouard Michelin agreed to advance Citroën a short-term loan, in addition to the existing debt, on the condition that he would be given an option to buy the company and that he offer up his own personal shareholding in the S.A André Citroën as a security. Moreover, he was obliged to undertake not to leave the company and attempt to set up a rival firm in partnership with the Americans or his friend Ettore Bugatti, with whom he was rumored to be having secret discussions. He was also required to allow the Michelin men to assume a role in the management of the Citroën organization, in order to implement immediately a program of drastic economies and redundancies and to set up a system of quality control to overcome the evident manufacturing deficiencies affecting the sales and production of the Traction Avant. Thus the exploratory visit of Pierre Michelin and Pierre-Jules Boulanger was extended into a permanent stay.

For the next few months, the hiatus of an unofficial creditor's moratorium held sway, as all involved held off from further action in the hope of not only saving their investment but also of preventing large-scale unemployment or precipitating a general crisis of confidence in the French motor industry, a scenario of events which could only benefit foreign manufacturers. Throughout this difficult post-natal period, work continued at a furious pace to remedy the car's faults while simultaneously maintaining output at the highest possible level, regardless of deficiencies, in order to maximize sales and revenue. In March the cars rolled off the line at the rate of 100 vehicles a day, then 200 in April, and 300 in May. At the same time an extensive testing program of was conducted, at first in North Africa and then later in metropolitan France. In June the car was entered in its first competition event, a 5,000 km tour of France and Belgium, completed within 77 hours. This was immediately followed by an excursion to Moscow and back, achieved successfully in 48 hours, without a single stop except to refuel. From these tests, as well as from the criticisms voiced by the car's first customers, it soon became apparent that in its 1303 cc form, the Traction was underpowered.

So in June 1934 the 7A sedan was replaced by the 7B,

Right: **By 1927, when this poster for the new Confort tire was published, the Michelin company had become one of Europe's largest industrial corporations, with factories in the USA, UK and Italy as well as France.**

rated as a 9CV, and equipped with an enlarged 1529cc version of Sainturat's OHV push-rod engine, having bore and stroke of 78mm × 80mm. In addition, a new, more powerful sporting version of the 7, the 7S (7 Sport), was introduced that same month, equipped with a yet larger 1911cc engine, with bore and stroke of 78mm × 100mm and rated at 11CV. Both these versions were made available with an all-steel roof as an option, but the following month this feature was adopted as standard. At the same time, both the 1529cc 7B and the 1911cc 7S light sedans were joined by two new variants, a soft-topped roadster/cabriolet convertible and a hard-topped fixed head coupe or faux cabriolet, both of them two seaters (but with an additional pair of exterior dickey seats at the rear), so that the would-be Traction Avant owner now had a total of eight different versions to choose from.

Although exceedingly generous by any standard, this offering was by no means enough to satisfy André Citroën. Despite the financial problems that were currently besetting his firm, and which were shortly to spell his own personal downfall, in September 1934, just prior to the

Also in June 1934, the improved 7B series Traction Avant with a larger 1529cc engine was introduced. In addition to the sedan, the line included two new versions, a drop-head cabriolet and a fixed-head faux cabriolet. The following month a special limited-edition series of the cabriolet was produced, finished to Concours d'Elegance standards, and with fenders painted in the same color as the body.

Left: This is the first example of the Traction Avant faux cabriolet or fixed-head coupe, which appeared in July 1934. Note that like all the other early examples of the Traction, its headlights and grille were chromed while a pair of chromed klaxon horns were mounted on the bumpers.

In September 1934 came a fourth version of the Traction Avant, equipped with a more powerful 1911 cc engine rated at 11CV and featuring an enlarged body, immediately recognizable by its wider track, longer wheelbase and deeper rear quarters. This type became known as the *normale* sedan and the original smaller version, the *légere* sedan.

October Paris Salon, he announced the full extent of his ambitious plans for the Traction Avant. To exploit the economies of scale, the range was to be enlarged and expanded by the introduction of a new, improved series of vehicles having larger, heavier bodies, with track increased from 1.34 m to 1.48 m and wheelbase from 2.91 m to 3.08 m. Each of these new cars would be powered by the 11CV 1911cc engine previously introduced on the 7 Sport. When added to the 7B series, the 11 series would form a complete family of models covering every purpose and price.

The intention was that the 11 series would comprise seven different models, a six-seater heavy sedan (the 11B or Onze Normale as it became known) a fixed-head coupe, a roadster and a coupe-de-ville, all sharing the same elongated wheelbase, plus two extra-long 3.27m wheelbase variants having six-light bodies; a six-seater limousine and a nine-seater seater familiale respectively. In addition, there would also be a four-seater light berline version, which of course was actually the existing 7 Sport, now renamed as the 11BL (or Onze Legere). Previously, no other French manufacturer had offered so wide a selection of variations on a single theme; rivals like Renault preferred to produce a multiplicity of individual designs that shared only engines and a minimum of other components, a practice which Citroën considered to be wasteful and uneconomic.

At the same time, in addition to the 7 and 11 series, yet another, previously unknown, deluxe, high-performance variant of the Traction Avant was announced. Described by its creator as the fastest yet safest series production vehicle in the world, this was the fabulous 22CV, the flagship model with which André Citroën planned to assault the territory held by such prestige marques as Delage, Delahaye and Bugatti. Powered by a brand-new 100 bhp 3822cc V-8 engine developing 79 hp at 3,500 rpm and coupled to a 3-speed gearbox, the 22CV was claimed to be capable of 140kph or 87 mph. Revealed to the public for the very first time at the October 1934 Paris Motor Show, it was intended as Citroën's riposte to Henry Ford's

***Opposite bottom:* Perhaps the most elegant, stylish — and rarest — of all the pre-war Traction Avant models, the Faux Cabriolet is pictured here in a typical Pierre Louys publicity photograph, taken in Autumn of 1934.**

celebrated V8 side-valve engine, the world's first, introduced on the 18-Eight in March 1933. Designed by Maurice Sainturat, Citroën's V-8 engine was, in effect, a doubled-up version of his 1911cc four-cylinder OHV engine (78 × 100 mm bore and stroke) with its two banks of cylinders inclined at 90 degrees and sharing a common block and crankcase. The overhead valves were driven through rockers by pushrods actuated by a single central camshaft located in the apex of the "V," above the crankshaft. A range of five separate versions of the 22CV was contemplated; a roadster and a standard wheelbase berline, plus a long wheelbase coupe-deville, a limousine and a familiale, the latter pair having six-light bodies. In fact, the coachwork of the 22CV series shared the same overall dimensions and appearance of the 11 series, the main difference appearing in its revised hood, fenders and frontal aspect. This featured a chromed radiator grille ornamented by a figure eight motif set beneath the traditional Double Chevrons, chromed double bumpers and large flared fenders incorporating faired-in headlights, located, with the horns, in a

Left: The full extent of André Citroën's hugely ambitious plans for the Traction Avant was revealed in this advertisement, published during the course of the Paris motor show in October 1934, to proclaim the adoption of front-wheel-drive across the Citroën line and announce the proposed 1934-1935 season's offering. But, alas, the top-of-the-line 22CV version never reached the showrooms.

No fewer than 12 examples of the Traction Avant were displayed at the October 1934 Paris Salon, including this impressive sedan version of the newly announced 11CV variant. The two-tone paint treatment of the 11CV was soon abandoned but the contrasting black fenders persisted on all the 7CV mocels until 1937.

streamlined housing unique to the V-8 car. Priced between 32,000 and 35,000 francs, the cost of the 22CV series would have been twice that of the basic 7CV, had any examples been sold.

Unfortunately, however, André Citroën's adventurous plans for the 22CV never came to pass and the car never entered series production. Indeed, apart from a brief appearance at the Brussels Motor Show later that autumn, the car was never exhibited again. Ultimately, all the known prototypes and demonstration/show cars were destroyed, and the V-8 car quickly disappeared from memory, leaving only the barest visible traces of its existence, even in photographic form. Thus it became a legend in the annals of French motoring history. Precisely how many examples were constructed is unknown, but the number was certainly less than thirty; ultimately all were destroyed or converted to 11CV form on the instructions of the Michelin men.

Undoubtedly, the 1934 Paris Salon was one of the most important motor shows to be held in pre-war France, as it saw the European unveiling of several technically significant cars, including the Chrysler Airflow and the Voisin Aerodyne plus many other essays in aerodynamic styling, from manufacturers such as Renault, Tatra, Hupmobile and Studebaker. Even so, the revolutionary Citroën Traction Avant range, which was being displayed at a public motor show for the very first time, was easily the most interesting and important debutante present at the Grand Palais d'Exposition. The show was a personal triumph for André Citroën; by the time that it closed, the total number of the various Traction Avant models that had been sold since the car's launch the previous April reached more than 10,000 examples. Its future seemed assured, together with that of its creator ... but alas by then it was all too late.

Top: **Naturally, the star of the show was the 3822 cc V-8 engine 22CV model, which was making its first and only appearance at the Paris salon. Three examples were exhibited — a cabriolet, a standard sedan and a long-wheelbase limousine or familiale with a six-light body — but none of them entered series production. A faux-cabriolet version is also known to have been built. All these prototypes were subsequently destroyed and not a single one survived.** ***Bottom:*** **In fact, the coachwork of the 22CV cars shared the same overall dimensions and appearance of the 11CV series, the main difference in their revised hood and frontal aspect — which featured a chromed radiator grille ornamented by a figure-eight motif, chromed double bumpers and large flared fenders incorporating unique faired-in headlights. Priced at 32,000–35,000 francs, the cost of the 22CV series was twice that of the basic 7CV.**

A month or so later, towards the end of November

By the autumn of 1934, production of the Traction Avant was in full swing at the Quai de Javel factory. A total of 30,548 cars were produced during that calendar year though output fell to 19,571 the following year, as production was interrupted in January 1935 to rectify the various technical faults that had marred the earliest examples and to improve the general quality of construction. In 1936 sales recovered, to 31,245 units.

1934, a small creditor by the name of Jean Ostheimer, owner of the Compagnie Franco-Americaine des Jantes en Bois, a supplier of bakelite steering wheels, which was owed a mere 60,000 francs, lost patience, broke ranks from the moratorium and put in the equivalent of a winding-up petition in the French commercial courts. Under French law, the Société Anonyme André Citroën was then required to deposit a statement of its financial situation at the Financial Tribunal of Paris. Under normal circumstances, a man of André Citroën's abilities would surely have found a way around this minor impasse, but by now he was a very sick man and had lost the physical strength and intellectual will to struggle on alone. Indeed he may well have already reached the realization that, far from being just a gastric ulcer that would heal in time, his illness was incurable and that he was doomed.

Unable to prove that its assets exceeded its liabilities, his company was declared insolvent and a state of judicial administration was imposed on December 21, 1934. To provide time for a permanent solution to be found, and to safeguard as many as possible of the 20,000 jobs still provided by the company, the SAAC was provisionally allowed to continue production of the Traction Avant at the previous level of trading, although initially its factories were closed for 10 days to allow an inventory to be carried out. A management committee was appointed by the court, comprising representatives of the three largest creditors, Lazard Fréres (Citroën's merchant bankers) the Comptoire Siderurgique (suppliers of steel) and the Société Michelin.

A few months later, Jean Ostheimer sold his business to the Michelin family. Cynics noted that his reward was an appointment as managing director of the tire company's American subsidiary. The affair remains a subject of controversy in France even today, and the Citroën family continues to maintain that the court's judgment was unjustified, in that André Citroën's assets (including the freeholds of his four Paris factories and other property interests) had been grossly undervalued. By this point the price of the company's shares, which five years earlier had topped 2,000 FF, had tumbled to just 52 FF.

Mindful of the repercussions that the debacle would have on their own fragile trading positions, the entire European and American motor industry closed ranks to witness André Citroën's collapse. The great gambler had rocked the boat once too often with his crazy ideas and overly-ambitious innovations. In these turbulent economic times, who among other motor-manufacturers would be rash enough to risk his own skin by jumping into unknown waters in order to save such an incorrigible adventurer and individualist? Fearing that U.S. interests might seize control of their motor industry entirely, just as the Americans had wrested away France's early lead in aeronautical engineering and air travel, the French government had proposed a merger with Renault as the solution, but this idea was rejected out of hand by André Citroën. Consequently, there was no other alternative for him but to admit defeat. In an agreement signed on December 15, 1935, the Michelin family took over the Citroën company lock, stock and barrel, acquiring a 57 percent controlling interest in its share capital in exchange for an agreement to assume responsibility for paying off all its debts. Moreover, in return for the surrender of André Citroën's own personal shareholding, it was agreed that he would be indemnified against personal bankruptcy. Although he was allowed to remain as titular head of the firm as Chairman following the judgment of the court, he was forced to relinquish all executive control to Pierre Michelin and P-J.Boulanger. Moreover, certain of his subsidiary companies, including the Société Anonyme des Taxis Citroën and the Citroën-Kegresse concern (makers of the caterpillar tracked vehicles with which he had staged his great geographical expeditions in Africa and Asia) were either wound-up or sold off. In effect, the Citroën company and its founder had been swallowed up in one great gulp by Monsieur Bibendum, the Michelin Man.

For a brief few weeks, André Citroën continued to make a regular appearance at the Quai de Javel, just as he had done almost every day for the past 15 years. But then in February 1935, he received a message from Pierre Michelin suggesting that it was no longer necessary for him to come to his office. In fact, under the circumstances, it might be best for all concerned if he stayed at home. By now his health was deteriorating visibly by the day, but far from aiding his recovery from illness, the suggestion came as a mortal blow. On reading the note, he broke down in the presence of his wife, devastated at the thought of being excluded from his beloved factories, the creation of which had been his life's work.

The shock of his dismissal proved fatal. On January 18, 1935, he was admitted to a private clinic in the rue Georges-Bizet, where a malignant tumor was diagnosed. All efforts by the doctors and surgeons to defeat the cancer (a course of treatment which culminated in a major operation performed on the 9th of May) proved unsuccessful. At 9am on Wednesday, July 3, 1935, André Citroën passed away. He was seven months short of his 57th birthday. Having built up Europe's largest car company from nothing in just 15 years, he had been left with nothing. Some said that he had died of a broken heart, the victim of political duplicity and treachery; others believed that his death was the inevitable result of the mental and physical exhaustion brought about by months of prolonged, and ultimately futile, efforts to save his firm.

André Citroën was buried on Friday, July 5th, at the

The Michelin tire company took an interest in the Traction Avant from the start, featuring it in their sales literature, as in this Michelin photograph showing a tire change in progress on an early 7CV.

Montparnasse Cemetery, in a short religious ceremony conducted by the Chief Rabbi of Paris, after being borne from the Quai de Javel in a horse-drawn hearse, followed by a long cortege of mourners. On his coffin, draped with a black velvet cloth embroidered in silver thread with the Double Chevron badge, were placed his insignia as a Grand Officier of the Legion d'Honneur. The following day, lavish tributes were published by the Paris newspapers in which he had so often made front page news. *Le Matin* described him as "the man who had popularized the automobile with bold new manufacturing and advertising practices," while *Paris Soir* followed suit by celebrating "the ideal modern businessman who had no qualms about using the most unusual forms of advertising."

The event did not pass unnoticed in England, a country which he often visited, and where he had established the first of his foreign factories, at Slough in 1926. In its obituary, *The Times* recorded that "his death removes from the industrial world ... one of the most striking personalities of post-war years." *The Daily Telegraph* went further, saying, "he was a man whose business achievements were astonishing. By sheer ability he succeeded in making his previously unknown name almost as famous as any in Europe. No enterprise was too great for André Citroën. An active brain impelled him to carry out one great commercial adventure after another. The greater the risk, the more the enterprise appealed to him."

Having lost his fortune, his company and the rights to the use of his own name, André Citroën never saw his optimism vindicated by the resounding success of the "new concept in motoring" that bore his name, nor indeed by the long line of avant-garde designs which followed it. Ironically, the Citroën Traction Avant was a gamble that paid off for everyone except its creator. Hailed by the press and public alike for its exceptional stability, exemplary handling and superb road-holding, it quickly became a legend. Indeed, as we shall see, its rapid commercial success allowed the company's new owners to repay all his remaining debts within two years of acquiring control and to embark on another odyssey of engineering exploration and achievement. The results would be just as great as those which its founder had attained.

3

The Citroën Traction Avant, 1934–1940 and 1945–1957

When the doors opened at the next Paris motor show, in October 1935, it was not André Citroën but Pierre Michelin who welcomed the President of France, Albert Lebrun, to the Citroën stand. For the first time since 1919, the founder of the Double Chevron firm was missing from the event, and undoubtedly his absence cast a shadow over the proceedings.

Pierre Michelin, the new *patron* of the Quai de Javel, was the fifth child and only surviving son of Edouard Michelin, the patriarchal figure who, with his elder brother André, had put the Michelin tire and rubber firm quite literally on the map, by patenting the world's first detachable pneumatic tire in 1891, and then later developing its famous brand of travel, hotel and restaurant guides for motorists and tourists.

At a board meeting held just a few days earlier, on September 30, 1935, Edouard had nominated Pierre as the *President-Directeur-General* or Chairman of the S.A. André Citroën, thus concluding the lengthy negotiations that the Michelin family conducted with the company's bankers and creditors to permit their takeover of the Double Chevron firm, following the events of André Citroën's bankruptcy and subsequent death, three months before. In fact, with the backing of the French government, the bankers had already refinanced the company by opening a 50 million franc credit in January 1935.

Pierre Michelin (1903–1937), Edouard's son, assumed effective control of the Citroën firm in July 1934. But a mere three years later, in December 1937, he met his death at the wheel of a Traction Avant while en route from Paris to Clermont-Ferrand. He was succeeded by his deputy, Pierre-Jules Boulanger.

To assist him in his mission of rescue and reorganization, Pierre Michelin had in turn appointed a certain senior Michelin executive, Pierre-Jules Boulanger, to take charge of the day-to-day running of the Citroën company's factories and supervise the work of its Bureau d'Etudes, or design and research department, and thus to become responsible for commissioning and approving prototypes. Unusually, P-J. Boulanger (of whom we will hear much more in later chapters) was not a member of the Michelin tribe, either by birth or marriage. His connection with the family had begun in 1906, when as a young man undergoing his period of compulsory military service he had become friendly with Marcel Michelin, the only son of André Michelin, who was serving in the same unit of the French army. Born in March 1885 at Sin-le-Noble, a village on the outskirts of Douai in northern France, Boulanger had been forced by family circumstances to abandon his Arts & Metiers education and to emigrate to the USA at the age of 23. Arriving on the U.S. west coast in 1908, he began to work his way up in the world the hard way, starting at the bottom as a ranch-hand in the Rockies. By 1910, after a brief spell as a tram driver in San Francisco, by 1910 he found himself employed as a draughtsman with a firm of architects in Seattle. A year later he had become his own boss, having founded a building and construction firm called Modern

Houses Ltd in the Canadian City of Vancouver, British Columbia.

But three years later, upon the outbreak of the First World War, Boulanger sold his business and returned to France to rejoin his former unit, the 25th Balloon Observation Battalion, eventually transferring to a reconnaissance squadron of the Service Aeronautique (the French Army Air Corps) where he became a specialist in aerial photography, flying behind enemy lines to observe German troop movements and artillery positions. By the end of the war, he was promoted to the rank of captain, having been shot down by anti-aircraft fire in 1917, sustaining serious injuries. For this exploit he was awarded several decorations for bravery and meritorious service, including the Legion d'Honneur and the honorary Order of the British Empire.

During the war, Boulanger had renewed his friendship with Marcel Michelin and on his frequent visit to Clermont-Ferrand had made a great impression on the Michelin family. After the Armistice, Marcel's uncle, Edouard Michelin, invited him to postpone his return to the USA in order to supervise a program of building work planned for the Michelin factory and headquarters, including the provision of housing for its expanding labor force. By 1930 Boulanger reached the top management echelons of the company, was accepted as an ex-officio member of the family, and as the trusted advisor and confidant of Edouard Michelin himself.

It is all too often assumed that, on its launch in April 1934, the Traction Avant had already been developed to the point of perfection and had reached its definitive form. However, the truth is very different. As we saw in the previous chapter, it had proved impossible for André Lefèbvre to achieve a miracle within the short space of time that elapsed between his arrival at Citroën, in March 1933, and the launch of the car in April 1934. It is hardly surprising, therefore, that the earliest versions of the car — a revolutionary, all-new design sharing no common parts with its Citroën predecessors— exhibited a woeful catalog of faults and problems as a result of its over-hasty development and premature introduction. Indeed, its first owners were put into the position of being unpaid test-drivers, liable to experience endless breakdowns which the staff of Citroën's sales and service network were unable to remedy, since these dealers and *garagistes* lacked both the technical know-how and the many special tools required. Only Maurice Sainturat's remarkably robust, reliable and fault-free OHV engine gave complete satisfaction, and without it the Traction Avant would surely have proved a complete fiasco.

So it was that throughout 1934 and 1935, Lefèbvre and his fellow engineers struggled to solve a succession of unforeseen difficulties— not merely to counter the criticisms of disappointed customers, but also to stem the outflow of cash on warranty claims, which had to be paid from funds that were already severely depleted as a result of low sales. The list of illnesses to be cured was daunting. First and foremost the *cocque*, or body-shell, lacked sufficient torsional strength so that it flexed and deformed on the road, to the extent that the doors often flew open unexpectedly or refused to shut. The welding-up of the panels was inadequate, so that the joints and seams let in water when it rained, allowing corrosion to form in the box sections. The brakes were prone to locking up and overheating, and both the torsion bars and stub axles often failed due to fatigue. The driveshafts were noisy and wore out rapidly; no less than six modifications were tried until a satisfactory alternative was found. Similarly, the fragile gearbox and its unusual system of actuating rods linking it to the "mustard spoon" change-speed lever on the dashboard was a constant source of trouble, jumping out of gear repeatedly, until a locking device was incorporated in the mechanism. And, as if that were not enough, the action of the steering gear was sloppy and imprecise, with a poor lock-to-lock travel that made parking maneuvers difficult. Consequently, during the gestation, nativity and infancy of the Traction Avant, the situation at Citroën was one of constant crisis in all departments, financial and technical alike.

Fortunately, however, one of the first emergency measures taken by Pierre Michelin on assuming control at the Quai de Javel had been to call in the services of Antoine Hermet, a first-class automobile engineer from the Michelin factory at Clermont Ferrand, to study the various technical problems besetting the new car, in order to assess its viability for further production and make recommendations on how it could be improved, if at all. Had M. Hermet produced an unfavorable report on his arrival there early in 1935, there can be no doubt that André Citroën's brain-child would have been killed, swiftly and unceremoniously, and replaced by a more conventional design. But after thorough tests and evaluations had been carried out, his verdict was that the vehicle's numerous defects and deficiencies could all be quickly remedied, and that it would be profitable to do so.

According to insiders, M. Hermet's role in keeping the Traction Avant alive in the difficult period that followed its birth has been greatly overlooked by automobile historians until now. Working closely with André Lefèbvre and the Bureau d'Etudes team, he was directly responsible for many of the improvements of design and construction that saved the car from oblivion and ensured its extended lifespan. Later, he went on to become head of the unique Super-Controle department set up by Pierre Michelin at Citroën, the first, true, super-quality inspection and control department established by any major automobile manufacturer.

Under M. Hermet's supervision, a constant stream of revisions and improvements was made to the original design throughout the next two years, so many, in fact, that on completion of the process, at the end of 1936, there was scarcely a common, interchangeable part left to be shared between the latest cars coming off the production line and those produced at the outset of production, at the beginning of 1934.

The first important consequence of the involvement of *les Michelin* in the development of the Traction Avant was that, by January 1935, completely new and redesigned suspension and transmission arrangements had been introduced, with no expense spared in either the methods or materials employed. At the front, both the Gregoire-Tracta and the subsequent Rzeppa drive shafts used on previous series-production cars (which had proved extremely difficult to machine with the required degree of precision) were replaced by American Glaenzer Spicer units with double crosshead universal joints at the outboard end and a single crosshead universal joint at the inboard end. Theoretically, this was a far less desirable solution to the problem of providing constant velocity power transmission but, in practice, it was simpler in construction and easier to manufacture. Similarly, the front suspension sub-assembly or cradle was strengthened and improved by the fitting of new wishbone-type upper links to the hubs, made of drop-forged steel, and located at their inner ends by phosphor bronze bushes. The horizontal torsion bars connected to the lower links were relocated in flexible rubber silent blocs to isolate the car from road-induced vibrations passing through the suspension. And, lastly, the original friction dampers, also mounted on the lower links, were replaced by telescopic shock-absorbers placed transversally between the lower suspension link and the cradle. At the rear, the trailing axle too was redesigned, the tubular cross-member linking the hubs being replaced by a lightweight cruciform section dead-axle, with any sideways movement of the whole assembly being restrained by a Panhard rod. Likewise, vertically mounted telescopic shock-absorbers replaced the vane-type Luvax dampers previously used. Inside the car a new type of tubular-framed seating replaced the pattern originally chosen by André Citroën.

Next, in May 1935, an entirely reworked body shell was introduced. Although its outward appearance was unchanged, internally it was massively reinforced to increase its structural stiffness and rigidity, and thus overcome its proneness to deformation and distortion. Then, at the October 1935 Paris Salon, an opening trunk-lid giving access to the luggage compartment was announced, allowing baggage to be loaded directly from the outside of the car, rather than through the passenger doors as before. The introduction of this feature, absent in the original design, was made possible by the strengthening measures incorporated earlier in the body shell. The provision of this downward opening trunk-lid made it necessary to move the license plate to a new location on the car's left fender, mounted on an upright metal panel. At the same time, the Traction's external appearance was altered further by the adoption of a painted radiator grille with flat-profile chevrons mounted in front of the bars, and by the relocation of the horns to a new position behind the grille so that the small chromed apertures in the fenders (which had been introduced in January that year) disappeared. On the original 7 of 1934, the horns had been fixed to the bumpers.

The Traction Avant range announced at the 1935 Salon for production during the 1935-36 season comprised eleven cars; three versions of the 7C, a sedan, roadster and faux-cabriolet; three of the 11L, a sedan, roadster and faux-cabriolet; and five of the 11, a sedan, roadster and faux-cabriolet plus a long-wheelbase limousine and familiale. In addition, the production of five conventional cars—two 7UA and three 11UA models—was continued. The range of paint colors adopted that season continued the two-tone schemes originally proposed by André Citroën for the 7 at the outset, in July 1934—navy blue, beige, pearl grey, claret and black, teamed with black fenders—except that pearl grey was replaced by olive green and steel grey. Indeed, this same selection continued with only minor changes (all of them special-order options only) until 1939, when a standard, universal black was adopted.

Interestingly, at the 1935 Salon it was also announced that a diesel-engine version of the RWD 11UA Rosalie car was to be produced, powered by a 1767cc compression-ignition engine employing Ricardo Comet combustion chambers and designated the 11UD. This engine had already been successfully developed during the course of 1934, in conjunction with the British firm, Ricardo Consulting Engineers, based at Shoreham in Sussex, with which Andrè Citroën had established a research and licensing agreement the previous year. This program of technical collaboration also foresaw the manufacture of a dieselized version of the 1911cc Traction-Avant engine, for service in taxi versions of the FWD car. In the event, limited numbers only of the former vehicle were ever produced, and none whatsoever of the latter, so that, under the Quai de Javel's new Michelin owners, the use of the Citroën-Ricardo diesel engine was confined to trucks and commercial vehicles only.

Although during 1935 production fell by 10,000 units (to approximately 18,000 cars from the 28,000 cars built in 1934) this output was clearly far more profitable; as a direct result of Pierre Michelin's improvements, the time taken to assemble the Traction Avant was cut from 955

Typical of the much improved models of the Traction Avant produced during the first half of 1936 under the new Michelin regime was the 1911 cc engine 11A sedan, the forerunner of the post-war Onze Normales. Outwardly, the car now presented a more sober, less elaborate appearance. Although the headlights remained chromed, the radiator shell was painted, with the chevrons, made from alloy, fixed in front of the grille bars. Also, the horns were relocated behind small apertures pierced in the front fenders.

hours at the start of 1935 to 535 hours at the end of the year, and to 480 hours in 1936.

That year saw the next, and perhaps greatest, technical improvement resulting from the Michelin takeover when in May 1936 the original Gemmer worm and peg steering box with its over-complicated linkages was replaced by an entirely new system working on the rack and pinion principle, the first time that this concept had been applied to a mass-produced automobile. A masterpiece of design, this cleverly conceived component exploited and enhanced the geometry of the suspension and, at a stroke, transformed the driving qualities of the car, to give it its enduring reputation for positive and responsive handling, coupled, of course, with leech-like road-holding and directional stability. Indeed, this direct-acting steering made it possible for the Traction's driver to change direction, swerve or take avoiding action rapidly with little risk of losing control or overturning, giving the car its reputation as the ultimate pursuit or get-away car, favored by cops and robbers alike. Placed in a new location below the gearbox and linked to the wheels by track-rods pivoting on internal ball-joints, the rack was now connected directly to the steering wheel by a column passing obliquely up through the body shell and bulkhead to the dashboard rather than by a relay shaft running horizontally across the engine compartment, as before, thus eliminating the vagueness and slackness that had compromised the handling of earlier versions of the Traction Avant. At the same time, the layout of the interior controls and instrumentation were also revised, by moving the speedometer, fuel gauge and other instruments from their original location in the center of the dashboard to a new binnacle located behind the steering wheel and projecting forward from the fascia.

By the summer of 1936, thanks to the very substantial investment made by Citroën's new owners, the development of the Traction Avant had at last reached the state of maturity, and the car was now *au point*. The teething troubles of its infancy had largely been overcome and it was an established success, recognized as an exceedingly robust, reliable and safe means of transport. It can therefore be argued that the New Concept in Motoring was as much a Michelin achievement as the creation of André Citroën. The Michelin family certainly thought so themselves. Writing to his father in February 1935, Pierre Michelin remarked that it was evident that the world at large — not merely the general public but also the company's bankers and suppliers— had so far failed to acknowledge the importance of their technical contribution at Citroën, or the true extent of the progress that had been made on improving the car over the past year. To which old Edouard Michelin replied "I ask myself how we can make it known that we are the fathers of the 7. Look how our technical staff has been collaborating with André Citroën for more than a year to get the car just right. It is thanks to our efforts that it is what it is today."

Moreover, now that the full potential of Lefèbvre's revolutionary design had been realized, the virtues of front-wheel-drive itself were fast becoming far more widely understood and appreciated among the general motoring public in France, who were returning to the showrooms. In fact, the worst effects of the Depression had passed and the demand for motor vehicles was reviving rapidly. The minutes of a board meeting held at the end of June 1936 reveal that, although all advertising and promotional activity had been suspended, and down-payments increased from 500 to 1,000 FF, orders continued to flow in faster than they could be filled; currently there was a backlog of 4,000 orders, the equivalent of a month's production. By September 1936, sales were running at the rate of 41,537 vehicles per year (as opposed to 30,950 during the low point of 1935) and Citroën had regained its position as France's premier car manufacturer, holding 26% of the home market that month, with sales of 2,758 vehicles. By March 1937, the backlog of orders stood at 8,000 cars—and that happy seller's market situation continued for years to come.

The range for the 1936/37 season announced at the October 1936 Paris Motor Show offered few differences from the previous year's offering except that the 11 series models were renamed as the 11B series, all previous 1911cc cars being referred to henceforth as the 11A series. The five conventional rear-wheel-drive cars remained in the catalog throughout the year. With one exception the same line-up continued during the following season, including the various 7UA and 11UA models, though these were eventually withdrawn from sale in the spring of 1938, by which time the viability of the Traction Avant had been established beyond any doubt. From that point on, the Citroën company built and sold only front-wheel-drive vehicles, the first major motor manufacturer in the world to entirely abandon rear-wheel-drive entirely throughout its passenger and light commercial vehicle ranges.

The sole new arrival in the Citroën catalog for the 1937-38 season was a utility version of the Traction Avant, the 11B Commerciale, aimed at a section of the rural population whose needs and requirements the Michelin men considered to be neglected. Thanks to its twin opening rear doors (the tailgate folded down and the window section lifted up) the Commerciale was a versatile dual-purpose vehicle, capable of carrying a 500 kg (1,100 lb.) payload. Derived from the long wheel-base 11B Familiale version, the Commerciale was essentially a family people-carrier that doubled as a van or light lorry, specifically intended for use by farmers, winegrowers and smallholders, or by country merchants, shopkeepers and tradesmen such as butchers and bakers. A contemporary sales brochure showed the vehicle being loaded-up with a wide variety of cargoes, including sacks, churns, boxes and barrels—and even live sheep and pigs. The rear passenger seat did not fold flat to form the load floor as in a modern station wagon, but could easily be removed to allow a false floor to be installed when transporting freight in the car's workaday role, and then replaced when it resumed its family-carrying duties.

Arguably, the Michelin brothers' idea of driving on a cushion of air rather than a solid circular block of rubber was as important a breakthrough in the technical development of the automobile as was the invention of the internal combustion engine. Certainly, the innovation improved immeasurably the comfort of drivers and passengers alike, and as their endurance was increased, so too was the range and mobility of the machine itself extended, transforming the automobile from a rich man's plaything into a practical method of road transport. In doing so the pneumatic tire not only gave an enormous impetus to the growth of the automobile industry, but it also boosted the fortunes of the Michelin family in particular.

Edouard and André Michelin belonged, in effect, to a clan or tribe of closely related individuals who could trace their descent back over many generations of intermarriage. Thus the Michelins and their network of kinsmen and women—for the most part merchants, lawyers, farmers and land-owners long established in the Auvergne region—were pillars of the local community and of the Catholic church, the epitome of middle-class respectability. The wealth that they had recently accumulated, almost by accident, through their shrewdly perceptive recognition of the commercial potential of rubber, had not changed their ways at all. No member of the Michelin family was ever to be seen at a race-course or night-club, much less a casino, the favorite haunt of André Citroën. Their deep religious beliefs had not only imbued them with a strongly ascetic work ethic, but had also made them parsimonious and somewhat puritanical, soberly bourgeois and utterly thrifty and unpretentious in their habits.

Even so, their horror of gambling did not mean that they were unwilling to back their hunches, or that as entrepreneur-industrialists they were afraid to risk their money on a promising venture. Consequently, throughout the previous 40-odd years, their profits had consistently been re-invested in further research and development. Having begun in 1895 by producing the first detachable pneumatic tire and then, in 1899, the first tire capable of withstanding speeds of more than 100 km/h (62 mph), the brothers had gone on to launch, in 1923, the world's first low pressure (2.5 bars) balloon tire, the Confort. In this, the tread-carrying rubber outer casing containing the pressurized inner tube was reinforced by layers of textile material, laid in a criss-cross pattern. By reducing friction with the road surface, this technique allowed the tire to run much faster without risk of overheating, and therefore greatly improved both its safety and service life. The Confort was normally capable of covering at least 15,000 km (9,323 miles), double that of ordinary contemporary tires. In 1932, the Confort was followed by

The Pilote wheels and tires greatly enhanced the already excellent handling and road-holding qualities of the Traction Avant and helped to establish its unrivalled reputation for superior cornering ability. The Traction's racy sports car image was typified by this 7C roadster-cabriolet, produced throughout the 1937-1938 season. Note that the cars of this pre-war period still retained the twin hood ventilation slats of the original 1934 design rather than the louvers seen on post-war cars.

the very low pressure (1.5 bars) Super Confort capable of lasting 30,000 km (18,645 miles), and in 1934 by the world's first rain tire, the Super Confort Stop, which featured a tread pattern molded, not cut, into its circumference, specifically designed to reduce the danger of skidding in wet conditions. The next great innovation from the Clermont-Ferrand firm was the Michelin Pilote tire, which made its first appearance at the 1937 Paris Motor Show. The Pilote was the world's first low-profile tire, with an aspect ratio of 0.80; in other words, its sidewall measured only 80 percent of the width of its tread. Designed specifically to enhance the road-holding and ride-comfort of high-performance cars, it duly became standard equipment on the Traction Avant range, in conjunction with the special lightweight wheels of the same name also made by Michelin. Designed to reduce unsprung weight and weighing a kilo less than their predecessors, these Pilote wheels featured a novel, slatted form of construction, the vanes between the hubs and rims acting as ventilating fans to cool the brake drums, which were deeply finned.

Automobiles were not the only means of transportation in which the Michelins took an interest. In the early 1930s they had introduced their experimental Michelin diesel-engined railcars, which featured rubber-tired wheels for better acceleration and braking and quieter running. Intended for rural rather than mainline intercity service these "Michelines" had been developed in conjunction with the Budd Manufacturing Company. Ultimately, the experiment was unsuccessful and they were withdrawn from service because of the excessive wear of their expensive rubber-shod wheels, but the idea continued to be employed on underground railways, including the Paris Metro, where such trains are still in use today.

By the time that it acquired the Citroën company in 1935, the Michelin firm had grown to become one of France's major industrial and commercial enterprises, employing more than 40,000 people worldwide and owning factories in the United Kingdom, Belgium, Germany, Italy, Spain, Czechoslovakia, Argentina and the USA as well as in France. Yet it was still far short of being a truly international organization, and retained an identity and culture that reflected its French provincial origins. Nevertheless, even at that point, the Michelins held global ambitions; to pursue these aims they had already disposed of their original agricultural equipment business and abandoned all their many other peripheral activities, including the making of golf balls and other sports equipment, to concentrate exclusively on their core tire-making and publishing activities, plus, of course, their reorganization and revitalization of Citroën, a company of similar size and stature.

Sadly, this success had not been achieved without pain and grief. Four years previously, in 1931, André Michelin had died at the age of 78, leaving the firm in the hands of Edouard who was assisted by his brother's only son Marcel and his own two sons, Etienne and Pierre. The succession seemed secure. But within a few months Etienne was also dead, having been killed while attempting to land an aircraft on the Puy de Dome, the extinct volcano that is the highest peak of the Auvergne mountains. Five years later tragedy struck the Michelin family yet again. On December 30, 1937, while driving along Route Nationale 7 between Paris and Clermont-Ferrand, to spend the New Year holiday with his wife and children, Pierre Michelin was killed at the wheel of his Traction Avant, at the village of Mormant, south of Montargis. Thereafter, for the following 13 years, the responsibility for running Citroën fell on Pierre-Jules Boulanger alone, though under the overall direction of, initially, Edouard Michelin, and Edouard's son-in-law, Robert Puiseux, who assumed control of the entire conglomerate following Edouard's death in 1940.

Meanwhile, the development of the Traction Avant continued to progress, slowly but surely. In February 1938, the French Ministry of Mines (which even nowadays acts as the equivalent of the British Department of Transport and the Environment with specific responsibility for examining prototypes and awarding Type Approval prior to series production) received a new submission from the Citroën firm, an addition to the Traction Avant range aimed at customers seeking higher performance. This was the 15-Six, the prestige flagship model that was eventually to earn the soubriquet *Reine de la Route,* as the foremost volume-production prestige car of France in the Fifties and Sixties. A true *Grande Routiere* in the tradition established by such marques as Delage and Delahaye, the 15-Six (actually rated as 16CV) was a spacious, luxurious but relatively inexpensive high-performance tourer, capable of cruising the *routes nationales* with unprecedented speed and security, and thus fulfilling the role that André Citroën had envisaged for his V-8 engine 22CV car, exhibited at the 1934 Paris Motor Show, but never produced. Given the policy of caution and restraint adopted by the Michelin management, however, there was no thought of reviving this 3822cc V-8 engine, nor even of incorporating some of the 22CV's other special features such as its streamlined, faired-in headlights. Instead, in the interest of achieving the greatest possible commonality of parts, the engine chosen was a 2867cc straight-six based on the 11CV four-cylinder Traction Avant engine, with the same 78mm × 100mm bore and stroke dimensions, due to its use of identical pistons and detachable wet cylinder liners. Producing 75 hp at 3800 rpm, the 15-Six had a top speed of 125 km/h, only 15 km/h less than that claimed for the 22CV. In fact, this six cylinder engine, again designed by Maurice Sainturat, packed a far more powerful punch than these figures suggest; its true performance can be gauged by its impressive torque of 191.3 Nm @ 1500 rpm.

The 15-Six body-shell was a modified version of that of the *Onze Normale*, reinforced at certain points. To ac-

This commodious 1938-1939 11A Commerciale, powered by the 1911 cc engine, was also typical of the period. The six-light long wheelbase body variants, dating from 1934, were currently available in three separate versions — the nine seater familiale (which had a row of three folding occasional seats between its front and rear bench seats), a six-seater limousine (no occasional seats), and the commerciale (which had a double-opening split rear door for the loading of freight). Note the Pilote wheels.

Responding to a widespread demand for greater performance, in 1937 Citroën's Michelin masters authorized the development of a more powerful top-of-the-line Traction Avant model, to take the place of the abandoned V-8 22CV. The result was the 15-Six, with a body derived from the 11CV Normale, but powered by a 2867 cc straight-six engine, rated at 15CV. The first five models, built in June and July 1938, were presented to Pierre Boulanger, Robert Puiseux and other members of the Michelin family. The 15-Six was commercialized in February 1939 in three separate versions, a standard sedan plus two long-wheelbase six-light cars, a limousine and a familiale. A small number of roadster-cabriolets were also built—at least three but certainly no more than six—for certain privileged customers. This is the limousine version.

commodate its larger and heavier engine and transmission axle cradle, its hood and engine compartment valences were extended forward, making it 110 mm longer overall. Its front track was 1487 mm (1660 mm on the 11BN) its wheelbase was 3087 mm (3090 mm for the 11B) and its overall length 4760 mm (4650 for the 11B). An entirely new three-speed gearbox and transmission were employed, together with a redesigned front cradle, enlarged to accommodate the bigger engine and gearbox, while the driveshafts, swivels, wheel-arms and torsion bars were also redesigned and beefed up. In order to reduce the length of the gearbox to the minimum, the compact layout adopted for its lay-shaft and differential required that the engine rotated in the opposite direction—counter-clockwise from right to left when viewed from the front, so that the car was referred to as the 15-Six G or gauche. In all other respects, the 15-Six followed the same technical conception as the 11CV Traction Avant models and, quite naturally, made full use all the various improvements that had previously been introduced on the other members of the family.

From the exterior, the 15-Six could be distinguished from the rest of the range by its painted radiator grille, with the chevrons fixed behind, rather than in front of, the grille bars, by the row of fixed ventilation louvers on the hood rather than the adjustable vents seen on the current four-cylinder cars, and by the two klaxon horns mounted on its front bumpers. With a few exceptions, the car was almost always painted black, with ivory-colored wheels which were of course Michelin's unique slatted Pilote type, shod with 185 × 400 Pilote tires, newly available that year. The headlights were chromed, but otherwise there was a notable absence of brightwork. Its interior fitments and furnishings were similarly subdued and restrained, with maroon cloth seats and a black-painted fascia; the layout of the dashboard instrumentation and controls was similar to that found on the four-cylinder cars.

Although the 15-Six was exhibited at the 1938 Paris show (a small pre-series having been built for Boulanger and other members of the Michelin clan in June/July that year) the first series-production examples of the berline or sedan did not appear until February 1939, priced at 36,500 FF in comparison with the 27,700 FF then being asked for the equivalent four-cylinder Traction model, the 11B Performance *Onze Legere*. The arrival of the six-cylinder sedan was closely followed by the appearance of two long-wheelbase versions, a limousine and a familiale, in March and April 1939 respectively. Later that year, a very small number of a cabriolet/roadster version were also produced (perhaps as few as five) for use by members of the Michelin family and certain other celebrities, but the launch and commercialization of this model, planned for the October 1939 Paris motor show, never took place.

For the 1938/39 season, the Citroën range (as exhibited at the October 1938 Paris Motor Show) comprised 13 cars, all of them Traction Avant models; the 1628cc 7C and the 1911cc 11BL (*Onze Legere*) both available in either sedan or roadster form; the 1911cc 11B (*Onze Normale*) available as a standard wheelbase sedan or roadster, and as a long-wheelbase, six-light limousine, familiale or commerciale; and lastly, of course, the new 2867cc 15-Six sedan, limousine and familiale models just described. The faux-cabriolet versions of the 7C, 11BL and 11B had all been deleted the previous month, in September 1938. From February 1939 onwards, the 7C became the 7C Economique, on account of various engine modifications which reduced its fuel consumption by 10 percent without affecting performance, while the 11BL and 11B were equipped with a new, more powerful, version of the 1911cc engine, the aforesaid Performance, with its output raised from 46hp to 56hp at 3800 rpm.

No traditional October Motor Show was held in Paris the following year, of course. The outbreak of World War Two (declared by France and Great Britain on Germany the previous month, on 3rd September 1939) prevented these celebrations (at which Citroën's proposed 1939/40 season's models would have been displayed) from taking place. But it did not stop the production of automobiles at that point in time. Throughout the *drole de guerre* or phoney war that followed over the next eight months, the Quai de Javel continued to assemble the Traction Avant, albeit in greatly reduced numbers since a large order for army lorries placed by the French government was given top priority. As it failed to meet the official French army specifications laid down in 1902 (which insisted on a separate chassis and high ground clearance), the Traction Avant had never been approved for military service; yet, to replace the motor transport losses sustained in the battles that followed the German invasion of France in April 1940, the authorities purchased substantial stocks of cars from Citroën and these saw action in the weeks leading up to the capitulation in June.

Among the last of the pre-war Traction Avant cars was this 7C model, photographed in Autumn of 1939. Following the outbreak of World War II, production was suspended in November 1941 and not resumed until June 1945. However, the configuration of the earliest post-war examples conformed in most ways to the pre-war specification and were equipped with Pilote wheels.

As might be expected under the circumstances, production of vehicles for the civilian market was severely curtailed throughout the winter of 1939-1940 and the output of all sports models ceased; no further series production of the 7C, 11BL or 11B cabriolets took place after August and September 1939 respectively. The range advertised (but not necessarily made available) in early 1940 included eight cars—the 7C Economique sedan, the 11BL Performance sedan (*Onze Legere*), the 11B Performance standard sedan (*Onze Normale*), plus the long-wheelbase 11B limousine (or *conduite interieure*) familiale and commerciale, and, lastly, the 15-Six in two forms, a standard sedan and a long-wheelbase limousine. Evidently, the provision of a choice of paintwork was also considered inappropriate and the cars assembled in 1939–1940 were all finished in standard black; the 7CV versions had yellow wheels, the 11CV versions red wheels, and the 15-Six ivory wheels.

Despite the reforms and restrictions introduced earlier by *les Michelin,* up to that point a surprisingly wide range of colors had been offered, though different to those seen under André Citroën's regime. From October 1936 until October 1939, the color choices for the 7CV included navy blue, Bordeaux red, olive green and black, always with black fenders and wheels. The same colors were available for the 11CV cars, plus dark grey, light grey, beige, blue and green — the last four shades metallic; however, on these cars the fenders were always the same color as the bodywork, but the wheels were a standard black, until the introduction of the Pilote type in 1938.

The invasion of France by Germany in June 1940 brought an immediate cessation of production for the civilian market, although assembly of the Traction Avant for official or military use continued sporadically over the next 18 months until it ended altogether in November 1941. No production of passenger cars whatsoever occurred throughout 1943 or 1944 at the Quai de Javel. Following the liberation of France in June 1944, the production of trucks was resumed within six months, but a whole year passed before a single post-war example of the Traction Avant sedan came off the Citroën assembly lines, in June 1945, one month after hostilities in Europe ended.

As a consequence of its continuing production of trucks, the Quai de Javel factory did not survive without aerial attack during World War II and it was bombed on three occasions, as were other targets among Citroën's nine satellite Paris plants. The first raid, made by the German invaders on June 3, 1940, severely damaged the administrative and design offices, while subsequent raids launched by the RAF and USAAF, on September 5, 1943 and August 7, 1944, respectively, hit the assembly lines, eventually putting them out of production altogether. Even so, the bombardment inflicted on the Citroën installations was far less severe than the punishment meted out upon the Renault factory at Boulogne-Billancourt (by the RAF in March 1942 and the USAAF in September 1943), which was virtually destroyed.

Undoubtedly, the reason for this more lenient treatment was that, unlike Louis Renault, Pierre-Jules Boulanger had refused to cooperate with the German authorities, more than was necessary to keep the Citroën firm in business and to safeguard the jobs of the 12,000 workers it employed — about half the pre-war number — throughout the four years of the Occupation. His stand in avoiding all personal contact with the Nazis and the *Verwalter* they had imposed on the factory had caused his name to be included on the Gestapo's blacklist of 67 prominent Frenchmen known to be hostile to the Third Reich, and who were under constant threat of being arrested and deported to German prisons or concentration camps. Only in recent times has information emerged establishing in any detail the exact number of vehicles actually assembled at the Quai de Javel during the war years; it seems that in spite of Pierre Boulanger's policy of non-collaboration, 37,190 vehicles—including 32,468 lorries and 4,722 cars—were produced in the 50 months that passed between July 1940 and the bombardment suffered in August 1944, when further production became impossible. The majority of these vehicles must have been purchased by the German military authorities. The combat service of the Traction Avant under French, German and, later, Free French Forces and Resistance colors is well documented by a multitude of wartime films and photographs.

At the first post-war Paris Salon, held in October 1945, Citroën exhibited three proposed models, all sedans, the 11B Legere and 11B Normale plus the 15-Six G, but initially, during the first year of post-war production, only the 11BL (*Onze Legere*), powered by the 1911cc engine, was manufactured, the various other models of the pre-war Traction Avant range being either deleted from the catalog or withdrawn temporarily. Henceforth only the 11CV 1911cc engine would be produced, the 7CV 1628cc version being discontinued, in deference to the provisions of the Pons Plan, described later in this chapter. Thus the casualties of war included the 7C Economy sedan and both the 7CV and 11CV versions of the roadster and faux cabriolet models, the production of which was never resumed after its cessation in 1938. The 11B (11CV *Onze Normale*) sedan, familiale and commerciale versions all survived, however although their re-appearance was delayed.

Indeed, for many months after the Liberation, work at the Quai de Javel was primarily concerned with the refurbishment of surplus American army trucks for civilian duties, as was the case at the other great automobile factories of France. Thus the 11B sedan did not return

As the flagship of the post-war Traction Avant line, the 15-Six was re-introduced in February 1946. However, in September that year, its Pilote wheels were replaced by the new, plain Michelin BM wheels, pictured here.

until 1947, while the long-wheelbase, six-light familiale and commerciale versions had to wait until 1953 and 1954 respectively. The same delay applied to the 15-Six model, which made its return in 1946, at first in sedan form only, but then as a familiale in 1953.

Considering its long career, covering a total life-span of 23 years, the technical evolution of the Traction Avant was much less complicated and eventful than that of any other major Citroën model. When assembly was recommenced in 1945, at first the car was produced in a form more or less identical to that of pre-war examples both inside and out. Its internal mechanical specification was unaltered and its external appearance unchanged, the only important visual difference being that the two adjustable, pivoting ventilation slats previously seen on each side of the hood were replaced by a row of louvers, as employed on the 15-Six model from the outset. Even the distinctive slatted Michelin Pilote wheels, originally introduced in 1938, were retained for a while, using pre-war stocks, until replaced by the new easy-clean, plain disc Michelin BM (Bon Marche) design, towards the end of 1947. The headlights on all three models now had a painted rather than a chromed finish, while the radiator grille was also painted rather than chromed. The Double Chevron insignia now took the form of fluted polished alloy strips, fitted in front of the vertical grill bars, as they had been between 1936 and 1940. Surprisingly also, a choice of four different paint colors was offered on these first post-war cars, built between 1945 and 1947, presumably due to the availability of pre-war stocks of paint. These colors were black, iridescent light or dark grey and Reseda (military green) which were teamed with either grey or ivory wheels with matching embellishers. Unusually, a few examples of the 15-Six built in 1946 were painted in grey, teamed with red wheels, rather than in the plain black that was generally standard for this model. In August 1946, the characteristic cast aluminum-alloy wheel spats associated with the post-war model appeared on certain examples and duly became a standard fitting right across the Traction Avant range the following season, 1947–1948.

In March 1947 came the return of the 11B Onze Normale sedan and the 15-Six sedan. The latter was fitted at first with the pre-war six cylinder engine which turned in a counter-clockwise direction but after only 240 examples of this type, the 15-Six G (or gauche) had been produced, it was superseded by a new version, the 15-Six D (or droite), equipped with an entirely new gearbox, though still having only three speeds. This box allowed the engine, which was also improved, to turn in the opposite, more normal, clockwise direction, just like the 1911cc Traction Avant engine from which it was derived.

For the people of France, life during the grim period between 1945 and 1950 was perhaps more difficult than throughout the four years of the Occupation. It was a time of universal deprivation; almost every commodity was in short supply including foodstuffs and fuel for heating and transportation. Essential industrial raw materials were also scarce and components of every kind severely rationed, especially automobile tires and batteries. Moreover, for car manufacturers like Citroën these problems were compounded by a lack of essential tools and equipment, since much of their vital machinery, which had been damaged by Allied bombing or requisitioned by the Nazis and carted off to Germany during the war, could not easily be returned or replaced, due to a shortage of foreign currency.

In an attempt to overcome these difficulties and ensure a speedy reconstruction of the French automobile industry, almost immediately after the Liberation, the Ministry of Industrial Production of the provisional government instituted a five-year plan, which remained in force between February 1945 and February 1950. Known as the Pons Plan, after its Socialist protagonist, Paul-Marie Pons, this directive stipulated that the principal constructors were required to confine their activities to a single well-defined sector of the market, to which they were to have exclusive access, amounting to a monopoly. The aim was to concentrate production among fewer firms, rationalize output, increase efficiency, maximize scarce material and labor resources, and to eliminate all duplication of effort as a result of unnecessary competition or wasteful change, purely for the sake of novelty, which the authorities considered undesirable. Under this somewhat bureaucratic and restrictive scheme, Citroën was authorized to continue production of the Traction Avant in its 11CV (and, later, 15CV) forms, together with trucks in the 2- and 3.5-ton class. But the cheaper end of the market for *voitures de tourisme* between 4CV and 8CV was left to others such as Renault and Ford (later Simca) to supply—hence the discontinuation of the 1628 cc 7CV version of the Traction Avant. The rate of production sanctioned was 387 vehicles per working day.

By the end of 1947, with 21,153 Tractions having been assembled and sold during the previous twelve months, production had reached about 40 percent of pre-war levels, and recovery was in sight. Even so, the supply of raw materials and components continued to present serious problems, so much so that it became necessary to introduce a more standardized and rational specification for the Traction Avant range, to reduce unnecessary duplication between models. Consequently, in effect from January 1948, for the next six years the Traction would be available painted only in black, with its interior trimmed and equipped in a far more austere and sober style than before. The elaborately decorative interior flourishes inherited from the André Citroën era disappeared forthwith and the car's seats, headlining and door panels were trimmed in plain grey cloth, greatly simplified from the far more elaborate style of furnishing introduced at the outset, although the tubular framed seats dating from 1936 were retained until 1949.

Despite this frugality and restraint, in the summer of 1948 the 15-Six received a new, fully-chromed grille (with the chevrons placed in front of the bars) plus large dome-shaped wheel embellishers, also chromed; the headlights stayed unchromed, however. The 11CV cars continued to be fitted with painted grilles, decorated only by a surrounding ring of alloy beading and, of course, the traditional Double Chevron motif also made from polished aluminum alloy strips. Similarly, the embellishers on the BM wheels, fitted to the 11B and 11BL models to replace the by-now obsolete Pilote wheels, were painted rather than chromed, though their plainness was relieved by the small chromed roundels at their centers.

In October 1947, the hood louvers employed on the 15-Six were adopted on the smaller 11CV cars as well, such as the 11BL or Onze Legere of 1949-1950 seen here. Note that its bumpers are curved in the center and that its windshield wipers continue to be mounted above the windshield. However, its wheel covers are of a simpler pattern, painted to match the wheels but with a small chromed roundel in their centers.

For the 1948-1949 season, the painted radiator shell of the 15-Six was replaced by a chromed grille, and for 1949-1950 the characteristic domed chromed hub caps appeared. Then for 1950-1951 a more elaborate pattern of bumpers, unique to the 15-Six, was introduced, as seen on this vehicle.

Initially, these BM wheels were shod with Michelin SP Pilote cross-ply tires, but from the end of 1949 onwards, as an optional extra, the Traction Avant could be ordered equipped with Michelin's new steel-belted radial tire, the Michelin X, which was launched at the October Paris Salon that year, exhibited on the Traction Avant, of course. The event marked a truly revolutionary breakthrough in the technology of transportation and a major milestone in the history of the motor car. By virtue of the way that it combined vertical elasticity (of the sidewall) with horizontal rigidity (of the tread surface), the Michelin X tire transformed the handling, braking and roadholding of contemporary automobiles and doubled the working life then expected of a tire, and in due course the principle was adopted universally for use on all types of motor transport.

Research work on this entirely new tire-making process had been conducted in secret at Clermont-Ferrand for the past ten years at least, but the war had delayed the work and it was not until 1946 that patents had been filed. Crossply tires, reinforced by bands of textile fibers in a criss-cross fashion, were comparatively rigid and inflexible in construction, and tended to lift off the road during cornering, breaking adhesion and causing skids. Michelin's solution was to make the tire sidewalls more supple, keeping the tread in contact with the road whenever the wheel was tilted out of true, through changes in camber or the side forces exerted when changing direction at speed. The secret of this superior grip lay in the way that the plies of fabric reinforcement were bonded to the rubber in overlapping bands running radially from the center-point of the tire instead of in the old criss-cross pattern. Moreover, to maximize the tire's traction and braking ability, the durable yet flexible tread on its circumference was reinforced by a metallic belt woven from finely drawn steel wires. Never before had it been possible to bond rubber to steel in this way — a complex process which remains difficult today, even by modern technological standards. Curiously, although the Traction Avant featured prominently in the earliest publicity material for this Michelin invention and that during the early 1950's, it was customarily photographed for Citroën's own advertising purposes, shod with the X tire, the first vehicle actually to feature the Michelin X as a standard fitment was the Lancia Aurelia, introduced in 1950. Evidently, it was not until the end of 1954 that production capacity at the Michelin factories had reached a sufficient volume for it to be adopted as standard issue on the Traction Avant also.

As we shall see in the following chapter, at the Paris Salon of October 1948, the three separate Traction Avant models displayed on the Citroën stand played a secondary, supporting role to the star of the show, the long-awaited Citroën 2CV people's car. So great was the atmosphere of drama and excitement surrounding the presentation of this new model that the older cars were left out of the spotlight altogether, completely overshadowed by the glare of publicity focused on the 2CV by the press. As a result of this launch and other developments, no other significant modification or improvement of any kind occurred to the Traction Avant range for another five years, except that in December 1949, on all three models, the tubular framed seats first introduced in 1936 were replaced by the type of seating referred to as Pullman, as seen on the first cars produced in 1934–1935. These seats were individual and non-reclining at the front and bench-type at the rear, but only those on the 15-Six had a folding central armrest. In October 1950 another minor change occurred when the 15-Six was equipped with a new, wider and more elaborate pattern of bumper bar, front and rear, intended to differentiate it further from the Traction Avant *ordinaire* In October 1950 the 15-Six also received a revised design of dashboard and a change of interior trim and upholstery fabric, from grey woven cloth to light-grey or blue-grey velour, with a matching headlining.

At the time of Pierre Michelin's death in 1937, the more sensationalistic among French newspapers spoke fancifully of a curse that, they claimed, had been cast upon the new owners of the Quai de Javel by the ghost of the man whose achievements they had supposedly usurped. The possibility that such a curse had indeed been heaped upon the house of Michelin was raised once again by the press when, by either a random act of fate or a cruel, preordained coincidence, almost thirteen years later, on November 11, 1950, Pierre-Jules Boulanger was also killed outright at the wheel of his Traction Avant while traveling from Paris to Clermont-Ferrand. Although he was undoubtedly a highly experienced and competent driver, when testing a 15-Six fitted with an experimental engine and four-speed gearbox intended for the Traction's forthcoming replacement, he somehow left the road and hit a tree, at a point on Route National 7 known as Brout-Vernet. He was succeeded as President-Directeur-General of the Citroën subsidiary by Robert Puiseux, a son-in-law of Edouard Michelin, who was currently the director of technical research at the Michelin company, a position he retained along with his new responsibilities.

Despite the popularity of the American Look in France at that time, as represented by the products of Simca and Renault, the Traction Avant of the 1950s was distinguished by an almost complete absence of brightwork. The only embellishments permitted were confined to the cast alloy fender spats and the decorative strip running along the flanks below the window line of the doors. On the 15-Six, this was a broad highly polished aluminum-alloy flashing; but on the 11BL and 11B, it was merely a thin strip of alloy beading. Another detail differentiating the two models was that the bigger car also had a pair of chromed electric klaxon horns mounted on its front bumper plus two special chromed filigree work 15-Six badges. One of these was located on its radiator shell, covering the aperture where the starting handle was inserted into the tube provided on the gearbox, while the other was fixed on its off-side rear fender; the 11CV cars had a plain oblong aluminum-alloy radiator grille embellisher to cover the starting handle aperture. The license plate on all three current models took the form of a panel mounted upright on the near-side fender, where it did not interfere with the opening of the trunk-lid or the spare-wheel cover.

All versions of the Traction Avant built before July 1952 and fitted with the small trunk carried their registration plates on a plaque mounted on the left rear fender, as on this 15-Six. Only one tail light was provided as this was all that was required by current French legislation.

However, in July 1952 came the first and only major change to the outward appearance of the Traction Avant to be introduced throughout its entire career. As a result of a widespread demand for greater luggage space, on all three members of the family the original downward-hinging trunk-lid with its external circular spare wheel housing was replaced by a new rectangular-shaped trunk which opened upwards. Protruding rearwards this "malle bombé"—which also accommodated the spare wheel and provided the location for a conven-

The only really major change in the Traction Avant's external appearance took place in July 1952 when the original pattern of luggage trunk door, with its integral spare wheel cover, was replaced by a rectangular shaped luggage trunk designed to counter criticisms of its restricted luggage capacity. Earlier, in the spring of 1951, another, more minor, modernization had occurred when the windshield wipers were moved to a new position below the windshield. Turn signals were also fitted, on the front fenders and rear quarter panels, at that time. All these modifications can be clearly seen on this 15-Six, built in autumn of 1953.

tional, centrally-positioned license plate — did not actually increase the overall length of the car. At the same time, certain other minor modifications were made. Most noticeably, the electric windshield wipers and their motors were mounted below the windshield rather than above it; front and rear turn signals and a new pattern of rear warning lamp were also fitted at this time, the latter mounted on the rear fenders. Inside, the layout and color scheme of the dashboard were revised again and a new type of metal internal window surround, painted grey to match the new dashboard, was featured, while the tops and sides of the seats and the bottoms of the door cards of the 11BL and 11B were given grey plastic inserts, to protect the grey cloth upholstery.

In July 1953 came the return of the long-wheelbase, six-light familiale version of the 11B, followed shortly after by a similar variant of the 15-Six; both types had been absent from the Citroën catalog since 1940. These familiales were full nine-seaters, thanks to the row of three folding occasional seats located in the foot-well of their rear passenger compartments. Later, a limousine version of both the 11B and 15-Six was also introduced, the only real difference being that, on these cars, no occasional seats were fitted. Measuring 4.96 meters in length overall from stem to stern, these 15-Six familiales and limousines were the longest of all the Traction Avant models.

From October 1953 onwards, two new colors were introduced across the Traction Avant range at last, to supplement the habitual plain black finish (relieved by contrasting ivory or pale yellow wheels teamed with ivory, pale yellow and, from June 1952 onwards, pearl grey embellishers or wheel trims) that had been standard since 1948. These new shades were pearl grey (with dark grey wheels and matching grey wheel trims) and Iceland blue (with blue wheels and contrasting grey wheel trims). The 15-Six was also available in smoky grey. The following year the color choices were further enhanced by the addition of midnight blue, air force blue (aka RAF blue), mist grey and heather grey, all of which were teamed with dark grey wheels and contrasting pearl grey wheel trims. Even so, black remained the most popular choice!

By now the Traction Avant was almost twenty years old, regarded with universal respect as a senior citizen among France's automobile population. Yet despite its well-established status as a cultural icon, its appearance and performance were often compared unfavorably with the attractions of its more youthful rivals, such as the Simca Aronde, Renault Fregate and Peugeot 203, the styling of which (as we have already noted) showed a pronounced Trans-Atlantic influence. In fact, the Renault Fregate, introduced in 1950 as "The Modern 11CV" was a commercial failure and quickly disappeared without ever threatening to overturn the popularity of its much older rival. Needless to say, Citroën's publicity material dismissed such criticism with disdain, loftily pointing out that, as a national institution, the Traction Avant was not

Top: A selection of colors became available at last on the entire Traction Avant line in October 1953. Customers could choose from mist grey, pearl grey, midnight blue and air force blue, all with matching wheels (though with the wheel covers painted in contrasting grey) as seen here. But the traditional black with contrasting ivory wheels remained the most popular choice. ***Bottom:*** In 1954 the Traction Avant celebrated its 20th anniversary. Having achieved the status of a French cultural icon, its familiar visage continued to dominate the traffic scene in Paris, seemingly outnumbering all its rivals put together. Over 52,000 examples were sold in France that year, although by then demand was falling.

In October 1953 the six-light, long-wheelbase 11CV Familiale model made a re-appearance in the catalog, having been discontinued before the war. It was followed seven months later by the 11CV Commerciale, illustrated here. The Familiale body was also made available in 15-Six form for the 1953-1954 season, but not the Commerciale. The entire rear end of the Commerciale hinged upward to give access to a vast 500 kg loadspace, in what was probably the first modern hatchback.

to be judged by the shallow criteria of fickle and transient fashion. "*Une ligne sobre et classique ne se demode pas*"—its sober and classical lines will never go out of fashion, it proclaimed.

Although its impending return was announced in 1953, it was not until April 1954 that the 11B Commerciale actually made its re-appearance in the Traction Avant line. The new version featured a fully-opening tailgate, which differed from the double doors seen on the pre-war examples in that it was a single one-piece structure comprising both the rear window and the recently introduced extended trunk lid, and thus it was probably the first true hatchback. Supported by spring-loaded struts, this rear door hinged upwards from the roof line to permit the loading of big and bulky objects; a couple of large wine barrels were suggested by a famous Citroën publicity poster advertising the Commerciale. In this post-war version, the rear load area and seating were trimmed in washable plastic, but the front seats were upholstered with the same grey cloth used in the other four-cylinder 11CV cars. No Commerciale version of the six-cylinder car was ever produced, either before or after the war.

No changes whatsoever were made to the 11CV versions of the Traction Avant throughout 1954, but the 15CV version underwent a revolution. For the past five years the Bureau d'Etudes had been conducting trials with an 11B sedan equipped with a novel form of independent suspension, the principles of which had been discovered and developed in secret experiments during the war. As we shall see in a later chapter, this unique Citroën self-leveling hydropneumatic suspension system (subsequently proven in nearly 50 years of service on more than 10 million vehicles but at that point untried in series production) relied on a rising-rate gas spring, which took the form of a spherically shaped metal chamber containing a fixed amount of compressible nitrogen held under pressure by a flexible diaphragm fastened to the circumference of the sphere. This oleo-pneumatic spring was linked hydraulically to the vehicles' wheel-arms by means of a piston moving in a cylinder filled with fluid.

This revolutionary technology had already been selected for installation on the Traction Avant's replacement, the DS19, soon to be revealed at the 1955 Paris Motor Show. But to gain practical on-road experience of the hydro-pneumatic componentry under normal service conditions, it was decided to fit the system on the series-production 15-Six, but on the rear wheels only, where it replaced the existing torsion bar springs and telescopic shock-absorbers. The result was the 15-Six H

The final incarnation of the Traction Avant was the 15-Six H, or Hydraulique, introduced in May 1954. On this model, the torsion bar springs of the rear wheels only were replaced by the gas springs of Citroën's hydro-pneumatic suspension system, soon to be employed on all four wheels of the DS19. With the system pressurized and the car raised to its normal running attitude, there were few tell-tale visual signs to differentiate it from its conventional counterpart, except for a badge on the rear.

or Hydraulique, announced in April 1954, and sold as an option alongside the conventionally sprung 15-Six D sedan; only two long-wheelbase limousines of this type were produced, however, and no familiales.

As installed on the 15-Six H, two of these unique oleo-pneumatic springs and their associated pistons were mounted to the rear sub-frame, and connected to the trailing suspension arms by means of push-rods. Bearing on the axle arms, the pistons and rods acted as rams or jacks to raise or lower the bodywork. Thus the correct ride-height was achieved by varying the supply of pressurized hydraulic fluid (supplied by an engine-driven pump), admitted to the cylinders and spheres through the action of a height-correcting device located on the rear axle. The vertical movements of the rear road wheels transmitted through the push-rods and pistons caused the hydraulic fluid in the cylinder to flow into and out of the sphere through multi-disc bump and rebound damper valves, the cushion of nitrogen in the spheres providing the springing effect. Therefore, no matter how heavy the passengers and cargo on board, perfect equilibrium was achieved under all road and load conditions, to ensure a smooth and stable ride at speed, even when traversing the poorly surfaced, pot-holed or cobble-stoned French highways of that era. As a bonus, as installed on the 15-Six H, the system also made it possible to jack up the rear of the car to change a wheel and tire, by moving a lever located in the trunk that was linked to the height-corrector device.

The greatly improved comfort, stability and security afforded by the new suspension system was quickly recognized by both the motoring press and public alike, so despite its considerably higher price (940,000 FF as opposed to 870,000 FF), the 15-Six H very soon began to outsell its sister sedan which was withdrawn from the catalog early the following year, although the 15-Six D Familiale continued in production until August 1955. The last 15-Six H sedan was built in July 1956; just 3079 examples had been produced, in contrast to some 42,000 conventional six-cylinder models.

When parked with its suspension system de-pressurized the 15-Six H could easily be distinguished from its conventionally sprung sister car by its low-slung attitude at the rear; but with the engine running and the car on the move, there were few visual clues to set the two vehicles apart. The two most noticeable give-aways were that the front suspension of the hydro-pneumatically sprung car had elongated, more flexible torsion bars (to give a softer more compliant ride in phase with the rear) which protruded from the front cradle well beyond the leading edge of the front fenders, and that its 15-Six badge was mounted centrally on the trunk-lid rather than on the right fender. The 15-Six H was powered by an improved version of the 2867 cc engine, developing 80 bhp at 4,000 rpm.

The final chapter in the story of the Traction Avant was written in May 1955, when all five versions of the 11CV series cars then available were equipped with an improved and uprated version of the original 1911cc engine, which by now had been in production for more than 20 years. This new engine, christened the 11D, achieved an increase in power output from 56 to 60bhp at 4,000 rpm, and thus offered higher performance and better flexibility. Benefiting from various modifications—including a revised cast-iron cylinder head with larger inlet passages and a raised compression ratio, strengthened crankshaft and con-rods with shell-type main and big-end bearings, revised pistons and valve gear and a cast alloy sump — the 11D engine was easily identified among its predecessors by the inscription cast on the spark-plug side of its cylinder block. In fact, the new motor was derived from the unit that had been specifically developed to power the Traction Avant's replacement, the DS19 sedan, which was launched later that year. Designed by Walter Becchia, this DS19 engine was based on Maurice Sainturat's 1911cc OHV Traction Avant design and shared the same bore and stroke dimensions, but by way of an improvement it featured an all-new aluminum cross-flow cylinder head which increased performance by a further 15 bhp, to 75 bhp no less.

The adoption of the 11D engine was really the only major revision to be incorporated in the Traction Avant's mechanical specification throughout its 10-year post-war career. Strangely, in view of its extended production life, no move was ever made to upgrade its electrical system from 6 to 12 volts, or even to replace its frail and inadequate three-speed gearbox, which (as we have already observed) was widely acknowledged to be its Achilles Heel. This was notoriously prone to the failure of its crownwheel and pinion, or the rupture of its casing if mistreated. Various far more sturdy four-speed alternatives were offered by specialist manufacturers, such as Duriez, to overcome the problem, but these were never fitted as standard equipment by Citroën.

Naturally, the arrival of the DS19, which entered production in October 1955, signaled the departure of the 15-Six from the Citroën range, the last examples being built in 1956, but it did not mean the exit of the Traction Avant altogether. It had originally been intended that the Deesse would supersede the Traction immediately and entirely; but as events turned out, the two cars continued to be assembled side by side at the Quai de Javel for almost another two years, until the advent of the ID19. In the course of 1956, 39,395 Tractions were made, but only 9,936 DS19s. However, the end was now inevitable. The last car, an 11B Familiale, left the assembly line on July 25, 1957, bringing to a close an era that covered three decades. Production of the Traction Avant had lasted a total of 23 years, 4 months and 15 days, a world record for longevity at that time, though, as we shall see, this feat was later broken by the 2CV. Between 1934 and 1957, a total of 700,961 examples were built at the Quai de Javel comprising 81,295 7s of all types, 105,109, 11AL and 11BL Légeres, 53,856 11A and 11B Normales, 2,424 15-Six models pre-war, plus 219,719 11BL Légeres, 193,311 11B Normales and 45,247 15-Six models post-war. Also, 56,750 cars of all types were built at Citroën's Belgian and British factories, making a grand combined total of 759,111 examples.*

**These figures are taken from Olivier de Serres' Grand Livre de la Traction Avant. Citroën's own figures say a total of 759,123 cars were produced: 88,066 7s between 1934 and 1941, 62,045 11s between 1934 and 1957, and 50,602 15-Sixes between 1938 and 1956.*

During that time it achieved the status of a French cultural icon, regarded by Francophiles everywhere as a symbol of uncompromising Gallic individuality, as idiosyncratic as pastis, petanque and Edith Piaf. Yet it was more than that. The Traction Avant was simply the first popularly priced, mass-produced car in which the motorist could cruise in confidence at a steady 100 kph in all road and weather conditions rather than the 60 kph which had previously been the norm. At its wheel, both novice and expert drivers alike could brake without hesitation and corner without apprehension, even swerving violently to avoid collisions without fear of overturning.

Insofar as it introduced (though not simultaneously) such key automotive systems as front-wheel-drive, chassis-less all-steel monocoque construction, hydraulic brakes, all-independent torsion-bar suspension, rack-and-pinion steering and radial tires (a combination of features once unique to Citroën, but which have since been adopted almost universally elsewhere), its significance was international. Inarguably among the most influential and widely copied automobile designs ever produced, it is surely the lineal ancestor of the modern family car.

The Michelin firm's famous symbol and mascot, Monsieur Bibendum, the Michelin Man, was born in 1898. In his modern slimmed-down form, and no longer seen drinking and smoking, he remains one of the best-loved and most widely recognized trademarks in the world.

Monsieur Bibendum, the Michelin Man

Established in 1889 as a limited liability company wholly owned by the Michelin family, the Société Commandite Michelin et Cie could trace its origins to 1832, when it was founded at Lavort in the Auvergne by two cousins working in partnership, Aristide Barbier and Edouard Daubree. Its principal original activities were the refining of sugar, the production of confections and, later, the manufacturing of farm machinery and pumps. Three years previously, Daubree had married an Englishwoman, Elizabeth Pugh-Barker, whom he had met in Paris where she was employed as a governess. Elizabeth Pugh-Barker was a niece of Charles Mackintosh, who had been first to discover the secret of dissolving natural rubber in benzene and to use this knowledge to waterproof garments, eventually producing the range of rain-wear clothing that bore his name. Elizabeth brought with her to the Auvergne the know-how for making toy rubber balls and other domestic articles; as a result, by 1863, Barbier and Daubree's company had expanded from its agricultural beginnings to establish itself as a manufacturer of a wide variety of vulcanised rubber components for domestic, industrial and agricultural uses, such as flexible hoses, drive belts and brake blocks used in farm machinery. By 1890 the firm had relocated to Clermont-Ferrand and passed into the ownership and control of the grandsons of Aristide Barbier, whose daughter Adele had married Jules Michelin, a local customs and excise official. The pair produced three children, a girl and two boys, André and Edouard Michelin, who became the true patriarchs of the Michelin industrial dynasty.

The eldest of the sons, André Michelin (1853–1931), trained as a civil engineer at the Ecole Centrale in Paris and later as an architect at the Ecole des Beaux Arts, but subsequently became involved in map-making and cartographical design at the French Ministry of the Interior in Paris. Eventually his interest in maps and guides led him to return to Clermont-Ferrand and join the family firm to take charge of its public relations and advertising affairs, and also to develop its publishing activities, including its famous series of road maps and touring guides for motorists, which were launched in 1900. The younger son, Edouard Michelin (1859–1940), set out in life by studying law, but then took up painting at the Ecole des Beaux-

Arts in Paris, intending to become a professional artist, supported by the generous private income he received from the family firm. Before long, however, he was forced to abandon this ambition and to embark instead on a remarkable career as an engineer, administrator and entrepreneur.

The crisis that provoked this change of plan occurred in the mid 1880s, following the death of the family firm's current owner-manager Ernest Daubree, the son of Edouard Daubree. Ernest had proved to be a competent leader and had provided the young Michelin brothers and their widowed mother with an ample income from the business in which they held a substantial shareholding. Unfortunately, when Daubree died in 1878 he was succeeded as managing partner by a lawyer, J.G. Bideau, who proved incapable, so much so that the business went into a steep decline. Within 10 years, the situation had deteriorated to such an extent that it threatened the financial security of the entire extended Michelin family. Consequently, in 1886 André and Edouard Michelin were forced to take the firm in hand and to re-organize and re-finance it, a decision which led Edouard to close his studio in Paris and return to Clermont-Ferrand to take charge of its affairs, on a full-time basis, at the age of only 27. Fortunately, although he had received no commercial or engineering training whatsoever, in the course of the following 50 years, his talent for business helped him transform a modest rural business into a substantial international organization employing more than 25,000 people.

Interestingly, both of these artistically gifted brothers found their wives among the same Parisian family, by marrying daughters of Auguste-Desiré Wolff, the Jewish-born former professor of music at the Paris Conservatoire and head of the Pleyel piano business. André married Wolf's eldest daughter Sophie and, later, following Sophie's early death, her sister Jeanne; while Edouard married a fifth daughter, Therese.

To begin with, the Clermont-Ferrand rubber firm had had no connection with wheels, tires or transportation whatsoever. But five years after Edouard's return from Paris, an event took place which not only brought about a complete change of direction for the business, but also eventually produced a spectacular transformation in the fortunes of the Michelin family as a whole. In 1891, while on a tour of the Auvergne, a passing British cyclist called at the Clermont-Ferrand rubber works, seeking assistance with the repair of a puncture. His machine was equipped with the very latest development in bicycling, the pneumatic rubber tires patented by John Boyd Dunlop in England in 1887, which had begun to supersede the solid rubber tires used until now. In this, the earliest form of pneumatic tire, the outer cover and its inflatable inner tube were actually fastened semi-permanently to the wheel by glue, and thus could not easily be detached, repaired and reaffixed to the wheel if damaged.

After struggling for more than three hours to repair this primitive Dunlop tire, Edouard had the visionary idea that led to the world's first detachable pneumatic tire for bicycles, an invention that he repeated four years later with a similar tire for automobiles. The Michelin cycle tire, patented in 1891, consisted of a flexible rubber inner tube containing air under high pressure, protected by an outer cover of canvas coated with a layer of harder rubber. This cover had wire hoops bonded into its inner edges, which allowed the tire to be secured tightly, but not permanently, to the wheel rims, initially by a series of bolts. Now it was possible to ride and drive in comfort on a cushion of air, instead of an unyieldingly hard and solid rubber ring — and, if it punctured, to rapidly remove and repair it.

The idea was convincingly demonstrated by a victory in the Paris-Brest-Paris cycle race that same year, and within 12 months some 10,000 cyclists were using Michelin tires. Four years later, driving the "Eclair," the car that they had built themselves using a Daimler engine, the

In this poster, published in 1967, Monsieur Bibendum proclaims the advantages of the Michelin X radial tire, which by now had become standard equipment on all Citroëns.

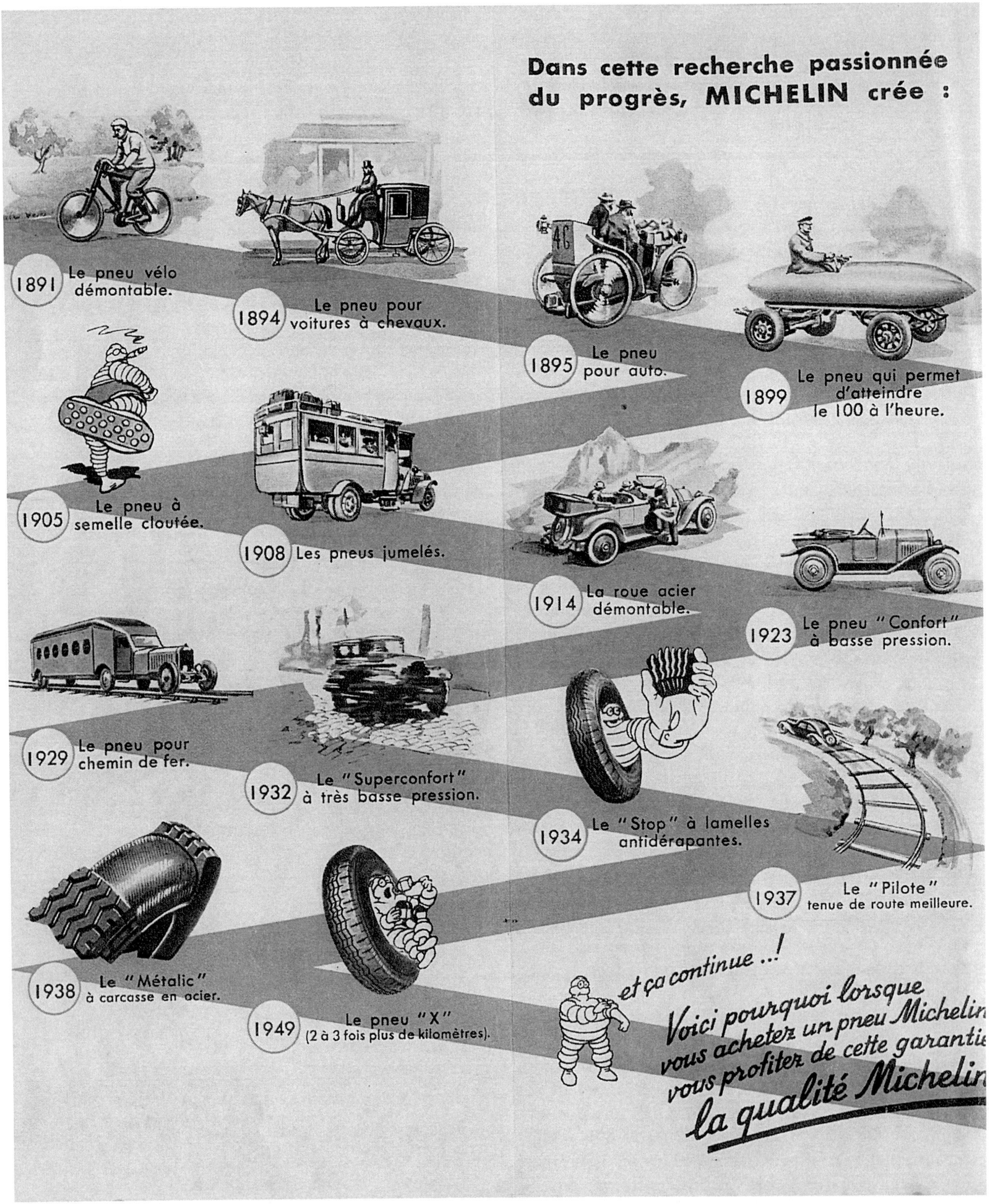

Monsieur Bibendum charts the passage of progress achieved by Michelin on the roads and railways of France, in an advertisement published in 1950 to celebrate the arrival of the Michelin X steel-belted radial tire.

Shown side-by-side here are the two coach-built ceremonial cars adapted from the 15-Six H Traction Avant for the Presidents of France. On the left is the limousine built by Franay in 1955. On the right is the decapotable constructed by Chapron in 1956. Commissioned by President Coty, who left office in 1958, they were used by his successor President de Gaulle throughout the following decade.

Michelin brothers convincingly demonstrated the application of the pneumatic tire to the automobile, by competing in the Paris-Bordeaux-Paris race of 1895. Although they finished last (and, indeed, were disqualified for changing tires—which lasted only 150 km —too frequently), they proved the value of their creation beyond question; the concept of the detachable pneumatic car tire (patented by Michelin in May 1896) was now an essential, inseparable and indispensable feature of motoring, as vital, perhaps, to the progress of road transportation as the contributions made by Daimler, Otto and Benz!

Enterprising and astute, the Michelin brothers prospered greatly in the motorcar boom which took place before and after the First World War and soon became figures of great importance in the French economy. Despite being cunning and secretive (so much that they were known in Paris as the old foxes of the Auvergne), they were certainly not backward or old-fashioned in their outlook. On the contrary, like a good many other entrepreneurs from a rural background, they proved to be extremely go-ahead in their business methods and embraced modern technology with enthusiasm. And although they were undoubtedly secretive to the point of paranoia, they also possessed a flair for publicity rivaling that of André Citroën himself; in 1898 they created their famous and ubiquitous Michelin Man trademark, Monsieur Bibendum, still regarded one hundred years later as one of the world's most widely recognized brand symbols.

The Two Presidential 15-Six Tractions

Early in 1955 the current President of France, Rene Coty (whose normal conveyance of choice was a Citroën 15-Six sedan), commissioned the *carrossier* Franay to build a closed state limousine based on the structural and mechanical elements of the newly-introduced 15-Six H. The styling of this car was actually the work of the well known designer Philippe Charbonneux, who later achieved fame with his work for Renault. The limitations imposed by the restricted budget required that certain parts be bought off the shelf from elsewhere—the door handles, for example, came from a Bentley and the windshield from a Ford Comete.

The car was exhibited at the 1955 Paris Salon and delivered to the Elysée Palace shortly afterwards. Unfortunately, insufficient attention had been paid to improving its cooling system, which is essential if a ceremonial vehicle is to spend long periods on parade, moving at a walking pace in the heat of summer when the flow of air passing through its radiator is inadequate. The result was that it over-heated and broke down ignominiously when conveying Queen Elizabeth II during her state visit to Paris in 1957. Later, in 1963, it was overhauled, modified and improved for the use of M. Coty's successor, President Charles de Gaulle.

The following year, 1956, M. Coty decided to add a new open-topped or *decapotable* parade car to the Elysée fleet, once again based on the 16-Six H, but this time the commission went to Henri Chapron. The styling of this second car was unabashedly American in its inspiration, with a kinked waistline at the C pillar, strongly reminiscent of the contemporary Chevrolet Bel Air. It saw service carrying visiting royalty and heads of state by the score for almost 20 years, from 1956 to 1974, throughout the presidencies of both General de Gaulle and Georges Pompidou.

4

The Design and Development of the 2CV, 1938–1948

Following the demise of its founder, the reputation of the Citroën marque reposed in the possession of the Michelin family for a full 40 years, from 1935 until 1975, more than twice as long as under André Citroën's ownership. Eventually, this second period in the company's history — the so-called Michelin-Lefèbvre era — came to be recognized as a time of remarkable technical progress, as great as, or perhaps even greater than, that which had gone before. But these advances were not made smoothly, at least in the first few years of the relationship.

As custodians of the Double Chevron firm's proud heritage and guardians of its destiny, Citroën's new owners were, paradoxically, both closely similar to and remotely different from the old regime in their business philosophy and corporate culture. On one hand, the Michelin tire firm was itself a pioneering, research-oriented company, dedicated to technical advancement, and it upheld the tradition of engineering excellence and innovation that André Citroën had established and espoused. On the other, it was run in an extremely cautious, conservative and parsimonious manner, which contrasted sharply with André Citroën's imprudent and overly optimistic style of administration. From the moment of their arrival in Paris, *les Michelins* began to introduce a frugal, hair-shirt style of business at the Quai de Javel, to the discomfiture of all those present. Five thousand factory workers and a thousand office staff were given notice, while many senior personnel (including Charles Brull, Charles Rocherand and Jean Daninos) left the company of their own volition.

Indeed, in the aftermath of André Citroën's departure, a chilly wind of change blew through the organization, equally radical and far-reaching as any experienced in a political revolution or coup d'état. Its effect was to sweep away all traces of the founder's existence. From then on, the name Citroën meant a marque, and not a man. Although the company's official title — the Société Anonyme André Citroën — was not changed, no further mention of his personality or deeds was permitted within the environs of the Citroën organization for many years to come, not even in its official company publications. The factory brass band, la Fanfare Citroën, was disbanded and the blasts of publicity that had constantly heralded his achievements throughout his regime were silenced; decades would pass before pretty girls appeared once again on the covers of Citroën brochures. Even the large art-deco desk and luxurious leather armchairs that he had installed in his palatial glass-walled office overlooking the factory's vast delivery hall were replaced by a more utilitarian type of furniture. To André Citroën's former associates and collaborators it seemed that he had been declared a non-person by the firm's new owners.

Although when assuming control the Michelin men insisted that they had held no previous interest in becoming car manufacturers and had formed no preconceived notions about the rights and wrongs of automobile design, in fact, the very opposite was true. As the owners of France's leading manufacturer of automobile wheels and tires, they were not without experience or ambition in the field and had, quite naturally, formed very strong opinions on the subject. For many years past they had nurtured schemes for a practical involvement in car production — and, indeed, for the production of a specific type of car. This plan they now intended to pursue. In short, when riding to Citroën's rescue, the Auvergnats had concealed a hidden agenda to enter the automobile manufacturing business in their own right, and they now had no intention of adopting a hands-off *laissez faire* stance in managing their new interest.

Above all, *les Michelin* subscribed to Cardinal Richelieu's maxim that secrecy is the first essential in affairs of state, believing that it also applied to affairs of industry and commerce. The ruling oligarchy that controlled and managed the tire-making firm operated as a kind of secret society, closed to the outsiders who did not belong to their number by birth or marriage. Austere and astute to the point of outright cunning (so much so that they were known as the old foxes of the Auvergne), Edouard Michelin and his close relations controlled and manipulated their interests by jealously guarding all technological and commercial information. Even the company's most senior managerial and technical employees were denied this intelligence, so that only members of the inner family circle themselves held a complete picture of all that was happening, and all that was planned for the future. In fact, their obsession with secrecy was so all-embracing that later, during the 1960s, when President de Gaulle visited their factory at Clermont-Ferrand and expressed an interest in seeing exactly how and where the new Michelin X radial tire was manufactured, his request for admittance to this most holy of inner sanctums was refused. By this time, the Michelin men had invested huge sums in perfecting the manufacturing technology of the steel-belted radial ply tire, much of which was considered by them to be non-patentable, and so, quite naturally, they were unwilling to expose themselves to even the remotest risk of industrial espionage!

This policy of absolute confidentiality and obfuscation was immediately replicated at Citroën, which had formerly been a relatively open and democratic organization. From the moment that *les Michelin* assumed control, an iron curtain descended to surround the company, equally as opaque and impenetrable as that which surrounded the Kremlin during the Cold War years, and for many years to come the Quai de Javel was referred to by journalists as *la maison de mystere*, the house of mysteries.

But for all their outward provincialism, the Michelin men were pioneering, forward-looking entrepreneurs who encouraged new ideas and invested heavily in fundamental research. From the outset they had dedicated themselves to achieving and maintaining the highest possible standards, in both the design and manufacture of their products and the quality of service offered to their distributors and customers. Indeed, had they not been so deeply committed to innovation, upon gaining control they might easily have put a stop to Citroën's progressive but risky policies, abandoned the Traction Avant, reverted to conventional products and treated their new acquisition as simply a safe captive market for their own products. Alternatively, they might even have sold the company outright—lock, stock and barrel—to one of the American giants, General Motors or Ford, which were both keen on such a deal.

Fortunately, at the time of the takeover they had already embarked on a course of research that was to lead inevitably to a truly revolutionary step forward in the history of transportation—the aforementioned Michelin X steel-belted radial-ply tire, patented in 1946. As we saw in the previous chapter, the principles of this technology had been mastered by Michelin as early as 1938, when it introduced its Metallic truck tire, the first to employ a reinforcing band woven from plies of finely drawn steel wire, bonded into the rubber of the tread. The previous year, 1937, it had introduced the world's first low-profile tire, the Pilote, specifically designed to improve the road-holding and handling of high performance passenger vehicles. Clearly, in developing and marketing these advanced products, Michelin had found it advantageous to foster a close association with an innovative car maker, to help ensure the proper familiarization of these radical concepts within the automobile industry as a whole. But now that the two firms were linked by common ownership, it would be possible to take this technical collaboration one step further. Not only would Citroën vehicles serve to demonstrate the safety and longevity of Michelin's new products on the road, but by cooperating synergistically with its new parent company, Citroën's designers and engineers would also assist the tire maker by producing, in due course, a range of advanced new products with suspension and steering systems specifically designed to complement and exploit the advantages of Michelin's tire know-how.

So it was that the demise of its founder led to a remarkable renaissance in the fortunes of the Citroën firm. Free to carry on its adventurous policies as before, but freed also from André Citroën's rash extravagance, it was soon set on course for a remarkable renaissance in its fortunes. recognized today to have been of seminal influence and significance in the story of the popular car, Indeed, it is no exaggeration to say that this second era of success amounted to a unique episode in the history of the automobile in that ultimately it produced a whole procession of designs including, of course, the Traction Avant, which the Michelins had rescued from disaster.

That this was so was entirely due to the remarkable two-man team that Edouard Michelin chose to manage his new motor manufacturing interests and supervise the technical collaboration between the two firms; his son Pierre Michelin and his *homme de confiance*, right-hand man, Pierre-Jules Boulanger. As André Citroën had observed when welcoming his saviors to the Quai de Javel in July 1934, in French the name Pierre (or Peter) also means

Pierre-Jules Boulanger (1885–1950), the architect turned industrialist who, as the *co-gerant* of Michelin (with Robert Puiseux) was responsible for running the Citroën firm between 1935 and 1950. Although he master-minded the creation of the 2CV, he did not design it in the proper sense. Nevertheless, he made the key decisions that shaped the vehicle, so that his austere personality and ascetic mentality gave the 2CV its Spartan character.

a stone; certainly, he had hoped that the pair would provide the solid foundations on which he could rebuild his business but, alas, the reconstruction took place without him. Working in tandem, over the next three years the two Pierres proved capable not only of restoring order and purpose to the tottering Citroën industrial empire but also of leading it on to even greater levels of engineering achievement than those set by its erstwhile leader.

Initially, Pierre Michelin took charge of the commercial, financial and administrative side of the company, while Pierre-Jules Boulanger supervised the running of its factories and oversaw the experimental work in progress at its Bureau d'Etudes, research and design office. However, as we saw in the previous chapter, when Pierre Michelin was killed in a car crash while en route from Paris to Clermont Ferrand in December 1937, P-J. Boulanger assumed total overall control of the firm and for the following 13 years, the burden of responsibility fell upon his shoulders alone.

To the old hands at the Paris factory, Boulanger seemed a most unlikely person to replace the ebulliently optimistic *bon-vivant* André Citroën as the master of the Quai de Javel. Completely opposite in both personality and physique, he was a dour, reclusive, introspective character who disliked flamboyant self-promotion and always avoided the free-wheeling socializing and junketing that so appealed to his predecessor. A tall, austere-looking figure with close-cropped grey hair and a trim grey moustache, he was habitually dressed in a quasi-uniform — grey suit, grey shirt and grey tie topped off by a grey felt hat and an enormous, rumpled grey raincoat. He was never to be seen without a Gitane cigarette dangling from his mouth, while in his pocket he carried a succession of little black notebooks, in which he jotted down his ideas, plans and observations, plus, of course, his impressions of the constant procession of cars that he tested personally. Some observers said that he was more like *les Michelin* than any of the family members themselves.

Again, in sharp contrast to André Citroën, P-J.B. was a keen motorist who loved driving and who knew intuitively when a car was right or wrong, sensing its roadholding vices and virtues through the seat of his pants and then fine-tuning its handling qualities with a stream of off-the-cuff suggestions. Cool, calm and decisive — almost to the point of seeming remote and authoritarian — P-J.B. inspired respect and confidence in all who worked with him and, like a stern but fatherly head master, he guided his school of unruly talents to new heights of achievement.

Upon assuming command of Citroën, Boulanger's first task was to draw up a plan of operations that would determine the company's model range for the next decade and beyond. In view of the situation just two years earlier, it was a plan of remarkable courage and audacity. The middle-class Traction Avant would continue, of course, but updated and revamped with modern, streamlined bodywork — a design referred to as the AX. Above that would be an all-new luxury car of advanced specification, code-named the VGD. A completely new front-wheel-drive utility van, the TUB, would also be produced. But at the bottom of the range, Boulanger proposed to build another completely new, clean-sheet design, code named the TPV or *Toute Petite Voiture,* an inexpensive, economical people's car aimed specifically at the agricultural and rural community, to be launched in or around 1940. Ostensibly, it was from this proposal, conceived in 1937, that the Citroën 2CV was ultimately born in 1948, after a gestation period lasting no less than eleven years!

Legend has it that the idea for the TPV hit Boulanger suddenly while watching the habits of the local Auvergnat farmers on market-day at Lempdes near Clermont-Ferrand, where he had his country home. Then, France was predominantly an agrarian nation, peopled by peasant farmers, small-holders and wine-growers living for the most part in widely scattered villages and small towns. And whereas the large industrial cities and departmental commercial centers were linked to the capital by the strategic Routes Nationales laid out by Napoleon, these small villages and market towns communicated via a network of rough country roads or rutted tracks, along which the farmers traveled by bicycle, pony-trap or horse-drawn wagon to bring their produce to market. What was needed, P-J.B observed, was a small, lightweight, all-purpose, go-anywhere car that even a farmer's wife could drive and maintain.

So runs the gospel story reverently handed down by Citroën's publicity department over the years. But the reality is less romantic. Like many other informed observers of the French auto-industry scene, P-J.B. and his Michelin masters believed that, for all his audacity, André Citroën had made only one serious mistake in his entire ca-

The 2CV was first revealed to the public at the 1948 Paris Motor Show when it was inspected by more than 1,300,000 would-be motorists. But on that occasion the hood stayed shut because the exact type and nature of its engine had still not been decided.

reer — to cease production of his little 7.5hp 5CV light car in 1926, without providing a similar vehicle to take its place. As we have seen, even though the coach-built 5CV was then still in great demand, it represented out-of-date design and technology to the progressive modernist, and he had no hesitation in replacing it with the bigger, all-steel bodied 11.4hp B12 model, thus abandoning the bottom end of the market and leaving open a lucrative gap for competitors such as the Peugeot Quadrilette and the Austin Seven (built under license in France by Rosengart) to fill. Moreover, in making his plans Boulanger would surely have known that another of these baby cars was just around the corner — the Fiat 500 Topolino, introduced in France as the Simca Cinq in April 1936, six months before it appeared in Italy. At that point in its history, the Simca firm was solely a builder of Fiats under license.

In reality, the true genesis of the 2CV took place not in Paris but at the Michelin plant at Clermont Ferrand, some two or three years earlier than is generally held to be the case. In 1934 Pierre Michelin instructed a Michelin engineer, Monsieur Chantaigner, to design and build a light-weight tire testing vehicle which would also serve as a test-bed on which to try out certain engineering ideas that he, Pierre Michelin, was currently considering. This vehicle is known to have been in existence by 1936, and its general configuration bears a striking similarity to the platform-chassis construction embodying projecting leading and trailing suspension arms, seen on the prototype 2CVs which appeared later, in 1937. Moreover, the present head of the Michelin family, François Michelin, recalls that, as a boy, age 10, he saw his uncle Pierre create a model from his (François') toy Meccano set to demonstrate the platform-chassis concept, saying, "This is what I want to get the engineers to understand."

Evidently, from the moment that they took over the Citroën firm, the notion of producing a French People's Car had already been under serious consideration by *les*

Michelin for some considerable time. As early as 1922 they had commissioned a nationwide survey to establish the commercial viability of such a product, using a questionnaire that posed; "In the USA, there is already a car for every 10 inhabitants, but in France there is only one for every 150 people. There, the automobile is a working tool employed by everybody, but here its use is confined to the rich. Why should this be so?" In October 1935, only three months after André Citroën's death, Pierre Michelin issued a specification for such a vehicle, based on the results of this survey. The proposed car, priced at 5,000 francs maximum, was to be capable of carrying four people at 70 to 80 km/h on a level road at an average fuel consumption of 5 liters per 100 km (47 mpg).

However, before any serious work on the project was begun, the Michelin men commissioned a second market research study to test their hunch that a vast, unsatisfied market existed for such a car in France. Over a five month period during 1936, a team of investigators led by Jacques Duclos (a former Michelin employee), toured the nation and asked more than 10,000 members of the public about their traveling habits, to discover their wants, needs, hopes and fears concerning car ownership. "How far and how fast do you need to travel?" "What do you have to carry with you?" "How much would you be prepared to pay for a car?" the Duclos survey asked. The results confirmed their intuition absolutely; not only farmers and country folk but also shopkeepers, artisans and tradesmen were interested in the proposition. The study also showed that 90 percent of first-time French car buyers opted for a used vehicle costing less than 10,000 francs, less than half the current price of a brand new Traction Avant.

Consequently, early in 1937, Pierre Michelin gave the go-ahead for the TPV project, and a team working at the Citroën Bureau d'Etudes in Paris began the task of building a prototype, based on and developed from the vehicle originally produced at Clermont-Ferrand by M. Chataigner; this, the first of innumerable prototypes, appeared later in 1937.

It therefore follows that when issuing his famous *cahier des charges* for the *Toute Petite Voiture*— the design brief which has since become enshrined among the myths and legends surrounding the Deux Chevaux — P.J. Boulanger was doing no more than specifying a reworked version of the design brief originally formulated at least two years earlier by Pierre Michelin, though with performance targets greatly revised in accordance with his own inclination towards simplicity and frugality. For example, road speed was reduced from 70–80 km/h to 60 km/h and fuel consumption cut from 5 liters/100 km (47 mpg) to an astonishing 3 liters/100 km (78 mpg).

As defined in P-J Boulanger's document, the TPV was to serve as a motorized pony-cart, transporting people who had no experience driving motor cars, or indeed owning machinery of any kind. No more than "four wheels under an umbrella," it was to be capable of carrying two farmers wearing clogs, plus fifty kilos (110 pounds) of potatoes or a small cask of wine, transporting its driver, passengers and cargo in the greatest comfort over the poorest roads, so that even when transporting a basket of eggs over a ploughed field, not one single egg would be broken. A woman should be able to drive and maintain it without problems, and it should cost no more than one-third of the price of the Traction Avant. Economy, practicality and versatility were what mattered to the potential owners he had in mind; the aesthetic appearance of the finished vehicle would be completely unimportant. But above all, Boulanger attached the highest priority to reliability and durability. "For the customer earning only 1,800 francs a month, a breakdown that costs 300 francs is a catastrophe," he later pointed out. "Even repairs and adjustments costing as little as 50 francs are unacceptable. We must therefore strive to achieve perfect quality as far as the key components are concerned."

Apparently, this revised design-directive was received with incredulity by the old-guard at Citroën's Bureau d'Etudes. Its chief, Maurice Broglie, protested that it was the most unreasonable specification he had ever received in his entire career, and that the proposal was unworkable. But Boulanger was adamant that his plan could and would succeed. France was facing great social changes, he pointed out. In the future, motoring would no longer be confined to the well-to-do; the poor and underprivileged also had a right to be mobile; the arrival of a French People's Car was inevitable, and with the blessing of the Michelin family he was determined that it would be a Citroën.

Having identified this vast market for a radical rustic vehicle of a kind that had never been built before, Boulanger began to recruit a team of the best technical brains in France, to replace all those who had left after André Citroën's departure. All manner of talents were engaged; intellectuals and academics (even an astronomer), artists and craftsmen as well as scientists and technicians. Priority was given to anyone who could promise new ideas, regardless of age, seniority or qualifications. This preference for self-taught talent lacking any formal engineering training was entirely typical of the Michelin mindset. Their innovative work on tire development had taught them the value of adopting a pragmatic, empirical approach to research. Disregarding established theory and dogma they prized intuitive practicality and originality of thought above formal academic qualifications or high professional status. Certainly, they avoided red tape and bureaucracy and rejected the stratified organizational structures and management hierarchies that seemed to stultify initiative in conventional business and industry. Indeed, many of Michelin's own top managerial and technical personnel (including the patron Edouard Michelin himself) lacked relevant academic qualifications. At Clermont-Ferrand it had already become a well-established dictum that engineers trained at the universities and *grandes ecoles* were blinkered by their education and thus incapable of the kind of lateral thinking that had produced the firm's greatest commercial successes. Similarly, in Boulanger's view, previous motor industry experience was also a relatively unimportant qualification for employment at Citroën. What mattered more was imagination and creativity, and a willingness to try anything new, even to the point of considering unreasonable or illogical solutions. "Even if only 10 percent of your work is finally used, you will have scored a magnificent success," he is reported to have said. When a Doubting Thomas rejected one of Boulanger's suggestions as being mechanically impossible, he was told to go away and think again. "We are not in the business of mechanical engineering — we're in the business of making cars," he exclaimed.

Despite this open-mindedness, in typical Michelin fashion the work itself was conducted in an atmosphere of obsessive secrecy, behind locked doors at the Bureau d'Etudes or hidden behind the three-meter-high walls surrounding Citroën's new test track laid out at la Ferte-Vidame, near Dreux, some 130 kilometers to the West of Paris. Here on instructions received from Clermont-Ferrand, P-J. Boulanger had acquired a 2,000-acre country estate of woods and meadows that had once surrounded a chateau, long since demolished. Nicknamed the "*pouponniere*" or nursery, the existence of the la Ferte-Vidame track was concealed from all but the few key personnel and test drivers directly involved. No one from the factory was allowed to know what was going on there, let alone staff from suppliers who might inadvertently spill the beans to rival firms. And, needless to say, inquisitive pressmen and photographers were declared *persona non grata* at any Citroën or Michelin establishment.

Overall control and coordination of the TPV project was vested in Marcel Chinon, an old hand at the Bureau d'Etudes who had been with Citroën since 1916. Chinon's responsibilities extended to liaising with those working on the engine, running gear, suspension and body, monitoring progress and preparing for production. In fact, his work on the project extended for moret than 20 years and continued long into the actual service life of the 2CV. But as his chief engineer and designer on the project, working under the overall supervision of Citroën's current head of research and development, Maurice Broglie, P-J.B appointed André Citroën's protégé André Lefèbvre, the brilliant engineer who had made such a vital contribution to the design of the Traction Avant which was by now an established and profitable success.

Evidently, Lefèbvre had already made a great impression on P-J. Boulanger and the Michelin men, who regarded him as their resident genius, giving him free rein to follow whatever lines of research seemed most interesting and promising to him personally, almost regardless of cost or ultimate commercial viability. "He's formidable — he thinks like us and does things the way that we do," old Edouard Michelin is reported to have remarked. The archetypal artist-engineer, Lefèbvre worshipped novelty for its own sake, taking a perverse delight in doing things differently and refusing to copy proven techniques and methods used successfully elsewhere. The more audacious, unconventional and complex a solution, the greater was its appeal. Nothing seemed impossible to him. In Lefèbvre's view, the only sin was to be unimaginative or unoriginal. Indeed, throughout the greater part of his 25-year service as the unofficial chief engineer and designer of Citroën's Bureau d'Etudes, from 1933 to 1958, its staff were forbidden to test, examine, compare or even possess the products of its competitors, lest their own inventiveness should somehow be diluted or compromised by external influences.

Most of the great designers in automobile history have been primarily designers of engines who sometimes had ideas on chassis design and sometimes not. But Lefèbvre was different. As we have already noted, thanks to his aeronautical background, he approached the priorities of automobile design from a different perspective than that adopted by most other leading engineers of his day. His mentor, Gabriel Voisin, had been perhaps the first aircraft constructor to build airplanes for sale to private customers rather than merely for personal purposes. Consequently, at the very outset of his career he had been made aware of the paramount importance of stability and controllability. Under Voisin's influence, he formed the view that the first duty of the automobile designer or constructor was to allow for lack of skill on the part of individual drivers. Therefore, he always took the view that his first priority was to improve the steering, braking, suspension and other factors affecting a vehicle's chassis dynamics, so as to offer higher standards of safety and comfort and general driving satisfaction through superior handling and road holding.

In adopting this standpoint, Lefèbvre had the absolute and unequivocal backing of his Michelin masters, who shared his point of view entirely. P-J Boulanger and the Michelins not only supported his radical thinking and endorsed his commitment to front-wheel-drive, but they also encouraged his investigations into the wider issues of suspension and steering design. As France's leading manufacturers of wheels and tires, they saw the architecture of the automobile from the same perspective, and regarded effective suspension, steering and braking ability as far more important than engine power in the synthesis of factors that ultimately governs a car's performance.

In fact, as early as 1930, they had begun to study vehicle dynamics in a methodical, scientific manner to measure precisely the role of the tire in determining the steering and suspension behavior of a car, and its roadholding and ride-comfort characteristics in particular. Upon taking over the Citroën company, they redoubled their examination of the relationship between the moving vehicle and the road beneath it, a function in which the tire plays the chief part, by embarking on a joint study of the concept known to both parties as *la liaison-au-sol*. Indeed, the exploration of this concept was central to the work of both the Citroën and Michelin firms for the next 40 years, with the aim of investigating all possible ways of ensuring a firmer and more constant contact between the wheel and the road, as determined ultimately by the grip exerted by the tire. The eventual result of this research partnership was the arrival of such highly advanced cars as the Citroën DS, SM, GS and CX and even, indeed, the 2CV, none of which could ever have been produced elsewhere. This close collaboration between these leading car and tire makers did not involve the complete integration of the two companies at every level, however; no actual merger took place and the two entities were run quite separately, so that technical dialogue occurred only at the highest levels of management, with little interchange of personnel. Whenever it was necessary for staff to be transferred from Clermont-Ferrand to Paris, or vice versa, they rarely, if ever, returned to their former positions. Clearly, *les Michelin* followed the management strategy of divide-and-rule, by favoring an organizational structure that compartmentalized the work of specialists operating in small dedicated departments, quite separate from, and normally completely ignorant of, the efforts of other teams working on different matters elsewhere. Communication between these groups or individuals was permitted through the center only, on a need-to-know basis, so that only a small select group of managers at the heart of the company had universal access to all information, and were able to form a complete overview of all activities in progress.

But to return to the story of the creation of the 2CV: in response to P-J. Boulanger's challenging design-brief for a cross-country vehicle that could also be cruised flat-out for hours on end, down the long, straight Routes Nationales of France, Lefèbvre set down three cardinal principles for the design and construction of the TPV. First, for maximum stability and ease of control in inexperienced hands, the car would have front-wheel-drive, with its engine and gearbox placed ahead of the front-wheel axis and its wheels positioned on all four corners. This would distribute weight to the front, placing the car's center-of-gravity as low and as far forward as possible. Lefèbvre observed that when you throw a hammer, it is the head not the handle that travels first. Similarly, when a car travels around a bend, it is best to have the greatest mass concentrated at the front end. To enhance this directional stability, the car would also be equipped with very positive rack and pinion steering—just 2.3 turns from lock to lock—and, moreover, it would also have a very pure steering geometry, free of bump-steer and fight-back effects.

Second, for maximum energy-efficiency and fuel-economy, the TPV would be made as light as possible—300 kgs at the most—using aluminum alloys instead of steel. Structural strength would come not from a conventional chassis or even a monocoque construction, but from a novel type of structure, a rigid rectangular pontoon or platform, to the corners of which the suspension and wheels would be attached, by means of two tubular cross-members. The all-independent suspension would take the form of swinging, crescent-shaped axle arms, leading at the front and trailing at the rear and sprung (initially, at least) by a system of multiple torsion bars. The engine and transmission would be fixed to mountings extending outward at the front, and placed so that the driving front wheels would pull the weight of the vehicle along as a man pulls a wheelbarrow or a horse pulls a cart. Likewise, the rear suspension arms and wheels would simply follow behind. The body work or superstructure would have no load-carrying role, but would merely act as an umbrella over the wheels, a lightweight shelter with no structural function other than to protect its driver, passengers, cargo and mechanicals from the wind and weather. To give these bolt-on aluminum body panels torsional stiffness, they would be swaged or corrugated in the manner pioneered by the German airplane designer, Dr. Hugo Junkers. Again, to save weight and expense, wherever possible waxed canvas would replace metal in the bodywork, for example in the roof and doors and the aircraft-type hammock seats. Since glass was both heavy and costly, all the windows would be made of Perspex. And third, to give a soft, comfortable ride over rough terrain and poor road surfaces, the fully independent torsion bar suspension system would be arranged to give an unusually wide degree of wheel travel up and down, so as to absorb the shocks and vibration encountered when traveling fast over ruts and potholes.

A tall, debonair, highly strung character, who habitually drank champagne and dressed in a white silk scarf and flying jacket, André Lefèbvre took little interest in engines, describing them scornfully as nothing more than hot and oily roasting jacks or turnspits. Responsibility for the design of the 2CV's power unit therefore rested entirely with the Bureau d'Etudes' engines department, under the direction of Maurice Sainturat who had designed the Traction Avant's power plant. The first prototype was powered by a 500cc BMW motorbike engine, but during those four years of frenetic research and development before the war, Sainturat's team of engineers experimented constantly with various ideas involving a host of different types and sizes of engine. Examples having one, two and four cylinders were all tried, but without achieving the absolute reliability and endurance in all operating conditions that Boulanger demanded.

Before the year 1937 had ended, around twenty TPV prototypes had been built and tried out at La Ferte-Vidame. The co-production of an architect and an aviator, they were strange-looking vehicles indeed. Little more than test platforms with makeshift seats and controls, the absence of bodywork forced the test drivers to wear leather flying suits which further accentuated the TPV's weird quasi-aeronautical appearance. By this point, completion of the TPV project had become a top priority for Boulanger. On one hand, he had already informed his Michelin masters that production would commence the following year. But on the other, he was obsessed with the idea that Renault was working in the same direction and that, unless he was quick, Citroën's great rival might beat him and be first to introduce a People's Car. And by now it was common knowledge that a similar project was under way in Germany.

Hence there ensued a period of feverish activity at the Bureau d'Etudes. Brainstorming sessions took place late into the night as the design team wrestled with technical problems in a highly charged atmosphere of urgency and secrecy. Despite several modifications to Lefèbvre's original proposals, certain basic flaws proved extremely hard to overcome. Most worrying of all was the difficulty experienced in actually assembling the prototypes, constructed as they were from duralinox and magnesium, materials that were inherently dangerous. Given the primitive technology of the time, welding the joints of the floor pan was found to be a hazardous operation, so that the cars tended to split and buckle along the seams when subjected to torsional stress. Strengthening cross members were required to keep the structure rigid, which added to the car's ever-increasing weight. One prototype suffered an electrical short-circuit which ignited the gas tank. When the flames reached the magnesium wheels and suspension arms, there was a blinding flash and the entire car literally disappeared in smoke. Worse still, these materials were scarce and expensive. At the outset of the project, Boulanger had reckoned on the cost of light alloys reducing sharply with their increased industrial use, but there was still no sign that this crucial downward price trend was taking place.

Moreover, Boulanger's insistence that, to save fuel, the TPV should be as light as possible was creating serious problems in another department. The difference between its weight empty (300 kg) and fully loaded (700 kg) was simply too great for its complicated interacting torsion bar suspension system to overcome. Set for a very soft ride with just the driver inside, the body sank down onto the road when passengers climbed on board; and whenever the brake was applied, the car pitched and vibrated, before diving sharply downwards so that its nose hit the ground. To prevent this happening, an anti-dive modification linking the suspension to the brake pedal was necessary. But then, when the testers put the all-important sack of potatoes in the back, the car pointed heavenward. Even the engine was still providing trouble. In its latest form it was prone to icing and refused to start in cold weather, below four degrees Centigrade. Its fuel economy and power output were also both disappointing, well below Boulanger's original specification. Nevertheless, in December 1938, after having personally tested a succession of no less than 47 different prototypes, P-J.B. declared that the TPV was ready for sale at last, and authorized that series production should commence the following May so that around 250 cars would be ready for the long-anticipated launch at the Paris Salon in October. In May 1938, an example was actually presented to the Service des Mines for approved.

Had the car appeared that year, however, it would surely have proved to be a commercial disaster, for although it might well have satisfied the engineers in its current state, it could never have pleased the public. To the inexperienced layman it would have been a mechanical nightmare. Routine engine maintenance such as topping off the oil required the removal of the front fender, and with no fuel gauge — not even a dipstick — it was difficult to avoid running out of gas. Highly charged with static electricity, the Perspex windows attracted so much road dust that they might as well have been made of frosted glass. The steering wheel and foot pedals were badly placed and the handbrake hardly worked. The doors and windows would not shut properly and the roof let in rain and drafts from the slip-stream so that, without a proper heater, the car's occupants were always cold and often soaking wet as well. And needless to say, no one had thought of fitting a starter-motor, or even a rearview mirror. To save weight, only one headlight was fitted, since this was all that French road traffic regulations currently required. A joke went round the company that a glow-worm would have been lighter and cheaper — and would have saved on the battery too!

But fortunately for P-J. Boulanger and the TPV, the October 1939 Paris Motor Show did not take place. On September 1st that year (the very day before the last example of the pre-production batch rolled off the line at Citroën's Levallois factory) the German Army invaded Poland. The following day, September 3rd, France and Britain declared war; shortly after that, the forthcoming Paris Salon was cancelled, causing the launch of the new People's Car to be postponed indefinitely. Now André Lefèbvre and his team would have ample time to sort out all the remaining minor problems!

By June 1940 the German Army had arrived in Paris, imposing a state of military occupation on the northern half of France and compelling the unwelcome presence of a German Verwalter or administrator upon the Citroën factories, in common with all other automobile firms lying within the occupied zone. A German order dated November 20, 1940, gave these military administrators total control over all commercial transactions, including the purchase of raw materials, the payment of wages and the sale of finished vehicles. In fact, their powers extended much further than just over control of production, to cover the use of technical information and the direction of technical staff. As related in the previous chapter, the orders issued by the Werwalter at the Quai de Javel (a certain Baron von Baumbach, a former Auto-Union manager) stated that the production of private passenger cars should cease forthwith and that Citroën (in common with the Renault and Berliet firms) should concentrate on the manufacture of lorries reserved solely for the use of the Wehrmacht.

Three months after the capitulation and partition of France, Edouard Michelin died at the age of 81. As there was no direct successor deemed to be of sufficient maturity and experience to be found among the immediate descendents of either André or Edouard Michelin (the heir presumptive, Edouard's grandson François, was currently only 14 and did not take up the reins of power for another 15 years), the role of *patron* fell to Edouard's son-in-law, Robert Puiseux, another long-standing employee, friend and confidant of the Michelin family, who remained in command until his retirement in May 1955. For the following ten years, until December 1950, these two faithful lieutenants, Boulanger and Puiseux, acted as joint custodians of the combined Michelin and Citroën businesses, which together formed one of the largest and most important industrial and commercial organizations in France at that time.

Then, as now, Michelin family members were soberly bourgeois and thoroughly uncosmopolitan; as devout Catholics and loyal republicans, they were relentless in their patriotic determination to uphold the interests and prestige of France. At the outbreak of the First World War they had encouraged the creation of a force of bomber aircraft with which to attack Germany, and financed the purchase by the French government of a fleet of 100 airplanes designed and built by Louis Breguet to a specification that André and Edouard Michelin had themselves proposed. As we have already noted, their sons had served in the embryonic French air force between 1914–1918, and Edouard's eldest son Etienne (father of François Michelin, the present head of the family) had been killed in an air crash in 1932 while attempting to land on the summit of the Puy de Dome.

Both Puiseux and Boulanger had also served with distinction as aviators during World War I (the latter winning many decorations for gallantry) and both were now united in their determination to defeat the recurring intrusion from Germany. Indeed, they roundly opposed everything about the Third Reich and Hitler's New European Order and despised even more the collaborationist Vichy regime led by Marshal Petain which governed the unoccupied zone. As supporters of General de Gaulle and the Free French Forces then rallying in England, they were convinced that the Wehrmacht's stay on French soil would be short and so, throughout the four years of the Occupation, in a variety of ploys, they steadfastly resisted all pressure to cooperate with the Germans, more than was necessary to ensure the survival of the Citroën and Michelin firms. In fact, in January 1943, following the German defeat at Stalingrad, they sent an emissary to de Gaulle in London, pledging support for the Free French cause and the Allied war effort in general.

As Clermont-Ferrand lay in the unoccupied southern zone of France, administered by the Vichy government, the Michelin firm was relatively undisturbed by interference from the ever-inquisitive Germans during the first two years of the war, although permits were required for travel between the Clermont-Ferrand and Paris factories. And although its factories were forced to produce tires for the Nazi war machine, the actual facilities were inviolate, so that the technological secrets hidden within them remained secure throughout the war. But in November 1942, following the Allied landings in North Africa, the Wehrmacht took control of the southern zone as well, ending the independence of the Vichy government. At the same time, measures directing the employment of labor throughout France were introduced, forcing thousands of skilled industrial workers to be deported to Germany, to work in labor camps under conditions of virtual slavery. This above all the other indignities inflicted upon them by the Nazis was the act that caused greatest outrage among the people of France, and which led to the formation of the French Resistance movement. Boulanger, Puiseux and other members of the Michelin family supported this secret organization without reservation, at great personal peril.

Indeed, in 1943, André Michelin's second son, Marcel Michelin (Boulanger's boyhood friend) was arrested by the Gestapo and sent to Buchenwald concentration camp where he died two years later, in January 1945. Marcel's eldest son Philippe fled to England where he served in the Royal Air Force, while his other two sons, Jacques and Jean-Pierre, remained in France as active members of the Resistance, in the cause of which they both eventually met their deaths. Similarly, André's daughter-in-law Marguerite (nee Puiseux, wife of his eldest son Jean and sister of Robert Puiseux) was interned at Ravensbruck, while his grandson Jean-Luc (son of Jean) was seized by the Germans and sent to work as a slave laborer in a factory near Munich.

Not surprisingly under the circumstances, Pierre-Jules Boulanger adopted an indefatigably hostile stand towards the Nazis. Even when faced with the confiscation of the Citroën factory's machinery and equipment, as related in the previous chapter, with the full backing of his Michelin masters he refused to cooperate directly with the German military and economic authorities and always insisted on dealing with the factory's Verwalter, von Baumbach, through his subordinates or other intermediaries. A profoundly serious and sober man, and a devout practicing Catholic (he was reputedly a Jansenist), Boulanger set himself the strictest moral standards. Throughout the Occupation he forbade his wife from buying bread, meat or butter on the black market or from obtaining any other articles, such as children's shoes, for which she did not have the appropriate ration coupon. By virtue of his position as Director-General of SA André Citroën, P-J.B. was one of the few citizens of Paris entitled to the use of a car for his personal needs, even on weekends. But Boulanger refused to exercise this privilege; when going home on Friday evenings and returning to work on Monday mornings, he traveled on the Metro.

Only when it came to deceiving the Germans was this rectitude relaxed. As a consequence of its work in constructing trucks, the Citroën firm was allowed unlimited supplies of gasoline throughout the war — but only for the purpose of fueling these trucks prior to delivery. By order of the Nazi administrator at the factory, all passenger cars in use by the firm had to be powered by the combustible gas produced by a wood-burning gazogene apparatus towed in a trailer behind the vehicle. The cars that traveled daily throughout Paris on Citroën business under the noses of the Germans appeared to be conforming to this rule, but, with Boulanger's full knowledge and approval, in reality they were running on gasoline with their tanks full of liquid fuel! Again, when it came to his attention that a small band of Citroën workers, known to be members of the Resistance, were being hunted down by the Gestapo, he helped these fugitives to evade capture by allowing them to hide for several days inside the case of the large clock that hung in the factory's delivery hall.

It is known that in July 1940 a technical fact-finding mission, led by none other than Dr. Ferdinand Porsche, arrived in Paris from Berlin to investigate rumors of a French rival to the Volkswagen. But despite promising a free exchange of information between Levallois and Wolfsburg, their enquiries revealed absolutely nothing. Questioned about the TPV, P-J.B. told the German authorities that the project was a commercial secret belonging to Citroën, not the Republic, and that he would not divulge such precious information to a Frenchman let alone a German.

In fact, on the outbreak of war, Boulanger had ordered that the 250 examples of the TPV so far completed be hidden for the duration, either at the Levallois factory or at the la Ferte-Vidame test track. Reliable witnesses have testified to the fact that large quantities remained under wraps at Levallois in 1943. But after the war, in 1949, with the car now an on-the-road reality (albeit in a rather different form, as the 2CV) P-J.B. ordered that all the remaining examples of the TPV be destroyed, together with many other prototypes and experimental vehicles dating from the André Citroën era. However, in 1968, a single example of the TPV was discovered at the La Ferte-Vidame test track and restored for publicity purposes. Later, in 1994, three more complete examples were uncovered there, having been hidden in a barn in a remote part of the estate, making a total of five surviving Citroën prototypes. However, some 50 years earlier, in 1947, the original Michelin prototype, dating from 1936, was found at the Clermont-Ferrand factory, where, as we have already noted, a parallel research project had been conducted before and during the Occupation. Disguised as a pickup truck to conceal it from the prying eyes of Germans, it had been thrown out as scrap after the Liberation, but fortunately it found its way to an automobile museum at Rochtailee-sur-Saone, the Musee Henri Malartre, where it stands to this day, as testament to the true origins of the 2CV. Although powered by a water-cooled engine, this car features the swinging leading and trailing axle-arms first conceived by Pierre Michelin, and demonstrated with his nephew's Meccano set!

Although the existence of the TPV was concealed throughout the war, it was certainly not forgotten. Relieved of normal commercial responsibilities and pressures, the design and development team at the Bureau d'Etudes was able to work on without interruption, in an atmosphere of clandestine creativity. Despite the fact that French car makers were forbidden to construct — or even to research and design — any vehicle whatsoever during the Occupation without obtaining the permission of the German authorities, Boulanger ignored the order, so that

At the following year's show, on October 7, 1947, all was revealed at last. The price quoted was now 228,000 FF, a considerable increase on the 185,000 FF announced the previous year. Series production commenced that month.

this was a period when imaginations ran rampant, unfettered by normal business realities. An agricultural tractor was another possible future product investigated at the time.

During the winter of 1940–1941, he initiated a cost review of the project, so that he would be ready to revive the car the moment that the war was over. Apart from obvious political developments, economic circumstances had already changed markedly since the outset. The materials and manufacturing costs of the original light-alloy design were already 40 percent higher and climbing fast, Boulanger calculated. A heavier steel-built car would now be inevitable — but that meant rethinking the suspension and even, perhaps, developing a lighter, more powerful engine. In fact, the whole scheme would have to be reconsidered.

Fortunately, the upheavals of war had caused several particularly talented engineers to change their jobs and join the Bureau d'Etudes, which, as a result of the damage sustained in the German air raid of June 1940, was now relocated in the former Mors factory at 48 rue du Theatre, a few streets away from the Quai de Javel. Chief among these new recruits was the highly gifted and experienced engine designer, Walter Becchia, who came from the Talbot-Lago design office at Suresnes to replace Maurice Sainturat, who had retired. Becchia was followed a year later by the carburetor expert, Lucien Girard, who also joined from Talbot-Lago.

Another infusion of fresh ideas on the project came from the Bureau's new official head of research Jean Cadiou (successor to Maurice Broglie), and also from the Italian sculptor and stylist, Flaminio Bertoni, who had made his reputation with the Traction Avant. Cadiou instructed Bertoni to produce designs for a new body shell in light-gauge steel, based on his proposals for the long since abandoned AX project, or Traction Avant re-vamp. Once more, Boulanger decreed that this Mark II TPV must have only one headlight, which Bertoni placed at the center of the hood, giving it a strange one-eyed appearance, like the Cyclops. Its simple flat-sided shape was due in part to the fact that the Germans had removed from the factory most of the heavy presses that would

P-J. Boulanger proudly explains the technical details of the 2CV's air-cooled flat-twin engine to a pair of French government ministers at the 1947 Paris Salon.

have been needed to produce a body with more shapely curves. At this point in time the revived TPV prototype still retained the original water-cooled engine and multiple torsion bar springing of the pre-war version.

By now, of course, Boulanger had no way of knowing if the missing presses would ever be found and repatriated after the war, and for a very good reason. On learning that his machine tools and presses were about to be requisitioned and sent by train to Germany, P-J.B. had arranged for the Resistance to be tipped off, so as to frustrate and disrupt the Nazi move. One night, while the railway wagons were still in the Paris marshalling yards, some members of the Resistance managed to swap the destination cards so that the freight cars ended up in the wrong places, scattered all over Europe. After the war, much time and effort was spent in locating and retrieving this machinery!

But either way, with or without the presses, this plain, functional no-frills styling, with its absence of adornment and ostentation, appealed to his aesthetic sensibilities. Although it would be stretching things to describe him as an intellectual, as a former architect P-J.B. was strongly influenced by le Corbusier and the thinkers of the Modern Movement who had attempted during the 1920s and 1930s to lay down comprehensive criteria of design covering all the products and artifacts of the modern industrial society. If, as le Corbusier claimed, a house was simply a machine for living in, then it followed that a car was just a machine for traveling in, and all design aims or considerations other than the purely functional were superfluous.

After the Liberation in 1944, work on the TPV was resumed in earnest, with a view to commencing production as soon as circumstances allowed. Initially, a finely detailed cost and viability analysis was carried out by Pierre Bercot (who later became the company's managing director) following which a radical, third, re-design program was commenced by the Bureau d'Etudes. This engineering project was headed by Jean Muratet, with overall body design work carried out by Maurice Steck, the bodywork specialist of the Methodes Techniques department, while questions of detail and styling remained the responsibility of Flaminio Bertoni.

For several years after the Liberation, the economic situation in France remained just as perilous as it had been during the war, if not more so, for now difficulties caused by continued shortages of raw materials, machinery and fuel were compounded by political instability and industrial unrest. However, by the end of 1946, the Citroën firm was well on the road to recovery, having turned out more than 10,000 examples of the Traction Avant sedan since production at its Quai de Javel factory had been resumed in June 1945. By now, plans to bring out a revised post-war version of the TPV were well advanced, and the design was beginning to resemble the car that would eventually appear in 1948, especially since the car had now acquired its unique and justly famous air-cooled, light-alloy, flat twin-cylinder engine. Conceived by Walter Becchia, this marvel of compact, weight-saving design and high-quality precision engineering, was intended to run continually for hours on end, even in especially arduous conditions. Designed within the space of a week, to the same 375 cc capacity and overall layout as Sainturat's earlier water-cooled design, this perfectly balanced engine combined extreme simplicity and reliability of operation with great fuel economy and efficiency. It could

One of the first official publicity photos of the 2CV, taken in September 1948. The Citroën Double Chevron badge on the hood grille remained in this form until October 1953, when the oval ring of beading surrounding it disappeared.

Left: **The 2CV's original 275 cc flat-four air-cooled engine plus its four-speed gearbox, as manufactured from 1949 to 1959. It powered the car to a maximum top speed of 40.9 mph and a 0–60 mph acceleration time of 42.4 seconds, yet returned an average fuel consumption of 54.7 mpg. The inboard drum brakes were not superseded by disc brakes until 1981.**

also be depended upon to start the first time, whatever the weather, although with no built-in self-starter this could only be achieved manually, with a starting handle.

Up to this point it had always been intended that the TPV, as conceived by Boulanger, would have a three-speed gearbox, but Becchia could not resist giving it four forward speeds. When Boulanger noticed this departure from his brief, he was furious. The farmer's wife would have enough problems mastering three speeds, let alone four, he maintained. In the end, a compromise was reached when Bechia succeeded in convincing Boulanger that the fourth speed was not another gear, but an overdrive.

The one remaining trouble-spot was the suspension, which, after revisions by Marcel Chinon, now featured compressible coil springs, mounted horizontally and interlinked front to rear. A great improvement on the expensive and complicated torsion bar arrangement used on the earlier prototypes, this system prevented pitching and gave the car a very comfortable ride, but at the expense of its road-holding ability. Some form of damping was still required to keep the wheels in contact with the road on rebound. The problem was that Boulanger refused to approve shock absorbers, the fitting of which would destroy the purity of his conception. Matters were finally resolved when Leon Renault revived his famous pre-war idea of inertia dampers, fitted to the ends of the axle arms, next to the wheels themselves. By describing these modifications as *batteurs* or beaters, this time P-J.B.'s objections were finally overcome and the system remained in use on the car for many years, until phased out in stages between 1965 and 1975, when conventional telescopic dampers were finally fitted on all models.

This photograph was taken at the Levallois factory in November 1949, where production had then been underway for a month. The roll-up canvas hood and trunk-cover are clearly visible. A metal trunk-lid was not added until October 1957.

Throughout 1945 and 1946, the car was subjected to constant, almost non-stop testing at la Ferte-Vidame, under Boulanger's personal supervision. By this point Lefèbvre's involvement in the TPV project had diminished; his creative energy was now focused on another major research project in progress at the Bureau d'Etudes, the so-called Voiture de Grande Diffusion which, as we shall see in a later chapter, was eventually to evolve into the revolutionary Citroën DS19. From then on the TPV was entirely Boulanger's baby and, as a result, the *patron's* personality and physique somehow became imprinted into the car, evident forever in its unique characteristics and appearance. In contrast to the average Frenchman, P-J.B. was tall and lean and wore a felt hat, not a beret, so that, to accommodate him, the car had to be given much more head room and leg room than that provided in other comparable contemporary small cars. On Sundays, he would exercise his privilege of driving on weekends by taking his wife and family for a test drive, each time driving over the same route at the same speed, to check that gas consumption never fell below 55 mpg.

P-J. Boulanger was a perfectionist and always found something to worry about. By now it was the car's weight that was causing him concern. With all the changes and modifications that had taken place, the weight had now reached more than 400 kgs—25 percent more than laid down in his original *cahier-des-charges.* The story goes that, in an effort to reduce this burden, he ordered a prototype to be stripped down completely and the parts weighed one by one, to see if each and every item could be made smaller, lighter or thinner, or simply be elimi-

The famous single-fold leaflet produced to publicize the 2CV in 1948, though advertising was hardly required to sell the car in its first few years. Throughout the early 1950s the waiting list exceeded five years' production (which rose to a rate of more than 21,000 sedans per annum in 1951), so that, initially at least, output was rationed and allocated to only the most deserving customers.

nated altogether. To monitor the precise weight of every component manufactured from that point onwards, a special department called the Service des Poids was set up — and Citroën's draftsmen were instructed henceforth to specify a nominal weight for even the tiniest, most trivial part shown on their drawings. But Boulanger's efforts were in vain — the weight kept increasing regardless, as more and more extra but essential items were incorporated into the design, such as proper window glass, a second headlight and a rudimentary heating system. Even so, he still drew the line at a conventional electric starter motor; his intention was that the car would be equipped with a recoil starter device, operated by a cord pulled from the drivers seat, in order to avoid the excess weight and cost of a battery, which would also require maintenance. In fact, a conventional electric self-starter was fitted on production models.

At the first post-war Paris Motor Show, held in October 1946, the newly-nationalized Renault firm revealed that it too had been engaged in the secret development of a French People's Car during the war. This vehicle, the Renault 4CV, was to be built in its factory on the Ile de Seguin in Paris, destroyed by allied bombing during the war, but presently being re-built and re-equipped with state funding. A conventional four-door, four-seater car, the Renault 4CV was powered by a 757cc engine mounted in the rear behind the axle, as on the VW Beetle. Indeed, the earliest prototypes of the 4CV, built in 1944, showed a very strong overall resemblance to the German People's Car, production of which was by now under way at Wolfsburg.

Sale of the Renault 4CV commenced one year later, in August 1947, under the provisions of the five-year Plan Pons discussed in the previous chapter. Amongst other measures, the Plan, introduced in 1945, had stipulated that Citroën confine itself to constructing the Traction Avant in its 11CV and 15CV forms, giving its arch rival Renault a virtual monopoly of the cheaper end of the market. Although he was a member of the committee formed to supervise the implementation of this plan, P-J.B. responded to the arrival of the Renault 4CV by issuing orders, in February 1948, that, after fourteen years of gestation, the TPV should at last be made ready for series

Above: In 1973, this example of the pre-war TPV prototype was discovered at Citroën's la Ferte Vidame test-track and restored for publicity purposes. When it was built in 1939, only one headlight was required under French law; to save weight, only one was fitted.

Much later — as recently as 1997, in fact — three other, similar prototypes were found hidden in a barn at la Ferte Vidame. Part of a pre-production batch of 250, built for the proposed launch in 1939, they had somehow escaped destruction and lain forgotten there for 60 years. Constructed largely of light-alloy and canvas, the TPV was powered by a water-cooled 375 cc flat-twin engine.

In fact, the oldest 2CV prototype extant is now known to be this model, which originated at Michelin's Clermont-Ferrand factory. Rescued from the scrap-heap just after World War II, it was certainly in existence as early as 1937, but it may even pre-date Michelin's acquisition of Citroën in 1934.

production. His plan was that its existence be revealed to the public for the first time at the next Paris Salon, in October 1948, with sales commencing the following autumn, in phase with the termination of the Pons Plan at the end of 1949.

It only remained to choose a name for the little car and to take some pictures for a publicity brochure — and, needless to say, P-J.B. supervised that job too. In truth, the whole idea of a fanciful name would surely have been completely contrary to a man of Boulanger's ascetic nature. Consequently, the completed Toute Petite Voiture was announced simply as the Citroën 2CV or Deux Chevaux, just as Renault had described its own 760cc engined People's Car as the 4CV. The 375cc engine of the original 2CV was designed specifically to fall into the lowest, cheapest bracket of the French road tax system; later models equipped with the larger 602cc engine were actually rated as 3CVs. In the *puissance fiscale* system, employed from the outset of popular motoring in France, the duty payable increases steeply with larger engine dimensions and outputs, according to a complex formula, as indeed was the case with the variable RAC system in force in Britain until 1948, when a fixed flat-rate system was in introduced. The rate

Left: **The primitive and rudimentary dashboard of the earliest 2CVs. Instrumentation was confined to an ammeter, while the speedometer (located near the bottom lefthand corner of the windshield) also served to drive the windshield wiper. There was no fuel gauge — the level of gas in the tank had to be measured with a dipstick!**

The first major revision of the 2CV's specification took place in October 1953 when, among other improvements, new seats covered with tartan fabric were introduced. But the color of the bodywork stayed a standard grey until late in 1959 when glacier blue also became available.

Throughout the greater part of its 42-year lifespan, the 2CV sedan was built at Citroën's Levallois factory on the outskirts of Paris. By 1963, when this photograph was taken, the output of 2CV sedans at Levallois had risen to more than 158,000 units a year.

Top: Although designed primarily for the use of farmers and rural folks, the 2CV soon found favor with the town and city dwellers of France. The standard of living of industrial workers rose rapidly in step with the economic recovery of the 1950s and their leisure time and holiday entitlement also increased. With its removable seats and fully opening sunshine roof, the 2CV was the ideal car for country outings and picnics, as this early publicity photo amply demonstrated. *Bottom:* In 1958, Citroën introduced a four-wheel-drive version of the 2CV intended especially for service on the roadless desert terrain of French North Africa. But this was no ordinary 4 × 4 design. It was powered by two separate 425 cc engines, mounted front and back, each one driving an individual axle. Its hill-climbing and cross-country performance was impressive. Apart from the engine ventilation louvers for its second engine, the 2CV 4 × 4 could easily be recognized by its spare wheel mounted on the hood.

of tax rises in stages from the small sum levied on engines under 400cc (2CV) to that charged on medium class two-liter car (11CV) but above 2.5 liters (13CV) it increases substantially. Bigger, more powerful engines above 2.9 liters (16CV) are subject to a punitive level of taxation. The system had actually originated in the late nineteenth century as a means of measuring the power output of steam-powered vehicles, hence the term *cheval vapeur* or steam horse.

When the TPV made its memorable first appearance at the Grand Palais d'Exposition just off the Champs Elysées on October 7, 1948, few of the 1,300,000 visitors who flocked to the show to catch their first glimpse of France's new People's Car could have predicted that it was destined to stay in production for 42 years and to sell almost 7,000,000 cars. Indeed its debut was panned by

By the end of the 1950s, the 2CV was well established as the favorite fun-car of the younger generation too, spelling freedom from routine and convention and an escape from needless expense. Citroën's publicity material cleverly developed this sense of mobility and independence, endowing the car with a lively character and personality much more in tune with the optimistic spirit of the times than the hair-shirt frugality of Boulanger's original conception.

the critics of the motoring press. Grave error ... a fiasco ... a total misreading of the market ... the ugliest car in the world ... these were some of the kinder comments. With the sole exception of a perceptive Swiss motoring journalist writing in the *Revue Automobile Suisse*, not one single reviewer had the foresight to suggest that the 2CV would become a landmark of motoring history and an enduring French cultural icon. Even Citroën's own dealers—steeped in the André Citroën tradition—thought that Boulanger had made a huge mistake. At a preview two months earlier they had begged him to change his plans, or at least to do something to beautify the car, but le patron was adamant—the 2CV was not meant to be a status symbol or object of prestige like other cars, and launch would go ahead regardless.

Although Boulanger was an administrator and industrialist and not an engineer, he was rightly identified as the father of the 2CV at its launch. As revealed to the world at the 1948 Paris Motor Show, this Spartan, quasi-monastic, utilitarian vehicle seemed to reflect his physique, personality and philosophy exactly, to represent a personal statement of engineering, aesthetic and cultural values. Yet, in truth, this radical form of rural transport was entirely a Michelin creation—a unique concept that the provincial tire-makers had long nurtured and dreamed of producing through their own resources, but which, by a chain of fortuitous events, came to be built and branded by Citroën. Surely, a car with such revolutionary engineering and social attributes could never have been proposed under the old André Citroën regime; nor could or would it ever be repeated when the time came for it to be replaced, under the new Peugeot management that was to follow when the Michelin men eventually gave up their ownership of Citroën.

The Michelin family themselves were certainly proud of the car and considered it to be their own creation. When François Michelin became chairman of the company in 1966, he continued to drive to work every day in his Deux Chevaux, until it was pointed out that this was considered by outsiders to be hardly an appropriate means of transport for the leader of a major industrial corporation. So, reluctantly, he exchanged his 2CV, not for a luxury limousine or a prestige sports tourer, but for the station wagon version of the Citroën ID19, another unique product of the Citroën-Michelin-Lefèbvre connection.

5

The Citroën 2CV, 1948–1990

Eleven years after it had first been mooted by Pierre Michelin and Pierre-Jules Boulanger, the 2CV finally made its public debut at the 1948 Paris Motor Show, which opened at the Grand Palais d'Exposition, just off the Champs Elysées, on October 7th that year. Few of the journalists who had assembled there to greet the new arrival from the Quai de Javel thought that the result had been worth the long wait, and with one notable exception the debutante was reported on with undisguised disappointment by the critics of the Continental motoring press.

Fortunately, the public thought differently. That year the Paris Salon attracted more than 1,300,000 visitors, only a handful of whom had any realistic prospect of buying a new vehicle in the foreseeable future, given the current perilous economic circumstances in France and the very low number of private cars then being produced. Yet all of these would-be motorists were impatient to catch their first glimpse of Citroën's new People's Car, about which there had been so much speculation. When P-J. Boulanger proudly unveiled the first three examples before the President of the Republic, Vincent Auriol, crowds surged onto the stand to get a closer look. Security guards had to be called in to prevent the public from forcing open the sealed hoods to inspect the mechanicals and to stop them bouncing the cars up and down to see the novel suspension in action. In fact, the hoods were empty; the final design and specification of the engine had not yet been decided upon. No matter! Thousands of orders were taken on the first day alone, and by the end of the proceedings more than 1.25 million visitors had flocked to the Citroën stand.

It was hardly surprising. Here at last was the means by which the ordinary Frenchman and his family could eventually become mobile. For little more than the price of a motorbike-engined cycle car—185,000 old francs—Citroën was offering a deceptively spacious and extremely comfortable four-door, four-seater sedan which, as a bonus, converted instantly into a removal van or pick-up truck. Its great advantages as a load and people carrier over its main French rival, the rear-engined Renault 4CV, were plain for all to see. The 4CV had first been exhibited two years earlier at the 1946 Paris show, although its manufacture and marketing had not begun until the autumn of 1947.

When, five years later, the right-hand-drive version, built at Citroën's factory at Slough, made its first U.K. appearance at the 1953 London Motor Show, it attracted lavish praise from the critics of the British motoring press. "The most original design since the model T Ford," said *The Autocar*, avowing that "Comment other than praise is confined to criticism of the position of the rear-view mirror," a trifling quibble considering the extraordinary contrast that the car must have made with competing contemporary British products. This opinion was later echoed by the rival magazine *The Motor* which described the 2CV as "A vehicle with almost every virtue except speed, silence and good looks." But perhaps the most glowing tribute came from the famous motoring journalist William Boddy, editor of *Motor Sport* magazine. In April 1954, after covering some 2,000 miles in six days touring the hills and valleys of Wales at the wheel of a Slough-built 2CV, he declared in his report, entitled "People's Car Reborn," that it was "a splendid, fascinating little car. Its designer, who must be a brilliant engineer indeed, has approached fearlessly the problem of providing a modern people's car. From now on I shall look with scorn at cars of low power output which employ heavy lumps of cast iron surrounded by water for engines, and I shall refuse to regard as an economy car any vehicle which does not give a genuine 60 miles per gallon."

In the aftermath of World War II France suffered an economic crisis of even greater severity than that which had occurred during the Occupation. Throughout the grim period from 1945 to 1950, virtually every commodity including food and fuel was in short supply, especially the raw materials and machine tools needed to build cars, a situation aggravated by the fact that during the war the factories of the French auto industry had been either ransacked for machinery by the Germans or damaged beyond repair by Allied bombing. Moreover, a severe shortage of foreign currency meant that it was difficult for Citroën and its suppliers to import new equipment to feed their production lines. Supplies of steel and other raw materials were still severely rationed (not to mention fuels such as coal and gas) and manufactured components of every kind were scarce, especially tires and batteries. Consequently, despite the huge pent-up demand for the 2CV exhibited by the hordes of potential customers who thronged the Citroën stand in 1948, almost another whole year was to pass before a single example was built and sold, in July 1949, production having actually commenced on the 23rd of June that year.

In its definitive and earliest form, the series A fitted with the original 9 bhp 375 cc engine, the 2CV was a four-door, four-seater sedan capable of 54.7 mpg, a maximum speed of 40.9 mph and a 0–40 mph acceleration time of 42.4 seconds. Designed by André Lefèbvre, styled by Flaminio Bertoni and engineered for production by Maurice Steck, it represented a structural concept unique in the history of the motor car, a system of construction which has never been repeated at Citroën or elsewhere. Its bodywork, which had no structural function and served only to enclose the occupants and protect them from the weather, was made from steel and rubberized canvas, and was painted all over with a standard matt metallic grey finish, including the wheels. The unladen curb weight of the little car was 508 kg (1,119 pounds) with the weight distributed fore and aft in an approximate 60%/40% ratio, which Lefèbvre considered to be the ideal balance.

The Deux Chevaux's simple but by no means unsophisticated bodywork was formed from just five major elements, fastened together with bolts rather than by spot-welds as was normal even then. Particular attention had been devoted to ensuring that the car would be both simple and inexpensive to manufacture and assemble using the barest minimum of machinery, and the use of complex, curved panel work requiring expensive press tools was ruled out. As the cost of human labor was then relatively cheap in comparison to plant, a reliance on manual assembly methods was not considered to be a great disadvantage. These five elements comprised the floor pan, the footboard, cowl and windshield pillar assembly; the two side members together with the doorposts; the three cross braces that supported the roof and the four doors; the four detachable fenders; and, finally, the hood, a one-piece structure that opened rearwards on a long single hinge fixed to the cowl. The upper surface of the hood was swaged or corrugated in the manner invented by the German airplane designer Dr. Hugo Junkers, to give it stiffness without adding unnecessary weight, while its front and sides were pierced by both grille and louvers, to enable a sufficient flow of cooling air to enter the fan through the front cowling and then to be vented from the engine bay.

In certain press reports at the time, the 2CV's bodywork was described as being of the cabriolet type, by virtue of its fully opening rubberized canvas roof, which extended across the top from the windshield right down to the rear bumper; there was as yet no opening metal trunk lid of the type eventually fitted, although the roof was pierced at the back by a small window made from solid glass, to give the driver rearward vision. In later years this removable, roll-back top was advertised as a sunroof, but its original purpose was to allow the carrying of awkward, oversize loads. The driver and passengers rode side by side in detachable tubular-framed bench seats, front and rear. These were covered in a plasticized fabric sprung by rubber cords, and both could be quickly removed to provide extra luggage space or for picnics by the way-side.

The rudimentary instrumentation of the 2CVA of 1949–1950s consisted solely of an ammeter located on a tiny panel attached to the steering column alongside the stalk-type lighting switch inherited from the Traction Avant; this gave the driver an indication of the condition of the car's 6-volt electrical system. The panel also housed an ignition key switch to turn the engine on and off, though starting was actually accomplished mechanically by pulling a cable attached to the contact switch on the starter motor; a proper solenoid starter mechanism operated by the ignition key was not introduced for another twenty years! As there was no dashboard as such, the speedometer was fixed to the windshield pillar, and the famous sliding push-pull gear selecting lever simply projected through the scuttle panel. The windshield wipers were also driven mechanically from the gearbox by the speedometer cable rather than by an electric motor. The car lacked turn signals and even a fuel gauge and the contents of the tank had to be measured by a dipstick. Heating and demisting was by a simple tube that admitted hot air from the cylinder heads into the cabin, while fresh air was obtained by opening a scuttle panel vent located immediately beneath the windshield. The one concession to sophistication was that a small hand wheel under the fascia enabled drivers to adjust the angle of the headlight beams by swiveling the headlight mounting bar, in order to compensate for the rise or fall caused by variations in the load being carried. A full width parcel shelf provided room for storing odds and ends and below this was the umbrella handle that served as a handbrake lever, of course acting on the front brakes.

The body was mounted directly onto the underlying platform chassis and its supporting outriggers, two pairs of which extended outwards on either side of the chassis frame. This chassis frame consisted of two box-section outer longerons, or side members, which extended along the full length of the car from front to rear and which were connected at intervals by bracing cross-members, plus two separate u-section inner side members which were attached to the inboard faces of the outer side members at the front and rear of the car, but which curved inwards at the central section of the platform, between the axle cross member mountings, to brace the platform floor in the front-foot well and rear-luggage well areas. For maximum strength and rigidity, the central section of the frame was enclosed on both its top and bottom sides by two large rectangular sheet steel panels welded to it, so that the resulting structure resembled a stretcher rather than a ladder with open foot rungs.

Also mounted directly to the platform chassis was the *bloc moteur*, or engine, gearbox and transmission unit, attached by means of rubber silentblocs, while the fuel tank was suspended from it at the rear. In addition, two substantial tubular cross-members were also attached to the chassis, being bolted to the frame at the corners of its reinforced central section, well within the car's wheelbase. At the ends of these cross tubes were located the massive taper-roller bearings upon which the 2CV's four crescent-shaped axle arms were suspended. Made from steel pressings, these arms extended either forward at the front or backward at the rear, the front pair described as leading arms and the rear pair as trailing arms. To their outer ends were attached the stub-axles and hubs that carried the road-wheels and, in the case of the rear arms, the rear drum brakes. This arrangement allowed the arms and their wheels to move up and down through a very wide arc, permitting an unusually high degree of suspension travel. The front axles had inboard drum brakes, mounted on the gearbox.

The 2CV's highly flexible suspension system was quite unique. Instead of acting completely independently of each other, the two axle arms on each side of the vehicle were linked via a shared suspension unit, comprising a double set of coil springs mounted horizontally in a tubular sliding-housing located under the bodywork of the car and fixed to the outriggers of the platform chassis. Thus the front and rear wheels were interconnected by means of these double coil springs in such a way that, when the front wheel hit a bump, the deflection of the front axle arm caused a tie rod to compress its associated coil spring, cushioning the blow. But because the rear wheel was connected by the same means to a second spring in the same sliding housing, this action had the effect of transmitting the motion to the rear to force the rear axle arm downwards, stiffening the suspension ready for the rear wheel to meet the bump in its turn. That way, shocks from ruts and potholes were completely absorbed; jarring and pitching was eliminated; and the travelers onboard, sitting well within the wheel-base, enjoyed an exceptionally smooth, stable ride, even over the cratered, cobbled roads, pockmarked with pot-holes, that were typical of the French road system in the 1950s.

Moreover, unlike all modern cars, the 2CV had no anti-roll bars to stiffen its suspension and prevent its body from leaning at an apparently perilous angle when rounding a bend at speed. Lefèbvre was one of the first automobile engineers to understand that there is no direct relationship between the force that makes a car's body roll when cornering and that which tries to overturn it. Indeed, a car that rolls a great deal may actually prove very difficult to overturn, while one that rolls little may be far more be liable to overturn unexpectedly since a vehicle's road holding ability is ultimately governed by the grip exerted by its tires on the road. In designing for the straight but bumpy rural roads of France and not the twisting, snaking country lanes of England, Lefèbvre took the view that anti-roll bars would tend to compromise the 2CV's finely balanced handling abilities and also spoil its ride. By transmitting lateral forces to the wheels and inducing them to lift off the ground when cornering, anti-roll bars might serve only to break the vital tire/road contact at critical direction-changing moments, causing a sudden loss of steering control. In fact, a certain degree of roll was actually an advantage, he believed, because it served to warn the inexperienced driver that the car was reaching the limits of tire adhesion. Thus, although by reducing roll he might produce a vehicle that looked safer to spectators, in reality its safety margins would actually be impaired, though with no corresponding gain in stability, security or ride-comfort. In short, he had discovered that there would never be any real correlation between a 2CV's pronounced body roll and the risk of overturning it, since the car's wide track and low center of gravity helped keep overturning forces firmly under control at all times, by ensuring that all four wheels stayed constantly planted on the road, remaining parallel to each other in straight line driving situations, to preserve optimum contact and adhesion between the tire footprint and the road. This achievement, which so greatly enhanced the safe, predictable handling and road-holding enjoyed by 2CV drivers, was among the first fruits of the program of research into the concept *of la liaison au sol* undertaken jointly by Citroën and Michelin in partnership.

Another unusual feature adopted by Lefèbvre to enhance the 2CV's handling and road holding was that the front pair of the Lockheed hydraulic drum brakes employed were mounted inboard of the hubs and drive shafts, in a position immediately adjacent to the gearbox, in order to reduce unsprung weight to the minimum, though the rear drums were fitted in the conventional position on the rear stub-axles. Moreover, the 125 × 400 Michelin steel disc wheels and Pilote tires chosen were lightweight and of very narrow section, so as to reduce the rolling resistance of the tires and also help minimize the gyroscopic forces induced when rotating at the extreme points of their suspension travel, which would otherwise have caused handling problems. Again, to damp out rebound and prevent wheel hop, early 2CVs were equipped with friction dampers located at the suspension arm articulating points and by inertia-weight dampers fitted in vertical tubes attached to all four wheel hubs. Eventually, however, these dampers were replaced by conventional hydraulic telescopic shock-absorbers, not fitted directly on the axle arms but slung beneath the car and working in a horizontal plane in conjunction with the mechanism that interconnected the front and rear axles.

Naturally, the steering system employed on the 2CV was of the rack and pinion type that had by then become customary at Citroën since its adoption on the revised Traction Avant in 1936. The rack was housed in the same cross-tube that carried the front suspension arms, and thus was located behind the engine at the leading edge of the chassis platform, well to the rear of the front axle axis. Movement of the steering wheel and its column was passed to the rack via the pinion, while the linkage from the rack to the front wheels was by long track-rods extending outward from its center and connecting with relay arms projecting rearward from the upper part of the hubs and wheel-carriers. These swiveled on large 17mm diameter kingpins located in phosphor-bronze bushes housed in the knuckles that formed part of the forging that supported the wheel hub and driveshaft bearings, thus connecting the whole three-stud wheel carrier assembly to the suspension arms. A notable feature of the 2CV's steering geometry was the way that the action of the suspension system allowed it to be adjusted automatically, according to the load being carried onboard. When weighed down with, say, four passengers and their luggage, the wheelbase was lengthened by 2 inches and its steering caster angle increased by 8 degrees, which had the effect of neutralizing any adverse influence that an increased load might have on the car's handling and roadholding qualities. Light, sensitive, direct and extremely accurate, this steering system enabled a 2CV to corner safely and predictably under all circumstances, and to cruise with remarkable straight-line stability. It also permitted a surprisingly tight turning circle of 33ft (10.6 m) with 2.5 turns of the wheel being required to move the wheel from lock to lock, so that parking maneuvers could be made with ease.

Perhaps the most remarkable of the 2CV's many innovative features, however, was its tiny lightweight air-cooled boxer engine, displacing 375cc and producing 9 bhp SAE @ 3,500 rpm and torque of 16.6 lb-ft @ 2,000 rpm in its original form. Featuring a pressure-cast light-alloy crankcase and detachable finned cast-iron cylinder barrels for its two horizontally-opposed cylinders, it had bore and stroke dimensions of 62 × 62mm and a compression ratio of 6.2:1. Designed by the ex–Fiat and Talbot-Lago engineer Walter Becchia (like his friend Flaminio Bertoni, an Italian expatriate) it was capable of cruising all day at 40 mph while returning a steady fuel consumption of 60 mpg, an extraordinary performance in an era when few popular family cars could exceed 50 mph in safety, even in short bursts. As such it was a complete contrast in every way to the large and complicated hunks of metal that are normally considered masterpieces in the evolution of the internal combustion engine. Among its contemporaries, only the engine of the fabled Jaguar XK120 (introduced in 1948, the same year as the 2CV) lasted anywhere near as long—for 38 years—compared with the 2CV engine's unbeaten record of 42 years in continuous production, which must surely rank it among the very greatest achievements of automobile design, and certainly the most enduring.

Becchia's reason for adopting the relatively expensive solution of an air-cooled, all-alloy engine for the 2CV was, first and foremost, its lightness and compactness compared with the water-cooled alternatives. Tipping the scales at just 41 kilos in bare form, minus its gearbox and ancillary equipment, the original 375cc unit was almost half the weight and bulk of a typical contemporary cast-iron water-cooled engine of similar performance. And not only was it made from a lighter material, it lacked the extra burden of a radiator and water pump and also the considerable weight of water required as a coolant fluid. But air-cooled engines saved more than weight; they also saved trouble. Hence, equally important deciding factors were reliability and ease of maintenance. In the late 1940s, at least a third of engine breakdowns could be attributed to cooling system problems—over-heating, icing up, or loss of coolant altogether due to failure of water pump or hoses. Not only did air-cooling overcome these problems at a stroke—there was nothing to freeze or to boil—but it also made for faster warming up of the engine (and hence significant fuel savings) and also far more effective heating of the passenger compartment. In fact, an air-cooled engine was considered to be thermodynamically more efficient than a water-cooled engine, since far less power was wasted in forcing air over the cylinders with a fan than in driving water through the engine with a pump.

Consequently, his brilliantly simple and logical design eliminated almost all the normal electrical and cooling-system trouble spots that affected the reliability of conventional engines of that era. With no fan belt to break, no radiator, water pump or hoses to leak and no coolant to freeze or cause corrosion, there was absolutely nothing to go wrong. By attaching the fan to the end of the crankshaft, and locating an oil-cooler in the resulting airflow, optimum working temperature was guaranteed for as long as the engine continued turning. Moreover, by disposing with the normal distributor and placing the contact-breaker on the end of the camshaft, working in conjunction with a double-ended coil to provide a spark at both plugs for every revolution of the crankshaft, consistently precise ignition timing was also ensured, despite the waste of a spark! Moreover, since there was no high tension current present at the contact breakers, the life of the points was also extended. In another move to reduce moving parts and simplify operation of the engine, the dynamo was attached directly to the block, interposed between the crankshaft and the fan in such a way that its revolving armature turned with the crankshaft and drove the fan rotor.

In short, the 2CV engine exhibited a sophistication and precision that completely belied its rough-and-ready sound. Manufactured and assembled to a tolerance of one micron, the fit between its cylinder heads, barrels and crankcase was so precise that gaskets could be dispensed with throughout. The integral crankcase and sump was an aluminum alloy casting, split vertically along the center line, and its two halves, with their respective cast-iron cylinder barrels, finned for cooling purposes; and their alloy cylinder heads were all bolted together in an exact, oil and gas tight fit without the need for the usual seals. The cylinder heads, which featured hemispherical combustion chambers and domed pistons, had their valves inclined in V-formation at a 70-degree angle, while the rocker gear was driven by pushrods located in tubes linking the crankcase and cylinder heads, and actuated by the single central camshaft, which was located in the crankcase immediately beneath the crankshaft. The camshaft also drove the distributor and the gas pump. Interestingly also, Becchia provided for harmful crankcase fumes to be extracted along a vent pipe by inlet manifold vacuum action, recycled through the carburetor and burnt off with the fuel in the cylinders, thus anticipating modern anti-pollution legislation by 50 years.

Another particularly unusual technical feature of the 2CV engine lay in the ingenious design and construction of its five-piece crankshaft and con-rod assembly. For maximum strength and perfect balance, the normal practice of using split big-ends with two-piece bearings retained by bolted-on caps was rejected in favor of one-piece conrods with sleeve bearings, fitted to the crankshaft at the assembly stage, the whole forming an extremely rigid and compact self-contained assembly. The two-bearing, two-throw crankshaft was built up with its associated bearing bushes and connecting rods into an integral unit before the crankpins were pressed into the webs, the pins having first been temporarily shrunk by immersion in liquid nitrogen. As the various component parts could not be dismantled and replaced independently, main-bearing failure meant that the entire unit had to be exchanged. Yet thanks to the low thermal and mechanical stresses inherent in Becchia's design, this was a very rare occurrence. Provided that the sump contained the correct amount of clean oil at the start of the journey, and that the grille muff was removed when cruising fast, the 2CV engine could always be relied upon to run flat out at maximum revs for hours and hours on end without ever missing a beat. At the outset of production, factory bench tests established its ability to withstand 100 hours at full throttle (5,000 rpm) without damage, the equivalent of traveling 50,000 miles flat out, without a stop.

Initially, power transmission to the front wheels was by cardan-type drive shafts having simple, conventional Hardy-Spicer type universal joints with needle-roller bearings at both their inboard and outboard ends, but these were replaced some fifteen years later when a Rzeppa-type ball-and cage constant velocity joint was employed at the wheel-carrier end. A four-speed gearbox was fitted, although on the gear-selector lever only three ordinary forward ratios plus reverse were indicated. The fourth position was marked with an "S" for *surmultipliee*, or overdrive, to overcome Boulanger's objections to the idea of a four-speed box, which he considered to be overly complicated and, indeed, superfluous.

When the 2CV made its second public appearance, at the Paris Salon of October 1949, the car was displayed with its hood open, so that its tiny air-cooled flat-twin 375cc engine was exposed for all to see in its definitive form. By now it had been fitted with a conventional electric starter motor, powered by a six-volt battery, though activated by pulling a cable running from the dashboard rather than by an electric circuit controlled by the ignition switch.

Series production, which commenced that month, took some time to get into its proper stride, so that only 924 models were actually completed by the end of the year. Since its unveiling twelve months earlier, its price had climbed by some 25 percent to 228,000 francs (the Renault 4CV cost 245,500 francs), although there were no complaints from customers on that score, and the waiting list of would-be purchasers continued to lengthen by the day. But very few had any hope of realizing their dreams, for it was still virtually impossible for private motorists to obtain a permit to purchase a car. Exports had top priority and the first examples sold on the domestic market went to customers who could claim to have a particularly deserving need, especially those in rural occupations, such as doctors, midwives, vets and priests. Also favored were the country shopkeepers, merchants, tradesmen, small-holders, farmers and wine-growers for whom the car had always been intended and who satisfied the stringent requirements of officialdom. By February 1950, some 1086 models had been delivered, all of them to the kind of drivers who, in Boulanger's words, "have to travel by car because of their work and for whom ordinary cars are too dear to buy."

From then on, as production built up little by little, the 2CV underwent a constant process of continual improvement and enhancement, both technical and aesthetic, extending over a period of almost 30 years, although these refinements were always minor revisions of detail and never major rethinks of construction or design. The process of evolution and amelioration began in April 1951 with the introduction of the 2CVAU Fourgonnette, or light van, which had first been shown to the public at the Paris motor show the previous October. Built, to begin with at least, at the Levallois factory alongside the 2CV sedan, the 2CVAU was equipped with the same 9bhp 375cc engine as the 2CVA and had a payload of 250kg (550 lbs). Its price in April 1951 was 273,000 francs compared with the 268,100 francs then being demanded for its sedan counterpart.

The 2CV Fourgonnette—often described as a little tin shack on wheels, on account of its corrugated steel walls and roof and its twin backdoors pierced by tiny oval peepholes—eventually played as important a part of the long-running success-story of the Deux Chevaux as did the more familiar sedan. Over the years, almost one and a quarter million were sold throughout the world (nearly a third of total 2CV production) to serve in hundreds of

The first example of the 2CV AU Fourgonnette, or light van, appeared in March 1951. Powered by the 375 cc engine, its payload capacity was limited to 250 kg (550 lbs.). In October 1954, the AU was replaced by the AZU Fourgonnette. Although its dimensions were no larger, this version was equipped with an improved and enlarged 425 cc version of the twin-pot engine. Note that the chevrons on the grille follow the revised pattern introduced the previous year.

different ways—as delivery vans for every conceivable type of trade and occupation, as ambulances and campers, and even as the official transport of the French country post service. As we shall see, over the coming 27 years, four successively improved and updated versions of the Fourgonnette van would be produced, the Type AU (1951–1954), the AZU (1954–1978), the AK (1963–1970) and the AKS (1970–1978), although regarding the latter, from April 1978 until May 1985, the basic design continued in the form of the Acadiane van, which combined the body of the 2CV Fourgonnette with the cab and mechanicals of the Dyane-6.

The Fourgonnette was never merely a 2CV platform chassis and engine crudely and hastily adapted for commercial purposes by having a van body grafted onto its back, however; although the mechanical specifications and chassis dimensions were identical, the chassis structure of the van was strengthened and its ride height raised in keeping with the greater loads that would be carried, so that it was always a slightly wider and taller vehicle overall. It also differed structurally from the sedan in that its floor was a flat pressing throughout its length; to give maximum unobstructed load-space, the spare-wheel was stowed outside in a neat compartment let into the left hand side of the bodywork, while the gas tank was hidden away in a similar recess on the opposite flank. Nor did the mechanical improvements successively made to the 2CV van follow exactly the evolutionary development of the sedans, at least initially. On some occasions, changes to the Fourgonnette (such as the fitting of more powerful engines) actually preceded those made to the Berline or passenger car variant.

By the end of 1951 the economic situation in France had been greatly improved and Citroën was now able to turn out the 2CV at the rate of more than 100 every week. Almost 15,000 examples were built that year, with output climbing to more than 21,000 in 1952. Nevertheless, throughout that era, the Levallois factory could never make enough cars to satisfy demand. As export markets took precedence, the supply of vehicles to French customers remained strictly rationed. A modest single-fold leaflet had been judged sufficient to launch the car, and throughout these early years, advertising was virtually non-existent. Owners' and drivers' enthusiastic tales of 2CV ownership alone were sufficient to publicize the car. Their word-of-mouth accounts were so favorable that second-hand models regularly commanded a far higher price than that asked for new cars, which ensured that the waiting list got longer and longer all the time. Although by 1952 production was nudging 400 cars a week, an eighteen-month wait was still unavoidable for every customer without exception, no matter how prominent or influential he or she might be. There was to be no queue-jumping—the incorruptible P-J.B. had seen to that. A government minister wrote to Citroën requesting a model for his daughter; a member of the Chamber of Deputies applied on behalf of a friend, but to no avail. Demand out-ran supply to such an extent that Citroën could choose its own customers, and the rich and powerful were given no priority. In fact, Citroën's dealers were permitted to make provisional contracts only, and after signing these the would-be buyers were visited by special inspectors, to check that they fulfilled Boulanger's social criteria and that they would undertake to supply Citroën with a written report on their experiences with the 2CV.

The process of evolution continued in October 1952, when the original metallic grey finish of both sedan and van versions (*gris metalisee*) was replaced by deep grey (*gris fonce*) paintwork with contrasting ivory wheels for the sedan but a uniform dark grey for the van. Next, in March 1953, the original drab grey seat coverings of the sedan were replaced by new fabric covers in a tartan design, available in a choice of three color-ways, to help relieve the austerity of the interior. Even so, the door trim panels remained in their original plain flat state, covered in grey plastic and unadorned by armrests. Six months later, in October 1953, the frontal aspect of all versions was modified slightly by the removal of the oval ring of beading surrounding the Double Chevron badge on the grille. At the same time, together with a number of other minor modifications to the controls and instrumentation, the color of the steering wheel was changed from black to grey. By 1953, Citroën was rolling out 400 models a week, both sedans and the newly introduced 2CV Fourgonnette. By 1954, production was up to almost 1,000 vehicles a week. Even so, throughout the mid–1950s, the waiting list of would-be buyers was never less than two years long. Manifestly the right car in the right place at the right time, the 2CV created an insatiable demand.

In October 1954, two new versions of the 2CV, the AZ sedan and the AZU van, were introduced as an option to the basic A and AU variants, which both continued in production—the A until August 1959 but the AU only until the end of 1955. The new vehicles offered the advantage of a more powerful engine, enlarged to 425 cc and developing 12 bhp, which had first been announced in prototype form in 1950 as a possible future power unit for the 2CVAU van. This 33 percent increase in power (achieved by increasing bore and stroke from 62 × 62mm to 66 × 62mm and improving the carburetion) boosted the top speed of both vehicles to almost 50 mph. A centrifugal clutch which disengaged automatically when the car was at a standstill with its engine ticking-over at low revs was also provided as standard on the AZ sedan, making driving easier in town traffic, although it also prevented the car from being push-started in the event of a dead battery. Again, for the first time on a 2CV, both AZ and AU versions were equipped with flashing turn signals but on the rear quarter panels only, in the form of a single lamp unit that shone both fore and aft. This improvement was subsequently fitted to the basic Type A and AU versions the following year.

During 1955, output of the 2CV exceeded 100,000 units for the very first time. Even so, despite the steady increase in the rate of production that had been achieved over the previous five years, the waiting list of would-be customers was scarcely reduced and the order book still extended at least two years. Consequently, the actual changes introduced across the range that year were confined to minor, though significant, revisions in the engine, suspension and electrical systems. Perhaps the most noticeable upgrade, from the driver's point of view, was that the dashboard of the cheaper 2CVA and 2CVAU models received the improvements that had earlier been offered on the AZ and AZU versions. Also, in April 1955, production of the 2CV Fourgonnette was transferred from Citroën's Levallois premises to the Panhard & Levassor factory at Ivry on the outskirts of Paris, Panhard having merged with Citroën in 1953.

In 1956, the 2CV catalog was expanded yet again by the introduction, in November, of a third sedan model, the AZL, fitted with such refinements as a heater and demister plus an enlarged rear window. Costing 392,000 old francs as opposed to the 352,000 franc price tag of the basic 2CVA, this deluxe model was inspired by a similar car currently being produced by Citroën's Belgian factory at Brussels, where 2CV assembly had commenced in 1952. Externally, the AZL could easily be identified by the strips of alloy beading that ran along its hood center-line, on the sill beneath its doors and also inset across the width of its bumpers. This feature was inherited from the Belgian-built models of that era which all made far greater use of polished alloy bright work than their French-built counterparts, by featuring such embellishments as wheel trims and fender skirts. The AZL also featured seats covered in blue or green plasticized cotton rather than the tartan cloth used on the remainder of the group.

Early in 1957, a third sedan variant, the AZLP, joined the 2CV family. This was fitted with a metal door or trunk lid instead of the canvas cover that had previously served to enclose the rear luggage space, an improvement that was subsequently introduced on the other two sedan models the following year. Also, at the Paris motor show in October 1957, Citroën exhibited a taxi version of the 2CV, powered by the 425cc engine and specially equipped to carry two passengers and their luggage. The front passenger seat was removed to provide extra luggage space next to the driver while a folding occasional seat for a third passenger was provided at the back, behind the rear seats. However, plans to put this vehicle into volume production fell through due to opposition from the taxi drivers of Paris, many of whom had already purchased Citroën's Traction Avant model for taxi use. They complained that a car as economical to run in city traffic as the 2CV would amount to unfair competition.

By the end of 1958, ten years after the first appearance of the 2CV, combined cumulative production of the sedan and van versions had at last reached more than 250,000 vehicles in total, with the number growing at the rate of 150,000 units per year as more and more models came off the assembly lines. By now the Deux Chevaux had more than fulfilled its maker's expectations and proved itself to be the ideal means of transport for farmers and country dwellers. No other car of its time could be relied on to travel so cheaply, so reliably and so comfortably over poor or non-existent roads, thanks to its flexible suspension and sure-footed traction. To exploit this cross-country potential to the full, Citroën decided to produce a specialist off-road version for mountain and desert use, particularly in French North Africa, where extensive oil and mineral exploration work was then under way. The result was the unique 2CVAW, otherwise known as the 4 × 4 Sahara, the world's one-and-only two-engined, four-wheel-drive car. With a separate 12 bhp 425 cc power unit and gearbox located at both front and rear, running either in tandem or front-only, the Sahara possessed truly exceptional climbing ability. Due to its very light curb-weight (650 kilos), optimum 50/50 weight distribution, low ground pressure and excellent traction, it could easily outperform most conventional heavy-duty 4 × 4 vehicles, and eventually it came to be regarded as one of the best-performing off-road cars ever developed. However, only 694 models were built between 1959 and 1967, 80 of which saw service with the Guardia Civil in Spain. No more than 25 are believed to remain in existence today, two of them in the UK.

The Sahara's two engines—one for each axle, front and rear—were controlled in such a way that both could be run together in tandem to provide double the motive power for cross-country travel or, alternatively, the front engine could be operated solo during normal road use. With both engines running, it could reach a top speed of 62 mph on flat ground, consuming gas at a rate of between 28 and 35 mpg; 47 mpg was claimed with only one engine running. Mounted on a specially strengthened chassis-platform, the body of the Sahara differed from that of the standard 2CV in a number of very noticeable ways, including a spare wheel mounted outboard in a recess in the hood; reinforced bumpers; fatter 155 section tires; widened, cut-away rear fenders; and of course the air-intake grille for its reverse-mounted second engine (located in a compartment behind the rear seats) clearly visible on its trunk-lid. The two gas-filler caps poking through the front doors were also unmistakable. The Sahara had twin fuel tanks—one for each engine—located under the front seats. When it first appeared in October 1958, the Sahara cost 815,000 old francs, more than twice the price of the standard 2CVA sedan; but when it was finally deleted in September 1966, this price tag had risen to 10,259 new francs

Next, with the 2CV's reputation as an indefatigable workhorse already spreading to the furthest corners of the world, Citroën began to explore its export potential by offering a PO (Pays d'Outre-mer) version especially equipped for overseas service. The company also set up assembly plants abroad using knock-down kits to exploit those foreign markets that demanded a low-cost utility car that would perform well in difficult conditions and across rough terrain. Two particularly interesting yet relatively unknown examples of this type were the Baby Brousse and FAF (Facile a Fabriquer) models, the latter being specially designed for easier construction or CKD assembly in third-world countries. A total of more than 33,000 of these two types were eventually produced overseas, mostly between 1968 and 1982.

Ultimately, the 2CV and its derivatives eventually came to be assembled in no less than fourteen countries besides France and Belgium, including Spain, Portugal, Yugoslavia, Rumania, Iran, Tunisia, the Ivory Coast, Chile, Argentina, Madagascar, Cambodia, Vietnam and the United Kingdom, which produced different versions at various times, put together from kits sent out from Paris. Production of the Deux Chevaux at Citroën's British factory at Slough (opened by André Citroën in 1926) commenced in 1953 but ceased in 1964. During that time Citroën Cars Ltd built a total of 1245 right-hand-drive examples of the 2CV, including 672 sedans, 231 vans, 131 pick-up trucks and 211 examples of its own unique fiberglass bodied coupe version, the Bijou.

Towards the end of the 1950s, the economic circumstances in France began to improve substantially, as was the case throughout Europe as a whole. Obtaining sufficient raw materials and component parts became less of a problem for motor manufacturers, who could now begin to relax the stringent restrictions and economies previously imposed as a result of shortages, though demand for private and commercial vehicles continued to outrun supply many times over. Even so, in September 1959, Citroën was able to offer its 2CV customers a choice of body colors for the very first time; now the Deuche could be ordered in glacier blue (with a matching blue fabric roof) as well as in the traditional grey paint that had been obligatory since the start of production. And, if that was not choice enough, the option of a Radioen factory-fitted radio was offered as well. Previously, in July 1959, the original 9hp Type A sedan had finally been withdrawn from sale, leaving only the AZ sedans and the AZU Fourgonnette in the catalog, all powered by the 12 bhp 425cc engine.

December 1960 saw the arrival of the first major facelift to the 2CV's exterior appearance when—on the AZL and AZLP sedans, but not as yet on the AZU van—the original one-piece corrugated hood was replaced by an entirely new design of hood, made up of three separate pressings. The hood itself had five ribs running fore and aft along its surface while, beneath it, the sides of the engine bay were closed by two separate side panels having recessed longitudinal ventilation slots instead of the primitive louvers

In October 1960, the 2CV got its first face-lift when the original corrugated hood was replaced by the entirely new design with a revised grille, as seen here on the 2CV AZAM of 1964. The AZAM boasted a higher level of trim including hubcaps and a more elaborate style of bumper. A metal trunk lid had replaced the original canvas cover in 1957, though initially on the AZLP model only.

as before. The new hood also featured a detachable aluminum air intake grille featuring a large Double Chevron emblem set into five horizontal bars, but this feature, unlike the hood itself, was later changed a number of times.

Within the interior of the car, further minor changes were made that year, including improved seats and seatcovers, together with stronger door-locks, while on the exterior the choice of a second new color was made available, a vibrant Panama Yellow teamed with maroon for the fabric roof and seat coverings. Before very long the previously limited selection of colors had been revised and expanded beyond recognition to include a wide palette of fresh, bright and youthful shades, including mist green, brick red, beige, sea green and Monte Carlo blue, each with a toning roof and interior trim, although rose grey remained available for traditionalists!

The 1961 model year saw further consolidation, with no major changes or introductions, except in three respects. Firstly, from July onwards, the AZU van received the new hood and grille that had been fitted to the AZ sedans the previous year. Secondly, from October onwards, the AZLP sedan was fitted with an up-rated engine developing 13.5 bhp at 4,000 rpm, which took its top speed up to 85km/h (53 mph). For the 1961–1962 season, buyers of the Fourgonnettes were also given an alternative to grey—cactus green and pastis yellow. And, thirdly, a specially modified commercial version of the AZL sedan was introduced, by the ENAC company rather than by Citroën. Called the AZC Mixte or combi, this was equipped with folding rear seats and rear door that hinged above the window rather than below it.

In September 1962, however, a completely new dashboard together with improved controls and instrumentation finally arrived across the range, which now comprised the AZL and AZLP sedans plus the AZU van, the basic AZ sedan having been discontinued at the end of 1960. At last the Deux Chevaux had a real dashboard with a modern steering wheel and a proper instrument binnacle boasting a conventional speedometer and fuel gauge, plus electric windshield wipers.

Next, in March 1963, the entire 2CV family was improved by the fitting of a further derivative of the aircooled flat-twin 425cc engine, developing 18 bhp at 4500 rpm and capable of propelling the Deuche to a top speed of 95 km/h (59 mph). At the same time, an entirely new sedan model, the 2CV AZAM, was introduced to head-up the range and offer Deuchistes a far greater degree of luxury and refinement than had been permitted until now, the letters AM standing for *amelioree* or improved. As well as featuring a lockable, hinged metal trunk-lid, its body boasted brightwork galore, such as polished alloy hubcaps, tubular bumper over-riders and a decorative strip along the hood center line. Inside there were further lavish touches to the trim, such as a vanity mirror and sun-visor for the front seat passenger!

In March 1963 the body design of the Fourgonnette vans was revised and modernized by the fitting of large rectangular windows to both the back doors and the side

Earlier, in 1963, the appearance of the Fourgonnette van (which had received the new hood in 1961) was changed again when its roof lost its distinctive corrugations. This is the new 3CV AK version introduced that year, powered by the larger 602 cc engine from the Dyane sedan.

panels, and by eliminating the swaged or corrugated ribbing above the waistline. The following month, however, an entirely new van, the 350 kg payload 2CV AK model, joined the range, powered by the 3CV 602cc flat-twin air-cooled engine from the recently introduced Ami-6 sedan, itself based on the 2CV's platform chassis and mechanical elements. Producing 22 bhp at 4500 rpm, this engine enabled the AK to reach the unheard-of top speed of 85 km/h (53 mph) on the flat! Introduced in response to a widely voiced demand for greater carrying capacity, the AK van had a usable interior volume of 2.10 cubic meters and a 350 kg payload (in contrast to the 250kg payload of the AZU) and was immediately recognizable by its longer body (20cm more floor length than the AZU) overhanging the rear wheels. Thereafter both alternative Fourgonnette versions, the AK and AZU, continued in production side by side until the end of 2CV production, successively updated and improved. Initially, at least, both were available in high-roof configuration, as a special order.

Interestingly, a special combi version of the AZU was also available in France for a number of years during the early Sixties. Called the Weekender and built by ENAC, this van featured a larger, panoramic side window on both sides plus two removable rear passenger seats, which made it an ideal all-purpose holiday vehicle for tourists traveling long-distances on low budgets. A camper version was offered too, fitted with a gas stove and wash basin stowed in the back doors. Two pickup versions (the Type AP, fitted with the 375cc engine and the AZP with the 425 cc engine) were also produced in limited numbers in France around the same time, by specialist firms rather than by the Citroën factory. These looked just like standard 2CV vans with the top half of the body cut off and a flat panel welded in to close the cab, unlike the Slough-built pickups which had rounded-off cab bodies built from specially manufactured pressings.

The next step in the gradual process of modernization and improvement took place towards the end of 1964 when all three sedan models then on sale—the AZL and AZA as well as the AZAM—each received forward hinged doors, improved seats (individual instead of bench type at the front) and lap-type seat-belt mountings, in order to comply with new EEC safety regulations. During 1964 also, the 2CV made motoring history by becoming the first vehicle ever to be fitted with Michelin X tubeless radial tires as standard; earlier, in 1960, tubed Michelin X 125 × 380 radial tires had replaced the cross-ply Michelin Pilote 125 × 400 tires originally fitted across the range.

At the next Paris Motor Show, in October 1965, a further major facelift for the 2CV sedans was put on public display. For the coming 1965–1966 model year, so it was announced, all sedan versions were to be equipped with six-light bodies having a glazed rear quarter panel, as had already been seen for some years on the versions built in Belgium. Also, yet another new style of grille was to be introduced, again made from alloy but this time consisting of just three, thicker, bars running laterally across the trim surrounding the fan aperture. The Double Chevron badge was now to be mounted on the hood itself, separately above the grille and not as a part of it, while the

A second revision occurred in October 1965, when the face of the 2CV was changed yet again and the chevrons were moved from the grille to a new location on the hood. Otherwise, things were much the same as before externally, except that by now a wider choice of paint colors was available, including yellow, green and red.

Top: **In September 1966, six-light bodywork was introduced for the first time on the 2CV but only in the case of the AZAM model seen here. Later, from 1968 on, it became a standard feature across the board. Note that the front doors are now hinged at their front edge and open forward, a revision made in 1964. *Bottom:* In October 1967 Citroën launched its intended replacement for the Deux Chevaux. Named the Dyane, this car was based on the 2CV's floor-pan and mechanical elements, including a 425 cc version of the air-cooled flat-twin engine, but with an entirely new, more spacious body. This was joined the following January by the Dyane-6, which had the 602 cc engine and by the Dyane-4 with an enlarged 435 cc engine. For the 1969-1970 season, both the Dyane-4 and Dyane-6 were given six-light bodies, the basic Dyane having been deleted the previous year. Ultimately, the newcomer proved far less popular than expected and was eventually withdrawn in 1984, leaving the 2CV to soldier on alone. A total of 1,443,583 Dyanes were built.**

bumpers and over-riders were fitted with a protective rib of black plastic material, said to be resistant to minor parking impacts or traffic accidents! On the technical side, fully homocinetic drive shafts replaced the simple cardan shafts with double Hardy-Spicer universal joints that were formerly used, while conventional telescopic hydraulic shock absorbers superseded the old friction dampers, though on the rear suspension only.

As things turned out, 1966 was the year when production of the 2CV sedan reached its all-time zenith, with a total of 168,357 units being assembled. But apart from this achievement, the mid 1960s was an uneventful period so far as developments in the overall story of 2CV evolution were concerned. The reason for the lull was that another new arrival in the range was expected shortly, to enlarge and extend the 2CV family. In August 1967, the birth of a cousin model, named the Dyane, was proudly announced. Designed by Louis Bionier, the veteran Panhard designer who had joined the Bureau d'Etudes when Citroën took control of this most ancient and illustrious of French marques in 1953, the four-seater Dyane sedan (built at the former Panhard factory) was clearly intended to eventually replace the Deux Chevaux, although this was not stated at the time. Combining the engine, suspension and underlying platform-chassis of the 2CV with completely new bodywork — larger, wider, stronger, more modern-looking and boasting up-to-date styling details such as integral fenders with faired-in recessed headlights— it was a fully fledged member of the 2CV or Type A family, as was indicated by its official designation, AYA.

At first the familiar 21 bhp 425cc flat twin air-cooled engine from the 2CV AZ was fitted, coupled to an Ami-6 transmission, but after just seven months' production this was soon replaced by a new, enlarged capacity 435cc version, developing 26 bhp. In January 1968, however, the original design was joined in the showrooms by a sister car equipped with the 28 bhp 602cc engine from the Ami-6, again using the Ami's transmission plus larger, more powerful drum brakes. Henceforth the pair of variants were referred to as the Dyane-4 and Dyane-6, respectively. Now it was possible to exceed 110 km/hr (69 mph) in a Deux Chevaux, while retaining the same frugal fuel consumption of an average 50 mpg (Dyane-6). Even so, the following year, in September 1969, the Dyane-6 was re-equipped with the recently redesigned and up-rated 602cc engine from the Ami-8, producing 32bhp. Both versions came in two levels of trim, Luxe and Confort, with a centrifugal traffi-clutch available as optional extras. A commercial variant featuring a fully folding rear seat was also supplied as an option.

The Dyane was Europe's first true volume-production hatchback car. With its full-height, fully opening glazed tailgate, it offered even greater load-space and cargo-carrying versatility than the 2CV although the empty well for the spare wheel in the floor of the rear load area was retained. So were the enclosed rear fenders, a styling feature common to all contemporary Citroëns. The earliest examples of the Dyane-4 had four-light bodies with the quarter panel left unglazed, but six-light coachwork was fitted on the Dyane-6 from the outset. From March 1968 onward, however, identical six-light bodies were fitted to both variants. On both types the front windows could be opened or closed by sliding them fore and aft, just like those of the Ami-6. Similarly, on both types the roof took the form of a removable fabric panel, as on the 2CV, but this time the front part could be folded back and left in a half-open position, without leaving the driver's seat, although attempting to do this when on the move was not advisable!

During its eleven-year production life, the Dyane went through the same process of mechanical evolution and improvement that applied to the 2CV, with revisions and changes made more or less in tandem. However, in September 1977, the Dyane-6 (but not the Dyane-4) became the first of the Deux Chevauxs to receive disc brakes, four years in advance of their introduction on the 2CV itself. However, the styling of the Dyane underwent very few revisions during its lifetime, all extremely minor. For example, in September 1972 the positioning of the door handles was inverted, while in September 1974 the treatment of the front grille was changed from the original stainless steel mesh to a black plastic fitment featuring horizontal bars, colored grey at first, but black after September 1980.

The Dyane sedan was produced in three special editions only, the first being the Dyane-6 Caban of April 1977. This was a limited series of 1,500 vehicles, painted dark blue with white wheels and a white roof, plus white coach-lining or decals on the hood, fenders and doors. The second was the Dyane-6 Capra of 1980–81, intended for the Spanish and Italian markets and easily distinguished by its GSA wheel trims, while the third was the blue and white Dyane-6 Cote d'Azur of 1982–83, which was imported into the UK.

Although in many ways a better, more practical, vehicle than the original 2CV, the Dyane failed to equal the long-term popularity of its cousins. Indeed many enthusiasts regarded it as an interloper in the 2CV family, entirely lacking the character and integrity of the true, authentic Deux Chevaux. Thus, by late 1975, the Dyane-4 had been deleted from the catalogs, superseded entirely by the Dyane-6. This was now available in two forms, the Dyane-6 Confort and the Dyane-6 Weekend, the latter distinguished from the former by its standard folding rear seats and removable covering panel over the wheel-well in the luggage area. But inevitably, at the end of the model year in July 1984, the Dyane-6 was also finally discontinued, having been made redundant by the arrival of Citroën's new Visa model in October 1978. Initially, in its 3CV Special form, this car also made use of the latest high-compression version of the 2CV's 602 cc air-cooled flat-twin engine, now producing 35 bhp at 5,750 rpm, a 25 percent increase in power output. In total, 1,443,583 models of the Dyane sedans were built during its eleven-year life-span, which turned out to be no less than 30 years shorter than that of the venerable vehicle it was originally intended to replace.

In May 1968, when students staged an uprising on the streets of Paris and car-workers downed tools and walked out on strike, bringing about a general state of political unrest that threatened the social and economic stability of the Republic, Citroën staged a minor revolu-

Top: **In October 1974 came a third and final revision to the design of the grille, in which the chevrons returned to their original location, but in a smaller form. But to the consternation of the traditionalists, this modification was accompanied by a change to rectangular-shaped headlights. By then, the sedan range had been reduced to just two models, the 2CV4 equipped with the 435 cc engine and the 2CV6 with the 602 cc engine, seen here. *Bottom:* In May 1968 came another Citroën first — the Mehari, a canvas-topped pickup which combined the engine and floor-pan of the Dyane-6 with a lightweight body formed from flexible, durable, non-corroding thermoplastic. 144,953 were built before production ceased in 1987. This is the Mehari Azur Special Edition of 1983, of which only 700 were made.**

tion of a technical kind — the introduction of its new off-road car, the Mehari. Although it was a simple and uncomplicated design in comparison with the Sahara which it replaced, the Mehari was no less interesting and innovative in automobile engineering terms. Named after the dromedary favored by Berber tribesmen for long distance travel in the desert, it was the first series production vehicle in the world to feature a lightweight body made of flexible, durable, non-corroding ABS thermoplastic.

Assembled at the Panhard factory at Ivry, with body parts supplied by the thermoplastic molding specialists, SEAB, the Mehari was a much more versatile design than the Sahara, and offered a far greater load-carrying capacity. More a pickup truck than a car, it was designed to serve a wide variety of tasks: agricultural and forestry work; light construction-site duties; a public service vehicle; and a practical, economical fun-car in the newly emerging leisure-vehicle and beach-buggy market. For

A little-known Mehari variant, also based on the Dyane-6, was the FAF (facile a fabriquer, facile a financer), a concept developed by Citroën to meet the needs of its African and Middle Eastern markets. Supplied in kit form between 1978 and 1982 for assembly abroad, the FAF was clad with simple, flat-sided body panels that could be produced locally without expensive press-tooling, though according to official figures only 2,295 vehicles were actually constructed.

this reason, initially it was fitted with only two seats, to qualify as a commercial vehicle for tax purposes.

In point of fact, the Mehari was derived from the Dyane-6 rather than the Deuche, as it shared the AYA's 602cc 28 bhp twin-pot engine and its platform chassis, strengthened to PO specification (*Pays d'Outre-mer* or overseas markets) to allow a 400kg payload to be carried. Normally, the Mehari had no doors or windows, so that its occupants were shielded from the weather by no more than a simple canvas folding roof with transparent plastic side-screens, although for cross-country work a metal under-shield was fitted beneath the engine bay to protect the sump and transmission.

The Mehari's bodywork—which was attached to the platform chassis by its supporting tubular steel framework—consisted of 13 separate panels, including the floor-pan, wheel-arches, dashboard, hood, tailgate and the optional doors, all vacuum-molded from sheets of robust, impact-resistant Cycolac ABS (Acrylonitrile Butadiene Stirene). Fastened to the frame by screws or rivets, these panels were colored by pigments added to the thermoplastic mix during processing and so required no subsequent painting, polishing or maintenance, except in the case of vehicles destined for service in hot countries. As ABS is sensitive to heat and ultra-violet light, cracks and stress lines tended to appear in cars exposed to strong sunlight for long periods, so in this case polyurethane-based UV-resistant paints were used for protection. At first, a choice of sage green, red and ochre bodies was available, but later yellow and white versions were also offered.

Throughout its production history, the design of the Mehari was changed only once, in 1978, when the grille was revised to incorporate new metal headlight mounting panels with integral turn signals. However, a special edition version, the Azure, intended as a beach buggy and thus equipped with a white body, blue doors and hood, and blue and white striped seats, was produced in 1983, while a fully enclosed version with a plastic hard-top was marketed by the ENAC company. In 1979, however, a four-wheel-drive version of Mehari was added to the range, but this time powered by one engine only through a conventional transfer reduction gearbox and a drive-shaft drive to the rear wheels. In this optional 4 × 4 mode, three of the four main forward ratios could be geared down, giving a total of seven forward speeds. For additional traction in rough conditions, a differential lock was also provided. The 4 × 4 Mehari could be recognized by its cow-catcher bumpers, different grille and hood-mounted spare-wheel similar to that of the Sahara. A total of only 1313 models had been built when sales were suspended in 1982, after only three years of production. Production of the standard Mehari continued for another five years until 1987, by which time no less than 144,953 cars had been assembled. It was never offered on the U.K. market at any point in its lifespan, since in several ways it did not comply with British Construction and Use and National Type Approval regulations.

But to return to the story of the evolution of the original Citroën 2CV itself, in August 1967 the AZU van was improved by the fitting of a new 425cc engine delivering

21 bhp at 5450 rpm. Some nine months later, in May 1968, its stable mate, the AK Fourgonnette, also received a new 602 cc engine rated at 3CV and delivered 29 bhp at 5750 rpm. Next, in July 1970 the 350kg AK-350 was transformed by a completely new and enlarged high-roof body with a payload of 450kg, easily recognizable by the fact that the strengthening corrugations in its side panels now took the form of indentations rather than protruding ribs or ripples; in this guise it was referred to as the AKS-400 van. Eventually, in 1972, the smaller 250kg capacity AZU-250 van also received this new style of bodywork.

The evolution of the Fourgonnette continued a stage further in 1972, when the specification of the AZU (the smaller of the two van options currently available) was revised yet again. Now it was offered with the 24 bhp 435 cc engine from the existing 2CV4 sedan, but mated to the gearbox from the 2CV6, in an economy version specifically intended for public service or Grandes Administrations use. Finally, for the 1976-1977 season, the side windows were removed from both types leaving the upper body sides plain and unperforated, but following much protest from customers, the side windows reappeared in September 1977. Following the consolidation of the sedan series as the 2CV-4 and 2CV-6 in 1970, the technical evolution of the two camionette versions, the AKS-400 and the AZU-250, continued in tandem, so that the vans simultaneously received the improvements introduced on the corresponding sedans.

By the end of the 1960s, the unmistakable sight and sound of the Two-Pot had become a familiar feature of both urban and rural life in France, as much to be seen and heard in the cities, towns and suburbs as well as in the country villages. The older it got, the more the 2CV seemed to appeal to the young and the young-at-heart, so that its erstwhile agricultural image had given way to a new-found classless status as the ideal cheap car for students, teachers and professionals as well as peasant farmers! But even though it had been on the road for more than 20 years, and more than 1,716,000 cars had been built, the Deux Chevaux was just approaching its adulthood, let alone its middle-age.

Just as the final curtain appeared to be descending on the 2CV, fate intervened once again to arrest declining sales and save the car from retirement, keeping it running for another two decades. The reason for its revival was the worldwide oil crisis of the early 1970s, which sent massive shockwaves reverberating through the motor industry as customers stopped buying big cars and searched for smaller, less thirsty vehicles instead. Suddenly, the 2CV was back in big demand again — not only in France and Belgium but also in Germany, Holland, Italy and Britain — as a new generation of drivers rediscovered its simple, frugal, rustic virtues. Once again, the Deuche was the right car for the time; a dependable, durable vehicle that would cover maximum distances with minimum effort and expense. Not only economically sensible and sound, it was also respectable from an ecological standpoint. With the blessing of environmentalists and the radical intelligentsia, its European sales took an upward turn to give the 2CV a new lease on life as the only real alternative for the alternative society, as far as personal transport was concerned.

In truth, the coming of the Dyane had been expected to signal the beginning of the end for the Deuche and so for the 1970–1971 season, the 2CV series was consolidated, leaving only two standard sedan models in the catalog. These were the AZL 2CV-4 (rated as a 2CV) and the AZL 2CV-6 (3CV), powered by the 435cc (24 bhp DIN) and 602cc (28 bhp DIN) engines from the Dyane-4 and Dyane-6 respectively. Each version incorporated all the improvements previously introduced on other models, plus a few more. Henceforth, the bumpers were sheathed with grey plastic instead of black as before, while the front turn signals (formerly located together with the rear indicators in a single unit mounted on the rear quarter panel) were set into recessed roundels on the front fenders. The rear lamp clusters were also enlarged and improved to house the rear turn signals. To improve the lighting system generally, in January 1972 a 12-volt electrical system was adopted for the first time, incorporating an alternator and a 25a/h battery. Inside, an entirely new instrument binnacle was fitted, plus a more modern twin-spoke steering wheel. Outside, identifying letters on the trunk-lid distinguished the 2CV-4 from the 2CV-6, the first time such badges had been used.

By now the technical evolution of the 2CV was more or less completed and the design had crystallized in the form that endured unchanged until the end of production. In the future, the only major revisions that were made were largely confined to improvements to the engines, which were invisible to the casual observer. However, a few minor, visible changes were also introduced from time to time. For example, in October 1974 a new type of headlight with rectangular lenses and housings was fitted, together with a new style of grille. Made of plastic, this grille had four thin lateral bars on which was mounted the Citroën Double Chevron badge, now returned to its original location. This grille — which remained unmodified until the cessation of 2CV production — came in three interchangeable versions, according to the individual model concerned; plain grey all over, plain grey surrounded by black, and grey surrounded by a chrome effect.

In September 1975, however, the traditional round headlights returned on the newly introduced 2CV Special but the rectangular type continued on all the Club variants until October 1987 when round headlights were re-introduced on these models too. That month also, telescopic hydraulic shock absorbers replaced the inertia dampers on the front wheels, while the following year a twin circuit-braking system was adopted, with a tandem master cylinder. In September 1975, the original 14:1 ratio of the rack-and-pinion steering was changed to 17:1 on the 2CV-6; and by April 1977 this improvement, made in the interest of lightness, had been extended to include the 2CV-4 Special base-level model as well. By now, the appeal of the standard 2CV-4 and 2CV-6 models had been boosted by a revised, even wider selection of jazzy colors (shades too numerous to mention here) and by new, gaily striped, jersey cloth upholstery.

Introduced to satisfy the purists, the 2CV Special was a Spartan, no-frills, back-to-basics version of the 2CV-4, intended to replace the Dyane-4, which was promptly withdrawn from sale. This economy model, powered by the 435cc engine from the Dyane-4, could easily be distinguished from the rest of the series as it reverted to the original body design and lost its rear quarter windows; it also had an even more rudimentary dashboard and a different kind of steering wheel (two spokes as opposed to one) and came with plastic Targa upholstered seating only. Thus, for the 1975-1976 season there were now five models in the series available in France: three sedans, the 2CV Special, the 2CV-4, the 2CV-6; and two vans, the 2CV-AZU and the 2CV-AKS, with prices ranging from 11,852 to 13,052 francs.

Thanks to the unforeseen demand occasioned by the energy crisis, worldwide production of the 2CV and its derivatives reached an all-time high of more than 370,000 vehicles in 1974. And to boost the 2CV's renewed popularity higher still, especially among its new-found market of youthful trend-setters, Citroën embarked on another marketing innovation — bringing out special editions, produced in limited numbers, usually for one season only, and aimed at fashion-conscious buyers looking for extra individuality and style. The first of these was the colorful 2CV Spot of April 1976, of which 1800 were made, all painted orange over white, with an orange and white striped roof. The Spot, which was powered by the 24 bhp 435 cc engine of the 2CV-4, was followed five years later by only 700 examples of the 2CV-007, based on the 2CV-6, introduced in October 1980. Painted in brilliant mimosa yel-

In April 1976, Citroën — the pioneers of front wheel drive and countless other engineering innovations — introduced another important feature of modern automobile design, the Special Edition, a clever device for giving old models a new lease on life. The first example, the 2CV Spot, painted orange and white and actually a version of the current 2CV-4, was indeed limited to 1800.

low, with 007 decals, including bullet-holes on its flanks, this car was built to celebrate the Deuche's starring role in the current James Bond film *For Your Eyes Only*, screened that year. Next, in April 1983, came the 2CV France 3 (known as the Beachcomber in the U.K.), and based on the 2CV-6. Limited to only 2,000 models, this car was painted in the blue and white livery of the successful French challenger in the Americas Cup yacht race that year. Then in 1984 the 2CV-6 Bamboo arrived, painted appropriately in a vivid shade of jungle green, while finally, in 1986, came 1,000 examples of the jokey 2CV-6 Cocorico, finished in white with red and blue sides and with its seats covered with a blue-jeans fabric, but sold on the French market only.

Offered 1983–1985 was the 2CV-6 France 3 special edition of which 4,000 were made to celebrate France's entry in the Americas Cup yacht race. A small number of right-hand-drive models were imported into the U.K. in 1984 and sold under the name Beachcomber. Appropriately, the color scheme was a nautical blue and white.

Earlier, in October 1980, Citroën had launched the most successful 2CV special edition of all, the art-deco style 2CV-6 Charleston; so successful with young buyers, in fact, that it became a standard model, remaining in the catalog for a whole ten years until the end of production. Two-thirds of all Charleston customers were under age 35. It was available initially in a two-tone burgundy and black color scheme, then later in canary yellow and black, and finally in a dark and light grey combination, with grey jersey nylon seats throughout. The Charleston—which had round headlights, initially painted black but

A highly successful 2CV special edition was the art-deco style 2CV-6 Charleston, introduced in October 1980. This version proved so popular that in October 1981 it joined the line as a standard series production car. Ultimately a total of 8,000 units were sold. The difference between the two types was that on the first, the headlights were painted (as seen here), but on the second, they were chromed. Both had chromed hubcaps.

Left: In July 1982, the Charleston appeared in a new color scheme, yellow and black, in contrast to the burgundy and black of the original. But as this version remained available for one year only, today it is regarded as the rarest of all the special editions. *Below:* Next came the 2CV-6 Dolly of April 1985, introduced in recognition of the Deux Chevaux's loyal following of female drivers (more than 40 percent of current buyers were female). It also duly became a standard model, continuing in production along with the Charleston until the end. Initially it came in no fewer than seven color combinations.

chromed from September 1981 onwards—was rivaled in popularity only by the Dolly, a special edition of the 2CV-6 initially produced in 1985 and 1986 when a total of 5,000 were sold. Introduced in recognition of the 2CV's loyal following of lady drivers (more than 40 percent of latter-day buyers were women), the Dolly was so well received that it became a standard model and continued in production to the end, alongside the Charleston and the basic Special and more lavishly equipped Club versions of the 2CV-6 then in the catalog.

In March 1985, the Dolly was available in three colorways—grey/red, grey/buttermilk yellow, and grey/white, each with an appropriately toned roof covering. But then, in October 1985, these choices were joined by white/buttermilk, red/buttermilk and white/green. Then from March 1986 onward, the combinations of buttermilk/midnight blue and white/red were added, making a total of eight possible color choices, although the first three possibilities were deleted at the end of the 1985–1986 season. Among the 2CV sedans, which normally were equipped with plain, unadorned wheels, painted rose-grey, the wheels of all seven of the various different special editions were fitted with small stainless-steel caps covering the central dome and lug-nuts only. The outer surface remained exposed, and painted yellow on the yellow/black Charlestons, red on the red/black Charlestons, silver on the grey Charlestons, and white on the Spot and Dolly models.

In October 1978, the 2CV reached its 30th birthday, but there were no special celebrations. On the contrary, the event was mainly noted for a drastic reduction in the series as earlier that year, in March, the 435cc 2CV-4 had at last been phased out, to be replaced by the new 2CV-6 Special. This version—with the rear quarter windows restored—was powered by a new, improved version of the 602cc engine, producing 29 bhp DIN. The 2CV-6 (which had earlier acquired the appellation 2CV-6 Confort) continued in the catalog, but was now referred to as

When production of the Dyane was discontinued in July 1984, its familiar features did not vanish entirely from Citroën showrooms. Instead its cab and fore-end panels continued in service on the Acadiane, a re-bodied version of the 2CV AKS fourgonnette, with a payload of 480 kg (1,057 lbs.). Introduced in October 1977, the Acadiane remained in the catalog until May 1987.

the 2CV-6 Club (to distinguish it from the Special) although it retained its former specification unchanged. At the very same time, the 2CV Fourgonnette light vans also came to the end of the road, replaced by the 480 kg payload Acadiane van, previously introduced in October 1977. The Acadiane was a hybrid vehicle formed by grafting the cab, fenders and hood pressings of the Dyane onto a lengthened and strengthened version of the platform chassis of the AKS van. Powered by the 35 bhp 602cc engine and gearbox also inherited from the AKS, it could carry an increased payload of 480 kg in its 2,270 cubic meter interior. Its name was derived from a marriage of the terms AK and Dyane. Produced at Citroën's Spanish factory at Vigo, the Acadiane remained available until May 1987 when it was phased out in favor of the new C15 light van, based on the Visa. Total production numbered 253,393 units, with 496,79 assembled during 1979, the high point of its career.

In June 1981, a special economy sedan version, the 2CV Special E was introduced, though it lasted for two seasons only, phased out in February 1983. Intended principally for urban use, it was equipped with a centrifugal clutch of the type last fitted as standard in the early 1970s. On all other models not equipped with the traffic-clutch, a diaphragm clutch replaced the toggle-type dry plate clutch previously used. Thanks also to its modified second gear ratio, the Special E returned an urban-cycle fuel consumption figure of 5.8 liters per 100 km (40 mpg), rather than the 6.8 liters (35 mpg) of the standard 2CV-6. Also, from September 1981 onwards, front disc brakes were fitted across the board, as they had been on the Dyane-6 since 1977. This was indeed a sensible improvement, for it was now possible to exceed 120kph in the Deux Chevaux, twice the top speed possible in 1948.

In 1986, the 2CV reached the zenith of its popularity in the UK, with peak sales of 7,520 cars recorded. Ten years after the suspension of British assembly at Slough, French-built RHD models had been re-introduced in 1974. Indeed, by the mid–1980s, the revived and rejuvenated Deux Chevaux had reached the summit of its international success, and scarcely a street in Europe could be traversed without encountering one. Total cumulative Citroën 2CV and Dyane production was fast approaching a staggering 6.5 million vehicles, of which almost 3.5 million had been built at Levallois. With CKD and Mehari output figures added, the total production tally for the 2CV family was reaching almost 7 million. Parked bumper to bumper, they would have formed a line nearly 17,000 miles long—or drawn up in rows with just a foot between them, they would have filled a car-park covering 24 square miles.

But, alas, familiarity breeds contempt among the car-buying public and inevitably the falling order levels for the 2CV in its own country gradually began to be overtaken by the strong demand still shown in its principal export markets—Germany, Belgium, Portugal and the United Kingdom. So, regrettably, the unavoidable decision was made to close down the old, out-moded Paris plant and concentrate production at Citroën's more modern facility at Mangualde in Portugal. Thus, on February 25th 1988, more than 50 years since the very first pre-war TPV prototypes were built there, the last French-built Deux Chevaux, a grey 2CV-6 Special, rolled off the assembly line at the ancient Levallois factory, the 3,418,347th car to have been assembled within its walls. Constructed a hundred years earlier for the Clement bicycle company and a Citroën factory since 1921, the Levallois building

At the close of 1987, the 2CV had been in continuous production at Citroën's Levallois factory for more than 40 years. By then, the plant was showing its age, as was the Deux Chevaux itself. So on February 25, 1988, the last car to be built there — the 3,418,347th in fact — rolled off the line and the place was closed without ceremony. Apparently, for many years past Citroën had been too embarrassed to allow visitors inside its walls to witness its ancient and outmoded facilities.

now possessed more profit potential as a property development site than as a museum of car manufacture, and so it was promptly and unceremoniously demolished to capitalize on its valuable inner-city location.

But although the threatened death sentence seemed at first to have been commuted to the lesser penalty of permanent exile, the end of the road was already in sight for Citroën's seemingly immortal Tin Snail. Previously, in March 1987, the deletion of the 2CV-6 Club (with rectangular headlights) had reduced the series to a two-car line-up, consisting of the 2CV-6 Special and the 2CV-6 Charleston (both with round chromed headlights). They were powered by the final 1975 version of the 602 cc engine producing 29bhp DIN at 5,750 rpm, which could be distinguished from its predecessors by its 8.5:1 compression ratio and additional emission control measures.

After a mere 30 months of further production at Mangualde, during which time another 42,000 or so cars were made, that assembly line was also condemned. Like the proverbial cat with nine lives, the 2CV had dodged the Grim Reaper before; a succession of fortuitous twists of fate and acts of providence had spun out its career and given it a string of successful roles on the motoring stage. But this time there could be no escaping the final curtain. Already, well before the end of 1989, Citroën had been forced to withdraw the 2CV from its showrooms in Austria, Switzerland, Spain, Holland, Italy and Scandinavia, as the car no longer complied with current construction and anti-pollution regulations in those countries. That left only France, Belgium, Germany and the U.K. where the car could be legitimately marketed, but in those places similar legislation was pending that would soon prevent its sale.

At precisely 3:00 pm on Friday, July 27, 1990, after almost 42 years of continuous production, the very last Deux Chevaux, a grey 2CV-6 Charleston, left the Portuguese production line. The final score had reached a staggering total of 6,956,895 vehicles, made up of 5,114,966

After the closure of Levallois, production was transferred to Citroën's factory at Mangualde in Portugal, for a further two years during which time another 42,000 or so cars were built. But there was no stopping the inevitable; despite its simplicity, the car was dependent on labor-intensive manual assembly methods and therefore costly to produce. So on July 27, 1990, the Portugese production line also was shut down. The final score had reached the staggering total of 5,114,966 vehicles of all types and derivatives. Not bad for a design condemned as a disaster on its first appearance.

2CV sedans and vans, 1,443,583 Dyane sedans, 253,393 Acadiane vans and 144,953 Meharis and other assorted derivatives. Not bad for a design condemned by the press as a disaster on its first appearance!

In truth, the 2CV had already exceeded the normal life expectancy of a motor car many times over, surviving well beyond its allotted time-span, to find itself in a world very different from that into which it had been born. Unequalled as a reliable and economical run-about for almost 50 years, it had been kept alive and preserved from the normal process of decline not by nostalgia and sentimentality but by the inherent, eternal qualities of its design. Condemned by the ignorant and ill-informed as unsafe and dangerous, it was, in the active sense of the word safety, one of the safest and easiest-to-drive cars ever offered to the motoring public. So much so that, at its wheel, even the most clumsy novice driver was able to survive the kinds of mistakes that spell disaster in less forgiving cars. But in the passive sense, its frail and fragile body (built for lightness and simplicity of construction) eventually proved to be overly vulnerable when exposed to modern dangers. Intended merely to shield its occupants from the wind and rain and not against the onslaught of forty-ton lorries, it was designed in an age well before the advent of expressways and freeways, when traffic densities were so light that it was a rare occurrence for two cars to meet and pass each other on a country road in France. Consequently, when involved in the kind of accidents and collisions that are almost inevitable in today's congested traffic conditions, the 2CV's driver and passengers were left unprotected from the mistakes of others and exposed to serious injury in even the slightest impact. As such, it was clearly ill-suited to a world in which the officially accepted test of a motor car's strengths and virtues was the ability to withstand a 15mph collision with a stationary ten-ton block of concrete placed in its path. For that reason alone, although the Deux Chevaux was greatly admired by other designers and manufacturers, its mixture of unusual features was never copied in toto elsewhere and so it remained a unique phenomenon in the history of the automobile!

Nowadays the French motor industry operates on a global basis and only the kind of products that promise all things to all people around the world go into production, shaped by the dictates of marketing and the rigorous disciplines of cost-accountancy and computer-aided design. Fifty years ago, however, the situation was very different. Working in a specifically French environment, without pressure to conform to the dictates of a vast amorphous international market, P-J. Boulanger and his Michelin masters had allowed André Lefèbvre and his team to solve a specifically French transport problem in an idiomatically French way, with a series of radical, inventive and original ideas that were at the same time entirely rational and logical. Ironically, it was these very qualities which eventually won the 2CV a completely new, international clientele among affluent young drivers who inhabited a motoring environment very different from the deprived and frugal circumstances for which the Deux Chevaux had originally been conceived.

6

The Citroën Type H Van, 1948–1981

The Traction Avant and the Deux Chevaux were not the only Citroëns to shape the motoring landscape of France in the early post-war years. At the second Paris Motor Show held following the Liberation, staged in October 1947 (a year before the first public presentation of the 2CV and two years before it was actually put into production), commercial vehicle owners and drivers of France were presented with another equally radical and idiosyncratic machine bearing the Double Chevron badge and similarly destined to become a national institution. Combining the uncompromising rationality of Descartes with the zany looks and personality of the popular contemporary comedian Fernandel, this strange, angular, corrugated tin-box-on-wheels, the unmistakeable Citroën Type H delivery van, very soon came to symbolize all that was individual, inventive and original about French automotive design, and the output of the Quai de Javel in particular.

The outcome of the second objective defined in Pierre-Jules Boulanger's master plan, laid down in 1935, and created by the very same team of engineers led by André Lefèbvre responsible for the 2CV and DS19 sedans, the Type H general-purpose light commercial van and truck was arguably not only the first of Citroën's many influential post-war designs, but also the most widely imitated among all its designs without exception. For whereas the 2CV and DS concepts, though greatly admired by other engineers, were never closely copied by other motor manufacturers, the revolutionary ideas advanced by the Type H series were soon adopted elsewhere, so that in its underlying technical specification, if not its exterior appearance, it set the universal pattern for the light delivery vehicles found in production today.

Not only was the Type H van the first commercial vehicle to offer front-wheel-drive, rack-and-pinion steering and all-independent torsion-bar suspension, it was also the first to adopt the layout and features now standard practice on modern-day vans, but unheard of then. Principally, these were a forward-control driving position; a walk-through cab with (normally) no separation dividing the front compartment from the rear cargo area, thus giving the driver easy access to and from the load-space without the need to dismount from the vehicle; sliding side doors to allow loading and unloading directly from the curb; and, last, a very low load-floor with no high step to be mounted in order to reach the interior. This latter advantage was emphasized by an extra-wide opening at the rear, formed by three hinged doors opening upwards and outwards, permitting effortless, walk-in access at street level.

This extremely practical and convenient layout was made possible by a novel form of construction employing a flat, load-bearing platform-chassis, instead of the traditional ladder frame under-structure normally employed on contemporary commercial vehicles to support the cargo floor. Another useful feature of the design was its ease of maintenance. Access to the H-Van's principal mechanical elements was unobstructed. And for repair or replacement the entire *bloc moteur* located in the nose — the engine, transmission and front axle assembly — could simply be detached and drawn forward as a single unit.

Undoubtedly, the Type H van offered commercial vehicle operators an unparalleled degree of practicality, versatility, safety and comfort for that era. Its small wide wheels (shod from 1960 onwards with Michelin X radial tires) were located at its corners for optimum handling and road-holding ability; while its low, wide platform floor ensured maximum stability on the move, thanks to its low center of gravity, even when fully loaded.

The world's first front-wheel-drive light utility van and the precursor of the post-war Type H series of commercial vehicles was the Citroën TU-B of 1939-1940. Less than 2,000 were produced before World War I broke out, powered by the 9CV 1628 cc engine of the 7C Traction Avant sedan.

The floor-pan itself was a punt-type platform structure, strengthened by substantial *longerons*, or side-members, running beneath it, these were linked to a series of cross-members to which were attached the engine and transmission and the front and rear suspension units. Along its lower flanks ran two hollow chambers providing additional stiffness; these contained, on the right hand side, the gas tank and, on the left, a compartment housing the spare wheel, an arrangement that was later adopted on the 2CV Fourgonnette light van introduced in 1951, as were the corrugated body panels.

Moreover, as the Type H van's two rear wheel-arches made only a minimal intrusion into its cargo-space, the actual freight-carrying capacity it offered in relation to its overall dimensions was particularly high. It was, in effect, a box or cube on wheels into which an extraordinarily wide variety of goods could be packed and transported. No other contemporary vehicle was so flexible or adaptable. So for more than 30 years, it acted as the standard delivery van of urban and rural France, serving in a hundred different roles and guises.

With minimal alterations to its bodywork this *bonne a tout faire*, or maid of all work, was easily modified to tackle a huge variety of jobs, becoming in turn a mini-bus, an ambulance, a fire-appliance, a police tender, a horse-box, a cattle-truck, a car-transporter, a tipper-wagon, a furniture pantechnicon, a workshop-on-wheels, a mobile post-office and even a motorized market-stall or café. Throughout the 1950s, 1960s, and 1970s, successive versions attended to the daily transport needs of three generations of French businesses. By the time production ceased in December 1981, more than 473,000 vans had been constructed, not just in France but also in Belgium and Holland where Citroën set up satellite assembly operations, in Brussels and Amsterdam.

Throughout its production lifespan, the Type H series was supplied by Citroën in two basic standard versions, a fully-finished panel van and an unfinished platform chassis, which came complete with all mechanical elements and a cab but no bodywork. Thus the great majority of all the Type H vehicles sold were produced by Citroën at its Quai de Javel and Aulnay-sous-Bois factories in Paris, from where the platform chassis, cab and mechanical elements all originated. However, assembly of the more unusual and exotic variations, including a number of special-purpose long-wheelbase or high-roof versions with extended bodies, was carried out under contract elsewhere by specialist low-volume firms such as Currus and Heuliez, which adapted the kits supplied by Citroën to meet the individual requirements of their customers.

Many of these non-standard versions were heavily disguised by their elaborate coach-building work and, lacking the characteristic washboard hood with its Double Chevron emblem, could not easily be recognized as a vehicle of Citroën origin. Perhaps the most celebrated examples of this type were the magnificent promotional vehicles created for the Aspro company by the *carrossier* Le Bastard, several of which took a leading part in the procession that traditionally led the Tour de France cycle race across France throughout the 1960s.

Actually, the Type H van was derived from a previous, pre-war Citroën design, developed in prototype form in 1938, passed by les Mines in May 1939, and produced in small numbers over the next twelve months, until the German invasion of France in June 1940. This was the TU series (Transport Utilitaire) utility light commercial vehicle which, like the 2CV and DS passenger cars, was produced as a direct result of

The Type H van was nothing if not versatile, playing countless different roles both in town and country throughout France, Belgium and the Netherlands. One of its longest-running appearances was as the *pannier de salade*, or paddy-wagon of the Paris police force.

The prototype of the revolutionary Type H van, which entered series production in 1947. The first truly modern delivery vehicle, it had all the features now commonplace, including front-wheel-drive; torsion bar suspension; a low, flat, unobstructed load floor; a walk-through cab; and, later, sliding side doors too.

Pierre Boulanger's original business plan, formulated on taking over management of the company. Powered by the 1628 cc four-cylinder long-stroke engine of the 7CV Traction Avant sedan (the TU-B, with a payload capacity rated at 1,020 kg) and, later, the 1911 cc engine of the 11CV Traction Avant (the TU-C, rated at 1,200 kg), the design boasted such advanced features as hydraulic brakes, rack-and-pinion steering and torsion bar suspension. However, it differed from the later Type H series in that its body was supported on a conventional chassis frame, to which the running gear and engine were attached. Its body was constructed from smooth flat steel and aluminum panels, with a roll-up canvas section forming its upper sides.

Similarly, the earliest versions of the Type H van also had canvas upper side sections, but the greater part of its structure including its doors and hood panels was formed from the ribbed or corrugated steel pressings that gave it its distinctive appearance. The whole design was arranged to allow for simple yet strong construction using only the most basic and simple metal-forming techniques, avoiding the necessity of expensive tools and presses which Citroën did not then possess.

The Type H van's boxy, angular, flat-sided shape was no styling accident, brought about by the whim of a designer bent on achieving originality at any price, but through sheer engineering logic. There was simply no other alternative, wholly viable constructional technique available to Citroën's engineers at that time. As we have noted, during the war the company's body presses had been requisitioned by the Nazis and removed to Germany; and without this tooling, more complex curved and rounded panels could not be produced. Thus, the firm's bodywork specialist, Pierre Franchiset, adapted the method pioneered in the 1930s by the German aircraft designer, Dr. Hugo Junkers, and employed in transport aircraft such as the JU52, which had served as Hitler's private plane. This gave strength and stiffness to thin-sheet steel sections that would otherwise have flexed and bent out of shape under load. The method of assembling the panels was also unusual. To reduce the need for welding to a minimum, they were slotted together using a type of tongue and groove technique.

In the aftermath of World War II France suffered an economic crisis of far, far greater severity than that which occurred after World War I. During those grim post-war years known to the French as *les annees grises,* virtually every commodity including food and fuel was in short supply, especially the raw materials and equipment needed to build motor vehicles. Following the depredations of the Occupation, during which the factories of the French auto industry had either been pillaged by the Germans or damaged by Allied bombing, machine tools were virtually non-existent. Moreover, a severe shortage of foreign currency meant that it was difficult for both Citroën and its suppliers to import new equipment to feed their production lines. So, even though the Plan Pons had by now run its course so that a free market in cars and car components was in the course of being re-established, components of every kind were still severely rationed, especially tires and batteries, not to mention gas and steel.

Thus the streets onto which the first examples of the Type H van emerged in the late 1940s were almost completely empty of motor traffic. Although the war had been over for the French for almost five years— Paris had been liberated in August 1944 —wartime conditions still prevailed. It was a time not just of universal restrictions and shortages, but also of industrial unrest and political uncertainty. Of the several million motor vehicles that had existed in pre-war France, less than 100,000 had survived the Occupation in working condition, and of these many had been converted to run on town gas or charcoal fumes, using *gazogene* equipment. In Paris and other major cities, horse-drawn cabs had reappeared on the streets, while in the country, horses, donkeys and oxen had been returned to work in the fields, orchards and vineyards.

There were few private cars on the streets— only occasional trucks or buses rumbling past old women riding ancient bicycles. According to contemporary observers, the whole somber picture was composed of a thousand subtly different shades of grey—a chiaroscuro effect formed by the stone-paved streets; the shabby, peeling stucco and louvered-shuttered windows of the apartment houses; the gaunt, bare plane trees lining the *grands boulevards*; and, of course, the metallic grey paint of the Citroën 2CV and H-Van, and universal black of the Traction Avant.

The first version of the Type H series to be commercialized entered production in June 1948. Known as the H, it had a length of 4.26 m, a height of 1.99 m, a wheelbase of 2.53 m, a track of 1.61 m and a payload of 1,200 kg. It was powered by a detuned version of the long-stroke 78 × 100mm three-bearing 1911cc engine used in the current 11CV Traction Avant sedan, producing 50 hp at 3,800 rpm. This engine was coupled to a three-speed gearbox designed specifically for the Type H, but the whole unit was mounted in a reversed position to that seen on the Traction Avant, with the engine set forward of the transmission, but ahead of the driven front wheels. Performance was never the Type H van's strong point; nevertheless, the torque available at low revs made for very brisk, flexible and tractable progress around town. Even when fully loaded, the van could be driven about in second gear all the time, with scarcely a need to change speeds up or down.

Four months later, in October 1948, a second version, the HZ, was announced, painted in the same grey metallic shade that was to remain the standard finish of the Type H vans for many years. Although its engine and overall dimensions were identical to those of its sister vehicle, its payload was reduced to 850kg and its top speed raised from 78 km/hr to 88 km/hr (55 mph), by the fitting of alternative ratios in its gearbox to permit a faster cruising speed. The idea was that while the H version would serve its original purpose as an urban delivery vehicle, the HZ would undertake rural and inter-city transport duties.

The following year, in October 1949, a third version, the HY, with a payload of 1,500 kg, was introduced; but notwithstanding its heavier capacity, it also had identical overall dimensions and the same engine and power-train. From September 1958 onward, production of the original 1,200 kg capacity H van was discontinued, to be replaced by a new improved version of the 1,500 kg HY, with a total overall curb weight of 2,925 kg as opposed to 2,600 kg.

Throughout its long service career, the technical evolution of the Type H range was slow but steady; small revisions were continually made, but none were large enough to alter the character or appearance of the vehicle, let alone to transform it. Most notable of these improvements were the changes made under the hood, which commenced in May 1955 when the improved IID version of the 1911cc engine (producing 60 hp at 4,000 rpm) was introduced, following its earlier appearance on the Traction Avant sedan.

In the eyes of Type H's customers, good fuel economy, low operating costs and general reliability and durability were much more important than outright performance. To this end, therefore, from January 1960 on, a British-made 1621cc Perkins 4/99 diesel engine was made available as an alternative on the HY only, though one year later this unit was offered on the HZ too. Next, in September 1963, an entirely new 9CV 1628cc (72 × 100mm) Citroën gas engine was introduced as an alternative to the original 1911cc (78 × 100mm) 11CV engine on both the HY and the HZ, which served to raise the top

Top: **This view of the Type H van, taken circa 1959, demonstrates clearly the sliding side door; fully opening rear doors; and low, flat load floor that made it such a practical and versatile delivery vehicle.** ***Bottom:*** **One of the last versions of the Type HY, built in the late 1970s. After three decades of production little had altered, except for the change to a single-piece windshield. Note that by then the Citroën Double Chevron badge on the grille had assumed its redesigned form.**

Besides serving the needs of French town and city businesses for more than three generations, the Type H van also did sterling work on the farms and vineyards of France, carrying agricultural produce and livestock alike.

For more than 30 years it also served as a mobile shop and market stall, as here. This is an early version with canvas side panels.

speed of the former to 92 km/h and 88 km/h for the latter. Finally, in February 1964, a new French diesel engine was announced to replace the Perkins unit formerly employed. This was an 1810cc unit, rated at 7CV, producing 50 hp at 4,000 rpm, built by the Indenor company (Industrie de Nord SA) co-owned by Citroën and Peugeot.

Over the years, a process of continual improvement was carried out on other aspects of the vehicle's internal layout and componentry, particularly on its dashboard instrumentation, minor controls and lighting equipment. But of major external revisions or redesigns there were virtually none, and in 34 years the vehicle's outward appearance change hardly at all. The biggest or most noticeable alteration came about in February 1964 when a new one-piece windshield was introduced to replace the twin screen with central division previously fitted. Then, the following October, the vehicle's famous radiator grille was also reworked, and the traditional Citroën motif (two large inverted V-shaped aluminum strips extending fully across its width) was replaced by the company's new, smaller, stylized Double Chevron badge, mounted centrally. At the same time, the standard paint finish of metallic grey, which had been the only choice offered for the past 17 years, was augmented by a new selection of three striking colors, off-white, pale blue and pale yellow.

And so things remained for the following 17 years, except that in November 1969 a new type of rear fender panel was introduced, rectangular in shape rather than semi-circular as before. Apart from that one single gesture towards modernity, no other significant or noticeable exterior modification took place before production was suspended in December 1981. From first to last, all vehicles in the Type H range were always fitted with forward-opening front doors, with the exception of those 10,000 or so vehicles assembled in Holland between 1963 and 1970.

In short, although it seemed shockingly avant garde at its first unveiling, ultimately the unchanging appearance of the long-lived Type H van came to represent a symbol of cultural identity for the French nation. Like the 2CV, it had played a vital role in the economic and social reconstruction of France, and its eventual replacement by its successor, the Citroën-Peugeot Group's new C35 van, was greatly mourned. Truly, with the passing of its familiar and much-loved visage, the face of France was also changed.

7

The Conception and Development of the Citroën DS, 1937–1955

"L'automobile — n'est que l'accessoire du pneu" — the automobile is nothing more than an appendage of the tire — said Edouard Michelin, defining the unique perspective from which he and his Michelin colleagues approached the subject of car design.

It is hardly surprising that the Michelin men adopted this radical viewpoint. As France's leading tire manufacturers they could hardly think otherwise. Because the pneumatic tire also functions as an elastic spring, supporting the weight resting on the wheel in such a way that its charge of air cushions the jolts caused by any irregularities in the road surface, it forms an integral part of the automobile's suspension system. So instead of regarding their tires and wheels in isolation, divorced from the car as a whole, they sought to improve the handling and ride comfort of road-going vehicles in general by taking a profound interest in all aspects of suspension design and attempting to integrate the tire more closely into automobile suspension systems.

Beginning in the early 1930s, they began to invest enormous sums in a wide-ranging program of fundamental research into all the parameters of suspension performance. Despite their notorious frugality when it came to purchasing routine business supplies such as drawing pins, paper clips and office furniture, their expenditure on these scientific studies was unstinting, requiring the acquisition of large quantities of highly expensive and sophisticated laboratory equipment. And this investment, of course, was made in addition to the substantial outlay required to conduct their continuing conventional tire development and testing programs.

Clearly, in the eyes of *les Michelin*, the springs of a car were its single most important component, to which all other parts and items including the steering, brakes, engine and gearbox, were subservient. They observed that the history of road transport was, in effect, the story of the centuries-old struggle to improve the performance of vehicle suspension systems. The invention of the wheel itself had not produced the great increase in human mobility that might have been expected, they argued, and its early use was confined to such machinery as pulleys, winches and potter's wheels rather than to vehicles used in transporting people and goods. Although the Romans had excelled as road-building engineers and had constructed horse-drawn chariots, carriages and wagons, their famous legions were armies of marching foot soldiers. The carts and drays that they used for carrying supplies and heavy equipment were far too uncomfortable for travel at any greater speed than walking pace because of their inadequate suspension arrangements. Similarly, the chariot races that they staged in their arenas claimed higher casualties than all their other dangerous gladiatorial combat sports, due entirely to the poor road-holding and directional stability of these primitive fighting vehicles!

It was not until two thousand years later that the English mastered the art of making spring steel in the early nineteenth century and applied this knowledge to build speedy, lightweight phaetons, a form of chariot in which the body was connected directly to the axles by flexible leaf springs, without a heavy intermediate undercarriage. Thereafter, it was possible for a man riding in a horse-drawn vehicle to travel as fast as a man galloping on horseback, without undue discomfort or risk of serious injury — a fact that the Michelin men acknowledged in a scholarly brochure explaining the thinking behind the

DS19's hydro-pneumatic suspension system, published in the 1960s.

As we saw in previous chapters, from 1935 to 1950, day-to-day control of activities at Citroën rested in the capable hands of Pierre-Jules Boulanger, an architect turned industrialist. Although by no means a trained automobile engineer or designer, when charged by the Michelin family with the job of turning around the fortunes of the Double Chevron marque, Boulanger laid down a plan of remarkable vision and audacity, one in which engineering excellence rather than commercial expediency was to be the guiding theme. His plan to revive and regenerate the Citroën marque envisaged the development of three new models, all of which — after a long gestation period caused by the unexpected interruption of the Second World War — duly became landmarks in the history of the automobile, just as the Traction Avant had done.

The first project, a small, lightweight, utilitarian people's car code-named the TPV or Toute Petite Voiture developed into the 2CV. The second, a front-wheel-drive forward-control delivery van known as the TUB eventually became the famous corrugated-panelled Citroën Type H utility vehicle, the inspiration for all post-war European delivery vans. And the third, intended to replace the Traction Avant and code-named the VGD (Voiture de Grande Diffusion or Mass-Market Car) ultimately became the Citroën DS19, the forerunner of the long series of D-type sedans, cabriolets and station wagons produced over a period of 20 years, and totalling some 115 different models.

Despite the mass-market inference of the phrase Voiture de Grand Diffusion, it is evident that the VGD was always intended to be an exclusive and sophisticated kind of vehicle, with an advanced specification, a deluxe automobile that would compete with the very best coach-built cars of its day. "I propose to produce 50 Talbots a day ... and sell them at a third of the price," Boulanger confided to his staff. Nothing survives of his design brief today, so the precise technical details of his plans will always remain a mystery. However, it is known that before World War II at least two versions of the VGD were foreseen — a four-cylinder type, the VGD 125 (capable of 125 kph) and a six-cylinder type, the VGD 135 (capable of 135 kph). In each case, the possibility of both front-wheel drive and rear-wheel drive, together with either water-cooled or air-cooled engines, was to be investigated. Naturally, overriding importance was to be attached to achieving the highest possible standards of ride-comfort, given the current state of French roads. As many of the major routes were still paved with cobblestones, this was the quality that French motorists valued above all else in a car.

So it happened that, under Pierre-Jules Boulanger's overall direction, many of the gifted engineers who were first recruited by Andrè Citroën to work on the Traction Avant project became involved in the design and development of the VGD/DS. Chief among these talents was the creator of the 2CV, André Lefèbvre, a designer of genius who spent a total of 25 years at Citroën's Bureau d'Etudes working in obscurity under the rules of secrecy imposed by the Michelin men, yet producing some of the most important and influential designs ever to appear on the road.

The first publicity photo of the DS19 shot in early 1956, following its launch at the October 1955 Paris Motor Show. The adventurous duo-tone colors schemes presented — champagne yellow with an aubergine roof was one option — were just as revolutionary as the engineering beneath the paintwork.

Another key member of the VGD/DS team was Flaminio Bertoni, who had been responsible for the body styling of the Traction Avant and, later, the utilitarian anti-car appearance of the 2CV. The son of an Italian stonemason, his early training as a sheet-metal worker had made him a practical craftsman with an intuitive understanding of materials. A far more primitive and pragmatic personality than the idealistic and highly sophisticated Lefèbvre, he was well able to translate the latter's avant-garde ideas and sketches into three-dimensional reality, and the two men formed a remarkable partnership. Together, in the DS19 they produced a car that has been rightly called a simultaneous masterpiece of engineering and aesthetics.

The third member of the quartet was Paul Mages, the man who invented the DS19's revolutionary hydropneumatic suspension system. A modest and unassuming man, he was nick-named the Professor by his colleagues, although he held no formal scientific or academic qualifications whatsoever. In fact, Mages was yet another of the *autodidactes*, or self-taught engineers, who flourished under the Michelin regime. He had joined Citroën in 1936 at the tender age of 17 without having graduated from either university or technical school. Later, when attempting to explain his invention he claimed that, had he received any formal training, he would never have produced such a novel device, since only a complete ignoramus would have been naive or foolish enough to have embarked upon such a difficult project. Despite his small size and rather timid, retiring nature, Mages possessed great intellectual energy coupled with a prodigious physical capacity for hard work and sustained concentration.

Responsibility for the development of the engine for the new car fell to another Italian expatriate who had found a congenial home at Citroën's Bureau d'Etudes, Walter Becchia. Born in 1903, he had begun his career with the highly successful Fiat Racing Department in Turin. In 1922, he moved to England and joined the Anglo-French Sunbeam-Talbot-Darracq firm, having been recruited by Sunbeam's famous managing director and chief designer, Louis Coatalen. Working at Wolverhampton, Becchia helped design the 2-liter 6-cylinder DOHC engine that powered the car in which Henry Segrave won first prize in the 1923 Grand Prix de l'Automobile Club de France at Tours, the first-ever British racing car to win a major Grand Prix event. By strange coincidence, André Lefèbvre also competed in this race, driving a Voisin. When the British side of the Sunbeam firm retired from racing in 1926 to concentrate on land speed record attempts, Becchia moved to Talbot-Darracq in France and soon found himself employed by a famous fellow Italian, Antonio (Anthony) Lago, who took over the French side of the business when the Rootes brothers acquired the Sunbeam-Talbot firm's British interests in 1934. Bechia's greatest contribution to the revival of the Talbot name was to design a new 3-liter straight-six engine with a novel type of cylinder head, that had hemispherical combustion chambers aspirated by twin overhead valves set at a V angle and operated by rockers driven by a complex arrangement of cross-over pushrods. This

A side view of one of the first hand-built DS19 prototypes — a right-hand-drive model bearing chassis no. 000010 — shot at Citroën's Slough Works in the autumn of 1955, prior to the commencement of production there in June 1956.

2996 cc T120 engine was duly uprated to 4.5 liters and 250 bhp, to power the Talbot Lagos that won the first three places in the 1937 French Grand Prix at Montlhery, a sports car event. These cars were capable of speeds of more than 150 mph.

In 1941, Pierre Boulanger persuaded Becchia to join Citroën to replace Maurice Sainturat as head of the Service Moteurs or engine design department of the Bureau d'Etudes, the latter engineer having retired some two years earlier. And so it happened that the creator of Talbot Lago's powerful racing car engines produced yet another tour-de-force employing the same hemispherical combustion chamber design — the tiny nine-horsepower motor of the 2CV! Endowed with a creative, Latin temperament in full measure, Becchia was not the slow, methodical type of engineer who ponderously weighs and measures the alternatives for weeks on end before coming to a decision. On the contrary, like his great friend and compatriot Bertoni, he was a kind of poet-mechanic who worked intuitively, constantly improvising and inventing just for the fun of it. He never got bogged down in details or minutiae, or lost in endless calculations. His gift was that he always saw a problem in its entirety and from a new perspective — hence the bold originality of his work.

However, as so many commentators have remarked in the past, the strong-point of the DS19 was not its engine but its chassis and suspension. Today, now that the roads of France are normally as smooth as the best in Europe and America, many critics find it hard to understand why Citroën took so much trouble to perfect the ride and road-holding of its new car, and in such an unconventional way, neglecting — in their view — the question of motive power. But in the late 1940s and early 1950s, driving conditions in France were even worse than they had been before the war, since the country's road network was still cratered and pock-marked in many places as a result of bomb damage. Before the opening of the Autoroutes in the 1960s and 1970s, the needs of Gallic motorists were perhaps unique among European motorists. To travel long distances quickly over the network of straight but narrow Routes Nationales called for the kind of car that could comfortably be driven flat out all day, steering and braking with unerring straight-line stability, overriding ruts, potholes and cobblestones of the *chausses deformes* without jolting the driver or passengers.

Consequently, Boulanger's original pre-war specification for the VGD stipulated that, to ensure a smooth and stable ride and reduce driver and passenger fatigue to a minimum, the car should be equipped with a very flexible suspension system that permitted an unusually wide amplitude of wheel movement, up and down, keeping all four wheels in contact with the road under all circumstances, just as had been developed for the TPV/2CV. The problem was that, fully loaded, the VGD would be more than twice as heavy as the 2CV. Plus, its projected top speed would be twice as fast, requiring a degree of flexibility until then unknown!

All suspension systems involve a finely balanced compromise between the conflicting demands of comfort and stability. For comfort, the springing medium should be soft and resilient, to cushion the driver and passengers from the shocks and vibration caused by uneven road surfaces. But for good road-holding and handling ability, it is essential that the tires of all four wheels maintain constant contact with the road, and that the pressure exerted on them stay constant, regardless of changes in the dynamic behavior of the car as it alters speed or course. If the suspension is too soft or spongy or the bouncing rebound of the springs is inadequately damped, the car's handling is impaired. If the suspension is too stiff or inflexible, comfort suffers. To complicate matters further, the operation of a vehicle's suspension system varies according to the load that is placed upon it, and the variation in weight between a five-seater sedan when full or empty can be as much as 700 lbs! Thus, when fully loaded, a soft suspension system tends to lose its resilience, allowing the car's body to sink down onto its springs. But when this is compensated for, by raising the ride-height, the car's center of gravity tends to be positioned far too high for good stability when the car is traveling lightly loaded. This being so, it followed that the kind of highly flexible suspension system demanded by Boulanger would not work satisfactorily unless the VGD's weight distribution could be kept constant at all times — an impossible requirement! Alternatively, a method had to be found to stabilize its body-shell at a constant height at all speeds and over all road surfaces, regardless of any variation in the carried load.

In theory, the arrival of German troops in Paris in 1940 and the cessation of normal commercial activities put a stop to further research on the VGD project. But in practice, although forbidden by the Nazis to engage in any design or development work, activities continued in secret at the Bureau d'Etudes, in an attempt to solve this engineering conundrum. With normal routine work at a standstill, the war years were a time when imaginations ran rampant at the Citroën Bureau d'Etudes, unfettered by ordinary business pressures. Throughout the Occupation, work on the VGD design project continued alongside the development of the TPV/2CV, and a number of different approaches using conventional methods were tried first, without much success.

The subject of power-operated braking and steering systems also kept these clandestine researchers busy during the war years. Experience with the six-cylinder version of the Traction Avant introduced in 1938 had shown that power-assistance was essential to ensure effortless control of a heavy and powerful front-wheel-drive car, at both high and low speeds. In the course of this experimental work, at some time around 1942, Paul Mages—then but a young and very junior braking-system specialist at the Quai de Javel—had a remarkable thought. Automatic adjustment of the ride-height of a vehicle could be achieved by harnessing the very same principles of hydraulics that were used in a braking system to transmit and amplify braking effort from pedal to drum! Furthermore, by replacing conventional metal torsion bar or coil springs with rising-rate gas springs (which, unlike metal, stiffen progressively under increased loads), a true load-compensating, fully-independent suspension system could be achieved at last.

The essence of Mages's idea was that instead of employing the normal mechanical linkages, a liquid could be used to transmit suspension loads from wheels to springs and also to regulate the ride-height automatically, by adding or venting fluid as required. Better still, besides enabling a heavy, fast-moving vehicle to remain in perfect equilibrium when traveling fast over poor road surfaces, the speedy response provided by the stored energy reserves of a central high-pressure hydraulic system could also provide instant, effortless power-operation of other driving control tasks such as steering and gear selection—and even for jacking up the car to change a tire! Mages had overthrown, once and for all, the time-honored dictum that the springing of a fast car had to be firm and inflexible for the sake of stability and safety. The principle of Citroën's unique self-leveling suspension system had been invented. Now only development of the technology remained.

As conceived by Paul Mages, the operation of this system would rely on the action of tiny slide valves located in the principal control centers, the pressure regulator and the height-correctors. These devices would open and close to direct pressurized hydraulic fluid, supplied by a constantly active pump, along various circuits to activate the suspension and brakes and to power the vehicle's steering, gear selection and clutch control mechanisms. At peak moments of demand, this pressure could rise to 2,500 psi—higher than that encountered in the barrel of a shotgun. Regardless of this pressure, in order to avoid friction in the most sensitive slide valve or piston units, it was essential that no seals or gaskets that would restrict the flow and prevent excess by-pass of fluid could be fitted. Although the pipe system itself would be fully sealed against leaks, the proper operation of the pistons and slide valves would have to be achieved entirely by ensuring an exact fit within the cylindrical bores, allowing just enough room for movement but no more. A certain amount of fluid would be permitted to escape so as to lubricate the moving parts. But even so, while the car was on the move, very little energy-absorbing work would be required from the hydraulic pump to maintain this pressure, even at high speeds.

By April 1944, a very primitive, prototype, low-pressure version of Mages' hydraulic system had been installed on a 2CV, ready for road testing. A year later, in July 1945, after hundreds of laboratory trials and thousands of test miles had run, the concept had been proved to be a viable working proposition. By 1947 it was judged good enough to demonstrate to Boulanger in person. And by 1949, Boulanger himself thought it sufficiently promising to show to his Michelin boss at Clermont-Ferrand, Robert Puiseux, this time installed in a Traction Avant. Staff at the Michelin factory were amazed to see a car that could raise itself off the ground, as if lifted by the psychokinetic force of levitation, and promptly called the vehicle "The Ectoplasm."

Robert Puiseux (Edouard Michelin's son-in-law) had succeeded to the position of Michelin supremo upon Edouard's death in 1940. Born in Paris in 1892, he had joined the firm in 1921 after a distinguished military career in the Great War, during which he had served in the artillery and then as an aviator in the army air corps. Al-

Robert Puiseux (1892–1991), chairman of the Société Michelin from 1937 to 1958 and President-Directeur General of Citroën SA from 1950 to 1958, seen at the wheel of one of the very first DS19s, outside the Michelin factory at Clermont-Ferrand.

though he had not enjoyed the benefit of higher education and was entirely without formal engineering training and qualifications, just like Edouard he proved to be a leader of considerable commercial acumen and vision and a worthy successor as patriarch of the Michelin dynasty.

Unfortunately (as we have already noted) in December 1950 while en route between Paris and Clermont-Ferrand, at the wheel of an experimental Traction Avant, Pierre-Jules Boulanger had an accident and was killed outright. His role as President-Directeur-General (Chairman) of the SA André Citroën passed to Robert Puiseux, who, effective January 1951, became ruler of both realms of the Michelin empire. Based at Clermont-Ferrand, Puiseux left the day-to-day management of Citroën to the control of a new managing director, Pierre Bercot, who was located in Paris. Bercot was himself assisted by a joint managing director, Antoine Brueder, who looked after administrative matters, in a job-sharing arrangement echoing exactly the relationship that had existed between P-J. Boulanger and Pierre Michelin twenty years earlier, when both had reported to Edouard Michelin.

Pierre Bercot (1903–1991), the joint General Manager of Citroën between 1950 and 1958, during the formative period of the DS19. After Robert Puiseux's retirement, Bercot in turn became President-Directeur-General (Chairman and Managing Director) of Citroën from 1958 until 1970. It was he who chose to make the Traction Avant's replacement a truly radical and innovative vehicle, a decision of remarkable courage and foresight.

Unusual among the hierarchy of the Michelin empire, Bercot was not a member of the family by birth or marriage. Born in 1903, he had studied languages (he spoke both ancient and modern Greek) before earning a doctorate in law. However, he had joined the Michelin firm in 1937 not as a lawyer but as an economist. In this capacity he was later transferred from Clermont-Ferrand to Paris by P-J. Boulanger, shortly after *les Michelin* acquired the Javel company, in order to undertake a study of manufacturing and operating costs. Over the years, he gradually became the de facto managing director at the Quai de Javel, with ever greater responsibilities continually delegated to him. Thus when Robert Puiseux eventually retired in 1958, this situation was formally recognized and Bercot took on full responsibility for Citroën affairs with the title of P.D.G, but reported to the new supremo at Clermont-Ferrand, François Michelin (Edouard Michelin's grandson) who had assumed control of the holding company, the Compagnie General des Etablissements Michelin, in May 1955. Four years earlier, Michelin's tire manufacturing and marketing activities had been re-organized by a subsidiary company, La Manufacture Francaise des Pneumatiques Michelin.

At this point in time, early in 1951, the work on the VGD carried out under Boulanger's directives had crystallized into the form of a strange-looking, round-snouted, hump-backed prototype, disrespectfully christened the Hippopotamus by those at the Bureau d'Etudes who thought that its somewhat outdated specification and appearance could be improved upon, now that P-J.B. was no longer on the scene. In forming this opinion, they had the approval of their new *patron*, Pierre Bercot. Taking stock of the situation, he recognized that by adopting a long-term view and delaying the production of a replacement for the Traction Avant for the time being, an opportunity existed for Citroën to create yet another truly advanced and radical vehicle that, once again, would give it a lasting lead over its competitors, just as the Traction had done some 20 years earlier. As a personal friend of General de Gaulle, he was quick to see that here lay the chance to build a car that would enhance the prestige of France as an automobile producer and industrial power, and so he readily agreed to a complete revision and updating of the project. Given the full backing of *les Michelin*, no expense was to be spared in making the Traction

One of Bertoni's sketches for the VGD, a design which was nick-named the Hippopotamus by the staff of the Bureau d'Etudes. This prototype was abandoned after P-J. Boulanger's death in 1950.

Avant's replacement the finest, fastest, most comfortable vehicle that had ever been produced by Citroën, using the very latest materials and methods. And not least among the innovations to be incorporated, of course, would be Michelin's own recent invention, the X series steel-belt radial tire, for which the car's suspension and steering arrangements would be specifically designed and engineered.

Without a doubt, this was the true moment of conception of the Citroën DS19. André Lefèbvre was instructed to carry out a total re-think of the VGD, employing hydro-pneumatic suspension technology and incorporating an extremely unusual and highly sophisticated front suspension layout, designed to exploit the advantages of the new X tire, which had been launched at the October 1949 Paris Motor Show. Clearly, the grand idea — though never explicitly stated — was that the new car should act as a demonstration vehicle to show off the virtues of the Michelin X tire to the outside world. By this point in time, the Michelin firm had already committed itself to developing the capacity to manufacture the X tire in very high volume, with the intention that it would eventually replace the conventional cross-ply tire completely throughout its product range.

Pierre Bercot was indeed a most unlikely figure to be given the task of running a major motor-car manufacturing firm, but then Citroën was not a normal industrial concern any more than was its parent company. Neither qualified in automobile engineering nor in business management, Bercot was a cultured and scholarly *haute-bourgeois* who held decidedly elitist views and viewed with disdain the mundane tenets of modern, consumer-led marketing, which he rejected. He whole-heartedly endorsed and promoted the radical engineering culture established by André Citroën and P-J. Boulanger, so that under his uncompromising direction, André Lefèbvre and the engineers of the Bureau d'Etudes continued to hold the final say in all matters of technical and production policy. Just as a doctor diagnoses an illness and prescribes a remedy, Lebfèbvre and his team gave Citroën drivers and dealers exactly what they thought was good for them. And the patients lapped up the medicine with an enthusiasm that bordered on the fanatical.

Naturally, Bercot's decision to proceed with the commercialization of Mages's hydro-pneumatic self-levelling suspension technology was fully endorsed by his boss at Clermont-Ferrand, the current *gerant* Robert Puiseux, who in 1951 gave the go-ahead for the huge investment required to enable Citroën to begin the manufacture of hydro-pneumatic systems and components. It had been Puiseux who, in 1944, approved the research and development program that led to the patenting of the radial tire concept by Michelin in June 1946. Later, in 1956, he displayed similar courage and foresight when he decided to abandon the production of conventional bias-ply tires altogether and authorized the company's future commitment to the exclusive production of the X steel-belted radial ply tire.

To function correctly, the various moving slide-valves and pistons employed in Mages' hydro-pneumatic suspension system required an ultra high-precision manufacturing technique that would ensure a degree of accuracy never achieved before in any area of industrial mass-production. In other words, before the DS19 could be produced, Citroën would have to develop a completely new metal-working technology involving the use of extremely sophisticated plant and machinery capable of working to one-tenth of a micron (0.0001 mm or 0.000004 inches), a degree of accuracy that until now had been confined solely to the specialized area of diesel pumps and injectors. Therefore, since this expertise did not exist elsewhere in Europe, the company would be obliged to achieve a virtual self-sufficiency in micron-standard manufacturing by designing and building the essential machinery and equipment itself, surely in itself a major feat of industrial skill.

Consequently, in 1954, Citroën opened at Asnieres near Paris a completely new factory dedicated to the production of hydraulic system components for use in the D series cars. At a time when other automotive component producers were content to work to tolerances of 0.2mm in normal practice (or to 0.02 mm in exceptional circumstances) Asnieres was, and remains, capable of adhering to standards 20 times more precise. Here, in a controlled, dust-free environment, technicians were able to work to the third decimal place — a far greater degree of precision than exercised in the Swiss watch industry — and produce more than 44,000 super-finished parts to tolerances of some 0.0005 mm (equivalent to one-fiftieth of the thickness of cigarette paper) every day, day in, day out, without difficulty. Initially, some 25 classes of diameters were produced and the slide-valves had to be matched to their bores by manual inspection. But within a few years of the commencement of production, the process had been greatly refined so that the number of classes was reduced in effect to one; all slide valves matched all bores, such was the accuracy achieved. Thereafter, these billions of identical, interchangeable slide valves and pistons were mass produced routinely like nuts and bolts, and no further human inspection or adjustment during assembly was necessary.

As we noted earlier, the first products of the Asnieres factory were introduced in April 1954, fitted to the Traction Avant 15/Six Hydraulique model. The achievement represented an extraordinary feat of industrial innovation, which could only have been contemplated — or considered worthwhile — by a parent company with the pioneering spirit to invest in change. But, of course, by virtue of inventing and developing the metallic tire (which also required the mastery of entirely new production methods), the Michelin firm had already shown that it possessed these qualities of industrial creativity.

To return to the story of the DS19, by 1952 the familiar streamlined body shape had begun to take its definitive form, fashioned by Lefèbvre, Bertoni and the bodywork expert Pierre Franchiset. Such features as the huge curved windshield and the detachable lightweight steel and aluminum panels mounted on a massively strong platform-chassis and passenger-cage had all been arrived at and agreed upon. But the small matter of engines had still not been resolved. Obsessed as he was by saving weight and improving aerodynamic performance, originally, Lefèbvre had specified a lightweight horizontally opposed engine, mounted ahead of the front axle so as to give the car a flat, sloping hood line and the lowest possible center of gravity. Accordingly, Walter Becchia, the designer of the 2CV's engine, had already produced two highly original six-cylinder prototypes with a boxer-motor layout, one water-cooled and the other air-cooled. Yet for all their refinement, originality and sophistication, these engines failed to produce the required performance and were subject to failure due to problems in the cooling of the rear pair of cylinders.

When by 1954 it was obvious that these technical problems could not be overcome — and that due to the expense of preparing for the production of the DS19's hydro-pneumatic componentry it had run out of money to fund the building of new engines — Citroën regretfully abandoned Becchia's prototypes. The Deesse would have to be powered by the old 1911cc four-cylinder Traction Avant engine, designed by Maurice Sainturat in 1934, but improved by a performance-boosting aluminum cross-flow cylinder head, designed by Becchia. To fit this old straight-four long-stroke engine aft of the front-axle axis (instead of in front as would have been the case with the much more compact sixes), it was necessary to install it in a niche, through the bulkhead, into the passenger compartment. This regrettable loss of interior space and the loss of the planned three-seater front-bench seat was one of the few compromises that Lefèbvre was forced to make on his original conception, but at least there was now free space in the nose to house the spare tire!

It was at this time that the DS19 acquired its poetic name, by a process that was decidedly prosaic. The various experimental prototypes produced successively, in answer to Boulanger's design brief, were referred to by the designations D1, D2, D3 and so forth, so that the VGD project eventually became known as the D project and the production part-numbering of its components were given the prefix letter D. When, early in 1955, the new aluminum-alloy cross-flow cylinder head came into being, it was known as the "*culasse Special*" and the "S" of Speciale was added to the prefix-letter D, to provide the prefix DS for the engine components concerned. This DS prefix was also adopted as a coded reference to other engineering matters connected with the prototype and thus gradually became known to those inside the factory who were allowed to hear about the new vehicle undergoing development in secret within the confines of the Bureau d'Etudes. Thus, when the time came to give the car a proper name for the benefit of the buying public, Citroën's Marketing and Sales people simply adopted this punning Deesse (goddess) appellation, which never entered official Citroën terminology. The factory remained faithful to the letter D, using this in combination with various other letters and numbers as the official, technical reference for the entire D series of vehicles.

While Becchia's abortive motive-power experiments were taking place between 1950 and 1952, Lefèbvre and Mages were busy developing other uses for the aircraft-style hydraulic power system required for the gas-oil suspension. Soon they had perfected a high-pressure twin-circuit braking arrangement that actually compensated for the load on board when distributing braking force front and rear, a novel design of disc-brakes for the two front wheels, a fully-powered rack-and-pinion steering system and, most ingenious of all, a hydraulically powered semi-automatic gear-selecting and clutch-actuating mechanism. Changing gears on the Deesse would require no more than a finger-tip movement on a tiny lever behind its famous single-spoke steering wheel!

All this design and development work took place in conditions of the utmost secrecy at the Bureau d'Etudes in the rue du Theatre in Paris, and at Citroën's test track at la Ferte-Vidame near Dreux, west of Paris, which was surrounded by a 12-foot-high wall. Surrounding the circuit were watchtowers manned by guards on constant lookout for intruders. If anything was sighted — even an aircraft flying overhead — a siren was sounded and the testers had to drive their cars straight off the road as quickly as possible and hide them under trees. Even so, word got around that the *Maison de Mystere* was planning something spectacular. In 1952, an enterprising journalist and photographer from the motoring magazine, *l'Auto Journal*, spotted a thinly disguised prototype being tested at Lefèbvre's country house in the south of France, and thereafter all the newsmen in the country were hot on the hunt for the biggest motoring story of the day. All kinds of speculation, including endless artists' impressions, were forecasted, including features of the new Citroën, which was widely expected to be as revolutionary as the Traction Avant had been. As a result of this publicity, the erstwhile steady sales of Citroën's ancient warhorse, now almost 20 years old, at last began to show signs of falling off. When, at the end of December 1953, *l'Auto-Journal* succeeded in revealing details that were embarrassingly accurate, Citroën management began a hunt for informers and gave orders for tooling and production engineering to begin, so that the car could appear onto the market at the earliest opportunity.

Even so, there was one final hitch to be overcome. In early 1954 came news that another major European manufacturer was planning to introduce a 2-liter model with a silhouette alarmingly similar to that of the Deesse. At that point in time, the car had a profile rather different from the one the public saw for the first time in October 1955. From the windshield forward, to the nose, the shape was the same, but from the windshield back the roof-line above the passenger compartment was higher and ran in a continuous curved line down to the rear bumper; the rear window and trunk lid were let into the rounded curve of the roof and there were long triangular quarter lights behind the rear door windows. After much deliberation, Citroën's management decided that, even though the press-tools for these rear panels had been made, they could not be used. To avoid all accusations of plagiarism, an alternative body-profile was urgently required. With his customary flair and creativity, Flaminio Bertoni quickly re-sculpted a new roofline with a flatter curve, a stepped-in, wrap-around rear window, solid quarter panels and a new trunk lid; while to disguise the step above the rear window and terminate the roof-line, he made tapering trumpet-shaped housings for the rear turn signals. At the same time, the fiber-glass reinforced plastic roof panel came into being, not only to reduce the weight of the superstructure and lower the vehicle's center of gravity, but to eliminate the requirement for further expensive press tools. Now the die was cast, there could be no further changes. The 15 years of gestation were over and the Deesse was ready to be born into the motoring world!

André Lefèbvre — Unsung Genius of Automobile Design

If André Lefèbvre had been an independent consultant, or even his own master at the head of his own firm, then surely his name would be recognized today as being among the greatest-ever exponents of automobile engineering and design. But instead of establishing an independent marque bearing his own name, he chose to devote his talents to designing cars for other men, working for the greater part of his life at Citroën in comfortable obscurity, out of the limelight and away from the attentions of the press. Consequently, as a result of the policy of secrecy and obfuscation imposed by his employers, during his lifetime, his talent came to be recognized only by his colleagues and a few knowledgeable connoisseurs. Today, almost forty years after his death, the significance of his work — and perhaps his very existence — are still relatively unknown and acknowledged in the automobile world.

Certainly, in placing his trust in so gifted a protégé, André Citroën ensured not only the success of the Traction Avant, but also the very survival of the Double

Chevron marque. Long after Citroën's demise, Lefèbvre continued to uphold the tradition of innovation and engineering excellence, established by his mentor, by producing that remarkable post-war string of radical, indeed revolutionary, cars that gave the Citroën firm its worldwide reputation for originality and unconventionality.

As the engineer in charge of design and development matters at Citroën for more than 25 years, André Lefèbvre was chiefly responsible for overseeing the chassis, power-train and suspension design not only of the DS19, but also the Traction Avant, the 2CV, the Type H van and innumerable experimental prototypes. Yet, due to the cloak of secrecy and obfuscation that shrouded research activities at the Bureau d'Etudes during the 1940s and 1950s, his contribution to the production of these seminally important vehicles remains largely unrecognized to this day, even among Citroën enthusiasts.

As we have seen, throughout this period the Citroën company pursued a policy of absolute self-sufficiency in every aspect of engineering and body design, undertaking all such activities in-house. No outside consultant stylists or design studios were ever employed. Moreover, its design staff was expressly forbidden to drive or dismantle cars from other manufacturers, in case the originality, integrity and inventiveness of their work should somehow be compromised or diluted. At the same time, an absolute ban on personal publicity was rigidly enforced upon all personnel, so that many of France's greatest automotive talents were employed at the Bureau's rue du Theatre premises in conditions of complete anonymity and obscurity, unknown to the outside world and unrecognized by the motoring press.

Born on August 19, 1894, at Louvres on the northern outskirts of Paris and educated at Lycee in Nantes, André Lefèbvre began his engineering career in the emerging French aircraft industry, having entered the Ecole Superieure d'Aeronautique in Paris in 1911, graduating in 1914. On completion of his compulsory two-year period of military service in March 1916, at the age 22, he joined the distinguished aircraft-building firm founded by Gabriel Voisin, remaining there for 15 years. Here he became the deputy and right-hand man of this famous aeronautical pioneer who collaborated with such men as Louis Bleriot, Henry Farman and even le Corbusier. Initially, Lefèbvre's work with Voisin involved designing military aircraft for the French and British air forces. But after the Great War, when Gabriel Voisin turned his attention to the motor industry, he helped to produce a series of very advanced luxury automobiles and racing cars, all showing a strong aeronautical influence. The first of these Voisins was the 18CV Type C1, powered by a Knight sleeve-valve engine. Originally designed by Artault and Dufresne in response to a commission from André Citroën, it was subsequently purchased — lock, stock and barrel — by Voisin when, on entering the motor industry in his own name, in 1919, Citroën decided that instead of continuing to produce the traditional type of European luxury car as he had done previously at Mors, he would make his name as the constructor of a truly popular car designed for the common man, mass-produced and mass-marketed in the American manner.

As was the custom during the Roaring Twenties, André Lefèbvre often drove these Voisin competition cars himself, as a member of its racing team. Thus (with the exception of Vincenzo Lancia) he became the only automobile engineer ever to have competed successfully in motor sport at the highest level. Most notably, in 1923 he finished fifth in the Grand Prix de l'Automobile Club de France held at Tours, driving a two-liter six-cylinder Voisin of advanced specification, featuring a revolutionary all-aluminum monocoque body, the first of its kind. The winner of this famous race was actually the Sunbeam Talbot driven by Sir Henry Segrave, powered by a 2-liter 6-cylinder DOHC engine designed by ex–Fiat engineers, Walter Bechia and Vincente Bertarione. By a strange coincidence, some 18 years later, in 1941, Walter Becchia joined Lefèbvre at Citroën's Bureau d'Etudes, where he was responsible for designing the engine of the 2CV and, eventually, that of the DS19 as well.

Later on, in 1930, Lefèbvre took part in a famous series of high-speed long-distance endurance runs staged by Voisin at the Montlhery circuit, in partnership with the Yacco Oil Company. These runs set many long-lasting records, especially the one for 48 hours of non-stop driving. In this epic run, the Voisin covered 10,560 kilometers at an average speed of 220 kph, with Lefèbvre and Cesar Marchand acting as co-drivers.

The economic problems of the Depression had a severe impact on the makers of luxury cars in France — and, being avant-garde, the Voisin firm was harder hit than most. The market for its expensive and eccentric products suddenly collapsed, and so in April 1931, Lefèbvre and Voisin were obliged to part company, although the pair were to remain close friends for the rest of their lives, consulting each other on every technical and automotive issue.

After an unproductive and uncongenial two-year stint with Renault, Lefèbvre joined Citroën in March 1933, having been recruited by André Citroën personally, on the recommendation of Gabriel Voisin, specifically to take overall technical control of his Traction Avant project then well under way at the Quai de Javel, but which had encountered certain technical problems of seemingly insurmountable difficulty. As Lefèbvre had already developed proposals for a front-wheel-drive car while working with Voisin, he was ideally qualified for such an assignment. Indeed, he was personally responsible for designing many of the Traction's most idiosyncratic features, including its unusual rod and tower gear selection mechanism and its mustard-spoon speed-change lever.

During his quarter-century service as de-facto Chief Engineer and Designer at Citroën's Bureau d'Etudes, Lefèbvre held no official rank or title in the company's hierarchy Although he never actually held an appointment as the head of that department, he was regarded nonetheless as the supreme authority and source of policy on all technical matters within the company. After the demise of André Citroën in 1935, he reported directly to the firm's new owners, the Michelin family at Clermont-Ferrand, who gave his advanced thinking and adventurous policies their total support and endorsement, allowing their resident genius carte-blanche to follow whatever lines of research seemed most interesting and promising to him personally, almost regardless of cost or ultimate commercial viability.

Bored by organizational and administrative matters, and totally uninterested in the symbols of power and status that motivate lesser men, Lefèbvre left the day-to-day running of the department to others and concentrated his energies and talents entirely on solving engineering problems, working at all hours and in all places. The archetypal artist-engineer, he worshipped novelty for its own sake taking a perverse delight in doing things differently and refusing to copy proven techniques used successfully elsewhere. Nothing seemed impossible to him. The more audacious, unconventional and complex a solution, the greater was its appeal. Throughout his career, both with Voisin and with Citroën, he was obsessed with the idea of adapting the principles of aeronautics to the automobile. Yet he never went in for the phoney streamlining that was so fashionable in the 1930s and which, as often as not, was aerodynamically unsound and merely concealed a crude chassis with a thin veneer of spurious sophistication.

A tall, dark, elegant, somewhat bohemian figure who dressed with style and drank nothing but water or champagne, he was evidently extremely attractive to women. Three times married, his life was one long passionate love affair with the motor car, punctuated by countless much shorter liaisons with innumerable pretty females. But the intense, good-looking Lefèbvre was not always so successful in persuading men to acquiesce to his wishes and desires. Like many other brilliant minds, he was high-strung and could often seem temperamental and impatient with those who simply could not keep up with the furious pace of his inventiveness. Consequently, he was confined in an isolated, inner sanctum in the Bureau d'Etudes, surrounded by a small staff of carefully chosen research assistants who could be trusted to understand his thinking and to carry out his instructions without contradiction, no matter how far-fetched they might appear at first sight. One of his draftsmen said that Lefèbvre would come to his drawing board almost every day with a new idea or device that he had just thought up and wanted to have produced and tried out. Another claimed that his boss had too many new ideas for the means available at the time.

But to understand exactly what André Lefèbvre achieved at Citroën — and to explain how it was that his Michelin bosses allowed him sufficient laissez-faire to realize those remarkable achievements— it is necessary to remember that, above all, he was man who loved driving fast. As a highly skilled and experienced former Grand Prix racing driver who had risked his life countless times on the track, he approached the problems of automotive design entirely from a driver's point of view. For Lefèbvre, the question of chassis dynamics always had paramount priority. From Voisin he had learned that lightness, balance, directional stability and aerodynamic efficiency were all ultimately far more important in determining a car's performance, handling and road-holding qualities than outright engine power. What ultimately determined the speed and safety of a car was the relationship between its moving wheels and the ever-changing road surface passing beneath it — the concept that came to be known in Citroën terminology as *la liaison-au-sol.* In this approach, all design objectives were held subservient to achieving optimum contact between the tire and the road, at all speeds and in all situations. Since that all-important tire/road contact governed the traction, acceleration, steering and braking abilities of a vehicle, under Lefèbvre's perfectionist philosophy, no effort was spared to develop sophisticated new suspension and steering arrangements that would guarantee this continuing contact, no matter what occurred to the driver or the car. His aim was always to improve the *liaison-au-sol* of Citroën vehicles to levels of refinement and security never before achieved by any other motor manufacturer.

It is no coincidence that throughout Lefèbvre's involvement in the design of the Traction Avant, the 2CV and the DS19, the scientists and engineers of the Michelin parent company were working toward the very same objective. Even before the war, the Michelin firm had decided to abandon rigid cross-ply tires and to concentrate its resources on the development and manufacture of a safer-running, longer-lasting alternative — the revolutionary, flexible, steel-braced radial tire, the Michelin X — first introduced (as an option) on the Traction Avant in 1949, then adopted as standard equipment from late 1954 on.

With global domination of the automobile tire market the ultimate objective, Citroën and Michelin operated in synergy in matters of research and development.

A constant exchange of information and personnel existed between Paris and Clermont-Ferrand. Surely, it was this long-term strategy on the part of the Michelin men that gave André Lefèbvre his power and prestige at the Citroën Bureau d'Etudes and which allowed him to pursue his adventurous ideas no matter what the cost.

Although he was forced by ill health to retire from the company prematurely in July 1958, André Lefèbvre continued to serve the Double Chevron marque until the end of his life. Having suffered a stroke which left him partially paralyzed, he learned to draw with his left hand and went on designing for Citroën, working from his home, until he died on May 4, 1964, at age 70.

André Lefèbvre—Key Career Dates

Born at Louvres, north of Paris	August 19, 1894
Entered Ecole Superieure d'Aeronautique, Paris	1911
Graduated from "Sup Aero"	1914
Joined Voisin aircraft firm	March 1, 1916
Left Voisin	April 30, 1931
Joined Renault car firm	May 1931
Left Renault	March 1933
Joined Automobiles Citroën	March 12, 1933
Retired from Citroën	July 1958
Died, aged 70	May 4, 1964
Service with Voisin: 15 years	
Service with Renault: 2 years	
Service with Citroën: 25 years	

Flaminio Bertoni

Although he was responsible for the shape and style of four of the most individual and instantly recognizable cars ever produced, Flaminio Bertoni, the stylist of the Citroën Traction Avant, 2CV, DS19 and Ami-6, remains virtually an unknown and unrecognized talent in the English-speaking world, not least among those who own and admire the very cars that he designed. Even in his adopted homeland of France, he continues to be regarded as *"un genie encore trop meconnu"*–a misunderstood and undeservedly neglected genius.

Yet experts on automobile and industrial design now acknowledge that Bertoni must be ranked among the most gifted and influential stylists ever to have worked in the motor industry, on either side of the Atlantic. His achievement was to create the visual appearance of a quartet of completely original and radical designs, all of them hailed as cult-cars and icons of creativity. On this evidence alone, he surely deserves a place in the pantheon of Heroes of Twentieth Century Automobile Styling alongside the other guiding lights of his era, such as Raymond Loewy and Harley Earle.

The son of a tailor, Bertoni was born on January 10, 1903, at Masnago, a suburb of Varese in Northern Italy, not far from Lake Como. He began work in 1918, at the age of 14, as an apprentice with a *carrozzeria* at Varese, la Societa anonima Fratelli Macchi, where he soon developed a profound ability and interest in automobile body styling and construction, and qualified as a sheet-metal worker. His outstanding talent as a draftsman, painter and sculptor were also quickly recognized by his employers, who transferred him to their design department and enabled him to study at the local art school at Varese. His first known design for a car body, a torpedo or open tourer, was produced in 1922.

In 1923, at age 20, he made his way to Paris, the City of Light, which was then the center of both the artistic and the automobile engineering worlds, where in June that year he found work as a designer and model-maker with the well-known, coach-building firm of Manessius located at Levallois-Perret. His employment there was brief, however, for by September he had moved to the rival *carrossiers*, Rothschild et Fils, based in the same locality. Here once again his stay was short, as within three months of his arrival, the firm went bust. Fortunately, one of its directors was none other than Lucien Rosengart, one of André Citroën's closest friends and collaborators. Recognizing Bertoni's great promise, Rosengart found a job for him at the Quai de Javel, where he started work as a bodywork stylist and designer on January 1, 1925. But within four months he was on the move again, having decided, for family reasons, to return to Italy and take up his old job as a draftsman with the Macchi brothers, where he remained until the end of 1929. Finding the environment at Fratelli Macchi conservative and stultifying, in 1930 he resigned and opened his own design consultancy at Varese, the Studio Technic di Carrozzeria Flaminio Bertoni. The next two years were spent designing car, bus and lorry bodies for various companies, though this work had to be sustained by his other freelance activities as a graphic artist, illustrator and book jacket designer.

By October 1931, however, he had returned to France, taking with him a girlfriend, Giovanna (Jeanne) Barcella, who was already pregnant with his eldest son, Leonardo, born in April 1932. To avoid a scandal, the pair had simply decided to run away to Paris, where Bertoni was fortunate enough to find another job, this time with the SICAL company (Societe Industrielle de Carosserie de Levallois-Perret) which held a contract to produce, in quite large numbers, a range of special bodies for Citroën's

C4 and C6 series of cars. Through this work he was able to resume his contacts at the Bureau d'Etudes, resulting on July 8, 1932, at age 29, in his rejoining the company to work on the development of the forthcoming replacements for the C4 and C6 models, and later on the Traction Avant. Initially he was employed only as a *maqueteur*, or maker of plaster styling models; but as the full extent of his talents became apparent to his colleagues and superiors, he gradually assumed overall responsibility for all matters of exterior styling and interior design at Citroën, working directly under successive chiefs of the bodywork section of the design office.

Although Bertoni had made his mark with his work on the Traction Avant, the period following the collapse of the André Citroën regime was a difficult time for all at the Bureau d'Etudes, where as a result of the economies introduced by *les Michelin*, staff numbers had been reduced from 40 to only seven people. In this uncertain atmosphere, Bertoni resumed and diversified his freelance activities, designing items for outside firms and entering various styling competitions, as well as exhibiting his sculptures. He also became a regular contributor to the magazine *l'Auto Carrosserie*.

As we have already noted, throughout the period during which Citroën was controlled by Michelin, the company pursued a policy of absolute self-sufficiency in every aspect of engineering and body design, undertaking all such activities in-house. No outside consultant stylists or design studios were ever employed. Consequently, Bertoni can safely be held solely responsible for the radical and innovative appearance of all the notable Citroën cars of his era. In addition Bertoni was also involved in a large number of important styling studies, prototypes and unproduced designs. His influence also extended to matters of graphic design and corporate identity. It was he who reworked André Citroën's original Double Chevron trademark and logo into the modern form employed today. But because research and development activities at Citroën were conducted in total secrecy and an absolute ban on personal publicity for employees and their achievements was rigidly enforced, throughout his career there, Bertoni worked in virtual anonymity. During the development of both the 2CV and the DS19, research work at the Bureau d'Etudes was just as closely guarded as at a Russian atomic weapons base. The rue du Theatre building became known as the Maison de Mystere, or House of Secrets, as impenetrable as the Kremlin. Consequently, Bertoni's contribution to the reputation of the Double Chevron marque — indeed, his entire presence chez Citroën — remained largely unknown to the outside world until many years after his death. So complete was this ignorance of his work, even among motoring journalists, that until comparatively recently, when knowledge of his contribution at last began to leak out, his work on the Deesse was still being attributed to Bertone (with an e) due to an elementary confusion over names, if not styles!

Small, dark and extremely energetic, with a large square head framed by thick sideburns, Bertoni was a workaholic who never stopped creating things, toiling late into the night and throughout weekends once an idea took hold of him.

He certainly didn't confine himself to designing cars. During his years at Citroën he kept up an impressive output of highly accomplished works of art — architectural drawings, charcoal sketches, clay statuettes and busts of his family and friends, including his boss, P.J. Boulanger. Colleagues described him as working like a demon, with a wicked gleam in his eyes, keeping them amused with a constant stream of witty remarks delivered in his Italian accent, which he never lost even after living a long time in France. According to one leading French journalist, he was a "force of nature," an "intuitive genius," blessed with an "electronic eye" for shape and form and who toiled at a "madcap pace." In his mind he could visualize the finished appearance of a car, or part of a car, from every angle, down to the tiniest detail, and sculpt it out of a solid mass of clay in less than a day. Another contemporary witness said he looked like a sorcerer in his cave, bustling around his trough of plaster and constantly chewing aspirins to fend off the incessant migraines caused by the motorbike accident that he had suffered during the war.

In June 1940, shortly before the invading German army reached Paris, the Citroën factory was bombed by the Luftwaffe. Although the company's production facilities were scarcely damaged, the Lutetia administrative building, which also housed the Bureau d'Etudes, was totally destroyed, creating a loss of the company's entire technical archive, including its engineering drawings. Immediately, the management and research staff moved south to Niort near la Rochelle on the Atlantic coast, until the political and military situation was stabilized, whereupon the Bureau d'Etudes returned to new accommodations in the old Mors car factory, located at the rue du Theatre in the 15th arrondissement of Paris, just off the Quai de Grenelle, a few steps away from the main Citroën factories on the Quai de Javel.

As the German Occupation spread inexorably southwards throughout France that autumn, communications between Paris and Niort became ever more difficult. But because of his Italian passport, Bertoni was able to travel without restriction and so, using his motorcycle, he became a sort of dispatch rider carrying vital parts and messages. Unfortunately, while undertaking one of these missions, he collided with a German armored car, an accident which almost cost him his life and left him crippled and subject to severe headaches for the rest of his days. When convalescing from his accident, Bertoni took a leave of absence from Citroën to study architecture at the Ecole National des Beaux Arts in Paris, earning a diploma — the formal qualification he had always sought. Later, in 1953, he was to be awarded the distinction of Chevalier de l'Ordre des Arts et des Lettres for his work as a sculptor. At this point in time Bertoni actually lived just a few doors away from the Bureau d'Etudes in an apartment further down the rue du Theatre, together with his second wife, Lucienne, nee Marondon, and their son Serge, Bertoni's second child, born in June 1949. Lucienne, also an Italian, was a talented dancer who had once been a leading member of the Corps de Ballet at La Scala in Milan. The pair had married in March 1947, at the ages of 44 and 37, respectively. Bertoni's eldest son, Leonardo, born in 1932, lived in Italy with his mother, Bertoni's first wife Jeanne Barcella, who had returned to her homeland after the break-up of the marriage in 1939.

Flaminio Bertoni died suddenly on February 7, 1964, struck down by a cerebral hemorrhage at the age of 61, having completed 32 years of service at Citroën. Throughout the greater part of this time, his role in the scheme of things had been to translate the adventurous ideas produced by André Lefèbvre and his engineering team into three dimensional form, while adding his own personal aesthetic vision and understanding, to produce avant-garde automobiles that could actually be manufactured economically in large volumes.

An exceptionally inventive and imaginative talent of the type that flourished under the Michelin regime, he was above all a practical hands-on craftsman with the gift — rare among visual artists — of being able not merely to appreciate the problems and pre-occupations of engineers but actually to assist them in their work. The remarkable originality and individuality of his imagination is obvious to even the most casual and uninterested observer. What seems all the more remarkable is his deep, practical understanding of the mechanical capabilities of the materials at his disposal, both new and old. As one of the very first designers to work with thermoplastics and glass-reinforced polyester resins as well as the traditional aluminum and steel, his grasp of the opportunities was total. The Citroën DS has often been described as a simultaneous masterpiece of engineering and aesthetics, as was recognized when it was awarded first prize in the prestigious 1957 Milan Triennale exhibition of industrial architecture and design, the first automobile ever to be thus honored. If so, then it was entirely Bertoni's achievement that, in this car, as with the 2CV, form and function were united with unsurpassed skill.

Flaminio Bertoni (1903–1964), the stylist of the DS19, photographed in 1950 with his second son, Serge, born in June 1949.

8

The Citroën DS, 1955–1975

As the whole world knows, at the Paris Motor Show on Thursday October 6, 1955, Citroën detonated what was described without exaggeration by the French popular motoring press as a bombshell. Unquestionably, the impact caused by the arrival of the DS19, entirely without warning, rocked the world's motor industry to its very foundations. The seismic shockwaves generated by the first sight of this sensational machine—the long-awaited replacement for the venerable Traction Avant—reverberated around the globe, exciting motoring professionals and amateurs alike. For although the advent of the car itself was not wholly unexpected, its appearance was truly astonishing in its originality and inventiveness. Nothing remotely like it had ever been seen before. Indeed, the technological contrast between this revolutionary vehicle and the conventional family sedans of that era on view at the Grand Palais des Expositions was so overwhelming that it seemed as if a machine from another planet had landed in Paris and parked on the Citroën stand. Yet although it had no traditional radiator grille to bear the famous Double Chevron badge, there was no mistaking that it actually came from the Quai de Javel!

Indeed, Citroën was so confident of the uniqueness and originality of its creation that almost until the end of its lifespan, the D series sedans bore no identifying badge or nameplate whatsoever, except for a small Double Chevron motif on their trunk lids—gold for a DS and silver for an ID model. It was not until 1973 that a plate carrying the maker's name was introduced again on the trunk lid. Ironically, the only brand name that was visible on the Paris show cars was the word Michelin, carefully picked out in black letters on its whitewall tires. From their familiar zig-zag tread pattern, these could be distinguished as Michelin X radials.

As a *coup de publicité,* the debut was a triumph, producing a vast outpouring of press reports and photographs. Citroën later calculated that the coverage devoted to the event around the world had been exceeded in recent times only by the death of Stalin. In France, quite naturally, the journalists gave the car a wildly enthusiastic reception. Paul Frere remarked, "The DS19 gives the impression of having jumped a generation in automobile history," while Jacques Ickx said, "Citroën has introduced, for 1956, the motor car of 1966." Even the British motoring press were impressed. Commenting on the new arrival, the technical editor of *The Motor,* the distinguished British motoring journalist Laurence Pomeroy, described the DS19 as "one of the biggest advances in production car design in the whole history of motoring." John Bolster of *Autosport* said that it was "a startling machine which at once renders half the cars of the world out of date." As things turned out, these predictions were somewhat conservative, for when production ended 20 years later, in 1975, the reputation of the Citroën DS19 as a motoring milestone had been strengthened rather than diluted by the passage of time.

Fifty years later, the boldly ambitious list of fresh ideas and innovations included in its specification still seems amazing. Highly complex beneath the hood and just as advanced behind it, the audacious DS19 was totally original in its conception and execution and bore no direct resemblance or relationship to any other car seen before or since. Never previously had a new car incorporated so many original and sophisticated ideas. Never subsequently has a mass-produced, mass-marketed car achieved so great an advance in safety, comfort and performance in one single step. Almost everything about it was completely new, so much so that it inherited very little from its predecessors in its engineering, construction and componentry.

The scene on the Citroën stand at the Paris Salon on Thursday, October 6, 1955. By the end of the day, more than 12,000 orders had been taken.

Here, of course, Citroën unveiled its unique hydropneumatic self-leveling fully-independent suspension, featuring rising-rate gas springs unaffected by changes in the loading of the car and interconnected by hydraulic fluid to allow constant ride-height and attitude adjustment of the chassis on the move. Coupled with front-wheel-drive transmission incorporating double leading arm suspension and center-point steering geometry, this allowed unerring control, stability and comfort when traveling fast over poor road surfaces. But, the DS19 also provided effortlessly accurate driving control, through fully-powered rack-and-pinion steering plus a semi-automatic gearbox and clutch actuated, as in an aircraft, by the same central high-pressure hydraulic system.

The DS19's ultra-smooth aerodynamic body was equally sophisticated, especially in the way that it was constructed with detachable panels for easier assembly, maintenance and repairs. So too was its high-pressure twin-circuit braking system featuring inboard-mounted front disc brakes operated by a novel *pedalo* or mushroom-pedal brake control device requiring the minimum effort or movement by the foot to operate, to save vital seconds of reaction time in an emergency. With its built-in automatic load-sensing capability, this device apportioned braking effort front and rear in order to provide the road-wheels with the optimum amount of braking effort which the tires could absorb without losing adhesion, thus reducing the possibility of the wheels locking during emergency stops—the first time such a system had been offered on a mass-produced car.

This impression of super-modernity was enhanced by the adventurous duo-tone color schemes in which the car was painted—champagne yellow body work with an aubergine roof, apple-green with white, pinkish rose-grey with turquoise—a sight that electrified French motorists accustomed to the monotony of driving only black or grey cars during the previous ten years of post-war austerity. Twelve thousand orders were taken on the first day of the

One of a series of stunning publicity photographs shot by master photographer Robert Doisneau in 1956, featuring a model wearing the latest New Look fashions by Dior. The DS and ID cars could always be distinguished by their wheel trims, the DS having large dish-type wheel covers as seen here. The roof of the DS also provided a clue, painted to contrast with the body color, unlike that of the ID which until 1969 was always white.

Paris Salon alone, reflecting a surprising willingness on the part of the public to buy an untried and untested product, having blind faith that its manufacturers possessed the ability to deliver the goods as displayed, in full working condition! Certainly, by the end of the show, it was apparent to Citroën that the problem was not any lack of interest in the car but a shortage of manufacturing capacity to satisfy the total of 80,000 orders that by then had been secured.

But if the DS19 caused astonishment throughout the outside world, it created an even greater shock within the Citroën organization itself, where up to that moment most employees had been as much in the dark about the car as were the general motoring public. So opaque and impenetrable was the cloak of secrecy shrouding the project that very few people either at the Quai de Javel or at Clermont-Ferrand (and certainly not among the company's dealer network) had any greater prior knowledge of the nature of the car than the inquisitive journalists of the motoring press. Indeed, it has since been calculated by one of the very few individuals who was actually "in the know" (and who was allowed to examine the car in prototype form six months before its launch) that, by the time the DS19 was revealed to the world at large, a total of fewer than 30 people within the entire company had been permitted to view it, in the metal, and gain an overall view of the way that it worked. Indeed, the obsession with confidentiality on the part of management was so complete that all those working on the development of the prototypes were given information on a "need to know" basis only. Thus, the engine and transmission specialists had no idea of the shape and style of the body into which their machinery was to be fitted; nor did the bodywork people know anything about the mechanical attributes and characteristics of the vehicle. Only Puiseux, Bercot, Lefébvre and their immediate subordinates, it seems, had sight of the overall picture, thanks to the highly compartmentalized organization of the enterprise, so typical of Michelin management methods.

Naturally, this situation led to problems in dealing with the various manufacturers who were contracted to supply the very few items that Citroën (unusually self-sufficient in most respects) was unable to make itself. For example, the glass manufacturer Saint-Gobain was at first given only raw dimensions for the novel panoramic wrap-around windshield; no drawings or other visual information were provided to show them how it fitted into the scheme of things, in case this might reveal the overall shape of the car. When the glass-makers found that they were unable to achieve the right shape from the basic dimensions alone, Citroën was forced to relent and provide a pattern.

The first few cars displayed at the Paris, London and Geneva Motor Shows in the autumn of 1955 were hand-built prototypes assembled in secret at the Bureau d'Etudes, but following this debut a larger batch of approximately 30 pre-production cars was assembled in the Quai de Javel factory proper for demonstration and publicity purposes. By the end of the year, only 69 cars had been completed, for use by members of the Michelin family and certain other privileged private buyers. It was to be January 1956 before series production began in earnest.

The next 500 standard production cars to roll off the assembly line were sold to carefully selected well-established Citroën customers (including members of the French diplomatic corps, in the hope that the DS19 would act as an ambassador for French technological prowess) and were kept under close observation. These first owners were instructed not to leave their vehicles overnight in public places, to show them off to strangers or to open the hood to reveal the workings of the hydraulic system to garage mechanics employed by rival car manufacturers. During the first six months of ownership they received regular fortnightly visits from a factory engineer, who made a full technical report detailing any necessary modifications that might be incorporated in future production. Should anything go wrong — and breakdowns due to hydraulic fluid leaks caused by faulty seals were commonplace — they were given a special hot-line number to call, to summon assistance from a flying squad of trouble-shooters who traveled about the country fixing the cars discreetly. As sales increased, so did the cries for help. At one point, these experts found themselves attempting to respond to more than 200 calls a day.

The normal Citroën distributors and service agents were powerless to assist, of course; no sales training or technical instruction on the car had been provided by the factory prior to the launch. There was no repair and maintenance documentation available whatsoever. Even if rectification was a simple matter, unless a visit from one of the mobile diagnostic specialists could be arranged, the car had to be returned to the Quai de Javel for attention. Launched with insufficient on-road testing and in-service development and without an adequate technical back-up among the dealer network, the DS19 was soon the subject of widespread rumors citing its unreliability. To overcome these negative impressions, a special rectification shop was set up at the Quai de Javel in October 1956 and remained open until April the following year, by which time the bulk of problems had been solved, although it was not until 1960 that the car was judged to be truly reliable in all respects. Clearly, the lengthy teething troubles of the DS19, resulting in a very high level of warranty claims, cost its makers dearly.

Similarly, the car received only minimal advertising and marketing support in its early years. As we have seen, after the war when the company's activities were masterminded by the ascetic Pierre Boulanger, expenditure on publicity was closely curtailed and the output of literature was confined to a few brief explanatory leaflets and instruction booklets. In the parlous economic situation that existed from 1949 to 1955, demand for Citroën's current products, the Traction Avant and the 2CV, exceeded supply to such an extent that there was simply no need to advertise, nor even to produce more than the most basic and rudimentary catalogs and owners handbooks. Word-of-mouth recommendations were enough to keep the order books full for years ahead. When the DS19 sedan arrived, however, the traditional Michelin policy of secrecy and silence was relaxed slightly, and an advertising feature in Paris Match involving the glamorous Italian moviestar Gina Lollobrigida was permitted. A series of brochures produced by the Draeger design and printing firm followed, commissioned by the new in-house advertising department that Pierre Bercot had set-up in 1954, headed by Claude Puech, a 25-year-old tyro who had previously been employed as a sales clerk. "Advertising was something I knew nothing about," Puech later recalled. "But since nobody else did either, I knew enough."

Bercot's advertising department became a kind of Bureau d'Etudes itself, researching, inventing and experimenting with new publicity methods and techniques. For example, it instituted the policy of employing only top-class photographers, designers and printers to illustrate the firm's products, commissioning such illustrious names as Henri Cartier-Bresson and Robert Doisneau to photograph the DS19, thus returning to the traditions established by André Citroën 30 years earlier. When Pierre Bercot took over complete managerial control from Robert Puiseux in 1958, the department and its activities were expanded. To handle literature and media advertising, in 1960 Puech engaged the services of his friend Robert Delpire, who had previously operated mainly as a publisher of photographic and other illustrated books, while occasionally advising Citroën on an ad-hoc basis. Delpire proceeded to set up a dedicated design studio and advertising agency, specifically formed to service the Citroën account under Puech's inspired overall direction.

Above: To counter rumors that the DS19 was experiencing production problems, in January 1956 Citroën photographed this assembly of finished cars in the delivery hall at the Quai de Javel factory to reassure customers that, three months after the launch, assembly was actually under way. Also visible are numerous examples of the Traction Avant, which was still in production there. Around 9800 DS19s were built during that year, as opposed to 25,000 Tractions. *Left:* Another early publicity photograph of the DS19, taken for a catalog published in 1959 and borrowing the imagery of the current *nouvelle vague* French cinema.

The Citroën Deesse has often been described as a simultaneous masterpiece of engineering and aesthetics, as was recognized when it was awarded first prize in the prestigious 1957 Milan Triennale exhibition of industrial architecture and design, the first automobile ever to be thus honored. Bertoni's individual effort was not acknowledged at that time, however, due to the absolute ban on personal publicity which Citroën's Michelin masters imposed on their employees.

Over the next 15 years, the Delpire firm produced a long succession of superb brochures, booklets and catalogs featuring the work of some of the world's greatest commercial artists, typographers and photographers, such as Sarah Moon, André Martin, William Klein and Helmut Newton. The copy for these booklets and brochures was usually written by Jacques Wolgensinger, a young journalist from Alsace-Lorraine who had been appointed as Citroën's director of Public and Press Relations in 1957, by Pierre Bercot, of course. The witty, stylish and intelligent work produced throughout the Delpire years, from 1960 to 1975, is recognized today as marking not merely a great renaissance in Citroën's advertising output, but also a rejuvenation of European automobile publicity as a whole. Similarly, the appointment of Jacques Wolgensinger marked a turning point in the company's relationship with the outside world; previously, under Boulanger's regime, the establishment of a public relations department would have been utterly unthinkable, but thereafter the veil of secrecy that shrouded its activities began to be lifted, inch by inch.

During the course of 1956, which saw the first full 12 months of series production, only 9,868 examples of the DS19 were assembled, alongside the car it was intended to replace, the Traction Avant, of which no less than 39,395 were built. The following year, this rate of output was increased to an overall total of 26,528 D-Series units, including 5,655 of a new and much cheaper sister model, the ID19, which had been announced at the October 1956 Paris Salon. Deliveries of the ID19 began in May 1957, replacing the Traction Avant, which ceased production two months later.

Ultimately, during the 20-odd years that elapsed between January 1956, when the Deesse production line opened at the Quai de Javel, and April 1975, when it closed, no fewer than 133 separate variants or derivatives of the original DS19 design were produced in a continual process of evolution and improvement. Ultimately, this grand total included 13 versions of the standard DS sedan, the performance of which was repeatedly enhanced by the introduction of new engines. No fewer than 10 successive, up-rated power units were eventually fitted to the DS series. To this tally can be added a further 41 Pallas, Prestige and Cabriolet versions, the characteristics of which will be examined later, together with the additional 75 sedans and station wagons belonging to the ID series, examined in the following chapter.

As related in the previous chapter, the DS19 had its origins in the third objective of Pierre-Jules Boulanger's master plan set down in 1937—the intention to replace the Traction Avant with an extremely advanced and sophisticated design, also featuring front-wheel-drive, and code-named the Voiture de Grande Diffusion or Mass-Market Car. Unfortunately, in December 1950, while en route between Paris and Clermont-Ferrand at the wheel of an experimental Traction Avant, P-J. Boulanger met with an accident and was killed outright. His post as President-Directeur-General (CEO) of Citroën passed to Robert Puiseux (Edouard Michelin's son-in-law) who became ruler of both realms of the Michelin empire, based at Clermont-Ferrand. Puiseux (who had succeeded to the position of Michelin supremo on Edouard's death in 1940) placed the day-to-day management of Citroën in the hands of a new managing director, Pierre Bercot, who was located in Paris.

Now that P-J.B. was no longer on the scene, Bercot quickly recognized the opportunities before him. By taking a long-term view and delaying the production of a replacement for the Traction Avant for the time being, Citroën had the chance to create yet another truly advanced and radical vehicle that, once again, would give it a lasting lead over its competitors. Moreover, as a personal friend of General de Gaulle, he was keen to build a car that would enhance the prestige of France as an automobile producer and industrial power, and so he readily agreed to a complete revision and updating of the project. Given the full backing of the Michelin family, no expense was to be spared in making the Traction Avant's replacement the finest, fastest, most comfortable vehicle that had ever been produced by Citroën, using the very latest materials and methods. And not least among the innovations to be incorporated, of course, would be Michelin's own recent invention, the X series steel-belt radial tire, for which the car's suspension and steering arrangements would be specifically designed and engineered.

Without a doubt, the accession of Pierre Bercot in 1950 marked the true moment of conception of the Citroën DS19. A total re-design of the VGD project was initiated, to incorporate hydro-pneumatic suspension technology and an extremely unusual and highly sophisticated front suspension layout, designed to exploit the advantages of the new X tire, which had been launched at the October 1949 Paris Motor Show. Clearly, the grand idea—though never explicitly stated—was that the new car should act as a demonstration vehicle to show off the virtues of the Michelin X tire to the outside world.

Given the unusual circumstances and objectives of its genesis, it is hardly surprising that in both its underlying structural conception and the methods followed in its production and assembly, the Citroën DS19 and its sister-vehicles were quite unlike any other mass-produced automobile ever manufactured, and it is worth looking at these various engineering abnormalities in detail.

Bodywork

In order to reduce tooling costs to a minimum, André Lefèbvre rejected the monocoque method of con-

In October 1962, the DS19 was given a new nose, designed to improve the aerodynamics and underhood air-flow of the car. The result was a 7 percent increase in top speed. Besides its redesigned underskirt with larger air-intakes to the radiator and disc-brakes, the new front end also featured an entirely different bumper with projecting triangular rubber over-riders.

struction as used in the Traction Avant and chose instead to employ many of the constructional principles that he had used so successfully on the 2CV. But whereas the infrastructure of the 2CV was no more than a simple, lightweight platform-chassis to which the mechanical elements and superstructure were secured, the structure of the DS19 involved a complex welded caisson which, when joined to the superstructure to form the body-shell proper, represented a fully integral load-bearing body-shell of enormous strength and rigidity. The principal structural units of this caisson, the front and rear sub-assemblies, were joined together by a pair of side-members running fore and aft, to form a punt-like structure to which were attached the floor-panels and also the pillars and cant rail that supported the roof.

The DS19's ultra-aerodynamic exterior bodywork was equally unusual, comprising fully detachable panels fastened to the superstructure by bolts instead of the conventional welded joints, for easier assembly, maintenance and repairs. Similar in conception to that of the 2CV, it had no structural function; the roof, doors, fenders and other panels were unstressed and served only to protect the car's occupants, cargo and mechanical parts. The doors and fenders were made of steel, but the roof panel — which contributed nothing to the structural integrity of the car — was normally produced from glass-resin reinforced polyester. The hood was made of aluminum, being the largest aluminum panel ever employed on a motor car. Initially, the trunk lid was also made from aluminum, but from August 1960 on, a steel version was fitted.

To show off this improvement on its stand at the Paris motor show, Citroën simply revised the sculptural model of the DS19 displayed five years earlier at the 1957 Milan Triennale exhibition.

The doors had no surrounding frame to hold the window glass in place; wind and water tightness was achieved simply by the pressure of the closed doors against rubber seals. Nor were they hinged in the normal way but pivoted on set-screws, attached vertically to the pillars, so that they could easily be adjusted to obtain the correct panel shut-lines. Similarly, the wrap-round glass windshield and rear window were held in place by a combination of rubber seals and screw fasteners and thus were also easily detachable. The use of these novel frameless windows, together with the lightweight roof panel, made it possible to achieve a big reduction in the size of the pillars, so that the total glazed surface area of the DS19 was more than 2.23 square meters, or 24 square feet, some 25 percent greater than that of its predecessor, the Traction Avant, providing remarkable all-round visibility and a sense of spaciousness never previously achieved in a mass-produced European car.

The Citroën DS19 was the very first car to dispense with the traditional radiator grille, a feature which had long been considered an essential part of automobile design, if only as a means of identifying the origin of a vehicle. As the hood was completely unpierced above the bumper line, the radiator received a flow of cooling air which entered the engine bay through a large aperture in the underskirt and openings in the bumper. Problems with over-heating (of the hydraulic pump rather than the engine) led to a re-think of this arrangement and to en-

Top: This publicity picture, shot in the shadow of the Eiffel Tower in Paris late in 1962, shows the air-scoops under the headlights which were added as part of the modifications introduced for the 1962-1963 season, to improve cabin ventilation. ***Bottom:*** The design of the new front end can be clearly seen from this action shot of the DS21M, which won the 1966 Monte Carlo Rally. A manual transmission version, the DS19M, had been introduced in 1963, and was preferred to the semi-automatic type by Citroën's competition team.

Above, top: The strikingly innovative dashboard of the early DS19, designed by Flaminio Bertoni. Made from injection-molded plastic, a revolutionary technique at that time, it had a lasting effect on the subsequent development of car interior design. Indeed, its influence can still be seen in the new cars of today. The single-spoke steering-wheel remained a Citroën trademark throughout the life of the DS and its successor, the CX. ***Above, bottom:*** In September 1961, a revised version of Bertoni's dashboard, designed under the supervision of the maestro himself, was introduced on the DS19. This had a two-tone finish with a black upper part and an off-white dashboard and instrument panel below.

Top and above: The structural concept of the D series sedans is exposed by these cutaway demonstration cars produced for exhibition and instruction purposes. The top vehicle is a 1967 DS21 while the bottom car is a later 1972 DS21. The massive side and cross members of the DS's punt-type caisson are clearly visible. The large vacant space in the nose in front of the radiator (removed in both vehicles) was used for stowing the spare wheel.

éditechnic

8
5
8
1
7
8
2
6
3
7
9
4
7
8

Left: In September 1968 this third design of dashboard appeared on the DS21, modified by a change to an all-black finish and the introduction of a combined ignition key and anti-theft steering lock located under the steering wheel. ***Right:*** The ultimate evolution of the D series dashboard occurred in September 1969, when this fourth design with a uniform charcoal grey finish was introduced across the board, on both DS and ID models. In fact, this is the version seen two years later when a foam-padded steering wheel was added.

Right: In November and December 1968, the reputation of the Deesse was hugely enhanced worldwide, thanks to its performance in the Daily Express London-Sydney Marathon, at that time the longest and toughest rally ever staged. Covering 10,000 miles across Europe, the Middle East, India and Australia, and passing through 12 countries, it involved 11 days of flat-out, non-stop driving, most of it in appalling weather and over abysmal dirt roads. This is the DS21 entered by the Automobile Club de France and driven by Vanson and Turcat.

Opposite top: The general arrangement of engine, gearbox and suspension of the DS can be seen in this cutaway drawing of a DS21. Note the inboard front disc brakes and the unusual twin leading arm half axles, which provided fully independent double wishbone suspension geometry. ***Bottom:*** This schematic diagram illustrates the principal functions and components of the hydraulic circuitry that actuated the suspension, braking, steering and gear-selection systems of the DS19 and later Citroën DS or ID models. A pump (1) driven by the engine camshaft through a belt and pulley-wheel arrangement, supplied fluid drawn from the reservoir (2) under high pressure to (3) the pressure regulator and its associated accumulator (4). This unit took the form of a gas-filled sphere attached to a cylinder, and operated in a similar way to the four oleomatic suspension units which acted as the car's springs (8). Fluid from the pump circulated constantly when the engine was turning, and was fed back to the reservoir if not required to maintain pressure in the suspension, braking, steering and other independent circuits, as directed by the distributor block (5). The pressure in the pressurized circuits was governed and maintained by the regulator at 2400 psi, in such a way that if pressure fell below 2000 psi, a supply of fluid from the pump was admitted, causing the pump to go under load to build up the pressure again. At other times the pump turned in an idling mode with its output bypassing the accumulator and returning to the reservoir. The amount of fluid admitted to, or vented from, the four suspension cylinders (6) was controlled by two height-corrector devices (7) located on the front and rear suspension arm housings, and reacting to the movements of the anti-roll bars (9) so as to maintain the self-levelling function of the independent spring units (8).

Left: This is one of the two rally-entered DS21s. Driven by Bianchi and Ogier, it took the lead half-way across the Australian outback. But, sadly, a mere 100 miles from Sydney, just one hour short of the finish line, and three-quarters of an hour ahead of the nearest following car, disaster struck when it collided head-on with a spectator's car which had strayed into its path, on a stretch of road that was supposedly closed and entirely free of oncoming traffic. The Citroën was wrecked, together with its driver's hopes of certain victory.

Left: The elegant profile of the DS21 of 1967-1968 showing the new cats-eye headlights. How can you tell that it is a DS rather than an ID model? Apart from the telltale presence of the gear-shift lever projecting upwards from behind the steering wheel, the clues are the large dish-type wheel covers, the stainless steel (or, later, alloy) sill covers under the doors and the dark-colored roof.

Throughout the 1960s and 1970s, the Citroën D-series cars made a major contribution to the Parisian taxi fleet, a testament to their inherent reliability and durability. Normally, the cheaper and more economical ID19 and later ID20 and D-Super variants were used but, on the evidence of its wheel-trims, this car belongs to the more expensive DS21 type.

The styling evolution of the D-Series cars reached its third and final stage in September 1967, when a new front-end with a revised design of bumper appeared. But the most striking feature of this facelift was the introduction of twin headlights, faired in behind glass covers. On the DS21 the outer, fixed, pair of lamps were self-levelling and moved vertically up and down according to changes in the attitude of the vehicle itself, while the inner pair of long-range lamps swivelled horizontally, their beams scanning to left or right in sync with movements of the steering wheel.

On April 24, 1975, the last DS sedan, a DS23 Pallas Injection Electronique, rolled off the assembly line at the Aulnay-sous-Bois plant, bringing to an end 20 years of continuous Deesse production chez Citroën. Actually, all was not quite over, as assembly of the DS Break continued elsewhere until the end of the year.

sure a better airflow, in September 1959, two polished aluminum (stainless steel from May 1961) exit grilles, resembling ashtrays and known as *cendriers,* were incorporated in the front fenders.

Yet another of the boldly original styling features of the DS19 were the unique rear turn signal housings, designed by Flaminio Bertoni. These were positioned at eye-level on the roof of the car, just above the rear quarter panel, where their signals could not be confused with the other lamps mounted below in the conventional position, on the rear bumper. The directional signals were housed in two flared conical tubes, made either from plastic or metal, resembling elongated ice-cream cornets, joined to a strip of stainless-steel trim that ran right along the guttering of the roof, linking the polished aluminum trunk hinges to the front windshield surround, in an unbroken band of brightwork.

On the DS19 prototypes and most cars built before September 1959, the trumpets took the form of long translucent red plastic moldings extending along the length of the quarter panel and slightly beyond, and which lit up along their entire length. These trumpets were teamed with C pillar trim panels made from either anodized aluminum, fluted with narrow corrugations, or plain steel plates painted in the body color of the car. However, a chrome-plated alternative was sometimes fitted, but generally only on the all-black Modele Administration cars used by the French government. These extra-long chromed indicator housings, which Bertoni called the "Trompettes de Jericho," ran almost the entire length of the car from the windshield back, and were always combined with plain black-painted C pillar trim panels. Later, from February 1958 on, these long chromed trumpets were replaced by shorter housings made from polished stainless steel and which extended no further than across the C pillar panels, henceforth also made from fluted aluminum. This treatment was soon standardized across the DS range, replacing the red plastic trumpets entirely, except on the all-black Prestige and Modele Administration cars, which continued to feature plain black C pillar trims, until superseded by the Pallas version in 1965, which adopted plain uncorrugated trims, made from anodized alloy.

From the outset in 1956, the ID sedans were fitted with black plastic trumpets teamed with plain painted C

This publicity photograph dates from 1960-1961 when stainless-steel turn signal housings became standard on all DS19 models. The model draws our attention to the "ash-tray"grilles inserted in the fenders that year, not as air intakes for the interior ventilation system but as vents intended to improve under-hood airflow and cool the hydraulic components. High engine compartment temperatures were causing the fluid in the hydraulic system to overheat in certain circumstances.

pillar trims, though in 1959 the trims were changed to the alloy type. In 1968, however, the plastic trumpets were replaced by the stainless-steel type on the new D-Super model and also the export version of the D-Special. However, the French home-market version of this base-level variant retained plastic trumpets to the end of production.

Great attention had been paid to the airflow under the car from the start, in the interest not only of fuel economy but also better handling and road holding. The floorpan of the DS19 was smooth and flat, with only the minimum of projections and cavities. Even the engine bay was shielded by an undertray, while the forward areas of the front wheel arches were enclosed by gusset panels. In September 1962, however, a completely new front end was introduced, involving an improved design of underskirt, bumper, hood and front fenders. Referred to in France as *le nouveau carenage* (new bow or prow) this incorporated revised and enlarged air openings and ducts in the underskirt for the cooling of engine and disc-brakes and also new slots in the fenders, located under the headlight units, to collect fresh air for the heating and ventilation system. The much improved aerodynamic efficiency of this new front end increased the car's top speed by 7 percent, from 150 kph to 160 kph.

The drag coefficent of the DS in its ultimate form was 0.37, as established by *Autocar* magazine in 1973 when testing a DS23 in the MIRA wind tunnel. This version, of course, featured the second and final face-lift to the front end, introduced across the D Series in September 1967 with revised bumpers and streamlined faired-in fenders incorporating twin headlights mounted behind glass panels. The two innermost long-range driving lamps were not fixed, but pivoted through a linkage to the steering so that they could swivel to follow curves in the road.

Interior

If the revolutionary exterior of the DS19 caused a sensation at the Paris Salon, then the very first glimpse of its futuristic interior must have seemed no less amazing.

Crammed with original and inventive ideas, many of them involving the first commercial use of certain new plastics and other man-made materials, its luxurious appointments came in spectacular contrast to the simplicity and austerity that had long characterized Citroën products such as the 2CV.

Indeed, the spacious seating arrangements of the DS19 marked a great advance in comfort and refinement. Although the intrusion of the engine into the passenger compartment robbed the car of foot-room in the front, the absence of a transmission tunnel or center console allowed the two front seats to be located close together, so that six people could be carried comfortably on short journeys. The front seats were of an unusual design, with high mounted seat squabs and low backs which, thanks to their generous foam-rubber cushioning, gave them the plump, rounded contours of small, well-stuffed armchairs. Adjustable fore and aft, they were also equipped with reclining backs, so that by turning a knob (or, later, pulling a lever) they could be lowered fully and, with further adjustment, be slid backwards to form full-length beds. Initially the seats were covered with a newly available smooth-faced jersey-knit nylon cloth, warm to the touch in winter and cool in summer.

But perhaps the most adventurous and sophisticated aspect of the DS19's interior was the range of striking colors chosen for the cloth upholstery. Royal blue, brick red, jade green and elephant grey were on the color chart in 1956, to complement or contrast with the equally vivid exterior paintwork—apple green, champagne yellow, aubergine and black. The following year metallic grey, turquoise blue and rose grey were added to the selection, which remained unchanged for the rest of the decade. Throughout the greater part of the DS19's lifetime, the footwells, front and rear, were fitted with light grey deep-pile carpeting backed with a thick layer of Dunlopillo foam.

The only significant change to the design of the interior trim and seating was made in September 1968 when the shape of the front seats was altered to give them higher, squarer backs for greater support, while the reclining mechanism was operated by a knurled wheel instead of a lever. However, the design of the dashboard was changed a number of times and went through three distinct stages of evolution. Described as "space-age" when it first appeared in 1955 (scarcely before the space-age had even begun), Bertoni's inspired design for the original dashbord of the DS19 was one of its most widely copied and lastingly influential features—a landmark in industrial design, using materials and manufacturing technologies unproven at the time; injection molding of such a large thermo-plastic (nylon) component had never been achieved before in any industry.

Finished in a standard black and off-white color scheme, this asymmetrically-shaped dashboard incorporated a sloping glove-box lid and, of course, the DS19's unique and justly famous single-spoke steering wheel, sheathed by white vinyl cord. Located immediately behind the wheel was a hooded instrument binnacle housing a speedometer (which had a vertical pointer that moved horizontally) plus a fuel gauge and ammeter, together with ignition, oil pressure and hydraulic pressure warning lights. The gear-selector lever was located on top of a molded steering wheel housing, while heating, ventilating and de-misting air entered through large adjustable louvers located on either side of the dashboard and fishtails at the base of the windshield.

With only small revisions, Bertoni's original design continued more or less untouched for five years, until in September 1961 a new yet very similar style of dashboard, also designed by Bertoni, was introduced. Again featuring a single-spoke steering wheel—but this time bound with black plastic tape—this facia was constructed of vinyl-clad steel pressings with a much reduced plastic content. The lower part was painted off-white while the binnacle hood and upper surface was matt black with a crackle finish. At last, provision for a radio was made, but on the passenger's side, well beyond the driver's reach.

When the manual transmission version of the DS19 arrived eighteen months later, in February 1963, this design of dashboard was adopted for that car also, with modifications to the hand and foot controls as appropriate. The cable and rod operated, column-type gear-change lever (similar to that fitted to the ID19) was positioned on the right hand side of the steering-wheel housing (on LHD cars). These arrangements continued on both semi-automatic and manual versions of the DS19 and DS21 until September 1968 when the entire dashboard ensemble, including the steering column, was colored entirely black on both types of car.

The third and final stage in the evolution of the DS's dashboard occurred in September 1969, when a completely new, universal pattern of facia with revised controls and instrumentation was introduced on all D Series models of every type. Flat and rectangular in aspect and made entirely from steel pressings sprayed with a charcoal-grey vinyl coating, this was topped by a protective, protruding over-shelf of soft grey-black vinyl-coated foam. Its predominant feature was the three large, circular dials located in a rectangular panel behind the steering wheel, comprising a comprehensive warning display with a large red hydraulic pressure warning light (signaling an imperative stop), a conventional revolving speedometer and a tachometer, plus the normal minor instruments and switches. As before, the main lighting, windshield wiper and turn signal controls were stalk switches mounted in the steering-wheel housing. The turn signals continued to be of the non–self-canceling type, as in all Citroëns of that era. In September 1971, the steering wheel was clad with safety-foam, while finally, in September 1974, a hazard warning light was added.

Engines

Throughout its life-span the Citroën DS range was constantly criticized for the perceived inadequacies of its engine, the performance of which was considered by many commentators to be disappointing and old-fashioned. As late as 1952, however, it was still envisaged that the DS19 would be powered by an entirely new engine every bit as advanced and sophisticated as its many other engineering innovations. By then Walter Becchia had produced a series of experimental lightweight, all-alloy, flat-six-cylinder air cooled engines, but due to cooling and other problems none of these boxer motors ever reached the stage at which they could have been adopted for series production. Thus, since there was no other affordable alternative available at the time, in a reluctant change of plan, Citroën was forced to equip the DS19 at its debut with a power-plant closely related to the four-cylinder 11CV 1,911cc engine of the Traction Avant, designed by Maurice Sainturat some 20 years earlier.

As re-engineered by Walter Becchia, this engine retained the basic features and dimensions of the Sainturat unit, such as its cast iron block, three-bearing crankshaft, flat-topped pistons and detachable wet cylinder liners, but included a completely new alloy cross-flow cylinder head which boosted output from 60 to 75 bhp. This head incorporated the feature which had proved such a notable success on Becchia's 2CV engine; hemispherical combustion chambers with inclined valves ranked in V formation and operated via pushrods by a single chain-driven camshaft in the block. The spark plugs were located centrally, reached through long tubes in the rocker cover, which necessitated the use of extension rods to connect them to the ignition leads.

Then in March 1961, the original 1,911cc DS engine was superseded by an improved version [type DA] of the same capacity, equipped with a crankshaft damper. The bore and stroke were unchanged, but various modifications to the valve and porting arrangements and the use of domed pistons (raising the compression ratio from 7.5:1 to 8.5:1) together with a down-draft dual-choke compound Weber 24/32 DDG carburetor, produced an extra 8 bhp. Although criticized as agricultural, just like the Traction Avant engine from which they were derived, these early long-stroke motors were outstandingly robust and durable machines, well capable of running flat out for very long periods without ill effect.

During the 1960s, Citroën continued to experiment with alternative engines for the D Series range, including an all-alloy 1,987cc four-cylinder 16-valve, twin-cam, twin carbureted unit designed by Walter Becchia, producing 145 bhp, enough to achieve a top-speed of 118 mph. Also from Becchia's drawing board came a 3-liter, 90-degree V-8 and an 1,800cc supercharged fuel-injected two-stroke V-4 which produced 120 bhp. But unfortunately there was never enough time or money available to advance these concepts through to the manufacturing and commercialization stage as other projects including the development of the GS range had a priority claim on the limited funds available.

However, from September 1965 on, the D Series received a completely new range of Becchia-designed four-cylinder water-cooled engines. Although they shared numerous features and dimensions with the previous series, this family of engines was actually substantially different, most notably in that they had five-bearing crankshafts and a higher compression ratio (8.5:1). Initially there were three versions; DV [1,985cc, 86 × 85.5 mm bore and stroke], DY [1,985cc, 86 × 85.5 mm] and DX [2,175cc, 90 × 85.5 mm]. The economy DY engine was fitted to the DS19A while the more powerful 2,175cc DX engine was reserved for the DS21, but the DV was used only on ID models.

As fitted to the DS19A sedan, the 1,985cc DY engine produced 90 bhp. But for use on the DS20 in Autumn 1968 it was uprated to 103 bhp as the DY2 and again to 108 bhp in Autumn 1971 as the DY3. The 2,175cc DX unit, employed on the DS21, was also up-rated twice; first in autumn 1968, as the DX2, when output was increased from 109 to 115 bhp through the fitting of larger inlet valves; and second, in autumn 1969, as the DX3, when output was increased again to 139 bhp by the adoption of Bosch electronic fuel injection, on the DS21 IE, capable of 117 mph, and which was the first mass-produced sedan to be equipped with such a system.

Finally, in September 1973 the DX, DX2 and DX3 engines were replaced altogether as power-plants for the DS by a further pair of engines, the DX4 and DX5. In these, the capacity was raised to 2,347cc through an increase in the cylinder bores (93.5 × 85.5 mm). This modification resulted in a power output of 124 bhp in the normally aspirated DX4 version fitted to the DS23 and 141 bhp on DX5 version fitted to the fuel-injected DS23 EFI.

It can thus be claimed that, thanks to these constant improvements, the last of the DS sedans was actually almost twice as powerful as the first; between 1956 and 1973 the claimed top speed was raised from 87 mph (DS19) to 116 mph (DS23 EFI) while fuel consumption remained almost constant at an average 28–30 mpg under all-around motoring conditions.

Transmission

Although sometimes mistaken — even today—for an unusual kind of automatic transmission, the gearbox of the DS19 was in fact entirely orthodox. The one unconventional feature of this ingenious two-pedal semi-automatic system was the way in which the gearbox and clutch were operated by hydraulic servo cylinders which relieved the driver of all manual effort when changing gears, but not of the task of deciding exactly what ratio to select, and when. Constantly modified throughout the first years of production, the system (which was always fitted exclusively to DS type models and never on the ID) underwent a major improvement in September 1960 when a centrifugal regulator was introduced. By governing the disengagement and re-engagement of the clutch at a pre-set engine speed, this allowed the car to stop in gear without stalling when the brakes were applied, or to creep forward at a walking pace when they were released. Thus although equipped with a conventional clutch, the vehicle could be controlled in slow traffic by use of the brakes and throttle alone, as with a true automatic transmission. Although extremely complex and expensive to manufacture and install, the whole arrangement was a most intelligent compromise between the two conventional alternatives.

From February 1963 on, the DS19 was offered with a four-speed all-synchromesh manual gearbox, and later from September 1970 with a five-speed manual box. Also, from December 1971, a fully-automatic Borg Warner transmission was made available, first on the DS21 and subsequently on the DS23, though in each case only as an expensive special option.

Braking system

The first mass-produced car to be so equipped, the DS19 and its successors were fitted with disc brakes for the front wheels (mounted inboard adjacent to the gearbox) but with conventional drum brakes at the rear. Actuated by two independent hydraulic circuits, front and rear, both containing fluid tapped from the vehicle's high-pressure hydraulic system, the system ensured that the braking effort exerted on the vehicle was never limited by the amount of force that could be applied by the driver's foot on the pedal, or indeed, by the travel of the brake pedal itself. In fact, the famous mushroom "pedalo" of the DS19 had little discernable travel at all — about 1 cm instead of the 5 or 6 cm common on conventional systems having a master cylinder!

On all DS models with semi-automatic transmission, the parking brake was applied by a foot pedal in the footwell where the clutch pedal of manual transmission vehicles is normally found. Spring loaded, it was released by a knob located under the dashboard. Alternatively, on the later manual transmission versions of the DS, a hand lever identical to that of the ID was used, mounted under the dashboard.

Clearly, the normal operating pressure of the D-Series hydraulic system — around 170 bars (2,470 psi)— was much too great for progressive and sensitive braking, so a device was provided to step-down this pressure, in the manner of a transformer. This also served to create a balancing back-pressure, giving the driver the essential degree of feel or feedback. Therefore, as in any conventional system; the force applied to the brakes was related directly to the effort applied to the pedal. Yet on the DS19, this was twice that provided by a conventional servo-assisted system — and thanks to the advantages of the mushroom pedal, it could be applied both instantly and effortlessly, allowing the driver to save vital seconds in an emergency.

The braking system of the DS19 was controlled by two brake control valves, located side by side under a panel in the footwell and operated jointly by the mushroom pedal. Each controlled a separate circuit, front or rear, and was fed by pressurized fluid stored in one of two special brake accumulators. In the event of an emergency, both brake circuits were isolated from the suspension and other hydraulic functions by a priority valve which ensured that a sufficient supply of fluid to activate the brakes was always available should a pressure failure occur elsewhere in the system. Pressure switches located at the pedal gear lit a warning lamp on the instrument panel to warn the driver of insufficient brake reserve pressure.

A further mechanical refinement allowed the braking force applied to the wheels to be distributed, front and rear, in direct proportion to the load actually being carried in the vehicle at the time, so as to avoid all possibility of the rear brakes locking up when the car was traveling empty and therefore much heavier in front, as tends to happen with conventional systems. Any significant variation in the load carried at the back of the car caused a change in the pressure within the rear suspension circuit, causing a change in the distribution of effort between the front and back braking circuits, as appropriate.

From May 1961 on, however, all DS19 cars were equipped with a revised and improved braking system of the type that had earlier been introduced on the ID19 Break (but not the ID19 sedans) in September 1959. In this modification, the hydraulic circuit powering the rear brakes was altered, so that the pressure supply was henceforth obtained directly from the rear suspension spheres. At the same time the diameter of the mushroom pedal was enlarged, in response to criticism that the original *pedalo* was far too small and overly sensitive, at least for drivers unaccustomed to the device.

Throughout the 1960s, Citroën continued to introduce numerous improvements and refinements to the hydraulic system of the D series cars. Perhaps the most important of these occurred in September 1966 when the last and most notorious weak point was eliminated. The red synthetic LSH2 hydraulic fluid that had previously been used could absorb water and become acidic at elevated working temperatures, which sometimes led to corrosion of steel components in the hydraulic system, with unfortunate results. From that point on all models were equipped with a completely new hydraulic system that used a green-colored mineral oil, LHM, which could not absorb water. At a stroke, Citroën's self-lubricating hydropneumatic suspension system became totally reliable and virtually maintenance-free.

Suspension & Hydraulic System

Developed specifically for the DS19 and still in use today on Citroën's top-of-the-line models, its unique self-leveling hydro-pneumatic suspension system relied on four rising-rate gas springs, one per wheel. These springs took the form of spherical metal chambers containing a fixed amount of compressible nitrogen gas held under pressure by a flexible diaphragm fastened to the circumference of the sphere. These springs were linked to the vehicle's axle-arms by means of pushrods connected to pistons moving in cylinders filled with hydraulic fluid. Bearing on the axle arms, the pistons and rods acted as rams or jacks to raise or lower the bodywork to maintain the correct ride-height in accordance with the action of height-correcting devices, front and rear, operated by the action of the anti-roll bars. The height-correctors varied the flow of pressurized hydraulic fluid (drawn from a constant supply provided by an engine-driven pump) to the cylinders and spheres. The movements of the road wheels, transmitted through the push-rods and pistons of the suspension cylinders caused the supply of hydraulic fluid to flow in or out of the spheres through damper valves.

Therefore, no matter how heavy the passengers and cargo being carried on board, perfect equilibrium was achieved on the move under all road and load conditions, to ensure a smooth and stable ride at speed, even when traversing the poorly surfaced, pot-holed or cobblestoned French highways of that era. As a bonus, the system also made it possible for the driver to jack up the vehicle to change a wheel, by moving a lever inside the car, linked to the height-corrector devices.

Wheels, Tires and Running Gear

Another unique feature of the DS19 and all other D series cars (also the Citroën Maserati SM) was the design of its front half-axles, which took the form of alloy castings carrying two curved wheel-arms, of equal length and similar shape, made from forged steel and mounted in a leading rather than a trailing position. These wheel-arms were located within their castings by four massive Timken bearings which enabled them to articulate up and down to provide, in effect, parallel double wishbone suspension geometry. To the arms were attached, by ball joints, the swiveling hubs carrying the road wheels and driveshafts. The pivot-points of these swivels were placed exactly in the vertical axis of the wheel, an arrangement which had the effect of keeping them positioned in such a way that an imaginary line drawn downward through them always bisected the front wheels and tires exactly, to pass through the center of the tire contact patch and hit precisely the point where the rubber tread met the road.

This unusual arrangement, known as *le pivot dans l'axe* or centerpoint steering, was a central tenet of André Lefèbvre's design philosophy, also ensuring uninterrupted contact between the tires and the road and conferring a positive self-centering action to the steering. By eliminating bump-steer effects, it prevented impact shocks and other reaction forces caused by irregularities in the road surface from being transmitted back to the steering wheel and from deflecting the car from its intended course. Even in the event of a high speed tire blow-out, the DS19 and its fellow-models could be relied upon to steer straight ahead and remain under the driver's full control during emergency braking.

The adoption of center-point steering was intended to exploit the characteristic vertical and lateral flexibility of the Michelin X radial tires with which the car was fitted. As already noted, the DS19 had been designed specifically to run on these tires, which with their successors, the Michelin XAS series, were mandatory equipment throughout the life of the model. Indeed, it was held that the use of any other type or make of tire could seriously impair the car's handling, road-holding and braking performance.

It also dictated the use of disc brakes mounted inboard adjacent to the gearbox in order that the very large hubs could be located well within the internal diameter of the wheels. It demanded, too, the use of a unique pattern of road-wheel, manufactured specially by Michelin. Deeply dished to provide adequate space for the hubs and swivels, these wheels were attached to the hubs by an unusual quick-release center fixing designed by André Lefèbvre. However, in October 1965 when the design of the original suspension arms, swivel hubs and driveshafts was modified, this unique center-screw mounting arrangement previously used was also discontinued and replaced by a conventional five-stud fixing.

Another peculiarity of the DS19's running gear was that, again in accordance with the theories espoused by Lefébvre, to increase its directional stability, the car had a narrower track at the rear than at the front—1,300 m (4 ft 3 ins) compared to 1,500 m (4 ft 11ins).

Steering System

Although it was fully powered by the car's high-pressure hydraulic fluid supply, the steering system fitted as standard to the DS19 was of the classic rack-and-pinion type. Nevertheless, it operated in a quite different way from the supplementary hydraulic rams fitted in conventional power-assisted steering systems, since no part of the effort exerted on the steering wheel was transmitted directly to the pinion all the while the unit was pressurized. Its action was extremely direct; movement of the road wheels from dead center to full lock took just 1.5 turns of the steering wheel, thanks to a gearing ratio of 12:1.

The steering column operated a rotating distributor device located in the rack-and-pinion housing, which sent fluid under pressure to the appropriate face of a double-acting piston attached to the rack, pushing it forward or back according to the direction in which the wheel was turned, left or right. The resulting steering motion produced by this servo action was transmitted via the track rods and relay arms to the swiveling hubs. At the exact moment that the steering wheel ceased to turn, however, the distributor valve cut off the flow of fluid in and out of the piston cylinder, so that the resulting equilibrium of pressure held the road wheels at the required lock angle without deviation, no matter what cornering forces were encountered. The result was that no shock could be felt at the steering wheel, whether it was caused by the wheel hitting a pot-hole or obstacle, or even by it suffering a puncture. Although there was normally no direct mechanical connection between the steering wheel and the front wheels, the system was designed so that in the event of an hydraulic pressure failure, a mechanical linkage between the steering column and the pinion was engaged, so that the car could be controlled manually in the conventional way.

Evolution

During the 20-odd years that passed between January 1956 and April 1975 when the model was withdrawn from sale, no fewer than 133 separate variants or derivatives of the original DS19 design were produced in a continual process of evolution and improvement. Ultimately, this grand total included 13 versions of the standard DS sedan, the performance of which was repeatedly enhanced by the introduction of new, more powerful engines. To this tally can be added 41 Pallas, Prestige and Cabriolet versions, plus an additional 75 sedans and station wagons belonging to the ID series of cars. Eventually, however, the two distinct branches of the D-Series family gradually grew together, until it was hard to differentiate between them at first sight. Eventually, in September 1971 the ID name was abolished altogether and henceforth all D-Series vehicles were labeled DS. Yet an underlying, basic difference in hydraulic circuitry between the original full DS and the simplified ID systems remained until the end.

Strictly speaking, the Paris-built DS sedan range produced for the French home market between 1956 and 1975 comprised in succession the 1,911cc DS19, the 1985cc DS20, the 2175cc DS21 and the 2347cc DS23. However, as the power output of the DS19 engine was uprated three times, and the DS21 and DS23 engines were available with either normal aspiration by carburetor or electronic fuel injection, there were 11 distinct DS versions. Additionally, the DS19, DS21 and DS23 were both equipped with either hydraulic semi-automatic or manual transmission while the option of a fully automatic gearbox was offered on both the DS21 and DS23, so that when these further transmission alternatives and other improvements are taken into account, the total reaches 18 separate entities. And, to add to this variety, the top-of-the-line option of Pallas luxury-level upholstery and trim was provided on all four successive DS types, while all four models were made not only as sedans but also, in very limited numbers, as limousines, in a version known as the Prestige. The DS19 was also built in a special version called the Modele Administration intended for official French government use.

On September 7, 1969, the millionth Deesse rolled off the line at the Quai de Javel. In France at that time, the D series range now offered no less than 24 different models, the majority in a choice of up to ten different color schemes. The basic line-up comprised four DS21 sedans in either standard or Pallas trim, two DS21 Prestige limousines and

Pierre Bercot shows President de Gaulle around the Citroën stand at the 1962 Paris Salon. Although the two men were close personal friends, the General was unable to penetrate the iron-curtain of secrecy that surrounded Citroën and Michelin affairs. On his visit to Michelin's Clermont Ferrrand tire plant in 1959, he was barred from entering the heart of the factory to view the production machinery.

two DS21 cabriolets, all available with a choice of semi-auto or manual gearboxes with either fuel-injection or normal aspiration; three DS20s (two sedans and a limousine); four ID21 station wagons or familiales also with either hydraulic or manual gearboxes; three ID20 wagons or familiales; and lastly two ID type sedans, the D Super and the D Special. And on top of that there were four commerciales and ambulances!

Finally, after numerous further changes and improvements, by late 1974, largely as a result of the unexpected arrival of the Energy Crisis, this huge Deesse range had been rationalized and reduced to a simple seven car line-up, consisting of five high-performance, luxury specification DS sedans, two medium class ID type sedans, the D Super and D Super 5, and a further ID type economy sedan, the D Special, plus two station wagons, a familiale and an ambulance. Earlier, in 1972 a new 124 bhp 2347cc engined car, the DS23 had replaced the old DS21. Initially at least, this engine was available in either electronic fuel injection or normally aspirated form, coupled to either a five-speed manual, a four-speed semi-automatic, or a fully automatic Borg Warner gear box.

In 1970, production had peaked, with no fewer than 103,633 new Deesses taking to the roads that year. But by the end of 1974, the number had dwindled to a little more than 40,000 units. So with the arrival of the new CX range imminent, from Citroën's new factory at Aulnay-sous-Bois on the northern outskirts of Paris, the Spring of 1975 saw the inevitable shutting-down of the D series production line at the Quai de Javel and the final closure of the great car factory that André Citroën had created on the banks of the Seine, in 1919.

On the 24th of April, the very last car, the 1,330,755th — a DS23 Pallas EFI painted metallic delta blue — was completed and another chapter in Citroën history came to an end. The Deesse had been in production for almost 20 years. At its demise, a small handful of two-liter cars from other manufacturers were just beginning to catch up with the standards of performance, comfort and safety that it had set at the outset in 1955. But none had come anywhere near to over-taking it outright.

The Deesse — Name or Misnomer?

Although a Citroën DS or ID model is universally known as a Deesse (pronounced "dee-ess"), this title (a pun on the French word for Goddess) was never used by Citroën in its official publications.

In Citroën parlance, the term DS refers to vehicles with hydraulic suspension, steering, transmission and braking systems based on the configuration found in the original DS19 of 1955. The term ID refers to the simplified hydraulic system offered on the original ID19 of 1956 which had a conventional manual gearbox. The DS cars were normally equipped with a hydraulically operated semi-automatic transmission although versions fitted with manual transmissions were also available from 1963 on, but by definition, ID cars were never fitted with the hydraulic gearbox at any time. Both DS and ID type cars shared the same oleopneumatic suspension system.

Over the years, this watershed between the two branches of the family — the Citroën D series — gradually disappeared as the ID models were fitted with more and more features originally exclusive to DS cars. From August 1973 on, the ID distinction was dropped altogether and the entire series was referred to by Citroën as the DS series. Strictly speaking, the Paris-built DS sedan range, produced for the French home market continuously between 1956 and 1975, comprised 11 distinct models; but when engine and transmission alternatives or improvements are taken into account, the total reaches 18 separate entities. The power output of the DS19 engine was uprated three times: the DS21 and DS23 engines were available with either normal aspiration by carburetor or electronic fuel injection; the DS19, DS21 and DS23 were both equipped with either hydraulic semi-automatic or manual transmission; while the further option of a fully automatic gearbox was offered on both the DS21 and DS23. And, finally, the additional top-of-the-line option of Pallas luxury-level upholstery and trim was provided on all four DS types, the 1911cc DS19, the 1985cc DS20, the 2175cc DS21 and the 2347cc DS23. In addition, all four models were made not only as sedans (berlines) but also, in limited numbers, as semi-limousines, in a version known as the Prestige. The DS19 was also built in a special version called the Modele Administration, intended for official French government use.

The Michelin X Tire

At exactly 8am on June 4, 1948, a messenger from the Michelin headquarters at Clermont-Ferrand walked into the French Patent Office in the rue de Leningrad, Paris, bearing a fat file of paperwork. The bulky dossier contained a patent application covering the technical principles and manufacturing technology of the steel-belted radial tire, the invention that Michelin's engineers had been perfecting over the past four years, and which was now set to revolutionize not just the tire industry but the entire automobile world at large.

The application was made in the name of Michelin's technical chief, Pierre-Marcel Bourdon, who had taken over the post following Marcel Michelin's death in 1944. Although he was not related to the Michelin family by birth, Bourdon had joined the clan by marrying Edouard Michelin's daughter Simone, thus becoming Robert Puiseux's brother-in-law and François Michelin's uncle. He was also the very same man who had accompanied André Citroën on the French automobile industry's trade mission to the USA in 1931, as the Michelin firm's representative.

In fact, Michelin's research into the steel-belt radial tire could be traced back as far as 1929, when attempts were made to improve the service life of the rubber-shod wheels of the Micheline railcars, by introducing various forms of metal reinforcement. But serious work on the concept had really begun in 1944 when a major investment in a program of fundamental research was approved by Robert Puiseux, who had taken charge of the company on Edouard Michelin's death in 1940.

The true begetter of the radial tire concept, however, was a certain Marius Mignol, who held no qualifications as a scientist or engineer whatsoever. He had originally joined the company as an accounts clerk in its sales department, where his skill in calculating foreign currency conversions with a slide rule had been quickly spotted by Edouard Michelin, who transferred him to the experimental department *tout de suite*, so that his abilities as a mathematician could be put to better use.

Before World War II there were two main technical problems facing tire manufacturers. First, how to overcome the heat generated through hysteresis by tires running under heavy loads, and which is not easily dissipated due to the poor conductivity of rubber, resulting in fatigue and failure. And second, how to prevent the distortions transmitted from the casing to the tread in fast or intensively run tires, and which leads to a loss of adhesion with the road surface. The tire is not only the most crucial part of a car, from the point of view of safety, but it is also perhaps its hardest working load-carrying component, supporting more than 50 times its own weight when moving under the most difficult conditions. All the useful tractive power produced by the car's engine and transmission passes through the small area of tread that forms the contact patch between the vehicle and the road, thus subjecting the tire to permanent stress.

Consequently, in the early 1930s, Michelin engineers had begun to study vehicle dynamics in a systematic, scientific manner, to measure the role of tires in steering, road holding, braking, suspension and ride comfort. Part of this research program had centered on exploring the questions of rolling resistance and directional stability, which entailed a study of how a tire absorbs energy and dissipates the resultant heat. It was already well understood that these heat build-ups and losses occurred separately in both the tread area and the side-wall region; but identifying and quantifying the exact source-points of the heat, and then tracing the flow-paths by which it escaped, proved to be a difficult task. In other words, it was impossible to measure exactly how and where, either in the side-walls or the tread, that the heat was being generated. Not having had the benefit of any formal technical education, Mignol was able to come up with the answer, which a professionally trained tire engineer would doubtless have dismissed as frivolous, facile and naive. "Make a special test tire without side walls," he suggested.

In the early 1930s, Michelin had begun a series of ex-

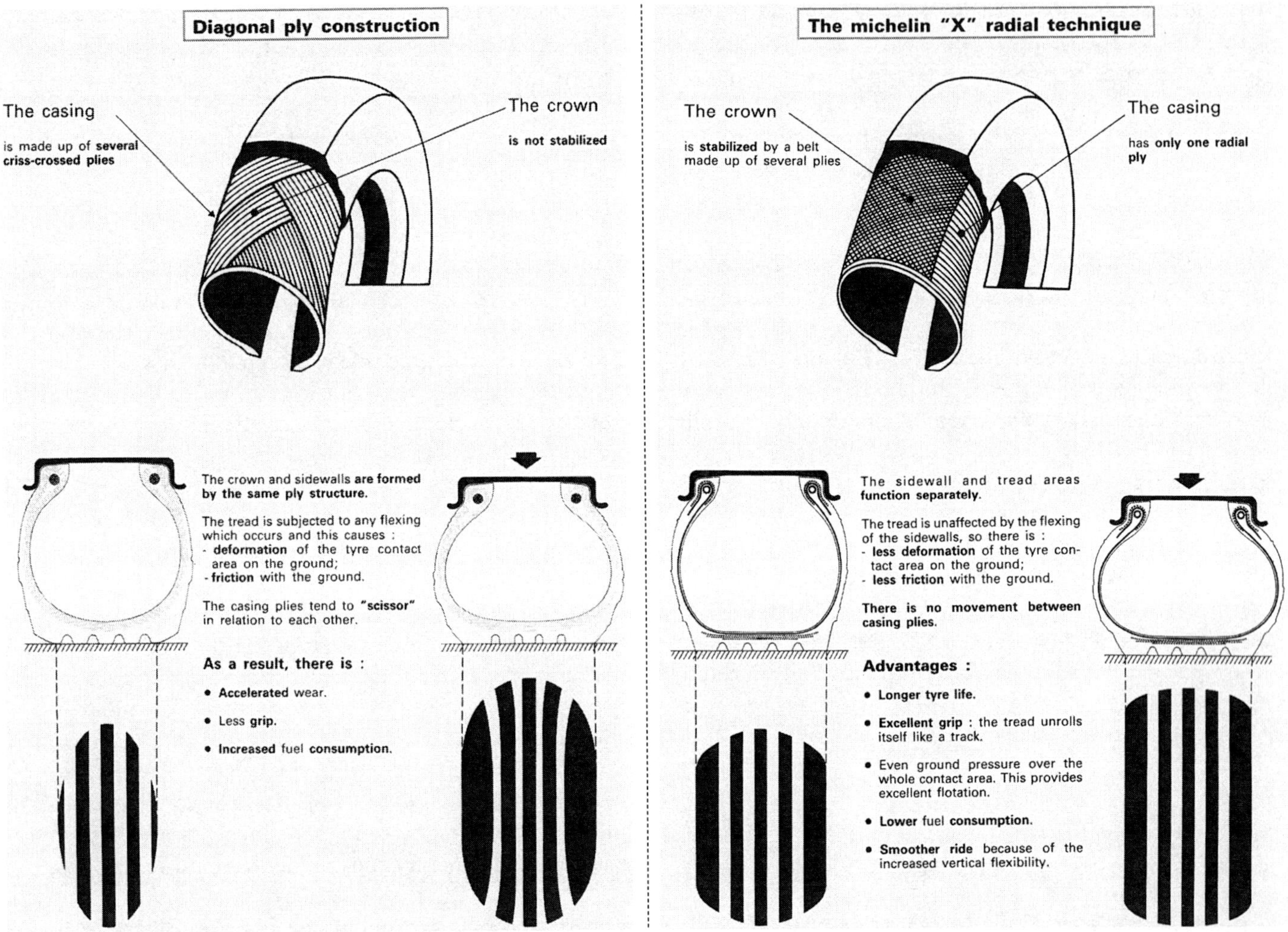

The Michelin X steel-belted radial tire (illustrated in the diagram on the right) was a revolutionary advance in the technology of transportation. The secret of its superior road-holding was that (unlike conventional diagonal or crossply tires, seen on the left) its sidewalls and tread areas functioned separately so that the tread was unaffected by the flexing of the sidewalls. As the wheel revolved, the steel-belt in the crown unrolled like the tracks of a tank, keeping the maximum area of tread in contact with the road, providing excellent grip under all circumstances. The X tire and its successor the XAS were standard, mandatory equipment on the Citroën D series cars as their steering and suspension were specifically designed to exploit the advantages of the parent company's invention.

periments designed to investigate the possibility of substituting the cotton textile cords used in reinforcing plies of truck tires with thin and highly flexible steel wires. As trucks got bigger and heavier, their tires required as many as 22 cord plies to achieve the required strength. Disliking the idea of simply adding more and more fabric, Edouard Michelin had begun to think of using stronger materials, such as finely drawn steel wire, and had eventually solved the extremely difficult problem of making these steel plies adhere to the rubber compound of the tire body, through the use of a powder coating. As a result, the first heavy duty metal-cord tires were tested in 1934 and marketed in 1938, for use on trucks and buses. By this time the company had also acquired the metallurgical know-how to produce the wire itself and to weave it into plies and cords, there being no other source of supply. Experience with these metallic tires showed that two or four steel plies not only did the job of 16 to 20 fabric plies but that the wear resistance of the tread was quadrupled, extending the life-expectancy of the tire from 10,000 to 40,000 miles.

To construct Mignol's sidewall-less test tire (nicknamed the *cage a mouches*, or fly trap, on account of its appearance) the tread area was anchored to the hub by a carcass formed from loops of wire spaced widely apart, running from bead to bead and located radially like the spokes of a wheel. Set at right angles to the crown, corresponding to a cord angle of 90 degrees, the loops were embedded in the thinnest possible sheet of rubber so as to offer minimal internal friction. High-speed running tests established right away that Mignol's tire ran with very low energy consumption and at very cool temperatures, showing that the heat problem lay in the sidewall area rather than in the tread region. Clearly, the explanation was that the heat build-up in a conventional cross-ply tire was produced not by the tread surface as it rolls along the road, but by the friction that occurs when the criss-cross reinforcing plies in the sidewalls rub together as they flex under a load. Lacking the normal cross-wise reinforcing layers of textile plies found in conventional tires, the thin walls and wire hoops of Mignol's experimental tire flexed without friction and exhibited very low rolling-resistance. Unfortunately, without the bracing effect normally provided by the sidewalls, and with the position of the wire hoops corresponding to a 90-degree cord angle—at right angles to the crown—the test tire was completely devoid of directional stability and would not steer satisfactorily.

Again, Mignol came up with the answer. " If the tire lacks stability because there's nothing under the tread, so that it lacks support, maybe we could put something in there, more or less in the direction of the crown line—nothing extra in the sidewalls, just under the tread, like some sort of a belt," he suggested. So to correct this defect, a second-stage test tire was made, incorporating a steel-cord belt plus two steel wire plies laid at the angle that had been found to give the highest directional stability in conventional bias-ply tires—at 20 degrees from the crown line, with one layer to the right and the other to the left. This arrangement proved to be the perfect triangulation required to stabilize the carcass and the tread.

When the experiments were resumed, even greater advantages were revealed. Not only did the new version of Mignol's test tire possess the required directional stability, but it also offered extraordinary cornering power. It ran even cooler than the earlier unbelted version, and the rolling resistance was greatly reduced. Also, as the test mileage mounted up, it was found that tread wear was minimal. Unwittingly, Mignol had stumbled on a novel and entirely superior principle of tire construction—a major advance in automobile engineering. Not only did the light and flexible sidewalls mean that the maximum footprint area was kept in contact with the road under all circumstances—even when the tire was tilted under lateral thrust—giving better grip and hence improved traction, braking and road-holding performance, but the steel belt construction actually extended the life expectancy of the tire.

Next, further research studies were conducted to determine the exact configuration of the new product. The construction method finally adopted involved a girdle laid radially under the tread made up of three plies of woven steel wire, with the layer closest to the tread being wider than the other two; but the steel wire cage supporting the side walls of Mignol's test tire was replaced by a single layer of cotton cord laid at a 90-degree angle to the crown. An 0:80 aspect ratio was chosen and the tire ran at inflation pressures as low as 25 psi. The familiar double zigzag tread pattern adopted was not new, however. Created by Marcel Michelin specifically to improve braking ability in wet conditions, it had made its first appearance on the Pilote Stop tire of 1937.

Limited production of the steel-belted radial began early in 1948, for large-scale field testing by selected customers all over France. At this stage, the product was referred to as the Pilote 165–400 SP or 185–400 SP, according to the size. In June 1949, however, it was renamed the Michelin X and put into volume production. Again, only two sizes were offered, 165–400 and 185–400, tubed of course, for use only on Michelin's own Pilote and certain other wide-rimmed wheels.

Naturally, the first examples went to Citroën for fitting on the Traction Avant, but as optional equipment only. There was no question of the Quai de Javel factory switching over to radials completely at this stage, as Michelin's manufacturing capacity was quite unable to keep up with the widespread demand, despite the premium price being charged. As the X tire could not be made on existing equipment, new machinery had to be introduced at the Michelin factories. And, of course, Michelin still had an enormous investment devoted to the production of the traditional crossply tire. It was not until the end of 1954 that supplies were sufficient for Citroën to be able to fit the Michelin X as standard on the Traction Avant.

In fact, the first car to feature the X tire as standard equipment was the Lancia Aurelia, introduced in May 1950; but by 1952, Alfa Romeo had also standardized the X tire for its 1900 series while Ferrari began to recommend it to its dealers and clients, though continuing to fit Pirelli products as original equipment. Indeed, it can be claimed that it was the Italian motor industry, rather than the French or British, that was first to recognize the advantages of the X tire.

Before long, the Michelin men realized that they had a major success on their hands. Consequently, in 1956, Robert Puiseux made the decision to commit the company to the exclusive production of the steel-belted radial tire only and to abandon bias-ply tires entirely. In 1956 the design of the X tire was simplified; the steel belts in the crown were reduced from three to two and the aspect ratio decreased to 0:78. Similarly, the cotton fabric employed in the casing was replaced by rayon, polyester or nylon. In 1964, the first tubeless version of the X tire made its appearance, on the Citroën 2CV and 3CV models.

During the 15 years between 1956 and 1970, no fewer than 15 new factories dedicated entirely to the Michelin X tire and its successors such—as the XAS, XVS and XZ—were built in France and abroad, an expansion that eventually transformed the Clermont-Ferrand firm into a substantial multinational business that traded in 140 countries worldwide, owned more than 75 centers of production and employed more than 130,000 people. By 1969, the company was making 30 million X tires a year. Today, the radial tire has completely eclipsed the cross-ply for use on private cars and light commercial vehicles, and Michelin products are used in virtually every transportation application involving the wheel—for cars, motorcycles, trucks, buses, tractors, earth-moving machinery and aircraft—even the NASA space shuttle. By any standard, this achievement was a monumental feat of industrial creativity and enterprise.

9

The DS Pallas, 1964–1975

By the early 1960s, the Citroën DS sedan had become an established commercial success, at least in France. Its teething troubles had been largely overcome and it was now attracting an enthusiastic following of both new and repeat purchasers, so that sales and production figures grew steadily year by year. It only remained to introduce a range of further performance and comfort-enhancing improvements that would increase this appeal at the top end of the market and win the car conquest sales from other prestige makes.

So, in response to a widespread demand for an even higher level of luxury and refinement than that provided by the standard DS sedan, in the autumn of 1964 Citroën introduced the DS19 Pallas, launching a top-of-the-line option that remained available to the very end of D Series production, albeit at a substantially increased price — 15,730 FF as opposed to 14,245 FF for the basic DS19 of that year.

Strictly speaking, the DS19 Pallas and its successors were not DS variants in their own right but simply represented an elevated level of trim and equipment. Named in honor of Pallas Athene, the goddess of wisdom and the arts and crafts, to whom the Parthenon in Athens had been dedicated by the ancient Greeks, they differed only in their interior and exterior finish. Their mechanical specification was always identical to that of the corresponding standard cars in the DS sedan range, with no engineering additions or improvements under the hood, except for additional soundproofing measures. Moreover, the Pallas treatment was confined exclusively to the DS19 and its successors, the DS21, DS21-IE, DS20, DS23 and DS23-IE. No ID models, sedans or breaks, were ever produced in Pallas form. And as these DS sedans trimmed to Pallas specification were never classed as specific models in their own right, it is impossible to calculate exactly how many were built, since no individual line of chassis numbers was ever allotted to distinguish them from standard vehicles.

When announcing the Pallas option, Citroën claimed that the new luxury specification provided no fewer than 41 different interior and exterior improvements and embellishments over the current standard DS19, including self-leveling headlights and auxiliary quartz-iodine long-range driving lamps, although these items were subsequently offered as extras on standard models. Thus the Pallas specification provided the ultimate in prestige and comfort short of a hand-trimmed coach-built custom-made car — of the type built by Henri Chapron on the DS chassis— and as such the DS Pallas sedans were ranked in the top echelon of European quality cars of that era. By 1973 the price of the DS23 Pallas had climbed to 27,000 FF compared with the 22,800 FF then being asked for the cheapest DS model then available, the DS20. In the U.K. that year the DS23 Pallas was priced at £2883, not that much less expensive than the BMW 520.

The Pallas version could easily be distinguished from the standard DS sedan by the stainless steel rubbing-strip with ribbed rubber inlay running along the flanks at the crease line of the doors, crossing the rear fender panel to surround the rear reflectors, and by the stainless steel beading fixed to the top and bottom edges of the doors. Again, instead of being corrugated as on the standard DS, the B and C pillar trim panels of the Pallas version were flat and smooth, made from brushed aluminum anodized to resemble stainless steel and carried an identifying motif not present on standard cars. On vehicles built before July 1972, this took the form of the letters DS ranged vertically, but on later cars a badge with the word Pallas set in relief within a rectangle was displayed. The wheel covers were also of a completely different design. Pressed from stainless steel, they had a flat, plate-like profile as opposed to the much more rounded bowl-shaped wheel covers fitted to the standard DS. On cars built before October 1965, the central boss had a decorative aureole shape with a circular band of indentations radiating out around it, but thereafter the central boss was plain and flat in profile. The true Pallas also featured a chromed trunk-lid lock and hinges instead of the normal aluminum, while the windshield wiper arms were also chromed. From October 1974 on, a laminated windshield was also fitted as a standard Pallas feature, as was a driver's seat height adjustment device.

Along the chassis side-rails, beneath the doors, stainless-steel closing panels were fitted instead of the aluminum trims fitted to the standard DS sedans—on ID sedans and breaks such protection was lacking altogether. Inside the doors, the outer sills were covered with detachable stainless steel protection plates etched with a chequered design, rather than the glued-on aluminum-effect vinylized cloth used on standard cars. On Pallas versions built before the introduction of the new front end in September 1967 and therefore fitted with single headlights, another distinguishing mark was the presence of two quartz iodine auxiliary long-range driving lamps mounted on the fenders, inboard of the main headlights. These differed from the normal optional Marchal and Cibie auxiliary lamps then available in that they had larger lenses and therefore were more bulbous in shape.

Inside a Pallas car, with the exception of the dashboard and principal controls, the trim and upholstery were altogether different from that fitted to the standard DS sedan, producing an effect that was considerably more stylish

Top: The most desirable DS? This is the DS19 Pallas, introduced in September 1964. All the exclusive exterior Pallas hallmarks are visible here, including the Marchal long-range lights, the special wheel trims and the rubbing strips along the flanks. Citroën claimed that the Pallas offered no fewer than 41 different improvements over the standard DS21. ***Bottom left:*** A full-frontal view of the DS19 Pallas, showing clearly the revised front bumper with rubber over-riders introduced earlier, in September 1962. The auxiliary long-range lights were a standard Pallas feature, through they were also often fitted as an option on the standard cars. ***Bottom right:*** The DS21 Pallas of September 1967, featuring the new frontal aspect with twin headlights introduced that season. The innermost of each pair of lights were long-range beams that swivelled with the steering.

As the top-of-the-line version of the DS, the Pallas was lavishly equipped and luxuriously trimmed and upholstered. Note the new high-backed seats introduced on all D series cars in September 1968 and also the distinctive padding on the doors, a unique Pallas feature.

and luxurious. First, the entire roof panel and cant-rail assembly, together with three-quarter panels, was lined and trimmed with a high-quality cloth head lining; whereas in the standard version, only the roof panel was covered with cloth, while the floor wells were covered with a high grade, deep-pile moquette carpet backed by a thick layer of foam rubber. Similarly, the engine bulkhead and the visible areas of the longerons or chassis side-members were also trimmed with the same color-matched carpeting instead of being covered by vinylized fabric, as on the standard DS sedans; while stainless steel tread plates, etched with a striated effect, were fitted at the door openings, separated from the carpeting by a further stainless-steel strip. The inner door surfaces were trimmed completely so that no metal showed, using a contrasting quilted leather-cloth material which covered the lower section of the door trim panels as well as the metal top surface above the panel and beneath the glass; this was given merely a painted finish on the standard DS. Below the trim panels was a stainless-steel kickplate, also etched with a striated effect. The door handles and window levers were chromed and, similarly, the recesses beneath the door handles were embellished with brightwork protective plates. Other deluxe interior refinements exclusive to Pallas cars were the limousine style passenger grab-straps, the elaborate interior courtesy lights with decorative glass lenses and the broad grooved aluminum accelerator pedal replacing the narrower steel version fitted on ordinary models. Even the hood release catches under the dashboard were more elaborate, with proper lever-type handles replacing the simple toggle-type cable pullers used on standard cars.

Second, the seats were even more generous in their proportions than those fitted on the standard cars, with exceptionally supportive cushioning; the backs were raised some 65cm higher than normal. Although covered with the same type of plain jersey nylon cloth employed on standard cars, the Pallas seats were upholstered in a more elaborate way, and distinguished by a distinctive pattern of stitching on the wearing surfaces. In later versions this took the form of wide sewn-in ribs or bands running upwards along the central section of the seat squabs and backs and over the roll-cushion tops, ending at the seatback support panels; ultimately, inserts of matching cloth with a contrasting texture were used to fashion these ribs. In fact, in the period between 1964 and 1975, three distinct patterns of cloth upholstery were offered as well as two different types of seat, the first type with the lever-operated reclining mechanism and the second type with the knurled knob introduced in September 1968. Initially, the material used for the central section was plain throughout, but from September 1969 to September 1973, a contrasting striped-effect two-tone cloth was introduced on the wearing surfaces in conjunction with a plain cloth of the same type and color on other areas. Finally, from September 1973 through April 1975, when the last examples of the Pallas were produced, the plain striped cloth was replaced by a similar type of two-tone jersey fabric in which the contrasting stripes took the form of a raised, tufted, waffle-effect design woven into the cloth. Irrespective of the color of the upholstery fabric employed, the embossed vinyl material used for the door trims and seatback rear panel coverings was off-white or light grey.

Third, certain minor controls and fitments were also given the special Pallas styling treatment, including the parking brake release knob, the parking brake foot lever, the heater control knob, the ashtrays and the sun visors. In addition, more often than not, Pallas versions were delivered fitted with many of the various optional extras available, such as head-rests, removable central-armrests between the front seats (the same folding armrests in the backseats were fitted as on standard cars), tinted glass and even air-conditioning.

Fourth, throughout its 10-year lifespan the DS Pallas was also offered trimmed throughout with high-grade leather, as an option available at extra cost. A choice of either black or brown hide was available, irrespective of the color of the exterior paintwork. If leather upholstery was fitted, the doors and seatback panels—and also the valance panel below the dashboard on the passenger's side, normally covered with carpet—were also clad with matching hide. When the overall design and construction of the DS's seats was improved in 1968, as previously described, the shade of brown leather offered was changed from light (*naturel*) to dark (*tabac*).

With one notable exception, there is no difference to be seen in paintwork between Pallas and standard cars, either in the quality of finish or in the choice of colors that were available—the options on the color chart for both body and roof colors and their permissible combinations (always toning, never contrasting) were always the same as those offered for ordinary DS19s, DS21s and DS23s. The single exception was that, when the Pallas was introduced in 1964, a shade of metallic paint became available for the very first time—Palladian Grey or *Gris Palladium*. In due course, a number of metallic paint shades were offered for the entire D series range including ID cars, albeit at extra cost; but even so, this type of paintwork was always a feature identified with the Pallas trim option, since the majority of Pallas owners chose this finish. Consequently, although metallic paint was never confined uniquely to Pallas cars, Palladian Grey always remained exclusive to the Pallas option and thus was unavailable on any other D series model. Black and metallic Mother-of-Pearl Grey (*Gris Nacre*), the replacement for Palladian Grey introduced in September 1968, were also colors strongly associated with the Pallas, particularly when combined with black leather upholstery. By tradition, black-painted Pallas cars were generally (though by no means exclusively) sold with either black leather or steel-grey cloth upholstery. In this refined and restrained form, the discreet refinements of the DS Pallas surely reached the summit of sophistication, epitomizing the very essence of Gallic elegance and chic.

Top: **The DS19 Pallas was superseded by the DS21 Pallas. The paint colors available remained the same as those offered for the rest of the DS range, except for gris palladium (palladian grey), which continued to be reserved exclusively for the Pallas version. The Pallas was, in effect, a prestige, special edition car, though with an identical mechanical specification to the standard DS19, DS21 and DS23 models.** ***Bottom:*** **The ultimate Pallas was this Prestige Pallas, built for French radio and TV personality Philippe Bouvard, who conducted interviews from the back of his car. All the normal Pallas features are visible, plus some non-standard items, including fog lamps located behind plexiglass covers in the underskirt and wheel covers taken from the SM.**

The Pallas Prestige

Not to be confused with the DS Pallas is the DS Prestige, first shown at the Paris Salon in October 1958 and introduced in DS19 form for the 1958–1959 season. This was a true limousine version, fitted with a central partition featuring a glass screen that could be raised or lowered by a handle. A radio telephone was also available as an optional factory fitting, making it the first vehicle so equipped ever to be offered commercially by a motor manufacturer. Normally painted an overall black, including its roof and flat-steel rear quarter panels, the DS19 Prestige had stainless steel turn signal housings. The interior was upholstered with grey cloth and carpeting in the passenger compartment, but with a black leather front bench seat for the chauffeur. To match this color scheme the inside faces of the doors were usually painted grey, with grey cloth trimmings on the door panels. Naturally, the conversion work was carried out by Henri Chapron.

The DS Prestige continued in the catalog until August 1971 when, now in DS21 form, it was replaced by a car known as the DS21 Prestige Pallas. Introduced the previous year, in September 1969, this had an interior fitted out to full Pallas specifications but with the inclusion of a central dividing partition with a retractable glass screen; unlike the Prestige, however, the Pallas Prestige was not a standard model and could be obtained only by special order. Although superseded by a DS23 version in September 1972, the Prestige Pallas remained in the catalog for another two years. Perhaps the most celebrated example of this type was the car owned by Philippe Bouvard, a French television journalist and political commentator who often conducted his ORTF interviews from within the leather-upholstered luxury of its rear compartment.

Aimed at France's leading politicians, diplomats, civil servants, military chiefs, industrialists, bankers and businessmen, the luxurious DS23 Prestige Pallas of the 1970s made an interesting contrast with the much more humble DS19 Modele Administration or Prefecture cars of the 1960s. These were the vehicles that carried government officials in France throughout that decade in their role as the official car of the Republic, under the patronage of President de Gaulle. Countless times, press photographs and newsreels of that era showed impressive convoys of these somber black vehicles parading through the streets of Paris, or assembling in the courtyard of the Elysée Palace on state occasions, their superior technical and aesthetic qualities somehow symbolizing the political and economic renaissance of France, just as *les Michelin* had envisaged when giving the go-ahead for the Deesse more than 10 years earlier.

The Citroën DS and General de Gaulle

Of all the Presidents of France who were known to have been Citroënistes (including the present incumbent, Jacques Chirac) the foremost and most fervent enthusiast was undoubtedly General Charles de Gaulle, who served as the first President of the 5th Republic from 1959 to 1969. His choice of a Citroën DS19 for his personal and official transport saved his life, and also, quite possibly, that of the 5th Republic also. On August 22, 1962, while en route from his residence, the Elysée Palace, to the Villacoublay military airfield on the outskirts of Paris (from where he intended to fly home to his country house at Colombey-les-deuxs-Eglises), he was attacked by terrorists of the outlawed OAS (Organization de l'Armee Secrete) a guerrilla movement dedicated to the continuation of French rule in Algeria, to which de Gaulle had recently promised independence.

In their attempt to assassinate the President, the terrorists set up a road-block at the Petit-Clamart crossroad and opened fire on the General's DS19 with machine guns as it passed, spraying it with more than 140 bullets. Although all the shots missed their target, who was sitting in the back seat, the rear of the car was badly damaged and its off-side rear tire punctured and completely deflated. Even so, by driving on three wheels only, the chauffeur

The interior of Monsieur Bouvard's car, which acted as a mobile studio, divided from the driver's compartment and complete with every comfort that a roving reporter could desire, including a radio telephone.

was able to mount the pavement and avoid the vehicles blocking his path before speeding away to safety at high speed. That de Gaulle's escape was possible was due entirely to the Citroën's self-leveling hydro-pneumatic suspension. No other contemporary make or model of car could have achieved this evading maneuver.

The General had first become a devotee of Citroëns when commanding the Free French Forces in England during the war, having been presented with an RHD version of the 15-Six Traction Avant sedan, built by Citroën Cars Ltd at Slough, for his official use. On becoming the leader of the provisional government of France after the Liberation, he continued to use a 15-Six for his official duties. Later, while out of office from 1946 to 1958, he maintained his interest in the Traction Avant, but purely as a private customer. On his election as President in 1959, however, he appointed Citroën as suppliers of official cars used by the central government and provincial administration of the Republic.

On state occasions he made use of the two ceremonial coach-built versions of the 15-Six H Traction Avant ordered from Chapron and Franay by his predecessor, President Rene Coty, but for his personal use he preferred a succession of DS19 sedans. These cars were normally equipped with full-length sunroofs, which enabled him to stand upright while on the move, to acknowledge the cheers of the crowd.

It was not until the last months of his Presidency that Henri Chapron was commissioned to build de Gaulle a special state limousine, based on the current DS21. This Super DS Presidentielle, painted dark grey with a contrasting silver-grey roof, carrying the license plate 1 PR 75, was presented to him in November 1968 by Pierre Bercot, which suggests that the Michelin firm may have picked up the bill.

Measuring 6.3 meters from stem to stern, this imposing vehicle was 13cm longer than the stretched Lincoln Continental then used by presidents of the United States of America, making it the longest vehicle owned by any head of state in the world at that time, a specific requirement of the commission. Another stipulation laid down by le General was that despite its great length, the car should have a turning circle tight enough to allow it to enter the courtyard of the Elysée Palace from the rue Faubourg du Saint-Honoré and pull up at the steps in a single maneuver, a feat that current U.S. presidential limousines could not achieve. The car was equipped with a

Thanks to its self-levelling hydro-pneumatic suspension, the DS could travel on three wheels in perfect equilibrium. It was this ability that saved President de Gaulle's life in the OAS assassination attempt of October 1961. Demonstrating this uncanny ability became a favorite trick among French stunt drivers, as on this occasion when a car was driven from Le Havre to Paris at an average speed of more than 80 km/h (50 mph) with one wheel missing.

Top: President Charles de Gaulle and his wife were both Citroën enthusiasts. As private motorists, they owned a long succession of Traction Avant and DS cars. On official duties during his presidency, however, de Gaulle regularly used a DS with a folding roof in which he could stand upright to acknowledge the cheers of the crowds. ***Bottom:*** The ceremonial DS21 built for President Charles de Gaulle by Henri Chapron in 1968. By presidential command, its overall length was extended to 6.3 m, to make it even longer than the stretched Lincoln Continental used by American presidents Lyndon Johnson and Richard Nixon.

standard DS21 engine, but the gearbox and cooling system were carefully modified to allow it to travel at walking pace for hours on end, even in very hot weather, so that it was not at risk of suffering a breakdown from overheating while on parade, the ignominious fate experienced by the Franay 15-Six limousine when transporting H.M. the Queen during her state visit to Paris in 1958.

Unfortunately, when building the car, Chapron had failed to consult the General about his preference concerning the division between the passenger's and driver's compartments. Consequently, as the car had air-conditioning, a fixed glass partition with no sliding window was installed. Alas, it seems that de Gaulle particularly enjoyed the chance to converse with his chauffeur, man to man, on these occasions, and had no intention of using the telephone intercom provided. So after enduring only a couple of these silent excursions, he returned to traveling in the Franay-bodied 15-Six H, and the Super DS was never used again. Eventually it was sold to a private collector.

10

The ID Sedans and Breaks, 1957–1975, and the DS and ID Cabriolets, 1961–1971

Although the majority of middle-class motorists in France welcomed the technical advances represented by the DS19, the Deesse concept did not meet with universal approval and acclaim, not even among Citroën enthusiasts. For many loyal customers it came as far too big a step forward from the Traction Avant and certainly much too much of a jump ahead in price, and well-publicized stories about its teething troubles served only to aggravate the doubts and criticisms of these die-hards. So in spite of earlier plans to delete the Traction from the catalog as soon as possible, this venerable but trustworthy old warhorse remained in production at the Quai de Javel throughout 1955 and 1956, alongside its intended replacement. In 1956, approximately 40,000 Tractions were built there, but only about 10,000 DS19s. As we already know, the last example of this obsolete but seemingly immortal design, dating back to 1934, was produced in July 1957.

By then, of course, Citroën had introduced a second branch of the D-series family, the ID19 sedan, as an answer to the many sceptics who had objected to the DS19's complication and expense. Hailed in the press as the poor man's Deesse, this was a much simplified manual transmission alternative, sharing the same basic engine, chassis, bodywork and suspension arrangements, but lacking the DS's fully-powered steering, braking and gear-selection mechanisms as well as most of its elaborate trim and interior refinements. First displayed at the Paris Motor Show in October 1956, the ID19 did not enter production until May 1957. Its name continued the punning theme established by its sister car, the Goddess, the letters ID signifying *Idee* or idea in French. Its price of 925,000 old francs (for the Luxe version) contrasted significantly with the inexpensive 647,000 francs charged for the Traction Avant in its final season, but it was still appreciably cheaper than that of the current DS19, which during the 18 months since its introduction had already escalated to more than a million old francs.

A supremely practical, reliable and economical car that provided an affordable alternative to the luxury and complexity of the DS19, the ID sedan continued in the Citroën D Series range until the end, though later it was marketed under the name of D-Special or D-Super. Ultimately, about 750,000 of the ID sedan type were produced, as opposed to slightly less than 500,000 DS sedans. In 1958, the first full calendar year of assembly in Paris, 28,654 ID19s were built compared to 20,419 DS19s. The following year, however, 43,131 IDs were made as opposed to only 13,853 DSs. By 1964, the split had settled to around 60 percent/40 percent in favor of the cheaper car — 45,218 IDs compared to 31,809 DSs— and this approximate balance continued until the end of production.

Over the years the status of the ID sedan gradually increased in terms of both the quality of its trim and equipment and the sophistication of its mechanical specification. Fully-powered brakes were soon introduced as standard across the ID range, in September 1961; and, ultimately, the fully powered steering system of the DS19 was made optional equipment, from October 1962 onwards, eventually becoming standard equipment on some versions though remaining an option on the remainder. By the 1970s, with engines of equivalent performance being shared between the two branches of the D-Series family, it was often hard to tell the DS and ID versions apart at first glance. However, one fundamental difference or distinction between the two types was permanently observed. No ID sedan was ever fitted with the braking and semi-automatic transmission systems of its sister vehicle and therefore its hydraulic circuitry always followed a simplified layout compared to that of the DS sedan, so that its brake pedal (on left-hand-drive cars) was always of the pendant rather than the mushroom-button type.

During the first seven years of its production, the ID19 range comprised two alternative versions, each with differing specifications, unlike the DS19 which appeared in one version alone, not counting the Pallas option. In fact, this two-tier trim level, Luxe and Confort, continued throughout the ID sedan's career, but with constant improvements and ameliorations in equipment. The first of these versions to be seen, the ID19 Luxe displayed at the 1956 Paris motor show, was powered by the same 1911cc cross-flow engine as was fitted to the DS19, but with modified carburetion and induction, de-tuning it to 66 bhp and reducing its top speed by 10 kph in comparison to the 75 bhp DS19. In both its internal and external trim and its standard equipment, the ID19 Luxe seemed noticeably stark and austere in contrast to the lavish apointments offered on the DS19. The alternative, the ID19 Confort, not shown in 1956 but also available from July 1957 on, was a far more lavish affair, trimmed and equipped to a level almost rivaling that of the DS19. Intended for drivers who preferred the ID's manual steering and gearbox to the unfamiliar controls of the semi-automatic car, but who admired the DS19's creature comforts, the ID19 Confort could even be delivered with Dunlopillo backed carpets plus seats and door panels trimmed just like those of the DS19 for a small supplement in its price, although its engine and mechanical elements were identical to those of the cheaper car.

In truth, from the beginning of 1958 through 1959, a third ID19 variant was produced, albeit in very limited numbers—some 390 in total, of which only one survives today. This was the ID19 Normale, introduced at the 1957 Paris Salon. Priced at 860,000 francs—10 percent cheaper than the basic ID19 Luxe model—this car was obviously intended as a consolation for drivers who had left it too late to buy a Traction Avant. Equipped with the 62 bhp 1911cc 11D engine from the Onze Normale, the ID19 Normale was indeed a base-level budget-priced model, available only in black and with only the most basic equipment provided both inside the cabin and beneath the hood. Its interior was restrained and somber in the extreme, with minimal instrumentation and merely a fixed-back bench-type front seat. The seats were upholstered with a blue plastic material while the door panels, entirely lacking armrests, were covered with plain black plastic. Brightwork was avoided altogether—all the polished aluminum exterior fitments found on the ID19 Luxe and Confort models were here painted black, as were the dashboard and the single-spoke steering wheel. Indeed, the cost-cutting measures even extended to fitting a hood made from sheet steel instead of aluminum and omitting the rubber strips that closed the gaps between the panels.

Another ID19 sedan version produced in low numbers was the ID Voiture de Maitre, an ID equivalent of the DS Prestige. Only 46 were built between June 1959 and June 1961. Based on the ID19 Confort and aimed at small-town dignitaries and businessmen intent on joining the chauffeur-driven classes, this car had a dividing partition with a manually operated glass screen. The bench type driver's seat was covered with a simulated leather fabric while the rear compartment was fitted out with grey jersey nylon cloth.

Apart from being improved by the fitting of two, successively more powerful, 1911cc three-bearing engines in September 1964 and September 1965 respectively, and subsequently a series of 1985cc five-bearing engines from September 1966 onwards, the two-model ID19 sedan range continued unaltered in basic concept for a full 13 years, although minor revisions and improvements in its specifications were incorporated annually, usually in step with the technical improvements made to the DS sedans. However, in October 1968, the range was expanded by the addition of the ID19B (also available in Luxe and Confort form) and the ID20 (Confort only) powered by different versions of the new 1985cc five-bearing engine from the DS, providing 91bhp and 103bhp respectively. Finally, in July 1969, purely for marketing reasons, the ID name was dropped, together with the Luxe/Confort distinction.

In 1959, an ID19 achieved the Deesse's first major competition success when, piloted by the three-man team of Coltelloni, Alexandre and Desrosiers, it won the Monte Carlo Rally. This shot provides a fine view of the original bumper and underskirt arrangements.

In September 1969 the ID19 became known as the D-Special although it kept the 91 bhp version of the 1985 cc engine. Note that the plastic rear turn signal trumpet seen on the earlier ID models cars continued in use on this model, the cheapest of the current D series range. Note also that although this car has the new front end introduced in September 1967, it retains the old style of door handles, which were not changed until September 1971.

Henceforth, all vehicles in the D series range were referred to as being a DS, even those of strictly ID origins. As a result, the ID19B was renamed the D-Special and the ID20 became the D-Super. In October 1971, the output of the 1985cc engine powering the D-Super was raised from 103 bhp to 108 bhp, but that of the D-Special was unchanged.

In July 1972 these two models were joined by another ID type, the D-Super-5, equipped with the 115 bhp 2175cc engine from the discontinued DS21, mated to the five-speed gearbox which had earlier been offered as an option on the D-Super of 1971. This car was capable of over 175 km/h or 110 mph. Thus, in the final months of D Series production, in early 1975, the range included only three cars of ID ancestry.

Essentially, the design and construction of the ID sedan's body shell and exterior panels was identical to that of its DS counterpart. Both were built on the same production line, using the same methods and materials; the ultimate differences between the two types resulted from variations in the engines, hydraulic systems and trim actually fitted to the common bodyshell design. Similarly, the running gear of the ID variants—axle arms, wheels, hubs and driveshafts—were always the same pattern as those employed on its sister vehicle, with improvements made in tandem to those appearing on the DS sedans.

Thus, the ID sedan always shared the same interchangeable panels as the DS sedans; as a rule, there were no differences in design or manufacture since all major and minor revisions made to the bodywork—including the adoption of new frontal aspects in 1962 and 1967—were made concurrently on both types. Even so, there were many minor differences in detail to be observed in the exterior finish of the ID sedans compared to their DS counterparts, not to mention the fact that the ID was offered in a completely different range of colors, though no less adventurous than those seen on the DS cars. These visible varia-

This is a D-Super, built in 1972, which had the new flush-fitting door handles. One of the last of the ID type models, the D-Super was powered by a 108 bhp version of the 1985 cc five-bearing engine. By this point in the evolution of the D series cars, differences between ID and DS models were harder to spot, as stainless steel rear turn signal housings were now fitted to all cars except the D-Special base model, which retained the plastic type—and then only sold on the the French market. But the characteristic small hub caps and white roof remain to indicate the D-Super's ID origins.

Apart from the many interior differences, the ID19 could always be distinguished from the DS19 at a glance by its white roof and its wheel trims. These were simple domed hub caps covering only the center part of the wheel, although the large dished wheel covers of the DS19 were generally fitted on export and U.K. market cars.

tions—including the omission of the DS's characteristic alloy sill covers and large stainless-steel wheel covers—resulted not only for economy, but also due to the need to differentiate the two strains of the D-Series family in the marketplace. By the 1970s, when the ID's status had been upgraded to the point of including most of the non-mechanical features of the standard DS sedan, albeit as optional extras, such minor external differences had been so diminished that they were scarcely noticeable to all but connoisseurs of the marque, especially since a common choice of paint shades was by now available for all D-Series models.

But on the original ID19 of 1957 the visible differences were obvious to all, with a marked absence of decoration and embellishment characterizing the appearance of the cheaper vehicle. Indeed, apart from the stainless steel bumpers, brightwork was almost completely absent. There were no chromed reflector housings on the rear fenders or protective alloy plates under the nose; the strip around the roof joint was the only shiny detail, while the trumpet-shaped rear turn signal housings were formed from plain black plastic rather than red plastic or, later, stainless steel. The headlight bezels were painted as were the plain steel rear quarter panels and the trunk hinges and rear reflectors were located in simple roundels. The door handles were of polished alloy outside and molded plastic inside, while the fiberglass reinforced polyester roof panel was completely unpainted, with its bare, translucent surface left exposed inside and out. Once again, there was no identifying badge or nameplate of any kind on the car, other than the two small chevrons on the trunk lid, silver as opposed to the gold of the DS19. The trunk lid itself was supported by a rod rather than a spring-loaded telescopic piston. Most noticeable of all, the wheels lacked the big dish-type covers of the DS19; their only embellishment was a small chromed disc that was fitted onto the head of the center fixing screw.

Gradually, over the years, this specification grew slightly less Spartan as, little by little, the ID was given more exterior brightwork, such as the chromed headlight bezels, fitted from July 1958 on. At the same time, the rear reflectors were encased in raised chrome mountings, but in 1960 these were sunk into the fenders, together with their chromed surrounds. In September 1958, the tiny wheel covers were replaced by larger, plain discs, although these covered only the central part of the wheel, leaving the outer painted surface exposed. These remained a standard feature or identification mark of all French-market ID models until the end of production. In 1959, the stainless steel roof surround-strip and trumpets from the DS were incorporated, together with polished alloy trunk hinges and fluted aluminum trims for the rear-quarter panels and center pillars. The striations were narrower — 3mm as opposed to 6mm on the DS. The following year, a polished aluminum trunk-lid catch was fitted and, on the Confort version, piston supports for the trunk lid.

Thereafter, the ID sedan was recognized chiefly by its roof. In Autumn 1962 this ceased to be plain translucent polyester and was colored white (by pigmentation of the plastic, not painting) so that throughout the 1960s the roof of an ID sedan was always in direct contrast to its body color and never matched or complemented it, as on the DS sedans, except in the case of white bodywork. From 1971 on, however, a toning roof in certain color combinations was allowed, but not on the D-Special which was restricted to a white top only. With the abandonment of the ID name that same year, the two former ID models, the D-Special and D-Super (and, later, the D-Super-5), were clearly labeled by badges at the rear. Initially these took the form of individual stylized letters affixed to the trunk, then open filigree letter-work affixed

One of the first publicity shots taken of the ID19 in 1957. The unique pattern of road wheel used on the early DS and ID cars is clearly visible, together with the original design of bumper and underskirt. The wheels were mounted on the hubs by a quick-release center fixing rather than with conventional studs.

to a chromed bar, and finally, from September 1972 on, solid alloy plaques with etched-in lettering.

As noted previously, the interiors of both Luxe and Confort versions of the ID sedans were always recognizably different from those of the DS cars, thanks to a contrasting style of furniture and fitments and the use of a wider range of upholstery materials. At first, both versions were sparsely equipped, with plain door trim panels having no armrests; front seats that, although similar to those of the DS in their overall shape, did not recline; and rear seats that had no central armrest. The wearing surfaces of these seats were upholstered in either jersey rhovynil (Confort) or nylon helanca cloth combined with leather-cloth (Luxe). A similar striated vinylized fabric covered the metal seatback support plates, as it was used on the DS. Although the longerons were covered with the same type of plasticized material as employed on the DS, the floor coverings were simple rubber mats on the Luxe and plain, non foam-backed carpet on the Confort. As we have already noted, in both cases the roofs were unlined, the door handles were of a molded nylon and the window winders were made from unchromed zinc alloy, with plastic knobs.

In September 1958, for one year only, the Luxe was equipped with a quite different style of upholstery featuring plastic-covered seats with inserts of a patterned fabric, called Broche, in the wearing surfaces. The same fabric covered the squabs and door panels, which now had small armrests. The following year, the Confort model got fully adjustable reclining seats, Dunlopillo backed carpets and door-cards with built-in armrests just like those of the DS, as standard rather than as an extra as before. The following year, the roof of the Confort was lined with grey cloth at last and a bench-type front seat was offered as an option, but the Luxe version remained unimproved, except for a change to a new type of upholstery fabric with a flocked-effect pattern, called Labyrinthe. In 1962, this fabric (used only on the ID Luxe sedans and wagons) was replaced by Nautilus, which in turn was superseded in 1966 by a hard-wearing vinyl cloth called Similoid Bufflon. For heavy duty use, this fabric was eventually replaced, in 1969, by a new, more comfortable high-grade vinyl fabric known as Targa. This came in two colors, black and tobacco brown, and two grades, one plain and one with a perforated surface, which were combined with the perforated type used on the central sections of the seats, due to its better heat and moisture dissipation qualities, and the plain grade used for the outer surfaces and the back-plates of the front seats as well as the door-trim panels. From Autumn of 1964 on, all ID models were equipped with door-trim panels that had odds-and-ends trays similar to those on the DS sedans, an improvement that further emphasized the gradually declining differences in interior equipment levels between the two types. Even so, the same distinction in armrests remained; Confort versions had the big, generously padded DS type, while Luxe customers had to be content with a smaller armrest-cum-handle made from expanded polystyrene covered with a vinyl skin. When the new, higher backed design of front seat appeared at the end of 1968, this class-distinction all but vanished altogether, for the same type of seats were fitted not only in both the DS and ID sedans, but also in both versions of the ID — Luxe and Confort together. With the exception of Targa, the upholstery material then used throughout the ID range was once again plain jersey nylon velour, with all previous patterned printed or textured fabrics having been discontinued.

When the amalgamation of the D series range took place in July 1969, the old distinction between Luxe and Confort trim levels was finally abolished, at least so far as the sedans were concerned. Thereafter, there was only one standard, Targa upholstered interior, available for the current ID type sedans, the D-Special and D-Super. However, the option of jersey nylon upholstered seats remained available at an additional price on the D-Super and, in the last years of production, on the D-Super-5 and D-Special as well.

To distinguish it from the DS19, the original ID19 of 1957 was equipped from the outset with a completely different pattern of dashboard made from sheet metal rather than injection-molded plastic, once again, designed by Flaminio Bertoni. But although there were a few shared features and design motifs—for example, the aggressive-looking ventilation louvers at the sides and the hooded binnacle that housed the speedometer behind the wheel—the ID's dashboard had little in common with the bold, asymmetric slopes and curves of the DS's molded nylon dashboard. Nor did it attempt to repeat the adventurous use of color. With a black upper surface behind the windshield, black louvers and an off-white center section, lower panel and glove-box lid, this was a much simpler two-tone affair, plain and flat in form. Visual interest was created mainly by a decorative strip of bright metal, horizontally striated, running under the center section and glove box and acting as a backing to a row of minor con-

In 1968 the Gendarmerie Nationale bought a trial batch of three ID cars for evaluation as motorway patrol cars. These were equipped with the 2175 cc engine, but modified by the addition of a Roots type supercharger which boosted power output to 150 bhp and top speed to 200 kph. Later, the Gendarmerie acquired several standard fuel-injected DS21-IE cars for the same purpose.

trols, including the ignition key switch and starter button, the ignition advance and retard control and the turn signal switch. This was actually the same curious clockwork timing device previously used on the Traction Avant. The manual gear-shift lever, straight, chromed and fitted with a white knob at its tip, protruded from the right hand side of a black-painted metal housing, together with the stalk switches operating the lighting, horn and windshield wipers. Although rectangular in shape, the speedometer in the binnacle was of the conventional revolving hand type. A clock was provided beneath it, alongside the fuel gauge, on the Confort model only. The rim of the large-diameter steering wheel was bound with white plastic cord except on the Normale version.

This design was revised in 1960 when a greater and more uniform range of switches was provided on the metallic center strip, to control the various extra items of electrical equipment then added to the specification of the car. The non self-canceling turn signal control, now fully electric, was re-located in the steering column housing. A hydraulic pressure warning light was not included until the following year, however, when power-braking was introduced.

In September 1964 the ID19 dashboard was changed entirely to a pattern more like that of the current DS19, with similar ventilation louvers and an all-black color scheme. Formed mainly from steel pressings sprayed with a textured black vinyl coating, now only the shelf beneath the windshield was plastic. But while the DS19 still retained its curving, asymmetric binnacle, that of the ID19 was abolished altogether and the new rectangular-shaped combined speedometer and instrument panel was set flush into the upper face of the flat dashboard panel with no cowl above or around it, except for an upper lip which ran the length of the windshield. As on the DS, centrally across the center of this panel was a dividing plastic bar in which the warning lights were placed, while the fuel gauge and trip/mileage indicators were located below it. To the right was another panel mounting an electric clock (on the Confort version only) and various minor switches. On the broad, angled lower face, which ran below this panel and the glove box lid, were ranked, from left to right, the ignition key switch and choke, a retractable ashtray and a pre-formed location for the radio. The steering column housing was also similar to that of the manual transmission version of the DS19, having a chromed aperture and finisher, while the chromed, cranked gear-change lever was now also the DS type. In September 1968, this scheme was slightly revised with the provision of a large hydraulic pressure warning light next to the clock. At the same time, a two-tone color scheme was adopted, with dark grey for the upper half and light grey for the lower, including the steering column housing and the column itself. Finally, in September 1969, the ID sedans adopted the new universal dashboard design featuring three round dials, as fitted thereafter on all Citroën Deesse models. Even so, the basic D Special model continued to be supplied without the clock fitted on all the other cars in the series.

With two important exceptions, the hydro-pneumatic suspension system and supporting hydraulic equipment fitted to the ID sedans was identical to that employed on the DS sedans. The same design of spheres, cylinders, height-correctors, main accumulator and reservoir were all present on the cheaper car. Indeed, these components were interchangeable subject to the accumulator and suspension spheres being charged at the correct pressure rating for the particular vehicle in question, and the spheres having the correct dampers. The differences were that, first, as the ID models had no hydraulic steering or gear-selector system, the high-output seven-cylinder pump fitted to the DS was not required. Therefore, the ID was equipped with a simpler single cylinder reciprocating unit, driven by an eccentric on the camshaft and therefore located on the left-hand side of the engine block, immediately behind the fan-belt pulley. And, second, since the ID was not equipped with power braking initially, it had no need for brake accumulators, so these were also omitted from the ID-type system. When power-steering was later offered as an option on the ID sedans, a greater output of hydraulic fluid was called for and thus the belt-driven seven-cylinder unit of the DS was fitted on cars so equipped, exactly as on the DS sedans.

Second, all ID19 models, both sedans and station wagons, were initially available with manual steering only. The rack-and-pinion system was derived from that of the DS but with the gearing ratio increased from 1:15 to 1:20 to compensate for the lack of power operation. Similarly, the diameter of the single-spoke steering wheel was increased to reduce the physical effort required to turn it; it now took four full turns to revolve from lock to lock as opposed to three. From March 1963 on, however, the fully powered steering system of the DS19 became available as an optional extra on the ID series. It remained so until cessation of production, and was never incorporated into the specification of the ID-type models. Even so, due to the ever-increasing performance of these vehicles, its fitment came to be regarded as essential by most private customers, so that relatively few cars left the factory without it in its final years.

Although all ID sedans were fitted with the same brake componentry as their DS counterparts (discs front, drums rear) during the model's lifetime a succession of no less than three quite different hydraulic systems were used to actuate these brakes. The first system, fitted during the first few months of production only, was entirely orthodox, save for the use of the same hydraulic fluid as the suspension system and for having no residual pressure-valve in the conventional master-cylinder employed. Linked to both front and rear circuits, this was operated by a pendant foot pedal in the normal way. Experience soon showed that the lack of power assistance was made worse by the abbreviated length and angle of operation of the pedal, which limited the pressure that could be applied to the cylinder piston by the driver. Moreover, for various technical reasons, this manual arrangement was found to be ill-suited to the efficient operation and adjustment of the front disc brakes, so it was quickly replaced.

In the second system, introduced early in 1958, the same general layout and components were maintained, but with the addition of a valve connected to the vehicle's front suspension, to offer a back-up supply of high-pressure hydraulic fluid in emergency situations. Fitted in an extension to the master cylinder, this valve opened only if the piston exceeded the limit of its normal maximum stroke, thus admitting high pressure fluid to both the front and rear brake circuits to increase the braking effort available. This sequence of events could happen not only during panic braking action, but also if wear on the friction linings had caused excessive clearance or if the supply of fluid in the conventional system was exhausted due to a leak.

Unfortunately, because this supplementary power source rarely came into action under normal motoring conditions, the control valve tended to stick in the open position when pressure on the brake pedal moved it, but was then released. This caused the high-pressure supply to enter the master cylinder and escape through the reservoir, spraying the engine compartment and hood of the car with hydraulic fluid, since the overflow pipe from the brake reservoir to the main hydraulic fluid reservoir was inadequate for the large volume of pressurized fluid attempting to flow through it. As the caster-based fluid used at that time had solvent properties similar to those of paint stripper, the results of such an occurrence were seldom appreciated by either drivers or dealers, even when an accident had been prevented by the extra braking force thus applied!

Therefore in September 1961, a third and final method was announced. Neither a conventional servo nor even another emergency-only device as before, this was a genuine fully powered system that at last made the benefit of high-pressure hydraulic brake operation available to the ID driver, just as it had always been to the DS owner. However, the simplified system used in this case was very different from the load-sensitive system employed on the sister vehicle, since there was no equivalent distributor valve arrangement to balance the braking effort applied fore and aft. Nor was there a means of varying the braking effort applied to the rear brakes in proportion to the load carried by the rear axle, even though the supply of pressure was taken from the rear suspension circuit. In the ID system, two sliding piston valves—one for each separate brake circuit, front and rear—were placed in tandem within a common cylinder, known as a *doseur de freinage*, or brake control valve. This was designed so that when the brake pedal was depressed, the front and rear brakes were not applied simultaneously; instead, the front brakes worked ahead of the rear, the response of which was briefly delayed by an ingenious interaction of the slide valves. Supplied by fluid tapped from the main accumulator (for the front disc brakes) and the rear suspension circuit (for the rear drum brakes) the doseur was actuated by an orthodox pendant foot pedal, rather than a mushroom pedal as on the DS.

To allow progressive and sensitive braking, and to ensure that braking effort was proportional to the effort exerted on the pedal by the driver, the doseur was also designed in such a way that when the required degree of deceleration was achieved and pressure on the foot pedal was sensed to be no longer increasing, the hydraulic backpressure acting on the valves moved them back into a position in which both the back-pressure and supply-pressure were cut off, so that the actuating pressure in the brake circuits was trapped or isolated and could not increase or decrease unless the pedal effort altered. This was the system subsequently used on the Citroën GS and, with a number of later improvements, on all the hydropneumatically sprung Citroëns that followed the Deesse, with the exception of the SM, including the CX, BX, XM and Xantia. The use of the doseur on the ID, together with the absence of a front brake accumulator, called for a greater volume of fluid to be held in reserve in the main accumulator, so its pressure was reduced from 65 to 40 bar to allow more fluid to enter the sphere.

Instead of the foot lever employed on the DS19, for the greater part of the model's lifespan the parking brake of the ID19 and subsequent ID sedans was operated by a quadrant-type hand lever located under the dashboard, to the left of the steering wheel, its handle positioned parallel to the facia. Separate pads were applied on the front discs only, of course. The brake calipers used on the ID were identical to those of the DS sedans and thus were updated from the old to the new type in 1965, in step with modifications made to the DS. In July 1970, however, a foot lever was introduced on LHD cars only, but with a different type of release catch to that on the DS. Instead of being a pull-type knob located under the dashboard, this took the form of a curved, wiry-looking lever mounted on the body to the left of the foot lever.

Apart from the anomaly of the IID power-unit used on the ID Normale, the engines fitted to the ID sedans were of the same basic design, construction and dimensions as those of the DS sedans, except for certain modifications in carburetion, aspiration and ignition, intended to increase fuel economy at the expense of outright performance. Ancillary items such as the radiator, air-cleaner, starter motor and fuel pump—but not the exhaust system—were therefore identical throughout. Initially, the engine fitted to the early ID19 Luxe and Confort of 1956–1964 comprised the bottom half of the DS19 motor, having an identical block with the same three main bearing crankshaft and flat-topped pistons, but topped by an entirely different cylinder head, which had an internal inlet manifold, a single choke Solex 34 PBIC carburetor and a conventional ignition system with a single coil. The camshaft had an additional eccentric to actuate the single-cylinder HP pump. Thus detuned, but with the same 7.5:1 compression ratio, it produced 66 bhp instead of the 75 bhp achieved in its DS19 form. However, from 1961 to 1964, the output of this original power unit was declared as 69 or even 70 bhp in sales catalogs and publicity material published in some markets; but according to the parts books at least, no change in any aspect of design, construction or componentry that would account for such an increase seems to have been made at any point throughout that period.

In August 1964, however, an improved version was introduced, which had the cylinder head with internal inlet manifold and various other features of the current 83 bhp 1911cc DS19 engine, including the Holset crankshaft damper, but retained flat-topped pistons and, of course, a 34 PBIC single-choke Solex carburetor mounted on a modified mounting block with enlarged porting. With its jetting and ignition arrangements also revised, this version produced 75 bhp at 4,500 rpm. One year later, in September 1965, this new engine was replaced by another, further improved 1911cc unit known as the DE, producing 81 bhp thanks to the use of a dual-choke compound Solex 32SDID carburetor and a higher compression ratio of 8:1 (domed pistons were used). Finally, in September 1966, this was superseded by an all-new five-bearing 84 bhp 1985cc unit, known as the DV, the first of the new generation of D series engines to be fitted to the ID.

Thus it can be said that, as a general rule, throughout the 1960s, the ID sedans always received de-tuned versions of the current three- and five-bearing engines fitted successively to the DS sedans, although the non-sedan ID variants such as the ID19 Cabriolet and the ID19 Break, both of which required extra performance, eventually used the DS19 specification engine in unmodified form, the Cabriolet from March 1962 and the Breaks from March 1963. Again, as a general rule, with the exception of the DE engine, single choke Solex carburetors were always employed on all the 1911cc and 1985cc engines used on the ID sedans up to October 1968, as opposed to the dual-choke Weber carburetors fitted to their DS counterparts.

But from that point forwards, starting with the ID20 introduced in October 1968, this trend was reversed. A need for greater power as well as economy led to regular up-ratings of the 1985cc five-bearing engines then being fitted, while the D-Super-5 sedan of 1972–75 was actually equipped with the 2175cc engine from the recently deleted DS21, with its specification unchanged. Again, the D23 Break of 1973–75 used a full DS specification engine.

Only in the matter of exhaust systems was the ID19 sedan ever in advance of its sister car. At first, it had twin circular-section pipes running straight down the car's centerline from the silencer located transversely in the nose and then canted outward to exit under the left-hand side of the rear bumper, on LHD cars. Fabricated initially from aluminum, the pipes were made of steel from May 1960 on. The down-pipe arrangements between the engine and the silencer were the same as the DS19 pattern, except that the ID19 Luxe version lacked a pre-expansion chamber. When the silencer was re-located under the front seat cross-member in September 1962, a single oval-section tailpipe was used, canted to the left at the rear on LHD vehicles, but running straight through to the tail on RHD cars. Upon the arrival of the five-bearing DX and DY DS21 and DS19/20 engines in September 1965, a secondary rear silencer was added, but not in the case of the DV engine of the ID19B, which did not receive this feature until June 1971. This rear silencer was connected to the main silencer by twin intermediate pipes and incorporated twin tailpipes, again angled to the left for LHD cars and running straight for RHD vehicles. The two types were interchangeable, of course!

Except for certain changes in ratios to suit the respective engines employed, the four-speed (and, later, five-speed) manual gearboxes fitted to the ID sedans were similar to, and interchangeable with, those used on the concurrently produced DS sedans with manual transmission, which entered the catalog in February 1963. Initially there was no synchromesh on first gear on the ID box, however; this was provided in September 1962. Three years later, in September 1965, in conjunction with the advent of the new five-bearing engines, the original D series manual and semi-automatic gearboxes were replaced by a completely new and improved design of gearbox on both DS and ID cars, except on the ID sedan equipped with the old 1911cc 81bhp engine, the production of which ceased one year later. Once more, the electrical and lighting arrangements employed on the ID sedans followed the pattern established by the DS sedans. Even the self-leveling and directional headlight systems introduced on the DS21 were ultimately made available on those ID models equipped with power steering, including Breaks, albeit only as optional extras. In the event that the latter was not ordered, on cars equipped with the twin-headlight configuration, the inside long-range lights were set in a fixed position.

Similarly, the tires and road-wheels fitted to ID sedans conformed to the practice followed on the DS sedans; 165 × 400 at the front and 155 × 400 at the rear and spare, with the changes from X to XAS tread patterns and in wheel diameter from 400 mm to 380 mm being made at the same time. However, the final change from 5 J to 5½ J rims was not made until September 1970, two years after the DS sedans. Initially, the center-fixing wheels used in the first years of ID production were painted to match the body color of the car, since without the large wheel covers of the DS, this painted surface was exposed. Pale blue, off-white and grey wheels were all seen on early ID cars, but after the introduction of the larger disc-type wheel trims, only white or grey was used. When the new five-stud fixing hubs came into use, the color scheme, off-white for 5J or grey for 5½ J wheels, again conformed to DS practice.

The Deesse Break

On the Citroën stand at the Paris Motor Show of 1958, held at the Grand Palais d'Exposition in the center of the city, two prototypes of a proposed series of semi-

commercial load-carrying variants of the DS concept were displayed, one an eight-seater Break, or station wagon, and the other a similarly commodious Familiale or family transporter. But that was not all. At the Commercial Motor Show staged at the Porte de Versailles exhibition hall on the outskirts of town, two further variations on this freight-carrying theme were also on view, a Commerciale or six-light commercial traveler's vehicle and an Ambulance.

The ID19 Break (and also the later DS21 and DS23 Breaks) came in four versions, a standard station wagon, a familiale, a commerciale and an ambulance, as seen here.

In the way that they offered a radical solution to the problem of moving light freight or merely the members of a large family plus their holiday luggage, these four vehicles were just as revolutionary as the sedan from which they were derived. The very first vehicles to combine the load capacity of a van with the speed and comfort of a fast sedan, they were destined to exert a similarly powerful design influence throughout the motor industry for many years to come, even anticipating the flexibility and utility of the MPV or people-carrier concept so fashionable today.

Inspired by the large and commodious American station wagons increasingly evident on the roads of Europe at that time, these vehicles employed the underlying structural and engineering principles of the ID sedans to exploit the technical advantages of Citroën's hydropneumatic suspension and braking systems, which offered considerable benefits when applied to a load-carrying, semi-commercial vehicle. Indeed these Break derivatives of the ID19 were specifically planned and designed to be the next logical step in extending the D series range and developing the Deesse concept. The result was a car that, even when loaded up to the roof with eight people and their baggage — a total payload of a massive 640 kilos was permitted — would ride and handle just as safely and securely as if only the driver was present inside. Full or empty, no appreciable difference could be felt at the controls at any speed, an advantage over conventional station wagon made uniquely possible by this self-leveling, rising-rate suspension system. No matter how much stuff was thrown into the back, the ID Break would always stay level with its nose positioned at the right attitude to ensure correct aerodynamic behavior and optimum fuel economy, and with its weight correctly distributed to ensure that its steering and braking performance would also be unimpaired.

Sales of these ID19 Break variants began one year later, in September 1959, when the definitive production versions of all four types — the Break (marketed as the Safari Estate in the U.K.), the Familiale, the Commerciale and the Ambulance — were introduced at the Paris Salon, ready to take their place in the French home-market catalogs for the 1959-1960 model season. Successively uprated and improved in step with the ameliorations made to the ID19 Sedans, this four-strong station wagon range was maintained in France and in leading export territories such as Holland and Germany, from 1959-1960 until 1970-1971, with the Break and Familiale continually offered in both Luxe and Confort versions, but the Commerciale and Ambulance in one trim level only, Luxe and Confort respectively. By the coming of the 1970s the line-up in France included at least 22 different versions, since with all four models there was a choice of either the 1985cc or 2175cc engine and either manual or hydraulic transmission. But from then on, this variety was gradually reduced, with the Commerciale deleted in September 1973. By January 1975, the final Break line-up in the catalog included the Break 20 Confort, the Break 23 Confort, the Familiale 20 Confort and the Ambulance 20. In fact, these four vehicles remained in production beyond the cessation of DS sedan assembly in April 1975. Since the CX

Opposite: The ID19 Break, or station wagon, introduced in September 1959. It was indeed the ideal vehicle for dog lovers.

Top: This is the familiale version of the ID19 Break, which featured two central folding, occasional passenger seats, plus bench seats front and rear, making it a full eight-seater. In contrast to the standard Break, the rear passenger seat was located toward the back and there were no folding seats in the luggage compartment, which was smaller. ***Bottom:*** On this later version, a DS21 Break, the layout of the folding rear occasional seats can be clearly seen, together with the split rear tailgate. The lower section carried two registration plates, so that the vehicle could be driven legitimately with this lower part open when carrying a projecting load, though the upper part had to be closed when on the move.

Break did not appear until September that year, six months after the arrival of the CX sedans, the DS Breaks continued to be made available to fill the gap, with stocks of the Break and Familiale remaining on sale throughout the year and well into 1976 in the case of the Ambulance. Between 1970 and 1975, further, more elaborate, versions of the Ambulance were constructed and marketed by various specialist constructors such as Currus and Petit, both of which produced a variety of elaborately equipped vehicles based on, or converted from, the standard factory-built ID20, ID21 and DS23 Ambulances.

Despite the great difference in appearance between the ID Break and ID sedan variants, the actual changes made to the underlying chassis and mechanical elements were surprisingly few. For although the Break appeared to be a much larger, longer vehicle, its wheelbase (3,125 mm) was identical. Its extra length over the sedan (5,026 mm as opposed to 4,874 mm for vehicles with new-style fronts, 4,995 mm compared with 4,800 mm for old-style fronts) was due entirely to the overhang of its rear door and tailgate unit. But because of the additional steelwork used in its construction, the Break was some 230 kilos heavier than the equivalent sedan, which resulted in an average reduction of 7 percent in its top speed and acceleration through the gears and a 4 percent drop in its overall fuel consumption.

Actually, instead of being assembled by Citroën, all French-built examples of these four variants were constructed by a specialist body-building company, Carrosserie de Levallois. This firm undertook the welding-up of the standard chassis parts as supplied by Citroën together with the construction of both the rear body subassembly that housed the glazed freight compartment and the tailgate unit. In fact, the Break, Familiale, Commerciale and Ambulance were all built using the same caisson or platform chassis infrastructure as the Sedan, modified by the use of thicker sheet metal for the inner face of the chassis side-box members. This provided additional load-bearing strength and allowed for the mounting of an extra jacking-point; unlike the sedan, the Break had two, positioned equidistant from the center point, to prevent undue stressing of the chassis when the car was jacked up with a full load in the rear compartment.

After completing the caisson and fitting the superstructure, the Levallois firm sprayed the resulting bodyshell, inside and out, with a light grey paint, rather than the black used for this purpose on the sedans. The same grey shade, *gris rose*, was also used to paint the tailgate and the roof, so that all the visible parts of the superstructure were the same color, with the exception of the area under the roof-rack where a slightly darker grey, *gris palombe*, was employed. From the 1969 model year on, however, this detail was abolished and light grey was seen throughout. Naturally, the fiberglass roof panel of the sedan was replaced by a large one-piece steel pressing bolted rather than welded to the superstructure. This roof-section featured an integral non-detachable roof-rack formed from aluminum rods, capable of carrying an 80 kg (175 lb) external load. The ribbed rubber sheathing on its leading edge was cleverly designed to eliminate wind noise by spiraling the air-flow so that it spread more cleanly and evenly over the roof.

The split tailgate was also of a novel and ingenious design, having a glazed upper part, held in the open position by a spring-loaded telescopic support, and a lower section which could be left open independently while the vehicle was traveling, so as to carry long, projecting loads. To allow this, it was fitted with two license-plate holders, so that the vehicle's registration number could be equally well displayed in either the open or closed positions. Initially, the rear window was made of a lightweight perspex material, but from early 1963 on, glass was fitted—US market models had glass throughout from the start of imports. Ultimately, in the final years of production the rear window was equipped with an electric heater/demister element but never with a washer/wiper device. Even when these became available and were fitted to most other makes and models of station wagons, they were found to be unnecessary on the Deesse, unlike the CX. The upper part of the rear door hinged from mountings on the cant rail, covered by a polished aluminum trim plate. At the junction between the door and the roof, the rubber door seal was also covered by an alloy trim.

Finally, after the fitting of the interior floor panels as appropriate (fastened by 8mm screws throughout instead of welds), the completed vehicles were returned to the Quai de Javel assembly line for installation of their engines, running gear and suspension and hydraulic systems by the factory, and for the fitting of body panels, seating and trim in the normal way. With the exception of the rear fender units, the body panels—front fenders, hood and doors—were identical to those of the sedan and therefore interchangeable, provided the glass of the rear doors was also changed to suit the difference in the window line between the sedan and the station wagon. The ID Breaks carried no distinguishing exterior trim-work or embellishments except for a decorative alloy strip on the rear fender panel and the rear-door hinge cover previously described.

To equip these vehicles for their routine task of moving far greater loads than were customarily carried by their sedan equivalents, all four variants were fitted with reinforced wheel-arms at the rear, plus larger diameter rear-suspension cylinders (enlarged from 35 to 40 mm) and rear spheres pressurized to 37kg per cm^2 instead of the 26kg employed on the sedans. The dampers fitted in these spheres were also specific to the Breaks. To provide extra stopping power, the rear wheel brake drums, cylinders and shoes were enlarged and the drums equipped with cooling fins. The front discs and calipers were unchanged from those of the current ID sedan, however.

Instead of the simplified twin-circuit braking system employed on the current ID sedans, the ID Break was equipped from the start with a more sophisticated set-up derived from that of the DS sedans, similarly controlled by a load-sensitive brake pressure distribution device and operated by a mushroom *pedalo* rather than a pendant pedal. An innovation incorporated from the outset, however, was a revised hydraulic circuit for the rear brakes. In this version, also introduced as an improvement on the DS sedan in May 1961, the hydraulic fluid supply was obtained not from a separate brake accumulator but directly from the rear suspension spheres so that the pressure available to operate the rear brakes was directly related to the loading of the rear suspension. This modification assisted further in ensuring that the braking effort applied on all four wheels was always related to the distribution of the load on board the vehicle, front and rear, so minimizing the risk of the rear brakes locking up under emergency braking when the load compartment was empty. This system can be distinguished from that of the ID sedans by the presence of a single brake accumulator supplying the front brakes, fitted at the front end of the left-hand chassis extension, as on the DS sedan. From the outset, the Break models were fitted with the seven-piston hydraulic pump from the DS, instead of the single-cylinder reciprocating type normally fitted to ID variants.

To begin with, the steering of the ID Break models was manual only, but from September 1962 on, DS-type power steering was offered as an option. From September 1970 it was fitted as standard throughout the range. All other additions or improvements made to the mechanical or structural specification of the ID Breaks and other derivatives, including changes to dashboards and controls, followed in step with those fitted to the equivalent ID sedans, year by year.

Initially the engines and transmissions fitted to the ID Breaks, Familiales and Commerciales were always of the same specification as those fitted to the equivalent ID sedans in the D-series range, with few modifications made in regard to the different purpose or workload of these vehicles except for a lower final drive ratio. From October 1964 on, however, the driveshafts on the Breaks were fitted with tri-axe inner constant-velocity joints, in advance of their appearance on the sedans.

However, in February 1968 a hybrid type of ID Break was offered for the very first time, on which a hydraulically operated semi-automatic gearbox of the DS type was fitted. Known as the ID19FH or ID21FH according to the engine employed, 1985cc or 2175cc, these cars were generally regarded as overly expensive for a semi-commercial vehicle, and relatively few were sold in France. Most examples of the limited numbers produced were exported, particularly to the United Kingdom where they were popular with well-heeled country gentlemen. For the benefit of these and other affluent motorists, from 1973 to 1975 the *hydraulique* Breaks and Familiales were finally offered in a version fitted with the 2347cc engine from the DS23 sedan coupled to either a five-speed manual or four-speed semi-auto box, to provide a true high-performance sportsman's estate. Unique in its era, the DS23 Break—capable of cruising at more than 100 mph fully loaded and still returning 25 mpg—was the forerunner of the high-speed sporting estate cars widely popular in Europe today. But despite the success of this vehicle, apart from a handful of special-order cars so fitted, the Break series was never offered with fuel injection variants of either the 2175cc or 2347cc engines or with the fully automatic Borg Warner transmission. Nor was it ever available in Pallas trim.

The extremely flexible seating configurations provided by the ID Break series were a great advance in practicality and versatility for the time. By virtue of the way that all the rear seats folded away beneath strong steel decking panels, where they could not be damaged, the interior layout could be quickly and easily adapted to meet changing passenger or load-carrying requirements. Moreover, the compact rear half-axle layout reduced the intrusion of the wheel arches into the body, creating minimal loss of interior space. The Break version itself offered the choice of either a fixed three-seater bench seat (Luxe versions) or two separate reclining seats (Confort versions) in the front and a fixed (Luxe) or folding (Confort) three-seater bench seat at the rear, plus two occasional folding rear seats or *strapontins* located under the floor in the rear luggage compartment. With all but the front seats folded down, the vehicle offered a completely flat and unobstructed load platform 2.11 meters long, providing a vast 2.30 square meters of floor space. The Commerciale was arranged in much the same way, except that there were no occasional seats beneath the rear floor, which was a fixed steel panel.

The accommodation of the Familiale was arranged quite differently, however. This necessitated a revised design of floor pan with a larger central well and with the fuel tank relocated behind, between the wheel arches. The fixed rear seat, carrying two passengers only, was positioned above it, directly between the rear wheels, thus

The ID Break in its final form, fitted with the 124 bhp 2347 cc engine from the DS23 sedan and known as the DS23 Break. Thanks to its self-leveling suspension and fully powered steering and brakes, it was capable of carrying a ¾-ton load at 100 mph plus, for long periods, with absolute stability and security. Note the built-in roof-rack.

leaving a small uncovered load space to the rear. In the intervening space behind the front seats were three forward-facing folding occasional seats, as in a limousine.

Two types of Ambulance were produced. The first, the Ambulance Mixte, was fitted with individual front seats and a folding rear bench seat that split in two parts, either ⅔ to the right or ⅓ to the left, an arrangement that was unheard of elsewhere then but which is universal today. The second, the Ambulance Amenagée, was equipped with a bench-type front seat and a single rear seat located on the right, plus a full-length, full-width removable stretcher-type bed positioned to the left. This configuration provided for a nurse or medical attendant to ride beside a patient. According to customer requirements, occasional folding rear seats were sometimes provided in the rear of both Ambulance versions, just as with ordinary Breaks. The trim offered was always of the ID Confort specification only.

By virtue of its smooth, stable, shock-free ride, the arrival of the ID Ambulance and its successors marked an enormous improvement in the transport of the sick and injured, particularly in the case of patients suffering from spinal injuries. Unlike the commercial van derivatives commonly used for ambulance work at that time, the Deesse concept with its low center of gravity was extremely suitable for medical purposes and easy to adapt by means of raised high-line roofs made from fiberglass which allowed extra headroom inside.

With the exception of the grey finish of the roof and caisson as already discussed, the body panels of the ID Breaks, Familiales and Commerciales were painted the colors currently offered on the equivalent ID sedans. The Ambulances were also available in the full range of ID Break colors, not just in white. As with the ID sedans, two trim levels, Luxe and Confort, were available for the Break and Familiale, but only one each for the Commerciale (Luxe) and Ambulance (Confort). As befitted the vehicle's role and status as a commercial or semi-commercial vehicle, cheaper Break Luxe trim and upholstery options were fashioned from a variety of practical, hard-wearing synthetic materials such as Labyrinthe, Nautilus, Similoid Bufflon and, finally, Targa.

The better-equipped Confort versions boasted nylon helanca cloth as used in the ID Confort sedans, but from September 1967 on, it was replaced by jersey nylon velour. Whenever cloth upholstery was fitted on the Break, a plastic apron-type cover was provided for the rear seat squab, to protect it when in the folded-forward position. The utilitarian Commerciale was fitted out with a light-yellow colored plastic material with an imitation reed pattern not seen on the Break. On all four types, the longerons— and also the inner surfaces of the wheel arches— were covered with the same grey plasticized material used on the sedans; the carpeting was the same as seen on the corresponding trim level of sedan, Luxe or Confort. Confort versions of the Break had a removable carpet to cover the decking plates in the luggage area. By the last year of production, the price and social status of the DS Break had become sufficiently elevated for plastic upholstery to be dispensed with altogether in favor of high-grade fabric seating and trim coverings, identical to those offered on the equivalent DS20 and DS23 sedans. Thus, the Targa option was deleted from the final models offered in 1974-1975.

With one notable exception, the dashboards and instrumentation fitted to the ID Breaks were always identical to those of the ID sedans, with all changes in the evolutionary sequence made simultaneously. The exception, of course, occurred in the case of the ID19FH and ID21FH models equipped with hydraulic gear selection introduced in 1968, for which there was no sedan equivalent. In this case, and also on the subsequent semi-automatic transmission DS23 Breaks, the same steering column housing and gear-selector lever used on current DS sedans was fitted.

Unlike the ID sedans, the ID Break series was fitted with a 12-volt electrical system from the start of production. Apart from this, there was no significant difference between the station wagon and sedan electrical and lighting equipment, with the obvious exception of the tail lights. The round lenses of these side lights, turn signals and stop lights (and on later models reversing lights also) were all mounted on a polished aluminum housing fixed to the detachable rear fender units, instead of on the body of the car itself.

The directional long-range headlights introduced on sedan models in 1967 were also available as an option on the ID Break models, with or without quartz iodine bulbs, just as they were on the ID sedans. The wheels and tires fitted to the ID Break range were always the same pattern as currently used on ID sedans, but of a slightly larger rim width —185 × 400 as opposed to 165 × 400. Unlike the sedans, however, the front, rear and spare-wheel tires were always of identical size. The Breaks were also equipped with the wider 5½ J rims in place of the 5 J type in October 1968, two years before these appeared on the ID sedans in March 1970. The 5 J rims dated from the introduction of the 380 mm five-stud wheels in September 1965, a change that was made simultaneously on all D Series models.

In France, the Breaks were always fitted with ID-type hub caps which covered only the central part of the wheel and the wheel nuts— or, on early cars, the central fixing-point. But export versions sold in the U.K. (as well as the cars made at Slough) were fitted with larger DS dish-type wheel covers.

The DS and ID Cabriolets

The last stage in the evolution of the Citroën D series range was the arrival, early in 1961, of the Decapotable or Cabriolet variant, which was actually related more closely to the Break than the Berline or sedan versions, by reason of its construction. Unveiled at a press launch held one month before the Paris Motor Show in October 1960, this superb two-door convertible or drop-head coupe first became commercially available in February 1961 in DS19 form (initially with semi-automatic transmission but from January 1964 with the option of a manual gearbox) and six months later, in July 1961, in ID19 form (with manual transmission only plus the option of fully powered steering and, later, fully powered brakes as well). To begin with, the 75 bhp and 66 bhp versions of the 1911cc engines were fitted to the DS and ID versions respectively, but from March 1962 the 83 bhp (DA) version was used for both. After September 1965, however, only the 2175cc engine from the DS21 was used on the Decapotable as supplied officially by Citroën.

There had been tentative plans to offer such a car in the range from the outset; from time to time Bertoni produced rough sketches indicating how he thought it might look. By virtue of the DS's strong and rigid platform-type chassis, it was obvious that the problems normally encountered when attempting to create a convertible from a sedan by dispensing with the roof would be avoided in this case. After all, the lightweight, non-stressed fiberglass roof panel of the sedan could be easily removed, allowing the car to be driven topless without problems. But despite this suitability for conversion to ragtop form with the minimum of structural modifications, Citroën had other more pressing priorities in those early days and the Decapotable project had to wait.

As often happens in the motor industry, the idea of exploiting the potential of the DS19 as the basis for a particularly stylish and elegant cabriolet was first developed not inside the Bureau d'Etudes but by an outside specialist *carrossier*, or coach-builder, Henri Chapron. Chapron had learned his craft before the war producing elaborate and expensive bodies for luxury, prestige marques such as Delage, Delahaye and Talbot-Lago. But with the demise of these Grandes Routieres, he had gone on to build special bodies for more humble mass-produced makes, including Citroën. In 1955, for example, he was commissioned to build a ceremonial Decapotable based on the 15-Six Traction Avant for use by President Coty on state occasions.

His first, private, essay on the Citroën DS theme, the Croisette cabriolet, appeared in 1958. In common with Chapron's other and later DS-based exercises, such as the Caddy cabriolet and the Dandy coupe, this design was constructed and sold as an individual business venture and never through the official Citroën sales network. Indeed, initially Citroën refused to co-operate on such freelance Deesse projects by supplying bare chassis and engines to coachbuilders like Chapron. So to produce his Citroën-based designs, Chapron had first to buy a brand new car from a dealer in the normal way and then dismantle it to obtain the parts he required. But then, in response to public demand, Citroën had a change of heart and commissioned the Chapron workshops to build an authorized cabriolet following Bertoni's original proposals, for sale through the Citroën dealer network. Four pre-production models are known to have been constructed by Chapron in 1960, three DS19, and one ID19.

The superb D series decapotable or cabriolet, introduced in October 1960, though production did not begin until the following year. Built under contract by Henri Chapron, it was a standard model available on special order from Citroën dealers throughout the 1960s and early 1970s in both DS (semi-auto or manual) or ID (manual only) form. It was usually referred to as the Usine, or factory cabriolet, to distinguish it from Chapron's own private efforts on the Deesse theme. The bumpers show this to be a post–1962 model.

Known as the Usine or Factory cabriolet (to distinguish it from Chapron's other efforts) the Decapotable was included in the Deesse catalogs from February 1961 onwards, available on a special order basis only rather than from stock. Its price throughout was almost twice that of a standard ID19 sedan. Refreshingly pure, clean, simple and unadorned in its styling compared with Chapron's own rather fussy and over-elaborate work, the Decapotable continued in limited production for 10 seasons, evolving technically with the development of the rest of the DS and ID range. After the first year of production, the engines fitted were as currently offered on the top-of-the-line DS or ID models; initially the 83bhp 1911cc engine, then the 109bhp and 115bhp versions of the 2175cc unit and, finally, the 139 bhp fuel-injected version of the 2175cc engine, with either semi-automatic or manual transmission as specified by the customer.

The chassis used as the basis of the Usine Cabriolet was a hybrid structure specially constructed for Chapron at the Quai de Javel and supplied with its engine and other mechanical elements and controls already installed. It was built using the standard shell of the D series sedan, minus the B pillar and roof supporting structure, but with the side-members of the chassis strengthened and stiffened in the same way as on the ID Break so that, like the Break, the Cabriolet had two jacking points. This was necessary in order to gain sufficient clearance when changing the rear wheel, shrouded as it was by a fixed rear fender panel. Due to its wider dimension at the waist, where the B pillar of the sedan was replaced by a new door post section providing extra space for the hood stowage area along the flanks, the cross-section of the caisson box member of the Cabriolet was also correspondingly thicker. An extension of the outer sill gave a pronounced triangular shape to the surface of the longeron forward of the B

With the introduction of the DS19 Pallas in September 1964, the Decapotable also assumed Pallas status by adopting such features as auxiliary driving lights and Pallas wheel covers. The stainless steel strips along its flanks had been fitted from the start.

The Decapotable in its ultimate post–1967 form, now fitted with the new "cats eyes" front end, and equipped with the 2175 cc DS21 engine. Officially, production ceased in August 1971 when the model was deleted from the catalog, but at least another three models, all private orders, are known to have been constructed by Chapron after that date.

pillar, so that the door recesses were different from those seen on the sedan, although they were clad with stainless steel trims in the same fashion as the Pallas sedans. The exposed steel surfaces of the body shell such as the outer face of the A pillars that on a sedan were black were here painted in the body color.

On this platform, Chapron installed the bodywork, seating, hood and other trim elements hand-crafted in his own workshops situated at Levallois-Perret on the outskirts of Paris, or purchased from various Citroën-approved suppliers. Involving completely different panel-work aft of the hood and front fenders, the Decapotable's body featured a new one-piece rear fender structure in steel, a new fiberglass trunk-lid and two new front doors that were 18 cm longer than the originals. These were produced by "cutting and shutting" two standard steel doors. To increase the stiffness of the body, they were fitted with double door-catches. Similarly, the rear bumper assembly was made from two standard stainless-steel units, so as to exactly resemble that of the sedan. The windshield glass was also identical to that of the sedan, but with the surround modified to accept the fasteners of the folding hood, which was made from black rubber-laminated fabric, unlined with the folding mechanism exposed, and fitted with a large rear window made from a transparent vinyl material. This could be opened with a zipper.

Overall length of the Decapotable was only 2cm longer than the sedan, but its weight in its original DS19 form was no less than 45 kilos heavier — 1,235 kg as opposed to 1,190 kg — a testament to the extra steelwork that went into strengthening the chassis and constructing the custom-built body-work. However, there was no significant difference in performance compared to the corresponding sedans. Fully carpeted throughout — even the chassis side-members were covered with a deep Wilton pile — and normally upholstered with leather only, the interior of the Cabriolet was trimmed to a very high standard, with features subsequently copied on the Pallas sedans when, later, this luxury option was introduced. Equipped with two individual fully reclining seats at the front and a bench-type occasional seat at the rear (narrower than in the sedan, to allow for the space occupied by the folded hood mechanism, but still providing sufficient elbow-room for two adult passengers) it represented the height of Parisian chic. The dashboard layout, controls and other instrumentation and interior equipment were identical to those found on the current equivalent standard DS sedans, except that the steering column was always black, but the interior lighting was provided by a fitting below the dashboard, on the engine bulkhead.

The exterior detailing also bore the unmistakable Chapron touch, featuring a wide chrome or stainless steel strip running down the full length of the car at the crease point of the doors, with a further chrome strip fitted along the bottom edge of the doors, both trims terminating in a splash-plate forward of the rear-wheel arch. Having no rubber insert, this upper strip was quite different from that fitted to the DS Pallas sedans, however. At first, standard DS type wheel ecovers were fitted, no matter if the car was built to DS or ID specification; but after the introduction of the Pallas version of the DS sedan in 1964, Pallas type wheel covers were used throughout. As we have already noted, Pallas-type stainless steel tread plates were fitted inside the doors when the material used became available, as

The spirit of the Swinging Sixties is personified as the model and singer Jane Birkin poses with one of the last examples of the Decapotable. A total of 1,365 Usine Cabriolets were built between February 1961 and August 1971 — 770 of the DS19 type, 112 of the ID19 type and 483 of the DS21 type.

were Pallas type closing plates running along the sills, underneath the doors.

The front headlight and turn signal arrangements were the same as those on the sedans but, curiously, between 1962 and 1965 round tail lights were fitted instead of the normal rectangular ones, except on the last few cars made from 1971 on which had standard rectangular rear lamp clusters of the type fitted on current DS19 Pallas sedans. Obviously, as the famous trumpet-style roof-level turn indicators of the sedans could not be fitted, the Usine Cabriolet was equipped with unique boomerang-shaped rear turn signal lights sited on the upper surface of the trunk panel. Forming the corners at the base of the hood, these were visible from both the side and back of the car. However, as lamps thus positioned were illegal in the USA, the cabriolets exported there had signal lights paired with the rear lights in the bumper.

As listed in the official Citroën sales catalog, a choice of no fewer than 13 colors was offered for the DS and ID cabriolets. With a further selection of 13 shades of upholstery and three of carpeting, this resulted in a permutation of more than 76 possible color combinations. But in fact, such was the nature of the car and its customers that practically any color was possible within the bounds of Parisian taste, subject to the approval of Monsieur and Madame Chapron.

The Usine Cabriolet, then available in DS21 form and powered by either the fuel-injected or normally aspirated 2175cc engine, was finally deleted from the catalog at the end of the 1970-1971 model year, production having fallen to only 40 units in 1970 compared with the 241 sold during the year of highest output, 1963. However, at least three more are known to have been subsequently constructed by Chapron as a result of private commissions received. The last, built on a standard DS23 sedan chassis originally manufactured in October 1974 and therefore fitted with the 2347cc engine, was delivered to its owner, the wife of a well-known English political personality, diarist and car collector, in early 1978, six years after sales of the Usine Decapotable ceased officially. This car was surely the last of all the Deesses to be built and sold; costing exactly 70,000 francs plus extras, it was undoubtedly the most expensive.

In total, 1,365 Usine Cabriolets are known to have found customers—770 DS19, 483 DS21 and 112 ID19—compared with a total 289 of Chapron's own Deesse-based cabriolet, fixed head coupe and limousine designs, including the Croisette, Paris, Caddy, Dandy, Palm Beach, Concorde, Leman, Majesty and Lorraine models.

In addition, once again as a result of private commissions, a small number of standard DS sedans were also modified and re-trimmed to extremely high levels of refinement and luxury by the Chapron firm, while in 1968 a special four-door Presidential limousine built on a stretched DS21 chassis was supplied to the Elysée Palace at the personal request of General de Gaulle.

11

The Ami-6, 1961–1969, and Ami-8, 1969–1978

By the late 1950s, motoring had become a recreational activity for the middle-classes in France, as elsewhere throughout Western Europe. As André Citroën had predicted, by then the automobile had established itself as an indispensable accessory, to be enjoyed as much for weekend and holiday excursions as for daily commuting or other business-related travel.

Increasingly, it was becoming a possession aspired to equally by women as by men, and for purely practical reasons. No other means of transport was more suited to the job of carrying a family's shopping or for taking children to and from school. But in attempting to satisfy this pressing new demand, stimulated by the dramatic increase in newly qualified female drivers, Citroën's dealers and concessionaires found themselves in a quandary. For although they had in their showrooms two of the best-selling cars in France — the cheap, practical 2CV and the costly, sophisticated DS19 or ID19 — neither vehicle could match the attractions of rival designs such as the Renault Dauphine and Floride, which were deliberately styled and promoted to appeal to feminine sensibilities. In short, between these two extremes a great new middle-income, family-motoring, market was opening up, in which the choice of purchase was greatly influenced — or perhaps even dominated — by the opinions of housewives who demanded comfort with economy as well as space and carrying capacity without undue expense.

As a legacy of the Pons Plan (which had actually excluded Citroën from the 6CV-8CV sector of the market), the company was placed at a disadvantage in that these new potential customers found the Deesse and the Deuche either too big or too small for their needs. Having been produced to cater exclusively to the needs of either the most affluent or the least well-off motorists, the *paysan* or the *haute-bourgeois*, these models were completely opposite in character. What was needed now was a new medium-class car which would put an end to this polarization and plug the large gap in the center of its model range through which much valuable business was escaping.

It seems that the efforts to define a medium-sized intermediate-class vehicle that would be, in effect, a halfway-house between the D and A series cars first began in the late 1950s with an ambitious project code-named the C60. This prototype combined hydro-pneumatic suspension with a flat four-cylinder air-cooled engine housed in a radically innovative body styled by Flaminio Bertoni, which resembled the DS at the front and the Ami-6 at the rear. But the proposal was abandoned in favor of a much less sophisticated stop-gap solution which reached production in 1961, as the Ami-6. Much cheaper to manufacture than the C60 would have been, this versatile and popular town and country sedan combined the proven mechanical elements of the 2CV with the avant-garde aesthetic appeal of the DS19.

Launched as "The world's most comfortable medium class car," this most individual of vehicles was the first Citroën model to be built at the company's brand new factory at Rennes-le-Janais in Brittany, opened by General de Gaulle the previous year. Based squarely on the mechanical conception of the 2CV but fitted with an all-new body of a very different design and appearance, the Ami-6 sedan and its successors and derivatives shared so many features and components with their 2CV cousins that they were always classed, in Citroën parlance, as members of the Type A family of vehicles.

Introduced in April 1961, the Ami-6 marked Citroën's entrance into the middle-income market in France. Based on the 2CV, and powered by a 602 cc version of the air-cooled flat-twin engine, its remarkable combination of space, comfort and economy soon made it a huge success. Ultimately almost two million of its various versions were sold. But its Gallic looks did not travel well, and elsewhere in Europe it was far less popular.

Although rarely seen outside its native land, the Ami range was destined to become another smash hit for Citroën — so much so that, like the 2CV before it, it lasted much longer than was originally planned. Between 1961 and 1971 1,127,649 Ami-6 sedans and station wagons found customers in France; and at the high-point of its popularity in 1966 when 180,000 were sold, the Ami ranked as the country's best-selling car by far. Later, between 1969 and 1979, healthy sales of the improved Ami-8 and Ami-Super versions continued to bear witness to the design's enduring strengths and virtues. An outstandingly comfortable and capacious small family car for its time, the Ami opened up the possibilities of cheap long-distance holiday or recreational motoring to a great many Gallic parents and their children. And yet, unlike the 2CV, its attractions never really caught on among British or German motorists.

Derived directly from the 2CV, the Ami models shared the Deuche's principal component systems— its durable air-cooled twin cylinder boxer engine; its four-speed front-wheel-drive transmission; its rack-and-pinion steering; its interconnected, all-independent suspension system and its platform-type chassis. Styled by Flaminio Bertoni, the Ami-6 shared numerous trim and styling features with the D Series range such as its unique single-spoke steering wheel, door handles and switchgear and its use, initially, of an unpainted translucent matt-white fiberglass roof panel. To save weight, maximum use of aluminum was made, for example in the bumpers, grille and trim-strips, which made its appearance seem stranger still. Yet the aesthetics of the Ami had little in common with the DS's elegant shape and style, and the car resembled a pop-eyed frog rather than a slinky shark! For some people, the Ami represented Citroën's attitude to design at its most unorthodox and original; the raw, uncompromising result of engineering logic and integrity. For others, the Ami-6 was quite simply the ugliest car ever made!

There was no distinguishing badge on the front, not even the Double Chevron sign, as on the 2CV. Its quirky appearance labeled it a Citroën so unmistakably that the fitting of an emblem was considered a superfluous extravagance by its makers. But besides its bizarre frontal aspect which presented a grotesque, tortured, grimacing expression to oncoming traffic, the Ami 6 sedan had another most unusual and unconventional visual detail — its reverse-sloping rear window. According to Robert Opron (who succeeded Bertoni as Citroën's chief of styling in 1975), this was no superficial gimmick but the only logical alternative available, given Bercot's insistence that the car should conform to the form of a sedan with a separate trunk. "Cadiou, the boss of the Bureau d'Etudes, had specified a classical three-box layout in his *cahier des charges,* although the overall dimensions really called for a station wagon layout. Bertoni found it impossible to divide the space available to accommodate both a large trunk and a passenger compartment providing sufficient headroom for the rear-seat passengers. The only answer was to gain cabin length at roof level by putting in the window the wrong way round." As a bonus, this solution also kept the large glass surface of the rear window clean and dry in wet weather. A distinct improvement on those of the 2CV, the side-windows on the Ami's front doors were of the sliding type; a similar arrangement was later fitted to the rear doors also. The spacious interior accommodation made possible by this layout was also enhanced by the car's flat floor and its wide bench seats, removable for even greater flexibility in loading, as with the 2CV.

Evolution

The first examples of the Ami-6 sedan as introduced in September 1961 were equipped with an up-rated version of the current 2CV engine, enlarged to 602cc and producing 21 bhp at 4,500 rpm, so that strictly speaking the car was rated as a 3CV. This gave the early Ami a top speed of 65 mph, slightly greater than that of the 2CV, with no loss in fuel economy which was claimed to exceed 50 mpg. Part of the secret was its lightness; its curb weight was only 1,428 lbs., some 350 lbs. less than most of its competitors, thanks to its notably thin external panels and its unpainted, translucent plastic roof. In September 1964, engine power output was increased to 26 bhp and then raised again to 28 bhp in September 1967, bringing the top speed up to almost 70 mph. This gave the Ami 6 a surprisingly fast yet economical long-distance cruising ability for a car endowed with so little outright performance. Just like the 2CV, the Ami 6 was far superior to the majority of small family cars of its era in the standards of comfort, roadholding and general ride quality that it offered. Despite displaying an alarming degree of body roll when cornering, its stability and handling were always entirely predictable and forgiving, whatever the conditions, while its tight turning circle (18 ft) made for outstanding maneuverability when parking. Truly, the Ami was driver-friendly in both name and nature. Regardless of its weird looks and eccentric styling, French motorists took it to their hearts and by 1962, the Ami-6 was rolling off the assembly lines at the Rennes-la-Janais factory at the rate of more than 600 units a day; by 1965 the production rate had overtaken even that of the 2CV. The ever-growing number of French female drivers on the roads comprised a significant proportion of this clientele.

Top: From the outset, the Ami-6 was marketed as woman's car — the ideal vehicle for shopping or taking the kids to school. This is one of a series of publicity photographs shot on location in Paris and published in a superb brochure designed by Robert Delpire. ***Bottom:*** Styled by Flaminio Bertoni, the remarkable originality of the Ami's unorthodox frontal appearance caused heated controversy. For some observers it represented the essence of pure engineering logic and integrity; others thought it was simply the ugliest car ever made. This is the station wagon version, the Ami-6 Break, which followed the sedan in September 1964.

In September 1964, the sedan was joined by the Ami 6 Break, plus the Ami 6 Commerciale, which differed from the passenger version in that it had no rear seats and was therefore exempt from tax; the glass side windows of the Break were retained. Quickly, the improved rear-end arrangements of these new variants eliminated all aesthetic objections to the lines of the sedan and widened the Ami's sales appeal by offering an unrivalled amount of load-carrying space — 53 cubic feet. One of the first inexpensive small station wagons ever offered to the motoring public, the Ami-6 Break turned out to be the ideal vehicle for small families, small businesses and small farmers alike. Boasting a payload of 300 kilos [660 lb] and 15 sq feet of load floor (with the folding rear seat removed completely, a 5'5" long object could be transported), the Ami 6 Break offered all the qualities of reliability, simplicity, versatility and economy provided by the 2CV, but with the bonus of a much greater load-carrying capacity into the bargain. It replaced the Deux Chevaux as the universal work-horse of France. Like the sedan, it was also offered with the option of a centrifugal traffi-clutch. Following the arrival of the Break, sales of the Ami 6 sedan declined substantially, to the point where, in 1967, no fewer than 135,046 of the former were manufactured compared to only 34,344 of the latter.

Top: **The remarkably spacious and comfortable interior of the Ami-6 is fully revealed here. The raked-back rear window was no styling gimmick as it allowed a larger trunk and greater headroom for rear seat passengers.** ***Bottom:*** **The absence of a transmission tunnel made possible by FWD allowed an unusual amount of space for driver and front-seat passenger alike. In fact, the wide front bench seat permitted a third person to sit between them, if necessary.**

For the 1968 model year, introduced in September 1967, two levels of trim were made available on both the sedan and Break, a standard Tourisme and a more luxurious and expensive Confort grade. Vinyl upholstery could be fitted on both, but jersey nylon cloth was seen on the Confort version only. Individual front seats were also offered as an alternative to the normal bench arrangement, plus various other extras such as windshield washers and a proper fan-assisted interior heating and ventilation system. A 12-volt electrical system was also introduced on all Ami models at this time, powered by an alternator. In May 1968, the range was augmented by a further new station wagon variant, known as the Ami-6 Break Club, a more up-market version immediately distinguishable from its fellows by its twin round headlights. The following October, for the 1969 model year, a similarly upgraded sedan model, the Ami-6 Club was added. Then finally in December 1968 the range was completed by the arrival of the Ami-6 Enterprise or Service Van, available in two forms, with or without side windows for the load compartment, which was particularly commodious thanks to its broad, flat unobstructed floor and wide rear-door aperture.

Relatively few of these vehicles were made, for in the Spring of 1969 the Ami-6 series was replaced by the Ami-8, launched in sedan form at the Geneva motor show that March. The big numerical increase implied by its name was slightly misleading, however, as the Ami's engine capacity and fiscal rating remained exactly the same as before. All that changed was the appearance of the car, which was given a major (and some say much-needed) face-lift to rejuvenate its time-worn looks. Inside, a completely revised dashboard was installed. Outside, at the front, the grille and headlight treatment was tidied-up (though the single rectangular headlight units rather than the twin round versions were retained) and the overhanging hood line was smoothed-out so that the Ami lost its toothless mouth and beetle-browed expression. At the back, the reverse-rake window was replaced by a more modern sloping fast-back look, though this improvement did not extend to providing a hatch-back door to the rear luggage compartment. In Autumn of 1969, the Ami-6 Break and Van versions were also upgraded to Ami-8 status with the same frontal styling modifications. As with the Ami-6, two different trim specifications of the Ami-8 sedans and Breaks were offered; the up-market Club version having a higher level of seating and equipment (with proper winding windows from September 1970 onwards) and the more Spartan and basic Confort grade. Although the first examples of the Ami-8 sedans retained an all-drum braking system, from the time of the launch of the Break versions in September 1969, all models were fitted with inboard mounted front disc brakes.

Finally, in January 1973, the Ami family was enlarged and augmented by the arrival of three new and very muscular cousins, the Ami-Super Berline (sedan), Break (station wagon) and Enterprise (service van). Rated as 6CVs, these were powered by a 55.5 bhp version of the 1015cc flat-four air-cooled engine from the recently launched Citroën GS range. With four times the swept-volume of the original 2CV power-plant, this power-unit was capable of pushing the Ami chassis up to a top speed of 87 mph! A four-speed all-synchromesh gearbox was fitted, operated by a floor-mounted stick-shift rather than the traditional push-pull 2CV-type dashboard mounted lever. To cope with all this extra performance, the Ami-Super models were equipped with disc brakes and a completely revised suspension layout, minus the front-to-rear interlinking seen on earlier 2CV and Ami types.

Although the Ami-Super offered Citroën customers a lot of car for their money, it was probably rather too much of a good thing and somewhat over-powered. Not surprisingly, production was stopped in late 1976 after just three years with only 42,000 or so having been built. But the 602cc Ami 8 sedan continued on sale for another two years until it was eventually replaced by the new Visa model which arrived in early 1978. The Ami-8 Break model survived for another year, until 1979. During its 17-year career the Citroën Ami had made friends with more than 1,840,000 continental customers!

During the lifespan of the Ami-6 from 1961 to 1969, many important changes took place within the Citroën organization on a corporate level. When Pierre Bercot took over its reins in

Top: **The uncluttered and uncramped driving position of the Ami-6. Notice the push-pull gear-shift lever from the 2CV and the single-spoke steering wheel from the ID. The door handles also came from the ID. *Bottom:* In April 1969, the Ami-6 was replaced by a restyled version, the Ami-8, with a new frontal aspect and a fastback (not hatchback) body. The name was misleading as the engine remained unchanged in size and performance. The first examples had no Citroën badge on their grilles.**

1958 upon the retirement of Robert Puiseux, he began to explore the possibility of forming cooperative ventures and strategic alliances with other motor manufacturers, with the intention of creating an extended partnership of automobile producers sufficiently large in size and capability to be fully competitive in world markets. The automobile industry was fast becoming a truly international trading environment, in which it was no longer possible to survive on the strength of domestic activities alone. By sharing its production facilities and purchasing power with such partners, he hoped to improve through economies of scale not just Citroën's competitive edge but its entire viability. By then the parent company Michelin had maintained control for almost 30 years, a period that — thanks to the success of the radial tire — had seen a dramatic upturn in its affairs. Yet having embarked on a massive program of expansion on its own account, Michelin could no longer afford to overlook Citroën's inadequate profitability — and certainly not to subsidize any losses that might be made by its subsidiary, as were indeed recorded subsequently, in 1969, 1970, 1974 and 1975.

Top: **The rear view of the Ami-8 sedan, which had a traditional interior layout with a trunk rather than a hatchback with a folding rear seat. Note that the rear door hinges beneath the window instead of above it.** ***Bottom:*** **In September 1969, the Ami-6 Break was also upgraded to Ami-8 status with the same frontal modifications. The main difference from the sedan was its extended rear roofline and fully opening tailgate. Note that the Ami-8 still retained the sliding windows of the Ami-6.**

The first of these ties, involving the oldest of all French car makers, Panhard & Levassor, founded in 1890, had actually been forged in 1953 when Citroën bought a 25 percent holding in the company, and an agreement amalgamating the Citroën and Panhard sales network was signed. Formerly a manufacturer of expensive luxury cars, Panhard had changed direction after the war to enter the popular "people's car" market and had begun to produce a series of extremely advanced and highly aerodynamic front-wheel-drive vehicles, built largely of lightweight aluminum and powered by small 850 cc air-cooled flat-twin engines. The precursor of the range was the Dyna X, launched in 1947. This vehicle was actually derived from the AFG (Aluminum-Francaise-Gregoire) prototype designed by Jean-Albert Gregoire in 1941. The thinking behind the Dyna X and its successors, the Dyna 54 of 1954 and the PL17 of 1961, a restyled steel-bodied version of the Dyna X, corresponded closely with Citroën's own design philosophy. A long and happy marriage seemed imminent.

The partnership was consolidated in 1955 when Panhard began producing the 2CV Fourgonnette at its Ivry factory on the outskirts of Paris and its chief designer Bionier joined Citroën's Bureau d'Etudes to become involved, amongst other projects, in the studies that eventually led to the Citroën Dyane. Ten years later Citroën took over the business completely, but in 1967 all further production of Panhard's current models (most notably the 24CT sports coupe, introduced in 1963 and capable of 160 kph) ceased and its illustrious name was consigned

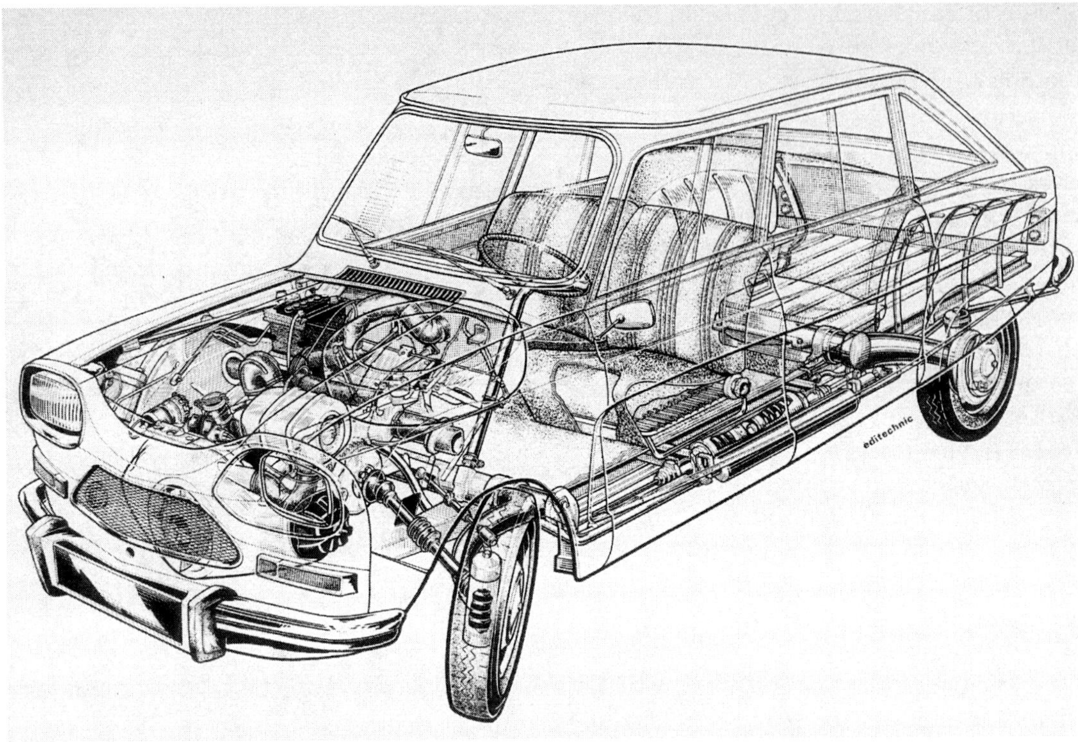

This cutaway drawing of the Ami-8 sedan shows clearly that its design was based on the 2CV's floor-pan, engine and suspension system. It also shows that the earliest versions of the Ami-8 sedan retained the inboard mounted drum brakes. But with the arrival of the Break version, inboard front disc brakes were adopted right across the range.

to motoring history, save as a manufacturer of armored cars and other military vehicles.

Next, in 1964, Citroën signed an agreement with the German firm NSU to undertake the study of rotary piston Wankel engines which at the at time were widely forecast as being most likely to replace the traditional reciprocating piston engine altogether. This accord was followed in 1967 by the creation of a jointly owned subsidiary, Comotor, formed specifically for the purpose of designing and manufacturing rotary engines. By 1969 this company had commenced production of a single rotor engine, which was exhaustively tested by selected customers in some 260 examples of an experimental car, the Citroën M35. Later, in 1974, a double-rotor version was produced to equip the Citroën GS Birotor model, of which only 874 were constructed. Naturally, NSU designed and built its own rotary-engined front-wheel-drive car, the Ro80 of 1967.

In 1967 Citroën acquired a majority (97 percent) shareholding in the truck and bus manufacturers Berliet, which dated from 1895. André Citroën had entered the commercial vehicle market in 1928 with considerable success, and since the war the Double Chevron firm had steadily expanded its activities in this area to become Europe's largest producers of light commercial vehicles and medium class lorries. The merger with Berliet was intended to increase Citroën's overall production capacity, and also to provide an entree into the public service vehicle and heavy truck sector of the market, which was Berliet's specialty.

The following year, on October 25, 1968, to be exact, Bercot announced the establishment of a far-reaching accord between Citroën and Fiat. The intention was that henceforth the two companies would cooperate closely in technical, commercial and manufacturing matters by means of a holding company, PARDEVI, in which Michelin would hold a majority shareholding of 51 percent and Fiat the remaining 49 percent. The plan proposed in these negotiations was that, ultimately, the ranges of both companies would be rationalized, integrated and harmonized to avoid any unnecessary overlapping of resources, so that both parties would be better placed in the battle against their common rivals Renault and Peugeot. As a result of the agreement, Citroën and Fiat began to collaborate on the design and manufacture of a new range of light commercial vans, the C35 (and the later C25) which replaced the Type H van, while Citroën's dealer network commenced distribution of the small cars built by Fiat's subsidiary Autobianchi.

This marriage of convenience lasted until 1973, when as a result of vastly changed trading circumstances the partners agreed to divorce, and Fiat returned its shares in Citroën to Michelin. It appears that a major cause of friction was that Fiat expected its French partner to abandon the production of the 2CV and its other A series models, so that the Italian company would have this market to itself, an idea that *les Michelin* found unacceptable. Thus Citroën recovered its independence (though it remained under Michelin control), but the commercial vehicle joint venture with Fiat continues to the present day.

Earlier, in parallel with the pursuit of this international strategy, Citroën had responded to the challenge of the establishment of the European Common Market in 1957 by embarking on the development of its own corporate structure, expanding its sales and distribution network and building new factories both in France and abroad to increase both domestic and export sales. Between 1955 and 1972, the size of the company doubled from 31,000 to 59,000 employees while factory floor space was increased by 79 percent from 1,118,000 sq meters to 2,001,000 sq meters. It was estimated that by 1971 there were more than 3,800,000 Citroën vehicles in service throughout the world, with 2,904,000 of them running on the roads of France alone, 25.7 percent of the overall national fleet. And what is more, by this time more than 80 percent of all tires sold in France were Michelin radials!

Top: **Finally, in January 1973, the Ami range was enlarged and augmented by the Ami-Super Berline (sedan), Break and Enterprise van. Powered by a 55.5 bhp version of the 1015 cc air-cooled flat-four engine from the GS and rated as a 6CV, the Ami-Super was capable of 87 mph. From its exterior, the Ami-Super could be distinguished by its revised grille with extra air-intakes beneath it and the rubbing strip running along its flanks. *Bottom:* From the interior, the give-away was the floor-mounted stick-shift gear lever located in a console, as fitted to the GS. Although the Ami-Super offered Citroën customers a lot of car for their money it was somewhat over-powered. Production was halted in late 1976 after only 42,000 had been made.**

By 1968, the Société Anoyname André Citroën had diversified its activities into a variety of different fields, to become a group of more than 70 associated companies, including Panhard, Berliet, Maserati and, of course, the original Citroën gear company from which the entire business had evolved. This diversity presented certain organizational and administrative problems, and so on the 27th of June that year (four months before the establishment of the PARDEVI accord) the company was reorganized under the control of a new holding company, Citroën SA, itself a Michelin subsidiary and headed by Pierre Bercot. The S.A. André Citroën, founded in 1922, was wound up. Of the 12 separate companies that were then controlled by Citroën SA, the two most important were the Société Automobiles Citroën, which was responsible for the industrial process of designing and constructing automobiles, and the Société Commerciale Citroën which was charged with the task of distributing these products. Initially, between 1968 and 1970, both these companies were headed by Claude-Alain Sarre, who was in turn succeeded as managing director, between 1970 and 1974, by Raymond Ravenel.

In November 1970 Pierre Bercot retired from his position as President-Directeur-General or Chairman and overall supremo of Citroën SA. He was replaced by François Rollier who since 1966 had been, together with

François Michelin, the principle *gerant* or chief director and controlling shareholder of the Michelin company. Unlike Messrs Bercot, Sarre and Ravenel, Rollier was a true member of the Michelin dynasty, closely related to the clan by marriage; his mother Marthe was the sister of Madeleine Callies who had married Edouard's son Etienne. When the young François Michelin was orphaned in 1936 (he lost both his parents before he was 10 years old), he was raised by Marthe Rollier alongside her own son who was 10 years older than the Michelin boy. So it was that François Rollier took the role of François Michelin's big brother rather than just his cousin; 30 years later, he became his fellow-director and business partner too. Not surprisingly, Rollier's appointment was taken as a sign that *les Michelins* intended to resume their grip on the reins of power at Citroën, and to bring to an end the period of relative independence and autonomy that it had enjoyed under Pierre Bercot's rule.

12

The Citroën Maserati SM, 1970–1975

As numerous motoring historians have acknowledged, the arrival of André Citroën on the French motoring scene in 1919 had divided the nation into two distinct parties, the Citroënistes and the Anti-Citroënistes. Yet the demarcation line separating these camps indicated far more than just trivial differences in car-buying preferences or prejudices. It was a watershed that defined other, more important, divisions in social, economic and political attitudes, distinguishing the progressives from the traditionalists and reactionaries. Far from being a simple boundary between Left and Right, it marked a cultural schism cutting across French society as a whole. The *intelos* or avant-garde factions tended to buy Citroën cars, since these vehicles were perceived to be more adventurous than the norm, while the conservatives, reacting against the iconoclasm displayed by André Citroën in his many activities, chose the more sober and conventional offerings of Renault and Peugeot instead.

The same observation held true in post-war years, long after André Citroën's demise. Throughout the 1950s and 1960s the marque was the fashionable choice among the intelligentsia, owned by countless famous artists, actors and film directors as well as leading architects and engineers. It was also the first choice of Francophile motorists in other European countries including the United Kingdom, where a market-research survey established that the firm's British customers tended to be educated at a higher level than the norm, with a high percentage of teachers and academics among them. Here as in France, motorists fell into two camps, those fanatically in favor of Citroën's individuality, and those who were against it, describing it as being merely quirky or eccentric. Citroën's insistence on fitting non-self-canceling turn signals, for example, was generally taken to be a typical indication of its capricious non-conformism.

By 1970, after almost 35 years of Michelin stewardship, the Citroënistes were most certainly in ascendance once again, and the Double Chevron company had recovered entirely from the problems of the past to regain its position as France's leading car maker, producing 750,000 vehicles annually. So great has been the fall in the popular image of the marque in recent years, that it is hard to describe and explain to those who were not motorists at the time just how commanding its pre-eminence was throughout that era, when its reputation for engineering excellence and its leadership in innovation were virtually unchallenged. Indeed, it was regarded as the supreme authority on technical matters within the automobile industry as a whole, recognized as the source of most, if not all, worthwhile new ideas by leading engineers, designers and motoring journalists of the period. For example, two of its most prestigious European rivals, Rolls-Royce and Mercedes-Benz, had both paid Citroën the compliment of adopting its hydro-pneumatic technology under license, for incorporation in the braking and suspension systems of their latest Silver Shadow and S-Class limousines.

Undoubtedly, Citroën owed this leadership to the size and strength of its Bureau d'Etudes, which with its associated laboratories constituted the foremost and best funded establishment of its type within the automobile industry at that time. Founded by André Citroën, it conducted, in conditions of the highest secrecy, long-term research into the widest aspects of transport technology. Whereas the research departments of the majority of other contemporary automobile firms were generally concerned merely with finding ways to shave a little off the cost of producing a car, the Citroën establishment investigated ways of maintaining a policy of continuous improvement in the company's products, so that each new offering marked a significant step forward. It did this by conducting programs of fundamental research as well as by examining specific matters confined to the vehicles currently under development. Under Michelin management, the Bureau was sub-divided into six departments—Moteurs (concerned with engines), Carrosserie (bodywork), Electricite (electrical and lighting matters), Poide Lourds (weight reduction), Hydraulique (hydraulic systems) and of course Liaison au Sol which looked into questions of chassis dynamics and suspension behavior. Long-term research was not confined to automobile matters as is born out by the aeronautical development work undertaken with Comotor throughout the 1960s and 1970s, involving the Wankel rotary engine. This resulted in a project to build a helicopter powered by a 180 bhp rotary engine, in association with the Nord Aviation firm. During the 1970s, the Citroën helicopter made some 200 test flights, reaching altitudes of more than 10,000 feet and speeds in excess of 200 km/h (124 mph), before the project was abandoned in 1979.

Throughout the early 1960s, the Citroën company had experienced a period of steady growth in both sales and profits. Encouraged by its commercial progress and confident in its future prospects, its board of management, then led by Pierre Bercot, had embarked on a policy of expansion, authorizing several initiatives that would have been considered quite impossible until then. Included amongst these plans was the building of a new factory at Aulnay-sous-Bois on the outskirts of Paris to replace the outdated facilities at the Quai de Javel and the opening of a new engineering research and development center at Velizy, to which the Bureau d'Etudes was relocated from its old home in the rue du Theatre, in 1965.

Also sanctioned by Bercot at that time was an ambitious research project intended to take the Double Chevron marque into completely new territory, the market for a luxurious high-performance Grand Touring car which would embody all the technical sophistication for which Citroën was renowned. Just like the Concorde supersonic airliner, which was also conceived around the same time, making its first flight in 1969, this scheme for a front-wheel-drive super-car featuring high-pressure hydropneumatic suspension, braking and steering was a *grand projet* with both commercial and political dimensions. Clearly, the intention was that this new flagship model would do more than celebrate the renaissance of the Double Chevron marque and demonstrate its world leadership in automotive engineering and design, but that it would also revive and re-assert the technological prestige of France, by reclaiming the Republic's supremacy in the Grande Routier class, lost through the demise of such exalted names as Delage, Delahaye, Hotchkiss, Talbot-Lago and Bugatti.

Doubtless, Bercot also hoped that the emergence of a true sports model from the Citroën stable would help to revive its fortunes in the North American market, which it had entered in 1956 with a disappointing lack of success. But whatever his exact intentions or inspirations, the research project he initiated—codenamed DS Sport—

Introduced at the Geneva Motor Show in March 1970, the Citroën Maserati SM was a two-door, four-seater, fixed-head coupe capable of a top speed of 137 mph in its original 170 hp carbureted form and 142 mph in the fuel-injected 178 hp version which came later, in 1972. It was powered by a 2670 cc all-alloy V6 Maserati engine derived from the Italian firm's earlier 4-liter V8 power-plant, used in its Indy sports car.

had the specific engineering objective of producing a vehicle capable of cruising at speeds of greater than 120mph for long periods with unprecedented comfort, safety and reliability, thus dominating the new trans-continental motorway networks that were then being opened across the USA, Canada and Europe. In the way that its design brief or specification combined the qualities of speed, stability and security, it evoked memories of Citroën's prewar super-car, the V8 22CV Traction Avant that André Citroën had displayed at the Paris Motor Show of 1935, but which the Michelin men had not permitted to enter series production. This was claimed to be the fastest, safest standard production car of its time.

The eventual outcome of the DS Sport project, of course, was the Citroën-Maserati SM two-door, four-seater coupe revealed at the Geneva Motor Show in March 1970, six months before Citroën's other major event of the year, the launch of the GS at the October Paris Salon. Representing an extraordinary synthesis that blended the qualities of a competition-bred sports-tourer and a luxury limousine, the SM offered levels of performance, comfort and safety unprecedented then and perhaps still unmatched today. An exotic blend of French style and Italian flair, it was the offspring of Citroën's relationship with the illustrious Italian racing car specialist of Modena, which had come under its ownership in March 1968. The Officine Alfieri Maserati could trace its origins to 1926, when the first cars actually bearing its famous Trident badge were built in the factory founded by the Maserati brothers, Alfieri and Ettore. In 1937, it was taken over by the industrialist Adolfo Orsi. By the mid 1950s, having achieved no fewer than nine Grand-Prix wins with its 250F Formula 1 car piloted by drivers such as Fangio, Moss and Hawthorne, Maserati's pedigree as a thoroughbred Continental sporting marque was rivaled only by Ferrari at that time, since Alfa-Romeo had long since quit the racing scene.

The nature of the SM and its genesis was entirely typical of the Citroën ethos and philosophy. It was a car built to delight the Citroënistes and to become the ultimate expression of the ideals and values of the marque. Little if any attention was paid to the normal disciplines of marketing and product planning in its development, which was led entirely by engineering considerations. Instead of seeking out potential customers and defining their needs and wishes through market research, Citroën built the SM to satisfy its own idealistic technical interests and priorities, fully expecting that the results would be interesting enough to stimulate these customers into seeking out the car! The fact that this very expensive, specialist vehicle could only be found in the showrooms of the general network of Citroën dealerships, displayed alongside its exact antithesis, the 2CV, did not strike those responsible as being in any way incongruous or inappropriate. Yet for the price of the SM in France at its launch (46,000 francs in March 1970, soon rising to 49,500 francs in January 1971) the would-be owner could have bought about seven Deux Chevaux (selling at 6,292 francs in standard 2CV-4 form during the first half of 1970). On the other hand, perhaps the company thought that, in Europe at least, given the projected production rate of 50 vehicles a day, enough buyers could be found within the community of existing customers without the necessity of having to look beyond these boundaries for buyers.

Actually, the project authorized by Bercot in 1964 had earlier origins and could be dated further back in time, to the heyday of André Lefèbvre. As a former Grand Prix racing driver, Lefèbvre was quite naturally interested in exploring the limits of front-wheel-drive transmission and in overcoming the problems encountered when the traction, braking and steering functions of a high-performance car are carried out by the forward driving wheels. A two- or four-door sports coupe version of the DS was certainly considered at that time, in addition to the famous *decapotable* drop-head cabriolet, but equipped with a far more potent engine than the current 1911cc motor. Many of the other talents involved in the design of the standard DS and ID sedans also contributed to the project, including Magés, Bertoni and Becchia, though the overall responsibility for progress was entrusted to a young engineer at the Bureau d'Etudes, Jacques Né.

By 1965, these ideas had been concretized in two DS based prototypes. The first, a short wheel-base convertible built entirely of light-alloy and weighing only 2,375 lbs., was powered by a mildly tuned version of the old three-bearing 1911cc DS19 engine equipped with two downdraft double-choke Weber carburetors and matched to a five speed gearbox. This car was capable of 109 mph, about 10 mph faster than the standard DS19M sedan of 1965. The second D Sport prototype was similar in conception, except that its four headlights were grouped in the center of the hood and concealed when not in use by an electrically operated sliding panel made from Plexiglass. It was powered by a twin-cam adaptation of the new 1985cc four cylinder five-bearing engine recently introduced on the DS19MA, producing 130 bhp as opposed to the 90 bhp of the standard car, enough to raise its maximum speed to around 115 mph.

In 1966 came a third D Sport prototype, referred to as the DXGT. This was again a short wheelbase two-door pillarless coupe version of the DS, but built of steel, which increased its weight to 2,710 lbs. Powered by a twin Weber conversion of the new 2175cc five-bearing engine of the DS21 sedan (introduced in September 1965) which boosted output from 109 bhp to 124 bhp, it was the first Citroën to exceed 120 mph. Apparently, it was envisaged that further trials of this prototype would see it powered by yet another, enlarged version of the classic Citroën four-cylinder power-plant, or even by one of the all-new V4, V6 or V8 engines designed by Walter Becchia which were then under development at the Bureau d'Etudes. But the fourth stage, built in 1967, served as a mule to test the new Maserati V6 engine which had speedily resulted from the technical cooperation agreement signed with the Italian specialists in September 1966 when Citroën acquired a financial interest in the Modena firm from its current owners, the Orsi industrial group. This arrangement was merely the prelude to the full merger established in March 1968 when Citroën assumed complete ownership and control, and installed its own executive, a certain M. Guy Maleret, as managing director.

As we have already noted, until the arrival of the DS19 Citroën had not previously participated in motorsport activities and did not establish a competitions department until 1960, in order to enter the ID19 in endurance events such as the Monte Carlo Rally. So the acquisition of Maserati promised not only to confer a sporting reputation upon the Double Chevron marque, but also to solve its perceived deficiencies in the engine department, at least so far as any plans to expand Citroën's *haut de gamme* activities were concerned. Other hybrid cars, to be marketed purely as Maseratis, were also expected to materialize from the marriage in addition to the new Citroën GT sports coupe, and these eventually included two outright sports cars, the Bora and Merak. The latter shared the SM's V6 engine, mounted amidships to drive the rear wheels, but both employed Citroën's high-pressure hydraulic steering and braking systems.

Work on this unit began shortly after the takeover early in 1968, when Maserati's chief engineer Giulio Alfieri was asked to produce a power-plant specifically for use in the proposed new car. The major design constraint was that its dimensions were to fall within the all-important *puissance-fiscale* rating of 15CV, which effectively limited its capacity to a maximum of 2.8 liters. The work was accomplished within three weeks, by the simple expedient of chopping two cylinders from Maserati's 4136cc V8 engine, used in its current Indy sports car, and then reducing the bore and stroke of the remaining six cylinders to 87mm x 75mm, giving a capacity of 2670cc. This configuration made for an exceptional compact and lightweight engine (just 140 kg or 309 lbs.) thanks in part to its short crankshaft. When coupled to its Citroën-made five-speed gearbox, the Maserati V6 could easily be installed fore and aft in the nose of the car, as in the DS, but without intruding into the interior compartment; similarly, the gearbox was located in front of the engine, ahead of the front axle.

The all-alloy engine comprised four main castings, two identical cylinder heads, and an upper and lower block, split along the center line of the crankshaft. The four-bearing crankshaft was located sandwich fashion between the latter castings, an expensive solution used only in the finest competition engines but which made for an exceptionally rigid and robust unit. The pistons ran in dry cast iron liners pressed into the upper block and

Naturally, this audacious and highly sophisticated design also featured Citroën's self-levelling hydro-pneumatic suspension and fully powered braking systems, first seen on the DS19, to which the SM was closely related. The result was an unprecedented combination of performance and ride comfort.

ranged in two banks opposed at a 90-degree angle, while the valve gear of the two identical cylinder heads (which had classic hemispherical combustion chambers with their inlet and outlet valves opposed at 75 degrees) were actuated by tappets driven by four overhead camshafts, two for each cylinder bank. The compression ratio was 9:1. The camshafts were rotated by long secondary duplex chains driven by a central jackshaft running in plain bearings and located in the V of the engine. This jackshaft was driven in turn by the crankshaft through a short primary duplex chain.

Unfortunately, this arrangement proved to be the engine's Achilles heel, for although the secondary chains were provided with automatic tensioners, no such arrangement was made for adjustment of wear in the primary chain. As the jackshaft also acted as a power-take-off point for various engine accessories including the distributor, water pump, hydraulic pump and air-conditioning pump, wear was inevitable, so that if the engine was overrevved, the primary chain was prone to jumping a tooth on its sprockets, with disastrous consequences. The engines of almost all the cars still running today have since been modified by the fitting of an automatic tensioner to the primary chain.

In its earliest form, employing three twin-choke Weber carburetors mounted centrally with inlet manifolds leading to each individual cylinder, left and right, the V6 engine produced 170 bhp DIN at 5,500 rpm. The majority of the 9,892 cars built in the first three years of production were aspirated in this way, with a claimed top speed of 136.8 mph and a 0–60 mph time of 8.2 secs. In July 1972, however, Citroën announced that, as standard, the carburetor-fed engine would be replaced by a version employing the computer-controlled Bosch Jetronic electronic fuel injection system; all other engine parameters were unaltered. This improvement produced a slightly increased power output of 178 bhp DIN, 8 bhp more than before. Although the acceleration times were unchanged, top speed was raised by 5 mph to more than 140 mph. But the greatest benefit under the circumstances was that touring fuel consumption was improved from 22.6 mpg to 25.2 mpg.

That these impressive levels of performance were achievable was due to the outstanding aerodynamic qualities of the SM's bodywork, which enabled an engine of modest dimensions to push this large and heavy car (curb weight was 1,450 kg or 3,200 lbs.) to high continuous cruising speeds (102 mph at 5,000 rpm in 5th gear, or 70 mph at 3,000 rpm) and to maintain them with perfect stability and composure for long distances. It took engines more than twice the size of the Maserati V6 to propel its rivals such as the Daimler Double Six (5343cc V12) and the Jensen Interceptor (6276cc V8) to similar top speeds. Styled in-house by Robert Opron, the bodywork benefited from extensive wind-tunnel work, which served not only to eliminate frontal turbulence but also to minimize the effects of crosswinds and the slipstream of other fast-moving traffic being overtaken. The reduction of drag was also assisted, of course, by the action of the SM's self-leveling suspension which ensured the optimum angle of attack under all circumstances. A drag coefficent of 0.34 was claimed by Citroën, 25 percent better than the DS.

Indeed this aspect of the design showed beyond a doubt that during its development in 1969 the influence of André Lefèbvre still held sway at the Bureau d'Etudes, some 10 years after his retirement. The shape of the SM conformed not only to the 60:40 ratio of weight distribution fore and aft that he considered ideal, but also to the tapering tear-drop shape that he consistently advocated. The car was nearly five meters long (4,893 cm) with a wheelbase of almost three meters (2,950 cm) but its maximum width of 1,836 cm occurred at the nose, the cross-

The SM at speed. According to ***Autocar***'s June 1971 test report, its performance was brisk. "First gear shot the SM up to nearly 40 mph, second to just short of 60 mph, and third on to nearly 90 mph. Fourth was good for 115 mph and in top we measured 135 mph." But the car's true forte was an ability to cruise the motorways all day long at 100 mph, with its engine turning at a leisurely 4000 rpm and its driver feeling completely relaxed, thanks to exceptional high-speed stability and security.

Top: **The aerodynamically efficient lines of the SM can be judged from this view which shows off its tapering curves. Its coefficient of drag was an unprecedented 0.34, 25 percent better than the DS, the previous benchmark. The car was 20 cms (8 ins) wider at the front than at the rear, in accordance with the theories advocated by André Lefèbvre.** ***Bottom:*** **Although it had no conventional grille bearing a Double Chevron badge to distinguish it, there was no mistaking the origins of the Citroën SM. Its unique frontal aspect was created by the full-width glass cover that enclosed the headlights and registration license plate. The inner pair of long-range lights were directional and swivelled with the steering to follow the curve of the road. Actually, the Double Chevron badge was located on the ventilation air-intake on top of the hood.**

section of the body being gradually reduced along its flanks resulting in a difference of no less than 20 cm (8 ins) between the front and rear tracks (1,526 cm and 1,326 cm, respectively).

The body-shell itself was a massive welded steel structure conforming to the classical three-box layout, possessing immense strength and robustness, as was subsequently demonstrated by the SM's brief rallying career. Although it was not designed specifically to be a competition car, on its first outing in the 1971 Moroccan Rally it took 1st, 3rd and 4th places, gaining Citroën the manufacturer's prize. Actually built under contract by the specialist low-volume constructors Chausson, its design resembled that of the DS except that it was a true monocoque in which the roof formed an integral part and contributed to the rigidity of the central passenger section. It consisted of two main units, front and rear, linked by large box-section longerons to which the floor pan was attached. The front unit extended forward from the firewall bulkhead to a cross-member located on the axis of the drive-shafts and beyond that to the nose, so forming a collapsible cage within which the engine, gearbox, axle-arm and steering rack assemblies were mounted. Similarly, the rear unit formed a bulkhead dividing the central passenger compartment from the conventional luggage trunk, at the same time providing a means of locating the rear anti-roll bar and the rear trailing arms and their associated suspension cylinders which were attached. Only the hood (made from light alloy), the front headlight panel, the front fenders, the side doors and the rear hatch door (raised and supported by two gas struts) were detachable. This latter element, with its large and extremely expensive double-curved glass rear window, was not a true hatchback at all, for the trunk-space (mainly devoted to carrying the spare wheel) was separated from the interior compartment by the rigid rear bulkhead so that the rear passenger seats could not be folded down. The SM's inherent strength continues to impress today. None of the owners and enthusiasts consulted were aware of any accident involving the car and resulting in a fatality among either drivers or passengers, throughout its entire thirty year lifespan to date, a quite exceptional record for this type of vehicle.

Although visually unique in every way, the SM preserved certain styling themes and details that had been established with the DS19, including the use of stainless steel for bumpers and other exterior fittings. The chromed mazak door handles were of the same pattern seen on the later D series cars, in fact. The SM also continued the tradition of faired-in rear wheels which by now had become an essential Citroën characteristic. But because the rear fender panels were welded permanently to the body-shell in a fixed position, small detachable spats were used to cover the wheels, and these had to be removed when changing a tire. These styling themes continued inside the car where the single-spoke steering wheel (heavily

Top: Besides sharing many of the major engineering features of the DS, the SM also followed the principal styling themes seen in other Citroën cars of the period, including the shrouded rear wheels and the use of stainless steel for the bumpers. It also borrowed certain specific trim parts from the DS and GS, such as the exterior door handles. This late example is fitted with the lightweight carbon fiber wheels developed for the SM by Michelin. ***Bottom:*** In the absence of a four-door sedan version of the SM from Citroën, the coachbuilder Henri Chapron produced this private venture, called the Opera, extended by 29 cm to a total length of 3.34 m. Just eight were built. Chapron also offered a cabriolet version, the Mylord.

Top: For a car regarded by some as overly complicated, the SM was exceptionally strong and durable, as was proven by its short rallying career. On the SM's competition debut in the 1971 Moroccan Rally, run under particularly demanding conditions, the single car entered (piloted by Jean Deschaseaux) won first prize. As the two DS21s also entered were ranked among the first four finishers, Citroën gained the manufacturer's cup. ***Bottom:*** Seen here airborne while competing in the Bandama Rally held in the Ivory Coast in 1973, this SM made a happy landing and went on to win 5th prize. Only eight cars among the 64 starters finished the course, three of them Citroëns, including the two SMs entered.

padded) and the curved, asymmetrical dashboard echoed Bertoni's original DS19 design, except that the three main dials on the instrument panel had unusual oval-shaped faces. Another novel feature — at least for Citroën — was the use of a large center console placed between the front seats, as seen in conventional high-performance RWD cars with a transmission tunnel. Although it was not required for any engineering reason, the console served to create an impression of power by housing the gear-shift and handbrake levers plus the radio and heating and ventilation systems. The steering wheel could be adjusted for height and reach, and the front seats (often criticized for lack of lateral support) with their integral head-rests, were also fully adjustable, though they did not recline to a horizontal position as the top part of their backs were designed to pivot forward to admit rear seat passengers. Considering the vast size of the car, the interior compartment, though comfortable and well appointed, was not exactly spacious and the rear seats were suited only for occasional use by adults. So, in truth, the SM was really a two-plus-two rather than a full four-seater as Citroën claimed. The interior was trimmed and upholstered with jersey nylon cloth as standard though leather was available at extra cost; tinted glass and air-conditioning were also optional extras.

The SM had a conventional cockpit layout with the gearshift located in a central console as on a rear-wheel-drive sports car, even though there was no transmission tunnel. Although the steering wheel was adjustable for rake and reach, the driver's seating position was often criticized due to lack of lateral support when cornering.

Naturally, the SM featured front-wheel-drive transmission and center-point steering geometry, both of which had become a *sine qua non* at Citroën. In fact the general design of its front and rear axle-arms, together with its front brakes, hubs and driveshafts, was identical to that of the DS, except that the front arms were mounted in a trailing rather than a leading position. Similarly, the layout and operation of the SM's self-leveling hydropneumatic suspension system followed that of the DS, using the same componentry, but with the gas springs having modified damper valve settings for a firmer, stiffer ride. The fully-powered, load-sensitive braking system, actuated by a mushroom pedal, was also taken from the DS, except that discs were fitted on all four wheels. At the front, the discs and their calipers were mounted inboard, as on the DS, with separate calipers for the parking brake which was operated by a conventional hand lever, rather than the foot-pedal employed on the DS. Many drivers new to the system found it over-sensitive, of course. The *Autocar's* road test reported that only 40 lbs. of effort on the pedal was enough to bring the heavy (3,400 lb.) car to a rapid stop from 70 mph, with more than 1 g retardation.

Although it shared the same general overall design and operating principles, the fully powered rack-and-pinion steering mechanism fitted to the SM was substantially different, however, and represented a major technical advance over the system employed earlier on the DS. Much thought had been devoted to improving this function, so the car would be capable of responding precisely and rapidly to the finest movement of the driver's hands on the steering wheel, as when making a rapid correction to its trajectory at high speed. At the same time, it was considered essential that this response would not be so overly sensitive as to be liable to amplify any small reactive or involuntary movements of the wheel, throwing the car off course. Consequently, the SM boasted an important new Citroën innovation, its variable Diravi (Direction a Rappel Asservi) hydraulically powered rack-and-pinion

Although presented as a full four-seater, the SM was, in truth, a two-plus-two, with restricted space in the rear. To make the interior look roomier than it was, Citroën used a particularly petite model in their launch-time publicity photographs.

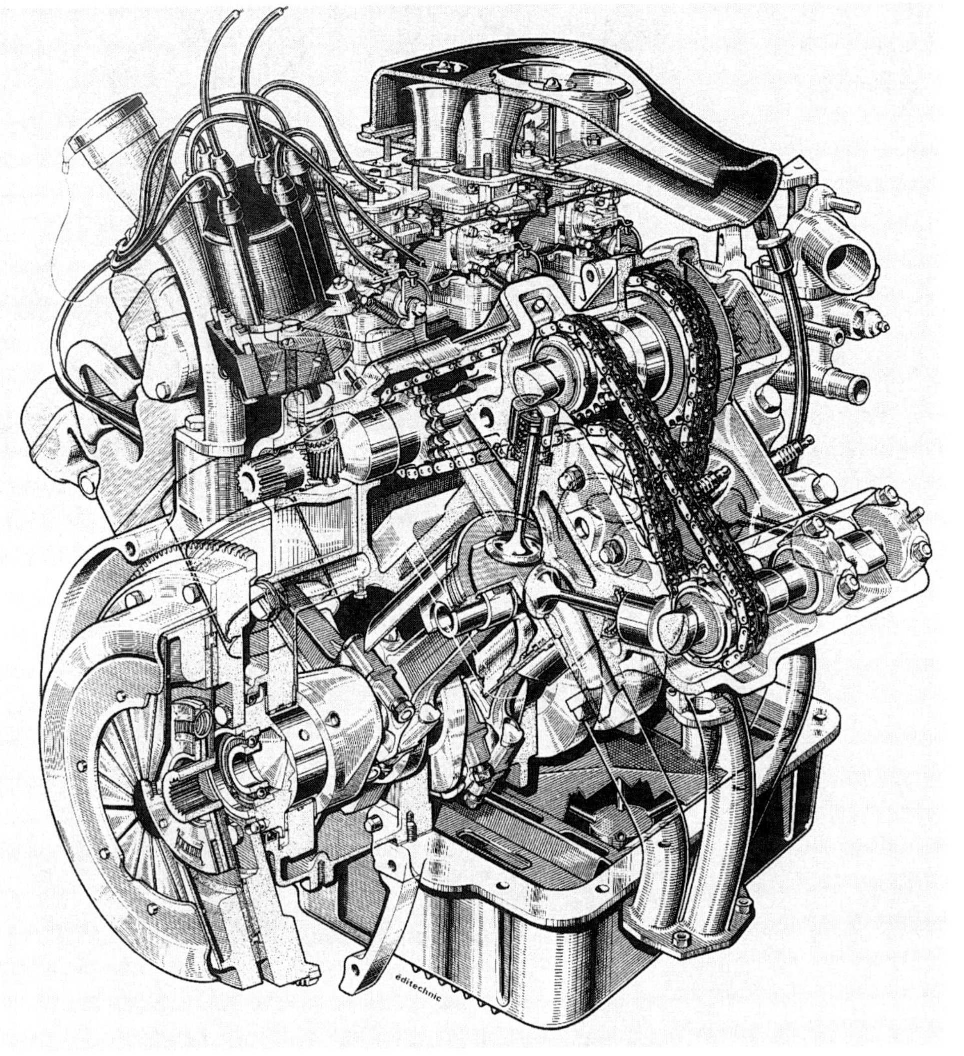

The principal details of the short-stroke Maserati V-6 engine are revealed in this cutaway drawing. Note the duplex chains that drove the four overhead camshafts via a jackshaft located centrally in the "V" between the cylinder heads. The jackshaft also acted as a drive for the engine accessories. Note also the unusual distributor; its two inner leads show that it is really two three-cylinder distributors housed within a single casing. Initially the SM was equipped with a five-speed manual transmission only. But largely for the benefit of the American market, in 1974 a three-speed fully-automatic gearbox was introduced, mated to an enlarged 2965 cc version of the Maserati V6 engine, normally aspirated with the original Weber carburetors.

steering system, known as Vari-Power in the U.K. market. A development of the principle introduced on the DS19, this revolutionary servo device, invented by Paul Magés and tested in the DXGT prototype of 1966, was exceptionally high-geared. The steering ratio of the SM was 9:4.1 (compared to 14:7.1 on the DS) so that one turn of the steering wheel, left or right, took the front wheels from straight-ahead to full lock.

As its name implied, the degree of power assistance provided by the Diravi system actually varied with the speed of the car. When the vehicle was at a standstill, the degree of assistance applied was total, to such an extent that the front wheels returned to the straight-ahead position when the steering wheel was released, with no intervention required from the driver. But as the speed of the vehicle was increased, and the angle of the steering lock became greater, the amount of resistance felt at the steering wheel rose proportionately. This result was achieved by the use of a centrifugal steering regulator driven from the front end of the gearbox in such a way that its speed of rotation was related directly to the road speed of the car. Bob weights inside the centrifugal regulator exerted leverage on a slide valve regulating pressure in the hydraulic circuit operating the steering rack in such a way that the force required at the steering wheel was constantly adjusted according to the circumstances. Additionally, by means of a cam and follower arrangement attached to the steering column, automatic self-centering action was provided, ensuring absolute and effortless directional stability when cruising fast on a straight course, as on a motorway. Conversely, when parking, virtually no manual effort was required to maneuver this heavy vehicle. As the system also eliminated all shocks and feedback from the front wheels, the end-result was to give the driver a feeling of maximum sensitivity and control when rounding bends at high speeds, even though, as on the DS system, there was no direct mechanical connection between the steering wheel and the tires. These were Michelin's latest high-performance XWX tubeless radials, also used on the Ferrari Daytona, but in this case fitted on special 6J wide-rimmed Michelin steel wheels with five-stud fastenings, manufactured specifically for the SM. Later Michelin produced a unique type of lightweight carbon-fiber wheels for the SM, available as an optional extra from July 1971 on. These were less than half the weight of the standard pressed steel wheels.

Last, the SM also boasted an extremely advanced lighting system featuring no fewer than six separate Cibie quartz halogen units. These were arranged in two rows, left and right, each consisting of a separate main beam, dipped beam and long-range beam. The latter inner-most unit was directionally controlled, pivoting on a vertical axis in response to movements of the steering wheel, an innovation that had been introduced earlier on certain DS models. But whereas on the DS these swiveling beams were mechanically controlled by a system of wires, on the SM the linkage was achieved by means of two independent hydraulic circuits. These lights were set to turn at an angle slightly in advance of the steering lock angle to illuminate the curve of a bend. Similarly, the level of the beams of each group of lamps was stabilized and controlled by an automatic self-leveling device, also hydraulically actuated, which enabled them to pivot on a horizontal axis to compensate for any changes in the vehicle's attitude in relation to the ground, as when accelerating or braking, but independently of the vehicle's own self-leveling suspension system. A damper prevented continuous action caused by transient movements. Both groups of lights (and also the frontal registration license plate) were housed behind a curved glass cowling that ran across the nose of the car to optimize the aerodynamic efficiency of the body. Unfortunately, this novel arrangement did not conform to U.S. lighting regulations and the cars supplied to that market had a simplified system comprising four conventional fixed position headlights with circular lenses, unshielded by any glass fairing.

By virtue of its short career — the shortest of any post-war Citroën model — the subsequent evolution of the SM was severely curtailed. In fact, besides the change to fuel-injection in 1972, its development was limited to the introduction, in October 1972, of a third, supplementary, 3-liter version, intended principally for the North American market. Citroën's experience in attempting to export the DS to the USA and Canada had shown that a fully automatic gearbox was regarded as essential by customers in these countries and had consequently entered into a liaison with the Borg-Warner company in England, with a view to adapting B-W's 35 epicyclical transmission used on the Rover P5 and Jaguar XJ6. A considerable amount of development work was involved in re-engineering this box for installation in a front-wheel-drive car (in conjunction with a Verto-Ferodo torque converter) since the drive had to be reversed by 180 degrees to return it to the differential, which required a two-shaft arrangement, the first of its kind. This automatic box duly become available as an option on the DS21 in December 1971 and then on the DS23, which replaced the DS21 nine months later, though it never found its way onto the DS's replacement, the CX, where a C-Matic semi-auto transmission was offered.

In fact, the Borg Warner automatic box was initially fitted to a limited series of 2.7-liter carburetted SMs made available in the USA in October 1971. However, to provide the increased torque demanded by an automatic transmission, the original 2.7-liter engine was soon superseded

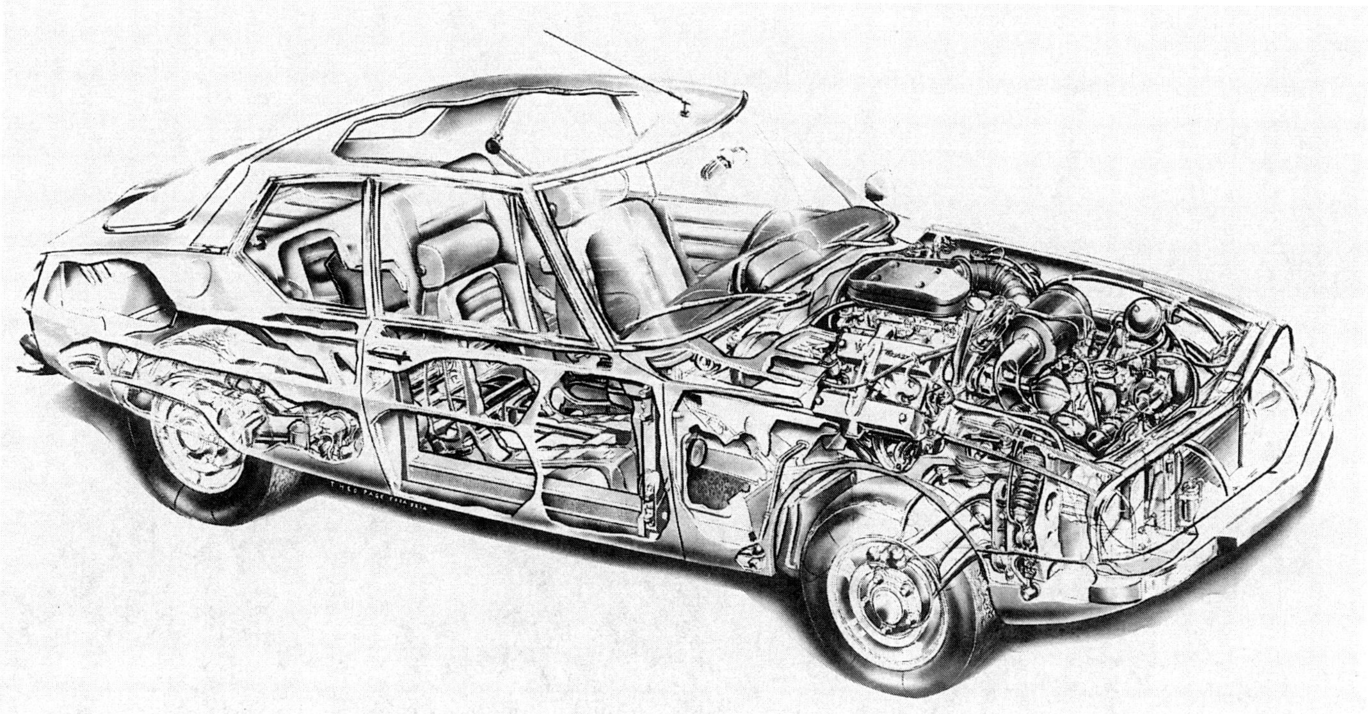

This cutaway drawing shows the general layout of the SM's engine, transmission and suspension systems. The position of the front off-side half-axle unit, with its trailing axle arms and associated suspension cylinder and sphere, can be clearly seen.

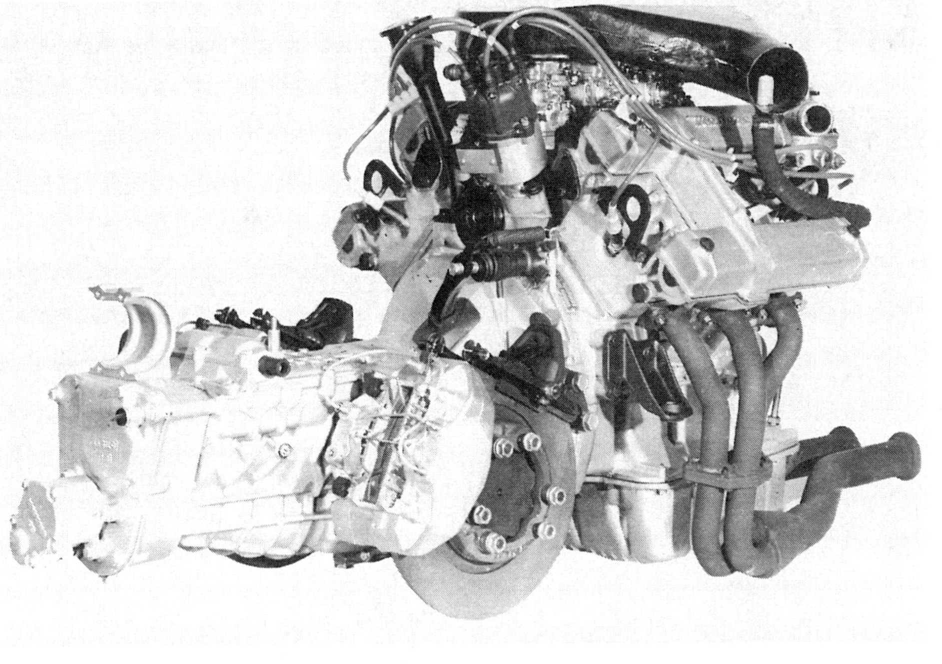

This is the 2670 cc V-6 Maserati engine with three twin-choke Weber carburetors fitted to the first version of the SM sold from 1971 and 1972, complete with its Citroën five-speed gearbox, positioned in front of the engine. Note also the inboard disc brakes and calipers mounted on the gearbox and the studs on the discs to which the drive-shafts were attached. Later post–1973 versions were fuel-injected.

on the SM auto model, by a new 3-liter version of the Maserati power-plant, with bores opened out to 91.6 mm, taking the swept volume up to 2965cc and the fiscal rating to 17CV. Moreover, as the Bosch fuel injection system used on the SM and DS had failed to satisfy U.S. emission control regulations, the current fuel-injected 2.7-liter engine, introduced in July 1972, could not be sold in the USA, with or without automatic transmission. So when it appeared, just three months after the 2.7-liter EFI engine, the 3-liter engine reverted to using the three twin-choke Weber carburetors of the original 2.7-liter engine. The power output achieved by this third and final power plant was 180 bhp, only 2 bhp more than the injected 2.7-liter, but torque was increased to 181 lb ft at 4,000 rpm, which was more the object of the exercise. Even so, the top speed was reduced by 15 mph to 127 mph, and touring fuel consumption to just 21 mpg. In September 1973, the 3-liter version was offered on the European market also, with the option of a manual transmission. Not surprisingly, very few of the total 1,612 of the 3-liter SMs built were sold on that side of the Atlantic.

In the early 1970s, the future of the automobile and the companies that built it looked bright indeed, the Citroën firm included. In 1970, the company built more than 600,000 cars for the first time in its history and greater than 700,000 in 1972. Even large, thirsty and expensive prestige cars like the SM were in demand. During 1971, 2,770 examples were sold in France alone, together with 922 in Italy and 513 in West Germany. It seemed at first as if Bercot's hunch had paid off handsomely. Initial reaction from both press and public was had extremely favorable. "Is all the expense and complication worth it?" asked the normally sceptical *Autocar* magazine in its Autotest report published in June 1971, concluding that indeed it was. "Getting back into other cars afterwards makes them, not the Citroën, seem odd and difficult, especially in regard to the steering. We feel that for a large and heavy car it sets new standards of handling and stability." Other motoring journalists on both sides of the Atlantic concurred that Citroën had succeeded in its am-

Avant-garde in 1972 and still advanced more than 30 years later, the SM is a design that has withstood the test of time. Clearly, its unique style and character have not dated, though they are still misunderstood, so that today it is undoubtedly among the most underestimated and undervalued of all the world's super-cars.

bitious task. In January 1972, the influential U.S. magazine *Motor Trend* voted the SM its Car of the Year. It was almost unheard of for this award to go to anything but an American car, and hopeful of succeeding at last in this previously unconquered territory, Citroën concentrated its SM sales effort on the North American market, selling 1,128 cars in the USA and a further 237 in Canada.

By the end of 1972, almost two years after the SM's launch, a total of 9,892 cars had found owners—868 in 1970, 4,988 in 1971 and 4,036 in 1972—numbers that were somewhat less than the planned production rate of 100 cars a week set at the outset. But, unfortunately, the following year both sales and production plummeted to almost half their previous levels. The reason, of course, was the onset, in the autumn of 1973, of the first Energy Crisis, an unforeseen event that spelled the end, temporarily at least, of glamorous but extravagant vehicles such as the Citroën Maserati. Following the Arab-Israeli Yom Kippur War of October 1973, the OPEC consortium of Middle-Eastern oil producers decided to reduce supplies of crude oil on the world market, which had the immediate effect of raising prices. Motorists recoiled in deep shock from the ensuing four-fold escalation in the cost of gas at the pumps, and also from the draconian speed limits that were then introduced across Europe in an attempt to conserve supplies. In West Germany (then Citroën's second largest export market) private recreational motoring on Sundays was banned altogether by the Federal Government for several weeks. Forced to re-evaluate the economics of motoring and to review their car-buying priorities, drivers delayed the replacement of their vehicles or turned to smaller, less thirsty, cars. A tidal wave of panic engulfed the European motor industry. For the first time since World War I, a brake had been put on the ever-increasing popularity and proliferation of the motor car. The French market alone was almost halved, and as its customers deserted its showrooms, the following year, 1974, Citroën's total production plummeted to 688,000 units, in contrast to the 750,000 vehicles assembled in 1973. This catastrophic down-turn in output, the second serious reversal in the company's growth to occur in eight years, caused another collapse in profits—a net loss of 999 million francs was recorded in 1974.

The Energy Crisis of 1973-1974 was indeed a defining moment in world history, and certainly a turning point in the story of the Double Chevron marque. Undoubtedly, it hit the Citroën company at a particularly bad moment; in fact, its impact turned the prevailing mood of optimistic confidence into one of bleak pessimism almost overnight. Having invested heavily in the development of three entirely new models, the GS, SM and the forthcoming CX, not to mention the Comotor Wankel engine research project and the construction of new production facilities at Aulnay-sous-Bois, Citroën was gravely exposed to this recession, far more so than most of its rivals, and severe counter-measures (including the mass redundancy of 4,000 employees) were taken to control the situation and reduce losses.

The disaster caused Michelin to reassess, once again, its relationship with its Citroën subsidiary, which was becoming increasingly difficult to manage and control. Michelin management concluded that, if they were to safeguard their own financial position at a time of political, social and economic uncertainty, they had little alternative but to abandon their interest in automobile manufacturing and to concentrate their resources exclusively on tire production. Observers noted that the current situation paralleled almost exactly the crisis that had led to their acquisition of Citroën forty years earlier, almost to the day.

The upshot was that, on June 24, 1974, a joint press communiqué was issued by Michelin, Citroën and Peugeot announcing plans for a collaboration between the erstwhile rivals that would amount to a complete takeover of Citroën by Peugeot. The press release stated that this co-operation of efforts and resources within the French automobile industry was the best response that could be made to the adverse circumstances then prevailing. The mutual objective was to create a group large enough to be fully competitive in the international arena and strong enough to withstand the realities of the global market, it declared. In fact, Citroën and Peugeot had already embarked upon a loose collaboration by setting up, in 1964, cooperative purchasing and supply arrangements such as the jointly owned diesel engine factory Indenor. Moreover, Peugeot had previously established a similar informal association with Renault.

The tie-up was, of course, a move that had the full backing and encouragement of the French government, anxious as ever to prevent the further ingress of Anglo-Saxon ownership within the strategic industries of the Republic. To this end, within four years Peugeot would also be encouraged to take over, in August 1978, the fourth largest of the major French car firms, Simca, from its owners, the American Chrysler Corporation, but in this case the move was actually initiated by the government and made possible by public funding.

So it happened that in December 1974 Peugeot acquired 38 percent of the share capital of Citroën and assumed overall command of the partnership. However, at this stage the two companies were administered by quite separate managerial structures. Having overseen the disposal of Michelin's interest in Citroën, François Rollier, the last of the Michelin men to hold the office of President-Directeur-General (Chairman and Managing Director) relinquished managerial control in favor of a Peugeot appointee, the production specialist George Taylor, who had made his name when running the Indenor diesel-engine factory (owned jointly by Citroën and Peugeot) and, later, Peugeot's assembly plant at Sochaux. As the new P-D-G of S.A. Automobiles Citroën, Taylor headed a three-man administrative directorate comprising the previous managing director under the Rollier regime, Raymond Ravenel, and Jacques Lombard, who represented Peugeot. This triumvirate reported to a six-man central council of administration headed by the current Peugeot Chairman and Chief Executive, François Gautier. That same year, the Berliet truck and bus division was sold by Michelin to the Renault group to form a partnership with Saviem.

Ironically, the following year saw the end of production at the Quai de Javel, when the last example of the D series range to be built there, a DS23 Pallas sedan, rolled off the assembly line in July 1975, terminating 55 years of car manufacturing on the site. During that time no fewer than 3,227,105 vehicles had been produced there, including 1,330,755 DS and ID models. Thereafter, production was switched to the new facility at Aulnay-sous-Bois in 1973. Actually, the Quai de Javel was to remain the Citroën company's head office for another eight years.

In September 1976, two years after the first *rapprochement,* Peugeot SA extended its holding in Automobiles Citroën to 89.95 percent via an exchange of shares effected with Michelin, and merged the automobile manufacturing interests of the Citroën and Peugeot firms completely under its direct control, by means of a holding company known as PSA, a contraction of Peugeot SA. The new PSA Group was directed until 1982 by Gautier's successor as PDG of Peugeot, Jean-Paul Parayre. Formerly a civil servant in the Ministry of Scientific and Industrial Development, Parayre had represented the French government in the long negotiations that had led to the takeover of Citroën by Peugeot, and which had been encouraged, fostered and to a large extent funded by the French government through grants and tax concessions.

The declared intention of the merger was that, henceforth, the two partners would combine to provide mutual technical, financial and administrative support, but although sharing joint manufacturing facilities they would retain their own distinct character and identity, producing their own individual models (with certain common components such as engines and floor pans) which would then be sold by autonomous distribution networks competing in every sector of the market. Thus, through a process of managerial reorganization and financial restructuring, the long-term survival of the Citroën marque was guaranteed, albeit in the hands of a new owner whose style and philosophy of management was very different indeed from the two regimes that had gone before.

Then as now, Peugeot, just like Michelin, remained a privately owned firm controlled by the family that bears its name, and which continues to be recognized as one of France's greatest and most powerful industrial dynasties. Located in the Belfort area of northeastern France, the company could trace its origins to 1810, when it had begun to produce hand-tools, ironmongery and kitchenware such as pots and pans. In 1885 it commenced the manufacture of bicycles (which it still makes today) before diversifying again by building, in 1891, the first automobile to carry its Lion badge, powered by a Daimler engine. As automobile pioneers, the two families were in close contact from the very start; in the Paris-to-Bordeaux road race of 1895, André and Edouard Michelin drove a vehicle equipped with pneumatic tires which they had built themselves using a Peugeot chassis and a Daimler engine, and which they had christened *l'Éclair*, or streak of lightning.

But there the similarity ends, for the discreet austerity of the Catholic Michelins did not correspond exactly with the self-denying, Calvinistic parsimony of the Protestant Peugeots. Whereas the members of the former family were generally artistic and creative by nature, unafraid of innovation and experimentation and quite prepared to back a promising idea, the latter were staid, conservative and unadventurous, acutely money-conscious and unaccustomed to taking financial risks by breaking new ground.

The first post-war Peugeot car had been the 1.3-liter 203, an entirely conventional rear-wheel-drive design, albeit outstandingly tough and well-built. Styled in the American manner currently fashionable in France, this model boasted independent front suspension by coil springs plus certain features borrowed from the Traction Avant such as rack-and-pinion steering. It remained in production until 1960, gaining for the company a reputation for rugged reliability and durability, and winning it an impressive share of export markets, particularly in Africa. Its success allowed Peugeot to acquire and absorb the old, established names of Chenard et Walcker and Hotchkiss. The 203 was followed by another best-seller, the 1.6-liter 404 sedan, a car of similar qualities and attributes but packaged with a more European look created by Pininfarina, the Italian stylists with which Peugeot subsequently established a long and enduring relationship. The 404 was replaced by the 1.8-liter 504 in 1973; but in the meanwhile, however, came the 204, introduced in 1965. This was an uncharacteristically original — indeed mold-breaking — FWD design, featuring a transversally mounted 956cc OHV engine, fully independent suspension front and rear and front disc brakes.

The strengths of the Peugeot Lion lay in production engineering rather than conceptual engineering and design. In marked contrast to Citroën and Michelin, it was a company dominated by the disciplines of cost accountancy, product-planning and market research, to which the design and engineering function was subservient. It had survived thus far, not by flair but by an unremitting perseverance in its quest for profitability, building cars down to a price, not up to a standard, and by carefully weighing the cost of every extra nut and bolt.

Upon arriving at the Quai de Javel in December 1974, in circumstances that compared with Michelin's takeover of André Citroën's empire almost exactly 40 years before, the new Peugeot rulers lost no time in making changes. Indeed, a veritable Inquisition of accountants and work-study experts descended upon the company, scrutinizing every aspect of its production costs and overheads with all the rigor of a Calvinistic Torquemada. No aspect of Citroën's activities would be allowed to continue unless proven to be self-financing. Apparently, the attempts to make savings extended to introducing the cheapest possible grade of toilet paper throughout the organization. These uncomfortable and disagreeable restrictions were not confined to financial measures either; the serving of wine in canteens and restaurants, a traditional feature of life chez Citroën, was also ended. Seven thousand compulsory redundancies were declared, though upon seeing this exodus and fearing further changes of a more fundamental kind in future, many of the old guard left of their own volition, including Robert Opron, who departed for Renault almost immediately, to be replaced by André Estaque.

Ironically, the only vehicle among Citroën's product portfolio to be affected by this clash of cultures was, of course, its flagship, the SM, which was declared to be an unnecessary and unprofitable extravagance, as was the entire relationship with Maserati. In May 1975, therefore, the Italian subsidiary was cast adrift by Peugeot and left to flounder before eventually being rescued by de Tomaso. But, in truth, this decision came as no more than a confirmation of an established reality. French market sales of the SM had already been terminated in July 1974, leaving the car available for export markets only; in fact, only 273 were built by Citroën at Javel throughout that year.

Earlier, however, in April 1974, a statement had been made by Citroën's Paris press office announcing the start

Commissioned by President Pompidou in 1971, the SM Presidential cabriolets were also built by Henri Chapron, using an extended long-wheelbase platform similar to that of the Opera. The top was operated hydraulically. Two were built.

of a cooperative venture between Maserati and Automobiles Ligier, a specialist low-volume constructor of sporting and racing cars located at Abrest near Vichy, and whose Ligier JS2 model, equipped with a Maserati engine, had already achieved success at le Mans. Although the press release did not say so explicitly, the move was a last ditch attempt to keep the SM project alive, by transferring both body production and final assembly from Paris to Abrest. During the 15 months that this agreement lasted, a total of 135 cars were built by Ligier, 21 in 1974 and another 114 in 1975.

Following the abandonment of Maserati, however, there was no way that production of the SM could continue under this arrangement. All that could be done was to dispose of the remaining stock of body-shells built by Chausson, rumored to amount to several hundred. But despite pleas from Citroën that these shells should all be completed as cars, the order came back from Peugeot that they must be sent to the crusher. The superb SM, the proud symbol of Citroën's superiority, was dead. Just like the Concorde, it had proved to be simultaneously a technological triumph and a commercial disaster. In just five years, between August 1970 and September 1975, exactly 12,920 were sold worldwide — 5,509 in France, 2,070 in Italy, 2,037 in the USA, 971 in Germany, 396 in Canada and 327 in the U.K., with the remainder finding customers here and there throughout the rest of the world, including the Middle East, Africa, Japan, Asia, Australia and, of course, other European countries such as Belgium, Luxembourg, Austria, Spain, Switzerland and the Netherlands.

All of them were left-hand-drive cars, of course. At the start of the SM project it had been decided that no provision would be made in its design for it to be built in a right-hand-drive version, and none were ever made by Citroën. Even so, several examples exist today, having been converted, either semi-officially or completely unofficially, by certain Citroën dealers — three in England and another five or six in Australia.

The Presidential SM Cabriolets

As the coach-builder most closely associated with Citroën, Henri Chapron lost no time in bringing out a drop-head cabriolet version of the SM, called the Mylord, which he presented on his stand at the 1971 Paris Salon. A relatively straightforward adaptation of the standard two-door car, the wheelbase and overall length of the Mylord were unchanged, and apart from the installation of a hydraulically operated folding hood, alterations to its

Despite their great size, the two presidential SMs were powered by the standard 2.7-liter carbureted engine. They were inaugurated in 1972 during the state visit to Paris of Her Majesty, the Queen and the Duke of Edinburgh. More than 30 years later, they are still in service and were used again during the state visit to Paris of the same Royals in April 2004.

styling were confined to revisions in the shape of its rear-end, made necessary by the replacement of the glass hatchback by a conventional trunk lid. This had a pronounced raised center section which gave a different appearance to the rear-end view, although the other aspects of the original design such as the bumper and its integrated light lenses were not disturbed. By 1984 seven of these cabriolets had been built for private customers who were happy to pay the considerably elevated price of 128,000 FF including tax for the exclusivity of owning one of these superbly elegant cars.

At the following year's show, however, Chapron went a step further by exhibiting a four-door limousine version of the SM, the Opera, built on an extended platform lengthened by 29cm (11.6 inches) with a wheel-base of 3.34m or 131.5 inches. Like the Mylord, this car had a conventional trunk, though with a lid that was plain and flat so that in profile, the Opera was more or less faithful to Opron's original design. Eventually, eight models of the Opera were constructed, selling at 165,400 francs, including tax.

Meanwhile, in 1971, Chapron had received an order from the Elysée Palace, inviting him to build two four-door drop-head cars for the use of President Pompidou for state or ceremonial occasions. According to tradition, these carried the registration numbers 2 PR 75 and 3 PR 75, as I PR 75 remained allocated to the Super DS which Chapron had built for General de Gaulle

in 1968. Both of these presidential cars (which measured 5.60 meters or 220 inches overall and weighed 1,780 kgs or 3,924 lbs.—14.5 percent longer and 22.8 percent heavier than the Mylord) were painted in metallic anthracite grey and trimmed in natural beige leather. Despite their great size, the engine fitted was the standard 2.7 liter carburetted version of the V6, and apart from an upgrading of the brakes and suspension, mechanical modifications were limited to a change to the final drive gearbox ratio to allow the cars to travel slowly in processions for long periods. This restricted their top speed to 180 km/h (112 mph). The cars were inaugurated in May 1972, on the occasion of the state visit to Paris of HM the Queen and the Duke of Edinburgh.

Having served four successive French presidents and their guests, both vehicles are still in service today, although they are rarely used. In May 1994 one of the pair actually visited England, when it conveyed President Mitterand on board the Shuttle train in the ceremonies that marked the official opening of the Channel Tunnel. Their most recent appearance took place in April 2004 when they were used again during the visit to Paris of HM the Queen and the Duke of Edinburgh almost exactly 30 years after their first appearance.

13

The Citroën GS and GSA, 1970–1986

As we have already observed, the Swinging Sixties certainly swung for Automobiles Citroën. As the post-war recovery of the French economy gathered momentum, the company's sales graph followed a steady upward curve throughout the greater part of the decade to reach, in 1966, an unprecedented high point. That year it produced more than 531,000 vehicles and captured 30.5 percent (1965) of the French domestic market, plus 9.3 percent of the total European car market (1966). Remarkably, this position of dominance was based on the outstanding long-term success of just two quite contrasting models that occupied opposing ends of the market spectrum — the cheap, practical 2CV and the costly, complex hydropneumatically-sprung D Series (DS19 & ID19).

Consistently throughout that time this pair of uniquely advanced designs had been numbered among the best-selling cars in France, catering to the needs of both the most affluent and the least well-off of motorists. Yet between the two extremes, Citroën had little to offer the great new intermediate-class market that was opening up, populated by middle-income drivers who demanded comfort with economy and space without expense, and who found the Deesse or the Deuche either too big or too small for their requirements. What was needed was a new car to oppose the more recently introduced offerings from Renault and Peugeot in the all-important 6CV-8CV (1000cc to 1300cc) bracket, a sales territory from which the Double Chevron marque had been absent since the war, and so to plug the large hole in the center of the its range through which so much valuable business was escaping.

The waiting was ended when Citroën's long-anticipated middle-class car, the Citroën GS, was unveiled at the Paris Motor Show in October 1970, a mere six months after the debut of the Citroën-Maserati. To have introduced, virtually simultaneously, two similarly innovative — yet essentially different and contrasting — models was a technical achievement quite unparalleled in motoring history. Never before had any manufacturer launched two such radically important designs within so short a space of time, or introduced virtually simultaneously two similarly innovative — yet essentially different and contrasting — models. Ten years had passed since the arrival of the company's last all-new cars, the DS19 and the ID19, (more recent introductions such as the Ami-6 and Dyane had been derivatives of the 2CV), but the interval had not been one of total inactivity. Although little new had emerged into public view from within the ultra-secret confines of the Bureau d'Etudes, behind the scenes a long succession of ultimately abortive prototypes had been investigated in an attempt to consolidate Citroën's reputation, not merely as an innovator and pioneer of unusual or eccentric technical solutions, but as mainstream volume manufacturer of cars that had true mass-market appeal.

In 1964, three years after the arrival of the Ami-6, the company embarked on a new, much more radical design project, code-named Vehicule F, intended for production in 1967. This time, the aim was to produce not one single new intermediate car, but a whole family of passenger and light commercial vehicles. Apparently, it was intended that, by using a modular approach, a wide range of models could be put together from a common inventory of systems and components, so that each one could be positioned to satisfy a particular individual category of customer or task, much as André Citroën had intended when launching the Traction Avant range. But ultimately this Project F was abandoned, for reasons that have never been entirely revealed or explained.

It appears that the design of the proposed body-shell

for the F series vehicles relied on a new constructional technique in which the sides of the monocoque bodyshell were formed entirely by large single-piece pressings having cut-outs for the doors. These pressings were joined to the roof panel by a raised seam running along the topline, and which actually formed a prominent styling feature of the car. As was its normal practice, Citroën had not patented this system, so as to avoid giving its competitors any clue as to exactly what new ideas were in preparation behind the iron curtain of its Bureau d'Etudes. Following the appearance in 1961 of Renault's first-ever FWD car, the Renault 4 (which Pierre Bercot regarded as nothing more than a plagiarized version of the 2CV), fear of industrial espionage at the Quai de Javel had verged on the borders of paranoia. Ever since the days of André Citroën, the Regie Renault (a nationalized company since January 1945) had been regarded as its greatest rival. Therefore when, as a result of either a fortuitous coincidence or the activities of a mole at the Quai de Javel, Renault announced that it had obtained a patent for a virtually identical system of construction (which it proceeded to employ on its R16 medium class hatchback sedan launched in 1965) Bercot was outraged, particularly as Renault demanded excessive royalties from Citroën for the use of the technique.

Jealous of his company's reputation for originality, he was adamant that the Double Chevron marque could never be seen to be imitating any of its competitors, and most certainly not Renault. In fact, the external appearance of the Renault 16 closely resembled the proposed new Citroën model. Dissatisfied with this and many other aspects of the car, he eventually ordered the cancellation of the F project, in April 1967, just six months before its scheduled launch at the forthcoming October Paris Motor Show.

Because the Vehicule F concept encompassed so many different variables, and thus had required the development of a great diversity of bodies and engines and their associated suspension and transmission systems (it is believed that even the possibility of hydrostatic transmission coupled with a Wankel engine was investigated) its abandonment proved to be an extremely costly setback for Citroën. Presses and tooling for the bodywork had already been ordered from Budd in the USA and had to be paid for; billions of francs in development costs were written off, and the financial ramifications of this wasted expenditure endured for many years, eventually leading to the merger negotiations with Fiat in 1968 and, later, with Peugeot in 1976, which will be discussed later in this chapter. However, there is little evidence to suggest that, had it gone ahead, the project would have produced the successful and profitable new additions to the Citroën range so greatly needed at that time. On the contrary, it seems that Project F was beset with many other unresolved technical problems, including troubles with certain of the proposed engines and suspension systems. It was rumoured that even the aerodynamic qualities of its bodywork left much to be desired.

With the scrapping of the Model F project, the need to fill the gap in the center of its model range became an even more urgent priority for Citroën. Thus, the ambitious multifarious marketing concept that had influenced the design and engineering thinking behind the abandoned vehicle was replaced by a new, far less complex design brief, with the intention of producing an alternative, stop-gap, medium class car within a very tight budget and time schedule. A mere two years was all that could be spared, a period that also saw the creation of the Citroën Maserati SM. The *cahier des charges* for Project G specified that the replacement should be a four-door, five-seater sedan, capable of 150 km/h (93 mph) and priced to compete with the conventionally engineered family car that was currently the best-selling automobile in France, the Renault 6. Moreover, on Bercot's insistence, it was to have a standard three-box configuration (with a separate trunk) instead of the radical hatchback layout that had been proposed and permitted for the Project F car.

Crucially also, its engine was to fall within the optimum 1000–1300cc or 6–7CV bracket, so that it would qualify for favorable rating under the French *puissance fiscale* system of road taxation, in which the rate of duty payable varies according to the size of the car and increases substantially with larger engine dimensions and outputs, as determined by a complex formula, instead of being subject to the fixed, universal rate levied in the U.K.. As has often been observed, this practice, introduced in its present form after the war, has had a profound and perhaps entirely adverse effect on the French motor industry. By favoring small cars less than 2 liters in capacity, it has made the ownership of larger high-powered machines of 3 liters and above (for which France was once renowned) prohibitively expensive, and thus has allowed a new breed of Grand Routier from Germany (where no such restrictions apply) to dominate the luxury, prestige, high-performance sector of the European market.

As so little evidence of the character and appearance of Project F has survived, it is impossible to judge how well it would have fared in the marketplace at that time. But there are no such doubts or mysteries about the success enjoyed by its replacement, the Project G. Built at Citroën's new factory at Rennes-le-Jannais in Brittany, opened by President Charles de Gaulle just two years earlier, the GS range was destined to remain in production for 16 years and to become one of Citroën's greatest achievements, ultimately selling more than 2,500,000 cars, second only to the 2CV. And yet, strangely, considering its many virtues, it has yet to achieve the classic status of its better known sister vehicles, the DS and SM, and become acknowledged as a cult-car or design icon by motoring experts and car collectors, at least in the Anglo-Saxon world.

Considering its very short gestation period, the GS was truly a technical tour de force, a hugely influential vehicle that represented yet another landmark in the history of the popular automobile. Although it was aimed at middle-class, middle-income owner-drivers, it was most certainly not middle-of-the-road. At a time when most average, ordinary, run-of-the-mill family sedans had cart-type semi-eliptic springs, live rear axles, crude drum brakes and even more uncertain steering arrangements, plus the aerodynamic efficiency of a flying brick, the GS represented an astounding combination of technical advantages and benefits, including fully independent self-leveling suspension. In short, the GS was a DS for the ordinary motorist, offering levels of comfort, performance and security normally associated only with cars twice its size and price.

Equipped with a durable air-cooled flat-four boxer engine, fully-powered disc brakes all round, rack-and-pinion steering, all-independent self-levelling hydro-pneumatic suspension and, naturally, front-wheel-drive transmission, the GS brought technical sophistication to the small family car and became the yardstick by which all the others were judged. And yet despite this wealth of engineering, its price was no more than that of its humdrum rivals, 12,100 Francs at the outset.

Not surprisingly, the following year the GS won the prestigious Car of the Year award staged by *Car* magazine, voted first by a wide majority of the international jury of 19 motoring journalists drawn from 11 countries. Scoring 11 first-place and six second-place votes, it finished well ahead of the field, which included the new Range Rover and, of course, the Citroën SM. Commenting on this success in the columns of *Car* magazine, the late L.J.K Setright remarked that "Without surrendering their aristocracy, Citroën have found the common touch, and motoring will never be quite the same again." To celebrate this victory, Citroën produced a special one-of-a-kind multi-colored version of the GS, painted with all the flags of Europe. This was pictured on the cover of its catalogs and used in its publicity campaigns.

The team responsible for the rapid design and development of Project G had been led by Alain Roche who reported to Citroën's new chief executive Claude-Alain Sarre, who had replaced Pierre Bercot on the latter's retirement at the end of 1968. The styling was the work of Robert Opron, assisted by Henri Dargent (exteriors) and Michel Harmand (interiors and controls) while responsibility for engine matters rested with a Monsieur Dupin. Naturally, its suspension was created by Paul Mages, the brains behind Citroën's hydro-pneumatic technology, who had worked closely with André Lefèbvre in the design of the DS19. It is hardly surprising, therefore, that although Lefèbvre played no part in this project himself (he had retired 10 years earlier, in 1958, and died in 1964), the resulting car was perhaps a much more faithful expression of his engineering credo than had actually been achieved during his time at the Bureau d'Etudes. Indeed, the GS incorporated many of the design concepts that he had intended for the DS19 in 1955, but which had been omitted due to the severe cost constraints imposed at that time. It also showed a marked conceptual similarity with the highly advanced Panhard Dyna X sedan, the old-established firm of Panhard & Levassor having recently been absorbed into the Citroën organization.

Chief among these features, of

This shot displays the pure, clean, simple lines of the first generation GS of 1970–79, styled by Robert Opron. No fewer than eight vivid color schemes were available, plus two trim levels, Confort and Club.

course, was an advanced, lightweight, flat-four-cylinder OHC air-cooled engine, located low in the nose of the vehicle, ahead of the front axle and with its integral clutch and gearbox inclined rearwards and downwards at seven degrees below the horizontal, to reduce the vehicle's center of gravity to the lowest possible point, as had originally been proposed for the DS19. In effect, a doubled-up version of the 2CV's power unit, sharing many of its features and constructed along the same lines, the original 1015cc version of this engine was rated as a 6CV, having over-square bore and stroke dimensions of 74mm x 59mm and a compression ratio of 9:1. Its specific power output was 61 bhp SAE @ 6750 rpm with 52 ft lbs DIN torque @ 3,500 rpm, enough to give the car a top speed of 147 km/h or 91 mph, not much less than the current 1985cc engined Citroën D-Super sedan. A gas consumption of 35–40 mpg at an average speed of 49 mph was claimed, or 29 mpg at a steady 68–70 mph, although a subsequent, perhaps more accurate, test by *Autocar*, published in March 1971, revealed an overall average of only 23.3 mpg (27.6 mpg at motorway cruising speeds), a fact that *Autocar* described, quite rightly, as being the most disappointing feature of the GS. At first sight, its acceleration did not seem to be particularly impressive either; *Autocar* recorded that it took the car 18 seconds to reach 60 mph from a standing start, although Citroën claimed 16 seconds. But quickness in sprinting away from traffic lights was never the objective so far as the GS's designers were concerned; what weighed more heavily with them was the ease with which the GS's driver could overcome drag and increase his speed when already on the move, by accelerating, say, from 60 to 80 mph. Therefore, propulsive matters were so arranged that, when traveling at a constant 75 mph, only 30 bhp of its engine's total potential power output of 50 bhp was absorbed, leaving a reserve of 20 bhp in surplus tractive effort available for accelerating away from danger, overtaking slower traffic or climbing gradients. Autocar's tests recorded that an increase from 60 to 80mph took just 24 seconds to achieve—quite an exceptional level of performance for a one-liter engine and an indication of the remarkable aerodynamic efficiency of the GS's streamlined bodywork.

The GS's extremely light and compact power unit comprised three main elements—a central crankcase containing the crankshaft, con-rod and piston assembly; four individual, detachable cast-iron cylinder barrels with light alloy pistons, each barrel being generously provided with cooling fins; and two cylinder heads, left and right, similarly well-equipped with fins and other heat exchange surfaces. The cylinder barrels were grouped in two horizontally opposed banks, both pairs fastened between the crankcase and their respective cylinder heads by eight long bolts which passed through the double cam-box assembly that formed the top or outer part of the cylinder head. The cylinder heads and the crankcase, with its integral sump, were pressure die-cast from aluminum alloy, there being no separate, detachable oil-pan.

Each bank of cylinders was surmounted by a single common cylinder head incorporating an integral cam-box, also cast from light alloy, housing the respective overhead camshaft, and the rocker arm mechanism that op-

The GS sedan had a conventional three-box configuration. The rear window was fixed, and access to the large trunk was through the door below it which opened upwards. As the door incorporated the central section of the bumper, there was no sill to impede loading.

erated the inlet and exhaust valves. Both pairs of overhead valves were set at 70 degrees to each other in V formation within the cylinder heads, which had hemispherical combustion chambers. Access to allow adjustment of the valve mechanisms in their respective cam-boxes was provided by removable dome-shaped steel covers, there being one for both sets of inlet and exhaust valves on each bank, or four in all. The valves were actuated by rocker arms which pivoted on short shafts, each set being driven by a single overhead camshaft, one for each bank, left and right. Each camshaft, right and left, was driven through a system of pulleys, sprockets and idler wheels by a separate toothed, rubber belt, powered by the crankshaft, but the left-hand belt also turned the separate pulleywheel that powered the oilpump. A short jackshaft, operated by an eccentric on the oil pump shaft, powered the hydraulic pump. Also revolving with the crankshaft and mounted directly to it was the nine-bladed nylon fan that blew cooling air through ducting to the fins of the cylinders and their associated exhaust manifolds. The central crankcase and sump was a two-piece structure, split into halves along its vertical center line and held together by bolts. Yet so precisely were these castings machined, to a tolerance of one micron in fact, that both parts together with their associated cylinder heads and barrels mated together in a perfect gas-and oil-tight union, without the customary gaskets.

Similarly, just as was the case with the 2CV, the GS engine's piston, con-rod and crankshaft assembly comprised a single integral unit, built-up under special conditions in the factory and thus incapable of being stripped down or dismantled for repair. In the unlikely event of a big-end bearing failure, the unit had to be replaced in its entirety. Unusually, the one-piece connecting rods had un-split annular big-end bearings which were sleeved over the crankpins. Thus, the whole crankshaft, with its two counter-balanced webs and three main bearing journals (which rested in conventional split shell-bearings), were pressed together hydraulically after first having been temporarily shrunk by immersion in liquid nitrogen.

Again, just like the 2CV, the GS had no radiator, hoses, fanbelt or water pump to fail, or coolant to boil or freeze. Thus there was virtually nothing to go wrong, since an oil cooler was fitted to ensure optimum working temperature under all climatic conditions. The 1015cc unit was designed to cruise flat-out for long periods at motorway speeds and to run for at least 60,000 miles without a major overhaul. In practice, a service life of 100,000 was regularly attained, an achievement which although commonplace nowadays was quite exceptional for its era. Consequently, the GS's engine soon earned an enviable reputation for its general durability and reliability, and was acknowledged to be extraordinarily quiet and refined for an air-cooled unit due principally to the extremely rigid construction of its cylinder barrels and heads and to the inherent dynamic balance of its horizontally opposed layout. Although it was capable of revving to 8,000 rpm, its short stroke meant that piston speeds were low, making for minimal wear and tear. Despite these virtues, the design had certain vices, including a reluctance to start in cold or damp conditions; the long inlet manifolds that curved down from the twin-choke downdraft Solex carburetor mounted on top of the engine led to a proneness to flooding of the plugs and combustion chambers. To overcome this defect, warm lubricating oil en route to the cooler was ducted through a hot-spot located at the point where the carburetor sat on the induction manifolds. Poor positioning of the distributor, low down on the block, also caused problems in wet conditions including a reluctance to negotiate fords or floods!

The frontal aspect of the GS was dominated by the large air-intake grille demanded by its air-cooled flat-four engine. Its superbly comfortable nylon jersey upholstered seats can be glimpsed in this shot.

Initially, the GS was equipped with a conventional diaphragm clutch and a four-speed manual all-synchromesh gearbox, located rearwards between the engine and the firewall. Transmission was by constant velocity driveshafts of equal length, each having sliding tri-axe couplings at its inner gearbox end, and Rzeppa ball-and-cage joints at its outer end. The 4½ J × 15 sized ventilated steel disc wheels employed had three-stud fastenings and were shod with Michelin 145-15 ZX tubeless radial tires as standard.

As a result of the research and development work undertaken during the course of Project F, the suspension and springing arrangements adopted for the GS were also completely novel, as was the use of subframe assemblies to attach the engine, transmission and running gear to the monocoque body-shell. The front subframe and axle unit consisted of a large arch-shaped yoke or upturned cradle which spanned the engine compartment from side to side, and from which the engine and gearbox were suspended on flexible mountings. At the base of its forward face the subframe—formed from welded-up steel pressings—had a large cross member to which the anti-roll bar was attached, while on the reverse face there were two rearward extensions by which it was bolted directly to the bulkhead and floor pan of the body-shell. At the shoulders of the arch were two outward-facing extensions that housed the spheres and cylinders of the front hydro-pneumatic suspension units, each of which were attached by a piston rod to a single solid upper suspension arm positioned immediately beneath them. This upper suspension arm, made from forged steel, was located rigidly to the sub-frame by a pair of tapered roller bearings. The front hubs were also attached to the cradle at this point by means of a lower wishbone link, made from pressed steel, which was secured to the subframe at its lowest point by two rubber and nylon silentbloc bushes.

The air-cooled flat-four engine of the GS, in its original 1015 cc form, sectioned to show key components. One of the two pulley wheels that turned the single overhead camshafts of each opposing pair of cylinder heads can be seen, together with the toothed rubber belt which was driven off the crankshaft. Note also the long, curved inlet manifolds. With the engine installed on the car, the cylinder heads were shrouded by metal ducts which directed a continuous blast of cooling air from the front-mounted fan (mounted directly to the crankshaft) across the finned piston barrels.

The upper and lower arms of this suspension subassembly operated as a parallelogram, but their axes of articulation were not exactly parallel. Instead, they were so constructed as to dip forward by 12 degrees when out of their normal horizontal attitude, in order to maintain a level attitude at all times and prevent lift or dive when the vehicle was accelerating or braking. Moreover, the geometry of the GS's front suspension was also carefully designed to follow the principles of center-point steering that had been established by André Lefèbvre on the DS19. The effect was that under all conditions of travel, the vertical line passing through the axis of the steering swivels coincided with the exact center point of contact between the tire and the road, giving excellent self-centering action and optimum straight-line stability. It was this feature, in conjunction with Citroën's hydro-pneumatic self-levelling suspension, that gave the GS driver the ability to maintain control when emergency braking, even in the event of a blow-out occurring on a front tire at high speed. However, the steering was not hydraulically powered, but relied on a conventional, manually operated rack-and-pinion system located on the bulkhead behind the engine and linked to the steering column by a relay shaft passing through two universal joints. Although the GS's 30-foot turning circle made for easy maneuverability when parking, in practice the steering was heavy to operate at low speeds, though it became progressively lighter and more precise as the car's speed increased. The directional stability and general predictability of the GS's handling and road-holding at high speed were greatly praised by all commentators. Even so, given that a hydraulic power supply was available on tap, it is surprising that power assistance was never provided, even as an option, throughout the life of the model.

The rear suspension arrangements were also a model of simple yet sophisticated design. Here a further, rectangular, subframe was attached to the body-shell by flexible rubber bushes, which also served to support and contain the fuel tank. To this subframe were connected the rear wheels, hubs and disc brakes, by means of a single trailing arms, linked together by an anti-roll bar. These arms, formed from steel pressings articulated on needle roller bearings, housed in a support tube attached to the forward cross-member of the subframe, were connected to levers that were attached in turn to the pistons of their own individual suspension cylinders. Together with its associated sphere, each cylinder was mounted horizontally within the u-shaped section of the subframe side-members. Thus, the whole rear-axle assembly formed a very compact arrangement which, unlike conventional, vertically mounted coil springs, struts and telescopic shock absorbers, made only a minimal intrusion into the interior loadspace of the vehicle.

As we have already noted, the GS was actually sprung not by the metal coil or torsion bar springs customarily used on the medium-class cars of that era but by Citroën's unique self-levelling hydro-pneumatic suspension system. Although not nearly as complex or costly a solution as is often claimed by its critics (since in practice the constant wear and tear and consequently high routine maintenance costs associated with conventional suspension methods are virtually eliminated), this was nevertheless an inherently expensive feature to be incorporated in a popular, mass-market car. The components and general arrangements employed were actually a simplified adaptation of the system seen in the earlier DS and ID models, the main differences being that, first, the hydraulic pressure was provided by a new type of hydraulic pump having a single rather than multi-chamber configuration and capacity. This pump was actually located within the engine crankcase and driven by the same mechanism that operated the engine oil pump. A new type of gas/oil sphere was also developed for use on the GS; this was manufactured in one piece from a swaged steel plate, rather than from two forged steel hemispheres screwed together, as before. Again, the ride-height of the car was regulated constantly by the action of two height-correctors, located at the front and rear of the vehicle, which automatically adjusted the volume of pressurized hydraulic fluid present in the system to maintain a constant level of ground clearance, though this could be adjusted or over-ridden by a manual lever located on the driver's console, to raise the under-body clearance when traversing rough ground or to facilitate wheel changes.

The second and even more notable improvement to Citroën's hydro-pneumatic suspension system introduced on the GS was that, following extensive research into its general characteristics and behavior, new, improved damping devices were fitted in the spheres and the rubber bump-and-rebound stops on the axle arms were repositioned. These measures resulted in a remarkable reduction in the tendency to roll, pitch and float for which the D series cars had long been criticized. It also virtually eliminated the handling problems previously induced by any sudden change of attitude, such as when crossing hump-backed bridges or encountering unexpected changes in the camber of the road, thus endowing the GS with leech-like cornering power.

Similarly, the GS's advanced, fully-powered, dual-circuit braking system, employing discs all round (10.6 ins front, 6.93 ins rear), was also a modified version of the system fitted to Citroën's ID sedans, itself a simplified version of the system found on the DS sedans and ID station wagons. As with the D series cars, the front discs and calipers were mounted inboard, adjacent to the gearbox, in order to reduce unsprung weight. The calipers and pads that formed the parking brakes also operated on the front discs, each being actuated by a separate cable linked to the handbrake lever. The pressurised fluid in the two independent circuits was distributed by a *doseur* or brake control valve, which was opened and closed by use of a conventional pendant foot pedal as on the LHD ID19 models, rather than the famous mushroom pedal device used on the DS19. However, a load-sensitive, pressure-apportioning device was incorporated in the rear circuit to prevent the rear wheels from locking-up during emergency braking, when the vehicle was running empty or only lightly loaded. The parking brake, applied by a handle mounted on the dashboard, acted on the front discs through separate pads and calipers.

The design of the four-door, six-light, five-seater body adopted for the GS sedan also broke new ground, at least for Citroën, marking as it did a return to the monocoque system first employed on the Traction Avant yet rejected for use on the company's previous post-war cars, to reduce tooling costs. Structurally, the body-shell comprised four main elements, the front section forming the bulkhead and firewall, which was linked to the rear section forming the trunk by a floorpan reinforced by robust side and cross members. This structure was linked to the roof panel and its integral tubular cantrail or ring frame by the upright windshield, door and side pillars, the whole construction forming a very strong and rigid safety cage for the driver and passengers. To the body-shell were attached the aforementioned front and rear subframe assemblies plus the front crossmember and undertray together with the headlamp panel, and also the doors, hood and front fenders. The latter were secured to the front structure by bolts to facilitate easy removal, whereas the rear fenders were permanently welded-on skins that formed the recesses into which the wheels retracted. Naturally, the GS was among the first French cars specifically designed to protect its occupants from injury in road accidents, through the use of collapsible panels that could be relied upon to crumple and deform in a scientifically predicted and pre-programmed way, to distribute stress and absorb kinetic energy in the event of a collision.

Top: In September 1972, the original 55 bhp 1015 cc GS engine, rated a 6CV, was joined by an alternative, enlarged 1220 cc version, producing 60 bhp and rated a 7CV. But apart from the badging at the rear, there were no visible external differences between the two models. The increase in top speed and fuel consumption was marginal, but greater torque at lower revs made for better acceleration. Even so, many drivers preferred the turbine-like smoothness of the smaller unit which could be spun to more than 6,000 rpm without complaint. Despite the modest power outputs involved, the smaller engined car could reach 149 k/hr and the bigger one 151 k/hr. ***Bottom:*** The great virtue of the GS Break was the way it eliminated the drawbacks of conventional station wagons. Its low, flat load floor was unobstructed by any intrusion from the suspension system or spare wheel (which was stowed under the hood) and there was no rear sill over which the baggage had to be lifted. The entire rear door and its integral bumper swung upward to give unimpeded access. And naturally the rear seat folded flat to offer a truly cavernous load space.

With its sloping hood, rounded flanks and flowing, swept-back roof-line, in profile the GS undoubtedly had a dynamic, sporting appearance, imparting an impression of speed and agility that was enhanced by its purposeful "wheel-on-all-four-corners" stance, with very short front and rear overhangs. However, to maximize interior space, its sides were deeply curved, as were the side window glasses, (the total glass area was no less than 30.03 sq ft), so that when viewed head-on its rounded outline could seem dumpy and ungainly. Another noticeable feature was its sharply cut-off fastback tail. Apart from its aerodynamic advantages, this Kamm tail allowed for a completely rectangular, flat-sided trunk offering no less than 16 cubic feet of unobstructed load space. Moreover, the rear bumper was integrated with the trunk lid that formed the rear side of the box. This lid opened upward to give free access directly onto the low flat floor — there was no cill or cross-panel to hinder loading, the necessary torsional stiffness provided by a fixed steel parcel shelf which formed the upper side of the trunk, which was closed-off from the passenger compartment by the removable (but non-folding) rear seat, as on the DS and ID sedans. As was by now customary at Citroën, the spare wheel was stored in the engine compartment, between the engine and the firewall.

As we have already noted, the GS's body was exceptionally aerodynamic for its era; its coefficient of drag was measured as 0.32, a figure which represented a 15 percent improvement on the Cd of the DS, which until now had been considered to be one of the most aerodynamically efficient cars in the world. The GS sedan measured up as being 5ft 3in wide, 4ft 5in tall (with the engine running!) and 13ft 6in long overall. Its curb weight was 880 kg or 1,940 lbs and its total laden weight, 1,295 kg or 2,855 lbs.

As mentioned previously, the exterior styling was the work of Robert Opron, who had succeeded Flaminio Bertoni as Citroën's chief stylist in February 1964, following the untimely death of the Italian maestro. It has often been said that the overall shape and configuration of the body-shell was based on rejected proposals produced by Pininfarina for British Leyland in 1967, but

The Break or station wagon variant was first presented at the 1971 Paris Salon. For the 1972-1973 season this versatile and extremely popular vehicle was available in both 1015 cc and 1220 cc engine forms.

naturally Citroën rejected this claim. However, Pininfarina's design certainly inspired the shape of the two other most significant medium-class designs introduced in the early 1970s, the Alfasud and the Lancia Beta.

A model of elegance and modernity, Opron's coachwork was plain and simple in its detailing, devoid of all unnecessary embellishment or cosmetic details, except for the use of polished stainless steel for brightwork such as the bumpers, door handles, window frames, gutter trims and wheel embellishers. Indeed, his work on the GS established certain enduring themes or motifs that became virtual Citroën trademarks, evident also on the SM and the later CX models. These included the pronounced kick-up line running to the tail from the rear wheel arches and, of course, the partial shrouding of the rear wheels. Initially, the flanks were left bare and there were no rubbing strips or other measures to protect the door panels, the lower edges of which overlapped the cills. Another notable visual feature of the GS was its large honeycomb-patterned air intake grille, required to admit sufficient cooling air to the fan, and also the novel trapezoidal headlights that flanked it. Produced by Cibie exclusively for the GS, these lamps embodied the very latest in vehicle lighting technology, including quartz halogen bulbs. The front sidelamps and turn signals were housed in a separate encasement located beneath the headlights.

The interior styling of the GS was similarly restrained, almost to the point of austerity. Its most radical feature was the futuristic dashboard, designed by Michel Harmand, then the head of interior design at Automobiles Citroën, which echoed the asymmetrical lines of Flaminio Bertoni's original creation for the DS19, sweeping upward from right to left in a shallow elliptical curve to encompass the instrument panel that lay behind the by-now-traditional one-spoke steering wheel. This dashboard featured one of the most controversial talking points of the whole car, a novel "magic eye" speedometer in which the figures moved rather than the pointer. Imprinted on a rotating drum, which revolved according to the speed of the vehicle, these scrolled past a fixed line marked beneath a magnifying lens, the whole display being permanently illuminated like a tiny television screen. A tachometer was also provided as standard equipment, adjacent to the speedo, but this took the more conventional form of a swinging pointer that moved upward in an arc through 120 degrees; a full range of warning lights was also provided to indicate low hydraulic or lubricating oil pressure, low fuel level and engine overheating.

The minor electrical controls consisted of push-buttons located on the dashboard, or stalk switches protruding from a cowling on the steering column. But perhaps more controversial still, for dyed-in-the-wool Citroënistes at least, was the method of gear selection chosen; this took the form of a conventional stick-shift lever mounted on the floor, or rather in a narrow and rather flimsy console, located in the front foot-well, extending back between the front seats. Apparently, this concession to orthodoxy was adopted at the very last moment in a momentary lapse of self-confidence on the part of the GS's manufacturers; originally it had been intended that a dash-mounted push-pull lever of the type used on Citroën's A series models would be employed, leaving room for an occasional third person to ride in the front seats, as was possible in the Ami-6. Instead, the space originally provided to house a 2CV-type sliding gear-shift lever on the dashboard, next to the steering wheel, was occupied instead by an unusual pull-out hand brake lever. For many drivers, unfamiliar with Citroën's customary

When introduced on the U.K. market in October 1971, the GS was given a different dashboard with round-dialed instruments to replace the revolving "magic-eye" speedometer of the French version, which Anglo-Saxon motorists found confusing. When sales got going in 1972, the GS1015 Confort cost £1159 (including tax), and the GS1220 Club £1315 (including tax), in contrast to the £1698 and £2281 (including tax) being charged for the D-Special and DS23 sedans. Not surprisingly, the advent of the GS caused a 145 percent increase in Citroën's U.K. sales.

eccentricities, this arrangement seemed even more confusing and difficult to use than the control that it replaced.

Initially, the GS sedan came in two versions, the Confort and the Club, and a choice of eight paint colors was available for both: white, beige, red, blue, grey, yellow, bronze and green. The Confort had a basic level of trim and equipment with leather-cloth upholstery and rubber floor coverings while the Club offered a more luxurious interior, with moquette carpets and a choice of either red, bronze, blue or green jersey nylon seat coverings to match, as appropriate, or alternatively black or brown Targa vinyl fabric (similar to the material used in the current ID20 and ID21 sedans and station wagons) plus a superior level of accessories and appointments, including reclining front seats.

Shortly after its Paris debut, the GS made its first public appearance in the U.K. at the 1970 Earls Court Motor Show, though in LHD form only. It had been planned to introduce the new arrival in RHD form the following April but it was not until June 1971 the first demonstrator cars were delivered to Citroën's British dealers. However, the delay served only to stoke interest rather than cool it down. Following rave reviews of the GS in the British press (and also the publicity generated earlier by the DS's performance in the 1968 London-Sydney Marathon and 1970 London-Mexico Rally), the order book was very soon filled to capacity, with sales stretching months ahead of production at the Rennses factory which by then was running at the rate of some 750 vehicles per day. The demand was described by Citroën Cars Ltd's current managing director as insatiable. Certainly, as a direct result of the introduction of the GS, in just one year total Citroën registrations in the U.K. shot up by more than 10,000 vehicles—from 6,992 cars in 1971 to 17,617 in 1972, the vast majority of them going to private customers, rather than business or fleet buyers as is the case with new cars today.

The GS was particularly well received by the motoring press in the U.K.. Reviewing the newcomer in August 1970, following its British press launch in County Donegal, Ireland, Geoffrey Howard of *Autocar* reported, "Not since the first Citroën DS has a new car been so full of technical novelty. From its aircooled, ohv flat-four engine to its self-levelling hydro-pneumatic suspension, this latest sedan sets new standards of ride and handling for small cars." His views were echoed by John Bolster writing in *Autosport* the following May, who observed, "For

Reflecting its importance to the future of Automobiles Citroën, the GS was launched in October 1970 with an unusually lavish advertising and publicity campaign, in which it was pictured among the sand dunes and gypsy horsemen of the Camargue.

fast driving on bad roads it is outstanding and it must be one of the safest vehicles that has ever been built. This is a low-powered sedan which some enthusiastic drivers will find more exciting than a sports car."

Criticism was confined to reservations about the unusual and unfamiliar "magic eye" speedometer. This led to the adoption of a completely revised instrument panel, having conventional round-dialed instruments, the only significant difference between the LHD and RHD versions of the car. The RHD dashboard itself was a simple mirror-image reversal of the original LHD design, however.

When launched in the U.K. in June 1971, the 1015cc engined GS appeared in a choice of either Confort or Club configurations, as in France, priced at £1,045 and £1,336, including sales tax, respectively, which compared favorably with British competitors in its market sector, such as the decidedly less sophisticated Triumph Toledo sedan, which cost £925, including tax. By autumn of 1972, the price of the GS1015 Club had risen to £1,159, including tax, or £1,315 including tax, in the case of the newly introduced GS1220 Club. Currently, the D Special was priced at £1,698, the DS23 at £2,281 and the SM at £5,342.

Evolution — GS

The first stage in the evolution of the GS range occurred in August 1971 when Citroën revealed the existence of three new variants—a four-door, five-seater Break or station wagon version for private customers; plus a four-door Commerciale Break; and a two-door, two-seater Service van for utility duties—all three of the trio powered by the same 1015cc engine in its original form. The Service van was available in two types—a normal enclosed van with steel side panels, and a fully-glazed version, resembling a hearse, which had two large unopening side windows extending along the length of its flanks, each formed by a single sheet of glass. All three types had the same rear door, featuring a window that curved round at its upper edge to meet the roofline. In common with that of the sedan, this door was unusual in opening right down to floor level; there was no cill or crossing panel at the rear to obstruct access to the interior as the bumper was attached to the door rather than to the body proper, which greatly facilitated loading and unloading. The GS Break offered a total 53.12 cu ft of loadspace with the rear seat folded and, like the Commerciale, it was available in either Club or Confort trim, but the Service van came in Club form only.

Although the GS's original free-revving 1015cc flat-four engine had been widely praised by motoring commentators for its smooth turbine-like response — more in keeping with a motorcycle than a car, it was said — many felt that greater reserves of torque were required, and at lower revs. Accordingly, in September 1972, Citroën announced the arrival of a second, enlarged version of its air-cooled boxer motor, increased in capacity to 1222cc (77 × 65.6mm) and developing 60 bhp DIN @ 5,750 rpm, enough to increase top speed from 149 to 151 km/h. This engine was immediately fitted in a new, parallel range of GS sedans, station wagons and commerciales bearing the GS-1220 badge, and rated at 7CV as opposed to the 6CV of the 1015cc version under the French motor tax system. Moreover, in addition to the standard four-speed manual gearbox, the option of a novel form of semi-automatic clutchless two-pedal transmission was announced.

This exclusive C-Matic system comprised a three-speed manual gearbox coupled with an automatically declutching, electrically operated, hydraulic torque converter which eliminated the need for a conventional clutch pedal. When driving around town it was necessary only to start off in first and then to select second gear on the move, and thereafter to use the accelerator and brakes only to speed up, slow down and stop as required, without further use of the gearshift lever. When reaching the open road, third would be selected to remain engaged continuously for progressive and flexible running, as with a conventional automatic gearbox. In France that year, the GS-1220 range comprised of nine versions—sedan, break and commerciale, each available in both Confort and Club form plus the two types of Service van in Confort form only. The GS-1015 range continued in production, but in four Confort versions only—sedan, break, commerciale and service van.

The following season, the 1974 model year, commencing in September 1973, brought no significant changes or additions to the GS range in France except that the three commerciale versions were deleted from the catalog. However, the 1015cc engine of the current GS Confort sedan, break and service van was improved by the adoption of certain modifications that had been introduced the previous year on the 1220cc engine, such as reinforced cylinder heads with improved cooling fins, revised induction and carburetor arrangements; the models that resulted were re-baptised the G-Special sedan, break and service van.

At the Paris motor show of October 1973, just one year after the launch of the Citroën Maserati SM, Citroën produced yet another trumpcard in its bid to retain its undisputed technical leadership of the European automobile engineering industry. This was the GS-GZ or Birotor, a modified version of the GS sedan powered by a Wankel rotary engine, coupled with a C-Matic *convertiseur*, or torque converter semi-automatic 3-speed gearbox.

In Autumn of 1973, Citroën announced the GS Birotor, a derivative of the GS, powered by a 1990 cc Wankel rotary engine. The Birotor could be easily distinguished by its larger wheels and the flared fenders needed to accommodate them. But the brave venture was unsuccessful; a mere 847 were sold before it was discontinued in 1975.

Proud of its reputation for advanced engineering and deeply conscious of the fact that the engines produced by the Service Moteurs or motive power department of the Bureau d'Etudes were unfairly perceived by critics as the weak point in its technical armory, Citroën resolved to rectify matters, and in a typically radical way. Under the direction of Pierre Bercot (President-Directeur-General from 1958 to 1968) the Double Chevron firm staked its future on the rotary piston concept, which had been invented by the German engineer Felix Wankel in the 1950s. Believing that the rotary engine's inherent simplicity and silence (apart from its revolving trapezoidal piston, it has no moving parts to cause noise and vibration, even at high speed) would lead inevitably to it superseding the conventional reciprocating piston engine entirely as a prime mover for motor vehicles, in 1960 Citroën entered into partnership with the German NSU company, forming the Comobil consortium to develop the Wankel principle under contract. The first fruit of this research program was the twin-rotor engine that powered the NSU Ro80 sedan, the world's first Wankel engined production car, launched in 1967.

Throughout the decade the company invested heavily in engine research and development, investigating all aspects of the mass-production and large-scale commercialization of the Wankel principle; 2 billion francs were spent in 1970 alone. The results were encouraging and led to the establishment in 1971 of the jointly owned manufacturing subsidiary Comotor, which built a dedicated factory at Alforweiler in the Saar province of Germany. The plant had a production target of around 500 engines per day, to be shared among the participants. At this stage it was anticipated that rotary engines would ultimately power all of Citroën's bigger models, including the forthcoming replacement for the D Series cars, the CX, a project which was already well under way.

Meanwhile, early in 1970 Citroën commissioned a specialist low-volume body-building firm, Heuliez, to build a limited series of 500 experimental vehicles, code-named the M35, intended as road-going test-beds, so that the proposed Citroën version of the Comotor Wankel engine could be thoroughly proven by ordinary owner-drivers, under normal, real-life conditions. The M35 took the form of a 2 + 2 coupe with a fastback

The Comotor Wankel engine opened up to reveal the arrangement of the trapezoidal double rotors within the combustion chamber.

body, based on the Ami-8 platform chassis but equipped with hydro-pneumatic suspension. Powered by a single rotor Wankel motor with a displacement equivalent to 995cc and developing 49 bhp @ 5,500 rpm, it was capable of reaching 144 km/h (89 mph) and returning an average fuel consumption og 8–10 liters per 100 km (23.5–29 mpg). A total of 267 were actually built over an 18-month period, ending in 1971. These cars were sold at a price of 14,000 FF (which included a comprehensive guarantee) to a panel of selected customers who were expected to use the vehicle for routine motoring duties and make regular reports detailing their experiences and running expenses. Unfortunately, though not unexpectedly, these reports revealed that, due to the poor thermal efficiency inherent in the Wankel concept, the Comotor engine displayed a disappointingly high consumption of both fuel and oil, far greater than the owners might reasonably have expected from its output and dimensions.

Until now, in an era of cheap gas, this disadvantage had not been regarded at Citroën as being a particularly serious problem — and, given the concomitant advantages, certainly not grave enough to prevent public acceptance of the Wankel motor. So at the end of 1970, Citroën's current chief executive, Raymond Ravenel, authorized its long-term commitment to the rotary engine and approved the program that resulted in the appearance of the GS Birotor some three years later. But before very long it had become quite clear that the Wankel's thirst was an obstacle of quite insurmountable proportions, for the very same reasons that had sounded the death knell of the Citroën Maserati SM.

In truth, high fuel consumption was not the only snag that signaled the end of the Wankel dream, at least at Automobiles Citroën. Experience with both the M35 and the GS Birotor (and the NSU Ro8O too) revealed the warning sign of high oil consumption caused by premature wear of the rotor-tip seals. This defect led in turn to engine failure after as little as 30,000 km of service, obviating completely the Wankel motor's promised advantages of outstanding durability and longevity. Consequently, when a detailed cost-benefit study of the rotary engine's prospects undertaken by Paul Mages concluded that the project would never pay the kind of dividends previously anticipated, Citroën was forced to abandon its commitment to Dr. Wankel's invention and further activity was suspended. Production of the GS Birotor finally ceased early in 1975, after only 847 had been built.

To avoid parts supply and warranty obligations, Citroën attempted to buy back all Birotors and M35s remaining in private ownership, and then proceeded to destroy all evidence of this still-born project. But a few cars evaded the crusher and are currently in the hands of museums and collectors. As is well known, after suffering grievous losses arising from warranty claims on its Ro80 engine, NSU was forced to give up the rotary engine concept and it was left to the Japanese firm, Mazda, to persevere with the development of Dr. Wankel's idea, which it did with notable success.

Although it was always a rare sight on the road, even in 1974, the GS Birotor could easily be distinguished from the standard GS by its exclusive metallic beige or dark brown finish, special badges and flared wheel arches which enclosed much larger wheels and tires than were fitted on the ordinary versions. It also carried a distinctive pattern of hub caps, the same as were later fitted to the CX series; these vehicles adopted a design of front axle, brake and suspension layout similar to that pioneered on the GS Birotor. Like the CX, the GS Birotor had its front disc brakes mounted outboard, on the hubs; because its engine and gearbox unit was mounted transversally, it was impossible to install the brakes in the inboard position as on the standard GS and GSA.

Notwithstanding the current adverse economic situation, in the autumn of 1974 the GS line was strengthened and broadened by the introduction of three new models— the GS Pallas and the GSX and GSX2 sporting sedans— so that the complete line-up, at least in France, now numbered 12 versions including six sedans, three station wagons and three service vans. The five pre-existing models, the G-Special sedan (still equipped with the 55.5 bhp 1015cc engine), the GS Club sedan (with the 60 bhp 1222cc engine), the G Special wagon (now available with either the 6CV 1015cc or 7CV 1222cc engine) and the GS Club wagon (fitted with the 1222cc engine only) all received detailed improvements inside and out, including seats of a new design and a fresh selection of paint colors.

First seen at the Paris Salon in October 1974, the GS Pallas was a luxury limousine in miniature, specially created to emulate the superlative ride-comfort and security of the big hydro-pneumatically sprung Citroëns but with the added benefit of small-car running costs. As such it offered many of the refinements previously associated only with the Pallas versions of the DS21 and DS23, and its price was similarly elevated; in the 1975 French catalog it was priced at 18,980 francs compared to the 17,880 francs then being asked for the standard GS Club sedan. These special features included a more elaborate facia with a finish that actually harmonized with the color scheme of the car, higher quality upholstery and headlining, and deep-pile carpeting on the floors and rear parcel shelf. The GS Pallas's specification also included additional sound-proofing measures that, in the words of a contemporary Citroën brochure, served to confer an atmosphere of hushed elegance and quiet sophistication. Externally, this version could be easily recognized by its large polished stainless steel hub caps and the typical Pallas rubbing strip running along its flanks. Moreover, as had been the case with the DS Pallas, it was offered initially in an exclusive metallic pearl-grey paint finish, although all the other colors of the GS line were available on demand; a black vinyl roof covering was also available as an option. Powered by the 1220cc engine only, as an option at extra cost, the GS Pallas was also available equipped with Citroën's C-Matic semi-automatic torque converter transmission, as were the GS Club sedan and the G Special and GS Club station wagons.

In September 1979 the GS was entirely revamped and re-launched as the GSA, powered by the 1220 cc engine only. The main improvement was the change to a hatchback body with a large fully opening tailgate, offering greater flexibility and versatility. This is the Pallas version, which featured a higher level of internal trim and upholstery, plus the distinctive stainless steel wheel covers.

The GSX2, on the other hand, was intended as a genuine sports sedan, aimed specifically at a younger, more fashion-conscious driver. Powered by an improved, more powerful, 65 bhp version of the 1222cc flat-twin aircooled engine featuring revised camshaft, carburetor and inlet manifold arrangements, and married to a new close-ratio four-speed gearbox, its performance was decidedly lively, so that its driver could exploit the GS's superb handling and roadholding abilities to the full. The GSX2 was capable of 155 km/h (96 mph) and could accelerate from 0 to 60 mph, two seconds faster than the standard 1222cc engined GS Club (top speed 151 km/h), and yet it returned 33.5 mpg overall as compared to 31 mpg for the standard car. To emphasize its sporting character, the GSX2 was given a particularly snappy appearance displaying all the latest motorsport trends and fashions, including an exclusive sunflower-yellow paint-job (although the normal current GS color chart also applied), a matt-black air intake

This cutaway drawing of the GS sedan shows how the engine was mounted far forward in the nose, ahead of the transmission axis and with the gearbox located behind it. The compact horizontal layout of the rear suspension arms and cylinders can also be seen.

grille and window surrounds, small central hub caps which left the greater part of the grey-painted wheels exposed, and long-range headlights. Inside, the facia was revised and the notorious revolving-drum speedometer and other instrument panel peculiarities of the standard GS models were replaced by round-dialed, clock-type Jaeger instruments. Special high-backed front seats were also fitted to accentuate the sporting image. The GSX1 was similar to the GSX2 in all outward respects, except that it was powered by the standard 55.5 bhp version of the 1015cc engine, as currently fitted to the G-Special sedan and station wagon.

Autumn of 1975 brought a visible revamp to the GS range for the coming 1976 season, in the form of a new treatment for the air-intake grille, with horizontal bars replacing the original honeycomb design; on the Special the grille was made from black plastic instead of grey, while on the Club and Pallas the bars were silvered. Also at that juncture, certain minor modifications were made to the various engines employed which enhanced fuel economy of all eight variants currently available, though at the expense of outright power output. The range now numbered five sedans, two station wagons and one service van. The latter was continued in its enclosed form only, the glazed version being discontinued as it was no longer held to be exempt from tax by the French authorities.

The next step in the evolution of the GS range took place in October 1976 when the dashboard with round-dialed instruments previously introduced on the GSX2 was adopted across the range. At the same time, minor alterations were made to the rear end of the car, including the lamps and badging, while the bumpers of the GSX and GSX2 became matt black, to match the window frames. The 1015cc engined service van was re-named the Entreprise.

A year later, in September 1977, the GSX2 was given a rear spoiler plus a new type of roadwheel lacking the customary ventilation slots; these solid wheels (which had stainless-steel wheel covers to protect the lug nuts) were subsequently adopted for the entire GS line. At the same time, the original 1015cc engine, still employed in the G Special, was replaced by a new, enlarged 1129cc unit (74mm × 65.6mm) developing 56.5 bhp at 5,750 rpm, to give the Special an improved top speed of 149 km/h (92 mph).

A further significant development took place in March 1978 when the first special-edition version of the GS, the Basalte, limited to 1800 examples only, appeared in France, although a small number were produced in RHD form and offered on the U.K. market. The GS Basalte was distinguished by its unusual color scheme, black overall but painted with horizontal bands of red running along its flanks, narrow at the waist but gradually increasing in width downwards towards the door bottoms. The Basalte also boasted large Pallas-type wheel trims, headlight wipers, long-range headlights, a sliding

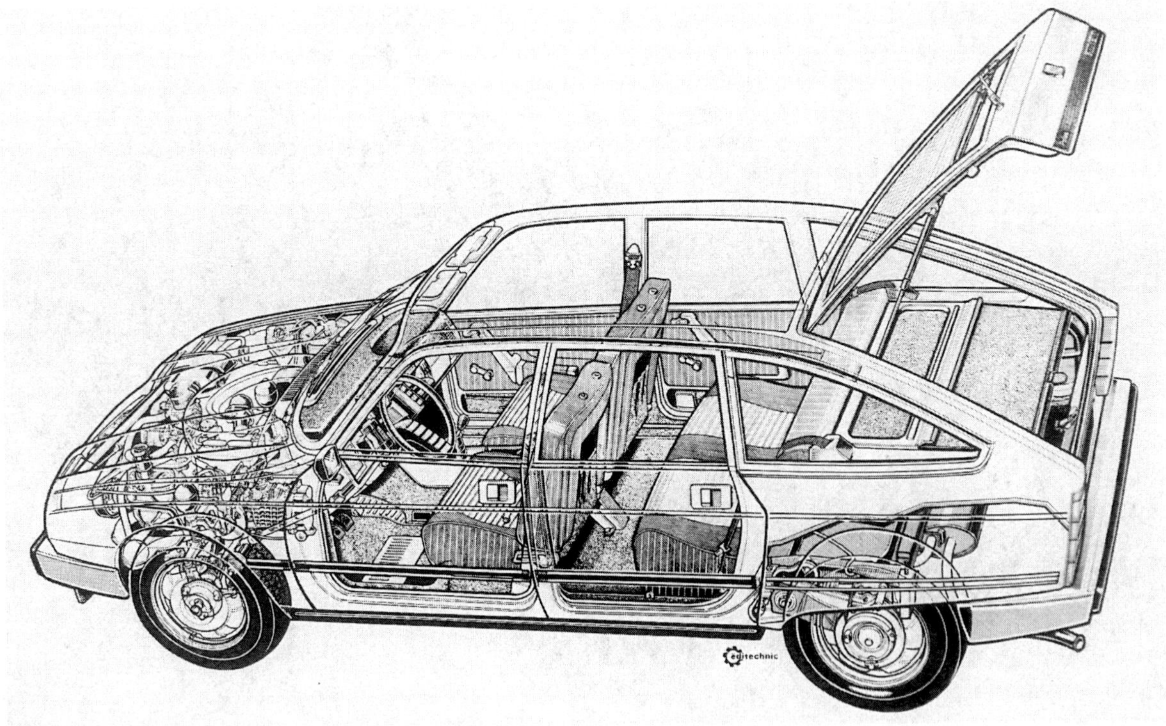

By comparing this second cutaway (showing the GSA) with the previous illustration, it can be seen how the box-like fixed metal structure of the GS's trunk was removed to create an open load-space, covered by a removable parcel tray.

Simultaneously, the GSA was offered in Break (or station wagon) form. This is the Break Club version of June 1984. All the characteristic external details of the GSA are visible here, including the matt-black door handles and window surrounds, the rubbing strip along the flanks and the grey thermoplastic bumpers, which replaced the expensive stainless steel bumpers of the GS.

metal sunroof and a unique red and black interior. In December 1979 came the GS Quartz, limited to 50 LHD units only, all of them painted white with contrasting black interiors.

The following September, for the 1979 season, the last major stage in the evolution of the GS proper was reached with the launch of the GSX3 model to replace the GSX2. A true 1300cc car, the GSX3 was equipped with a new, improved version of the four-cylinder air-cooled boxer motor, with bore and stroke enlarged to 79.4mm × 65.6mm giving a swept volume of 1229cc. This produced 65bhp DIN at 5,500 rpm, permitting a top speed of 158 km/h (98 mph). Presented as the ultimate GS sporting sedan, the GSX3 had all the special exterior and interior appointments of the GSX2 model including a rear spoiler, though its characteristic plastic three-spoked wheel-trims were grey rather than black.

Evolution — GSA

In September 1979, the GS entered its second generation with the arrival of the GSA, first exhibited at the Paris Salon that October. The event was heralded by an award-winning advertising campaign demonstrating the model's unique safety features, its superb roadholding and its incomparably smooth and comfortable ride. This, the advertisements claimed, was a motoring experience that could only be compared to the sensation of traveling on a red carpet that was constantly unrolled before the car, smoothing out all the undulations in its path.

Powered by the 7CV 65 bhp 1299cc version of the flat-four air-cooled engine previously introduced on the GSX3, the GSA was available initially, for the 1980 season, in either Club, Pallas and X3 sports sedan form plus a Club Break. However, the 1129cc G-Special sedan, stationwagon and Entreprise van continued in production in their original GS form. A 4-speed manual gearbox was standard on the GSA Club and Pallas sedans (plus the optional 3-speed C-Matic semi-automatic transmission, of course), but a 5-speed manual gearbox was standard on the GSA X3.

The GSA amounted to a complete redesign of the original GS concept, at least so far as the sedan version was concerned, as its new bodywork was entirely different in structure. The previous conventional three-box layout was modified by the provision of a fully opening tail-gate, to offer a modern hatchback arrangement as had originally been proposed to Citroën's management by the Bureau d'Etudes some ten years earlier at the prototype stage, but rejected by Pierre Bercot as being inappropriate for a private passenger car. The fixed steel parcel shelf formerly enclosing the trunk space was removed, so that the luggage space was united with the passenger compartment, the rear seats of which could now be folded down to form a long flat load-floor, as in the station wagon version. The space thus formed was enclosed by a large glazed, fully opening rear door which gave the car its sloping fast-back roofline. The result was that the difference in the total useable internal volume or loadspace now offered by the two respective versions, sedan and station wagon, was governed by the difference in the height of their roofs at their rear extremities.

From the outside, the GSA could be easily distinguished from the GS by a number of changes to its exterior detailing and embellishments, with the polished stainless-steel brightwork of the original design giving way to matt-black plastic fittings, such as door handles, window frames and rear-view mirrors. Similarly, the bumpers were now made from grey molded polypropylene with black shock-absorbing inserts, front and rear. Attached to the underside of the front bumpers were a pair of small flaps, mounted just ahead of the front wheels and projecting forward into the airstream. A feature peculiar to the GSA and not seen on the GS, these flaps acted as air dams to ensure an adequate supply of cooling air to the engine fan at high speed. Similarly, the redesigned front grille was also made of injection-molded black plastic. A revised pattern of tail lights was also adopted, while rubber side-strips— running along the entire length of the bodywork, not just across the doors— were fitted throughout the range, not merely on the Pallas version. Initially, a narrow strip of black paint appeared on the door bottoms of all cars, while the rear closing panel under the hatchback door of the sedan was also given the same black paint treatment. Initially also the roadwheels fitted across the GSA line reverted to the ventilated type with small stainless-steel disc hub caps, except that now the slots were circular in shape, rather than oval.

There were also a number significant changes to be seen inside the car, including a new pattern of seats. The most noticeable interior revision, however, involved the dashboard, which was completely redesigned — and in a radical way — by Michel Harmand, who had conceived the original version, and whose work (as we shall see in the following chapter) had been such a notable feature of the Citroën CX. This new design featured a novel square-shaped instrument panel flanked by two cylindrical satellite pods mounted on extensions that projected forwards and outwards from the dashboard itself, on either side of the single-spoked steering wheel, well within reach of the driver's finger-tips. The pods housed all the switches and buttons operating the lights, horn, windshield wipers, turn signals (non self-cancelling, of course) and other electrical equipment. The instrument panel itself was notable for the return of the revolving drum speedometer (the Pallas and GSX versions also had a similar type of tachometer) but its display area was mainly devoted to an illuminated diagram showing an outline of the car, pictured as if on a television screen. Radiating outward from this pictogram were a number of lines linked to the warning lights that indicated hydraulic or oil pressure failure and the necessity of an "imperative stop," plus other minor conditions such as excessive front-brake pad wear not necessarily requiring an immediate halt. The impression thus presented of innumerable, ever-present threats and dangers peculiar to the GSA must have been most disconcerting for new owners, who doubtless feared that they were about to be subjected to an endless series of inevitable electrical and mechanical breakdowns. But for those drivers who knew of its inherent reliability from experience, the sight of this colorful control panel, lit up both by day and night as if on an aircraft's flight deck, was not regarded as unduly ominous or off-putting!

The next stage in the evolution of the GSA range was reached in August 1980 when the G-Special sedan also adopted the new five-door body and became known as the GSA Special, as did the equivalent station wagon version, both cars being equipped with the 6CV 1129cc engine coupled with a 4- or 5-speed gearbox, according to choice. The GS Entreprise (a version of the former Service van) was discontinued and replaced by the GSA Fourgonnette Entreprise, based on the GSA Break, but with a two-door panel-van body. This was available powered by either the 1129cc or 1299cc engines and with either a 4- or 5-speed gearbox. Thus, the GSA line for the 1981 season totalled seven versions. The cheaper GSA Special versions were given plain jersey cloth seats and vinyl-covered door facings, while the Club versions also had plain jersey upholstery, but with ribbed jersey cloth inserts on the wearing surfaces of the seats. The door panels of the Club were also more elaborate, with fabric partly covering their surfaces and armrests in conjunction with vinyl, but the Pallas versions had ribbed jersey cloth throughout.

The following year, for the 1982 season, the GSA Special was equipped with the 65 bhp 7CV 1299cc engine while a new base model (available only France), referred to simply as the GSA was introduced, powered by the earlier 6CV 1129cc engine. As fitted to the GSA Club, Pallas and X3 models, the 1299cc engine received certain modifications including a transistorized magnetic-impulse ignition sys-

The last incarnation of the GSA sedan was the GSA Special, introduced in 1982, equipped with an enlarged 1299 cc version of the air-cooled flat-four engine. It was finally withdrawn in 1987.

tem that reduced both fuel consumption and emissions, but without adversely affecting performance. But besides the introduction of this ECO engine, the changes made were confined to cosmetic matters; for example, the black-painted bumpers formerly exclusive to the X1 and X3 variants were fitted, across the line.

In September 1982, for the 1983 season, the Club version of the GSA sedan (but not the Break) was deleted from the line, although a new, cheaper, version of the GSA X3, the GSA X1, was introduced, identical in mechanical specification to the X3 but lacking certain refinements of trim and equipment. Earlier, in April that year, the first special edition version of the GSA sedan had appeared, limited to 1,500 examples only. Painted in black with a blue coachline and named the Tuner, this car—sold only in France—was noted for its superior stereo radio-cassette system, supplied by Phillips.

The GSA X1 and GSA X3 were semi-performance models aimed at younger drivers. Available from 1983 to 1985, they were equipped with suitably sporting trim and accessories.

Next, in July 1983, the base model GSA (with the 1129cc 6CV engine) was withdrawn from the catalog leaving just four sedans—the Special, X1, X3 and Pallas plus the Special and Club Breaks and the Entreprise van. Similarly, the option of C-Matic transmission was also discontinued. However, in October 1983, the 1984 season's line-up was augmented by the appearance of a further special edition, the Cottage, a particularly luxurious and well-specified version of the GSA Break. Only 2000 were built, but none were exported to the U.K.. Equipped to Pallas standards, this car was immediately recognizable by its standard alloy wheels, of the type previously fitted to the GSA Pallas only, and as an optional extra.

Also during the 1982-1983 and 1983-1984 model years (and for the U.K. market only) another special edition was produced, the GSA Pallas SE sedan. Besides all the usual Pallas refinements, this deluxe model featured such extras as alloy wheels, front fog lights, a sunshine roof, tinted glass and was available in a choice of either black or pearl-grey metallic paintwork, with a red coachline. Finally, the last of the GSA special editions, announced in July 1984, was the Chic, offered only in France. Based on the GSA Special, this car featured metallic pearl-grey paintwork teamed with black bumpers, black window-frames, and a band of black skirting on the lower part of the doors, plus tinted glass, alloy wheels and a rear spoiler; only 1,200 were constructed.

For the following and final season, 1986, the GSA range was reduced to four models—the GSA Special sedan, the GSA-X3 sedan, the GSA Special station wagon and the GSA Fourgonnette Entreprise—all powered by the 65 bhp 1299cc engine coupled with the short-ratio 5-speed gearbox. At the end of July 1986, the GSA was discontinued altogether in favor of the new BX range of sedans and station wagons, which had actually been introduced four years earlier at the 1982 Paris Motor Show. By then a total of 2,440,610 had been built during the GS/GSA's 15-year career (GS: 1,874,754. GSA: 565,009. GS Birotor: 847) of which no fewer than 106,645 cars found owners in the United Kingdom.

Thus, this highly original air-cooled, flat-four design had proved to be Citroën's second most successful model ever, at least in terms of sales that it achieved. Compared with its predecessors and contempories, only the 2CV (which went on to enjoy an extended lifespan more than double that of the GSA) achieved higher popularity. And of its successors, not even the BX (2,315,739 produced in 12 years) or the AX (2,425,138 in 12 years) achieved better commercial results.

Truly, the GSA was the car that saved the Citroën company from extinction, by enabling it to overcome the crisis years of the 1970s when the Double Chevron marque very nearly disappeared under the weight of its severe financial difficulties. But more than that, the GSA was also the achievement that reasserted Citroën's claim to superiority in engineering matters, and which pointed the way ahead for other manufacturers. Unquestionably, it represented the benchmark against which all other contemporary small cars were judged, at least as far as comfort and safety were concerned. Above all, it proved that cars of high technical quality could be produced—and sold profitably—in large quantities, and that engineering excellence was actually recognized and demanded by the mainstream motoring public at large.

Despite this achievement, however, its reputation has been neglected in recent years, at least in comparison with its better known stable-mates, the DS, SM and 2CV, which are more appreciated and sought-after by collectors. Too often perceived as being a ladies' shopping car or family run-about, woefully underpowered on account of its 1100cc–1300cc specification, the GSA's true performance and abilities were ignored and, indeed, remain so today, even among Citroën enthusiasts. Surely, a reassessment is called for. Had this excellent vehicle and its superlative air-cooled boxer engine been produced in Germany, bearing a Volkswagen or Porsche badge, there can be little doubt that its present-day status among classic car buffs would be very different indeed!

14

The Citroën CX, 1974–1989

At exactly 4.30 p.m. on Sunday, September 1, 1974, a procession of 20 cars of unfamiliar design but unmistakable origin entered the Place de l'Etoile in Paris. After driving past the Arc de Triomphe and down the Champs Elysées, the motorcade reached its destination and pulled up outside the main Citroën showrooms of the French capital, bedecked for the occasion with blue and yellow flags bearing the Double Chevron emblem. The new 2-liter CX2000, the long-awaited replacement for the 20-year-old DS/ID series, had arrived at last. The cars in question were not entirely in brand new condition, however. Over the previous three weeks they had been test-driven for a total of more than 100,000 miles on the rough gravel roads of Swedish Lapland, north of the Arctic Circle, by 400 members of the European motoring press. These punishing tests completed, the cars had then headed south on a 2000-mile non-stop journey through Sweden, Germany, Belgium and northern France, to be presented to the world at large in Paris.

Actually, the CX2000 had been launched in France just four days earlier, on the 28th of August, 1974, to great acclaim from the motoring press and general public alike. This enthusiastic reception was endorsed the following year when the new arrival went on to win three major prizes, the first car ever to hold these trophies simultaneously. First, in January 1975 it was voted Car of the Year by a panel of 49 journalists from 14 European countries, winning the award by a wide margin. Second, in February the French motoring press presented it with the Prix de la Securite in recognition of its outstanding safety features. And third, at the Geneva Motor Show in March it received the ultimate accolade from 170 international design experts, the Auto Style Award.

Although the fact was not fully realized by the public at the time, the CX was destined to be the last true Citroën, a car conceived and produced by an independent Citroën management and design team according to the principles established by André Citroën's protégé, André Lefèbvre. As we saw in a previous chapter, during the year of its birth, 1974, following the collapse of its partnership accord with Fiat, Citroën's current owners, the Michelin tire concern, had opened negotiations for the sale of the company to its erstwhile rivals, Peugeot, a company with an altogether different character and philosophy. These arrangements were eventually concluded two years later when, with French government backing, the Citroën and Peugeot marques were merged within a reorganized and financially restructured management framework known as the PSA Group, controlled entirely by Peugeot interests. Though the intention was that the two marques would retain their own identities, it was in effect a shot-gun marriage, a union of convenience between two very dissimilar partners, made necessary not so much by common interests and shared philosophies but by current adverse economic circumstances. As a result of this merger, Citroën's Bureau d'Etudes experienced an exodus of personnel, both voluntary and enforced. Among the departees was the designer responsible for the exterior styling of the CX, Robert Opron, who left to join Renault in 1975.

Indeed, the Autumn of 1974 had not been exactly an auspicious time to launch a large executive-class car. As related in previous chapters, the outbreak of the Yom Kippur Arab-Israeli War the previous October had led to massive economic shockwaves, felt around the world, as the Middle East producers cut supplies of crude oil. By January 1974 the cost per barrel had quadrupled, bringing with it a commensurate increase in the price of fuel at the pumps; the age of cheap energy had ended. Consequently, in the months leading up to the unveiling of the

The CX-2000 in its pre-production form, photographed in Lapland during its press launch in the summer of 1974. Its restrained and sober lines, devoid of all ostentation and embellishment, were in tune with the times.

CX, an attitude of caution — even pessimism — had held sway among its makers, in stark contrast to the optimism that had existed at the inception of the project three years earlier. Yet despite these fears, the CX quickly established itself in the European market. During its first full year of production, 1975, more than 96,700 units were produced, a mere 200 or so less than the 96,900 DS/ID models built in 1973. But the following year, 1976, production soared to more than 112,000 units, proving to its supporters and detractors alike that Citroën had yet another winner on its hands.

Four years earlier, however, when the *cahier des charges*, or design brief, for the CX had laid down at the beginning of 1971, a mood of confidence prevailed at Citroën, due largely to the enthusiastic reception currently being extended toward the GS. Even so it was never doubted that it would be difficult to build a successor to the DS/ID series good enough to satisfy the over-optimistic expectations of Citroën's partisan supporters and clientele. Nevertheless, the company was determined to ensure that the new car would offer yet another great step forward by representing a major improvement over its predecessor in all the major areas of design, construction and performance, and especially in matters of handling and road-holding.

As well as including all the familiar advanced engineering features such as front-wheel-drive and hydropneumatic suspension that had already been pioneered by Citroën research, it was intended that Project L (as it was then called) would exploit a whole range of new attributes and advantages born of marketing and manufacturing studies, to make the avant-garde a more practical and affordable proposition for both the company and its customers alike. Simplicity rather than complexity was the watchword, while comfort, safety, economy and ease of maintenance and repair were the prime objectives.

Thus, despite the existence of other, more radical, proposals, the Project L prototype finally took shape as a traditional three-box six-light sedan, but of unconventional appearance and unorthodox engineering. Its styling, which bore a strong family resemblance to that of both the SM and the GS, was again the work of Robert Opron. His design embraced a number of distinctive themes seen on earlier Citroën cars and which had already become established as virtual trademarks. Most noticeable of these motifs were the shrouded rear wheels enclosed by removable spats, the pronounced kick-up line running from the rear wheel arches to the tail and the use of expensive stainless steel for the bumpers and other brightwork. In fact, on the instructions of the previous President-Directeur-General, Pierre Bercot (who had retired in 1970), it was company policy to use only this durable high-quality material for decorative purposes, in preference to the chromium-plated mild steel used elsewhere; this was thought to be inferior and unacceptable, since it tarnished or deteriorated all too rapidly.

It was Bercot who had ruled that the CX should be a conventional four/five seater three-box sedan with a separate trunk, rather than a hatchback as had already been pioneered by Renault with its rival R14 model introduced in 1972, and, indeed, Citroën itself with the Traction Avant Commerciale built between 1938 and 1941 and again from 1953 to 1957. The CX sedan was actually smaller than its D series counterparts, at 181 inches long overall and 68 inches wide, 12 inches shorter and 3inches narrower overall. Its 112-inch wheelbase was also shorter by 11 inches, though with an unladen weight of 2,788 lbs it was only 27 lbs lighter. Its smooth, fluid, streamlined shape resulted in a significant improvement in aerodynamic efficiency, however, achieving a drag coefficient of 0.30, a figure unrivalled by any other large contemporary sedan except the DS, which was rated at 0.29. It was this performance that gave the car its name, CX, the equivalent of CD in French engineering terminology. The CX also demonstrated an exemplary resistance to cross-winds as was subsequently proven in a series of tests staged by a German motoring magazine. When driven at 100kph past a bank of wind machines its deviation from a straight line was shown to be only 80cm, whereas some others among the 10 cars tested wandered off course by as much as four meters! The smooth, flat underbody of the CX, made possible by its front-wheel-drive layout and the absence of driveshaft, transmission tunnel, rear axle and differential, created a partial venturi effect, sucking it down onto the road and improving the adhesion between tarmac and tires.

The 1985 cc engined CX-2000 was equipped with wheels and hubcaps that were identical to those first seen on the GS Birotor. The CX got its name from the French expression for coefficient of drag.

In the interest of better visibility, the CX also boasted a greatly enlarged glass area of no less than 31.5 sq ft, far larger than on the DS, due largely to its huge, deeply curved 9.6 sq ft safety glass windshield which was swept by a two-speed windshield wiper having a single blade, some two-and-a-half feet long. Another novel feature was its large, raked, concave rear screen, sloping backwards across the enclosed trunk space and enveloping it within the passenger compartment. This screen was cleverly shaped to allow the passing airflow to scour its surface and keep it free of moisture. As long as the car was traveling at a reasonable speed, excellent rear vision was ensured even in very heavy rain and therefore no rear window wiper was required. The box-shaped, 16.8 cu ft capacity trunk had no high sill to impede loading and was closed by a short right-angled lid that was neatly integrated into the structure to form the Kamm-type tail panel. The spare wheel was stowed under the hood, as on all Citroëns of that era except the SM.

The system of construction and assembly employed on the CX series also broke new ground in automobile design. Firstly, unlike the caisson structure of the DS, its body-shell was a conventional monocoque, with a massive one-piece floor pan pressing reinforced by two large box-section sill members, intended to provide maximum resistance to side impacts. This base was further strengthened by the two cross-members on which the seats were mounted, and by the three hoops—effectively constituting roll-over bars—which formed the main door and window pillars of the superstructure. To these were attached the two lateral roof side rails that ran fore and aft from the base of the windshield to the extreme rear end of the car, forming a protective cage for its occupants. At either end of the passenger compartment, two bulkhead panels crossed the structure, the back completely isolating the trunk space from the interior.

Second, the body-shell itself was attached by means of flexible rubber silentbloc mountings to a separate under-frame or formed by two longerons or side-members which were permanently joined by rivets to the front subframe holding the engine, transmission and suspension sub-assemblies, and to the rear sub-frame holding the rear axles and suspension. By linking these sub-frames together into a single unit, which acted as a semi-chassis, the longerons imparted great structural strength and rigidity to the total body structure, resisting any tendency of the body-shell to twist or bend when in motion. Furthermore, the exceptional torsional stiffness achieved by this unusual arrangement ensured that perfect alignment between the front and rear axles was maintained under all conditions, and thus made possible the highly accurate steering and exemplary directional stability for which the CX was noted. Additionally, these rubber mountings helped to improve the sound insulation of the car, by isolating the cabin from the running gear acoustically and filtering out the noise and vibration generated by the engine and the tires. Initially, 16 rubber silentblocs were employed, eight on each side of the car, but from September 1977 on, this number was reduced to 12, the front and rear pair of the six bushes located on the longerons being eliminated to prevent resonance from being transmitted to the cabin.

The front sub-frame and axle unit was made up of a massive arch-shaped upright yoke, or cradle, which was joined to the forward extension of the longerons with a wide flat cross-member closing-off its base, while another smaller cross-member was located at the extreme forward point of the longerons, at the nose of the car. At the shoulders of this arch were two outward-facing extensions that housed the front suspension units. The transversely-mounted engine was placed immediately forward of this cradle, attached to it low down by flexible couplings and high up by two sturdy steady-bars fastened to built-in brackets. The front hubs were also attached to this cradle by means of a single forged-steel upper arm located rigidly by a tapered roller bearing, and by a lower wishbone link, secured to the sub-frame by two rubber and nylon silent-bloc bushes, as was the anti-roll bar which was actuated by a rod and a ball-and-socket joint.

The rear sub-frame was somewhat simpler, comprising two rearward extensions of the longerons between which the fuel tank was located. Joining this pair of extensions was a large tubular cross-member, to each end of which was attached a short tubular housing containing a pair of tapered roller bearings. Suspended from these bearings, and articulating from their centers, were the two aluminum trailing arms comprising the rear axles. The spheres and cylinders of the rear suspension system were placed horizontally within the deepest section of the sub-frame and attached to the axle arms by piston rods, while an anti-roll bar was placed between the arms and secured to their inner sides. Thus, the whole rear axle assembly formed a very compact arrangement which, unlike conventional vertical coil springs and struts, made only a minimal intrusion into the interior load-space of the vehicle.

This unusual system of construction also enabled a different method of assembly to be followed at the new factory, located at Aulnay-sous-Bois on the northern outskirts of Paris, which had been constructed specifically to produce the CX. The complex design of the DS, which required countless threaded screw fastenings and hydraulic unions to be connected manually, had made it a particularly time-consuming and labor-intensive vehicle to assemble. Consequently, much production-engineering thought had gone into simplifying assembly operations for the new car. The two-part structure of the CX overcame these problems and made it possible for the monocoque body to be welded-up, painted, fitted with its doors, windows and electrical loom and then partially trimmed in advance, before being finally united with its underframe, to which the appropriate engine, running-gear, hydraulic system and other mechanical components had already been attached. In fact, the semi-finished bodies were held in a huge automated storage rack called an auto-stocker, to await completion on the assembly line at a later stage, when the lighting and electrical equipment was added, the seats and carpets installed and the wheels and bumpers fitted, in accordance with a specific computer-generated order.

The radical design of the CX's interior fittings and furnishings was perhaps more influential and trend-setting than any other of its many innovative features, and remained widely admired and copied in the automobile industry for years to come. The work of Michel Harmand, this established new standards for safety and comfort, and by its adventurous use of new materials it created a particularly light and airy driving environment. First and foremost it featured a dashboard of revolutionary conception which echoed Bertoni's earlier achievements on the DS19. This dashboard was formed from a single symmetrical plastic molding that swept in a gentle curve from one side of the car to the other, sloping down steeply from the base of the windshield in another concave curve to a large, lockable drop-down glove-box positioned high in the passenger foot-well. At either end were eyeball ventilation outlets. A remarkably harmonious fusion of ergonomics and aesthetics, Harmand's avant-garde design, imaginatively futuristic yet at the same time sober and restrained, created a sense of uncluttered spaciousness never before achieved in the passenger compartment of a private car. The instrument panel was set into a separate binnacle of elliptical shape, described in a contemporary road-test report as "a bisected flying saucer hovering above the dashboard." This *lunule*, as it was christened in France, was located just below eye level behind the tradi-

The design and construction of the CX's interior was among its most revolutionary features. The dashboard, with its instruments displayed in a binnacle, was particularly advanced. Note the central console housing a stick-shift gear lever and the reclining front seats upholstered with nylon jersey cloth.

The "lunule" or instrument binnacle in close-up, showing the revolving speedometer and tachometer displays. The minor switches operating the lamps and windshield wipers were grouped ergonomically at either end, so that they could be operated by the fingertips, without the driver's hands leaving the steering wheel.

tional Citroën one-spoke steering wheel. Attached at both ends of the binnacle were pods containing all the minor controls operating the electrical equipment. There were no conventional stalk switches on the steering column; instead the rocker switches in the pods could be operated by the driver's fingertips without the need to lift a hand from the steering wheel. The instruments in the binnacle comprised a speedometer and tachometer of the same revolving drum type as seen in the GS, plus a full range of warning lights that monitored the status of the motive power, braking, suspension and lighting systems.

Together with the radio, the main controls of the CX—the gearshift lever, the parking brake and the sliders for adjusting the heating and ventilation system and also the ride-height of the car—were placed in a large central console, located between the front seats, extending forward to the facia, in an arrangement which copied the system introduced earlier on the GS. Once again, this departure from previous practice was dictated by marketing rather than engineering considerations. Citroën had proved on the ID19 that it had mastered the design of an excellent cable-operated manual gear-shift lever located on the steering column and also a bulkhead-mounted parking brake. These allowed for the front seats to be positioned closely adjacent to each other, in a semi bench-seat configuration, and thus left the front foot-well entirely free of obstructions. But market research showed that the buyers of European executive cars favored a floor-mounted gear-stick, even on a front-wheel-drive car having no conventional transmission tunnel or intruding gearbox. Similarly, they preferred that the shifter of the automatic transmission provided later on the CX should also be found in this position, despite the habit of American manufacturers to locate this control on the dashboard behind the steering wheel, just as Citroën had done on the semi- and fully-automatic versions of the DS.

The one-piece panels cladding the interior surface of the CX's doors were also a strikingly original feature of the design. Colored the same shade as the dashboard unit—blue, grey or beige—they were formed from molded plastic, padded with foam and sheathed in vinyl. Into these panels were set recessed roundels housing the radio speakers and handles for raising and lowering the windows, on the versions lacking electric lifters. The door catches were integrated into large pistol grip door handles, in such a way that no potentially harmful metal fixtures and fittings protruded into the passenger compartment. The seats of the CX2000, upholstered with jersey nylon cloth, were also of an entirely new pattern, the result of an intensive program of ergonomic and medical research designed to achieve yet higher standards of comfort and security. To match the interior trim, and contrast with the dashboard, steering wheel and center console, the seating was either caramel, blue-green or vermilion in color, while the roof lining was light blue or beige. Though perhaps not quite as strikingly original as the colorful interiors that had characterized the DS, the whole effect was completely diffferent from the somber blacks and greys in fashion today.

Under the hood, however, the CX was rather less revolutionary. It had originally been envisaged that the next big Citroën would be powered by a completely new Wankel rotary engine, a product of the Comotor joint-manufacturing venture discussed in Chapter 13. But development problems and delays, aggravated by new priorities of the energy crisis, ruled against this adventurous but thirsty option, a fortunate move as things turned out, in light of the severe problems that NSU later experienced with its Wankel engined R080. Instead, Citroën decided to install in the CX an improved version of the outstandingly robust and economical four-cylinder 1985cc power unit that had been introduced in 1965, and which in various forms had previously powered the DS19A, DS20,

ID20, D Super and D Special cars. Thus, in its first incarnation as the CX2000, the CX was powered by a four-cylinder 1985cc engine (bore:86mm/stroke:85.5mm) producing just 102 bhp at 5,500 rpm and rated in the optimum 11CV tax bracket. In this case, however, the unit was ameliorated by the addition of an external cartridge-type oil filter and various other modifications imposed by its new employment, including revised layouts for both inlet and exhaust manifolds. Classical in design with a cast-iron block, removable cast-iron wet cylinder liners, a five-bearing crankshaft, light alloy pistons and a light alloy cylinder head with hemispherical combustion chambers having two valves per cylinder inclined at 60 degrees and operated by pushrods driven by a camshaft mounted high up in the crankcase, this engine represented an innovation only in that, for the first time on a Citroën, it was mounted transversely and inclined toward the front by 30 degrees. Installed in this position, the weight of the combined engine and transmission unit was concentrated ahead of the front wheels, in accordance with the principles established by André Lefèbvre, but which (as we have already seen) it had been impossible to achieve with the DS19. In fact the entire weight of the CX was concentrated forward and distributed 60:40 between the front and rear wheels.

Naturally, this set-up called for completely different arrangements for the CX's front-wheel-drive transmission than had been seen on a Citroën until now. These included a new four-speed all-synchromesh gearbox placed on the left-hand side of the engine bay, in line with the crankshaft. This was driven through a normal dry-plate diaphragm clutch, and operated through a rod and cable linkage by a stick-shift lever located in a central console between the front seats, as on the GS. Actually, two gearboxes were offered; a standard and an economy version with appropriate ratios, final drive being 13:62 in the former and 14:61 in the latter. The constant velocity driveshafts were identical and of equal length, the nearside shaft connected directly to the differential, but the offside shaft powered through an intermediate jackshaft running across the back of the engine to a relay-cum-support bearing attached to the sump. In all other respects the shafts were similar to those used on the DS, with tri-axe joints at the inboard and Rzeppa ball-and-cage couplings on the outboard ends. Due to the location of the engine/gearbox unit, however, the CX's front disc brakes (powered by the car's high-pressure hydraulic system) could no longer be mounted inboard, as on the DS and GS. Therefore the ventilated 10.24 in front discs (9.19 in on the rear) and their calipers were placed in the conventional position, integrally with the hubs, as were the independent calipers and pads that constituted the emergency or parking brakes, acting on the front discs and actuated by means of cables running from a conventional hand lever located on the central console. The rear brakes were also of the disc type, instead of the drums used on the DS. The braking system was fully powered, of course, with separate twin forward and rear circuits energized by the car's central high-pressure hydraulic servo-system. A conventional lever-type foot pedal was fitted, however, rather than the mushroom button of the DS; this actuated a brake control valve that distributed fluid to each of the circuits at a pressure proportional to the effort exerted on the foot pedal. Later, a compensating valve was fitted to the rear circuit, to ensure a more progressive braking action on the rear brakes according to the load being carried in the back of the car, so as to reduce the risk of locking-up the rear wheels upon emergency braking.

As expected on a big Citroën, the CX featured the same unique self-leveling hydro-pneumatic gas/oil suspension system that had been developed and refined with such success on the DS and GS models; that is to say, its springs took the form of four spheres containing nitrogen gas under pressure, each one linked to the wheel by a piston moving in a cylinder attached to the sphere and bearing on a quantity of hydraulic fluid held under pressure in the cylinder and its associated sphere. The constant ride-height and ground clearance position of the vehicle was controlled by two height-corrector devices, positioned at the front and rear of the car and operated by the action of the anti-roll bars, which admitted pressurized fluid supplied by the pump and accumulator of the central hydraulic system, as required. A lever on the console allowed the driver to select one of three height settings, the highest used when changing a wheel.

However, the design of the mechanical elements of the CX's suspension system owed more to the GS than the DS. The front axle sub-assembly comprised two forged-steel transversal arms linking the hubs to the front subframe, and connected also to the front suspension units and the anti-roll bar. These arms operated as a parallelogram, but their axes of articulation were not exactly parallel. Instead, they dipped forward by 12 degrees in order to maintain a level attitude at all times and prevent lift or dive when the vehicle was accelerating or braking. Just as was the case with the DS and GS, the CX's front suspension was designed to follow the principle of center-point steering; under all conditions of travel the vertical axis of steering swivel passed through the hubs and wheels to meet the exact point of contact between the tire and the road. It was this feature, in conjunction with Citroën's self-leveling suspension, that gave the CX driver the ability to maintain absolute directional stability and control when emergency braking, even in the event of a blow-out occurring on a front tire at high speed. Initially, steering was controlled via a manually operated rack-and-pinion

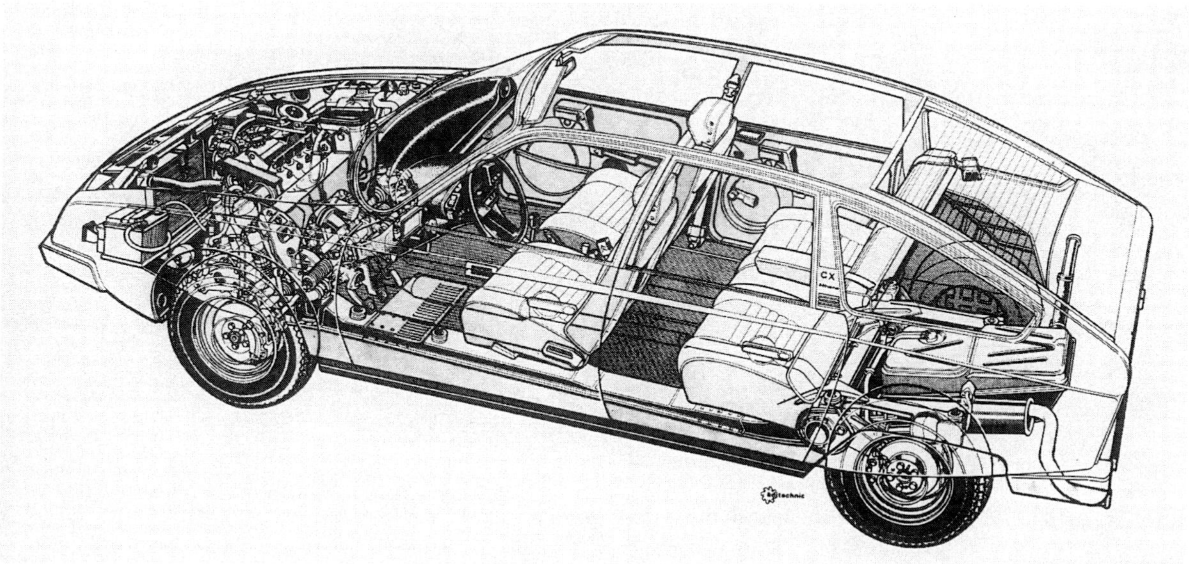

The construction of the CX can be seen from this technical diagram. The body-shell rested on two sub-frames, front and rear, and on two longerons which ran between these subframes, a unique arrangement which gave extra torsional stiffness and ensured correct alignment of the wheels under all circumstances.

system located behind the engine but, as we shall see, optional power steering was introduced later on.

The CX was fitted with smaller, 5½ J size, wheels than were employed on the DS/ID series vehicles, and the method of securing them to the hubs (by bolts instead of studs and nuts) was also different. Naturally, Michelin tubeless radial tires were employed throughout. Initially, on the CX2000 and CX2200 models sold on the French market, 185SR14 ZX pattern were fitted on the front wheels and 175SR14 ZX pattern on the rear and spare wheels.

Evolution — Series 1

In light of the adverse economic situation prevailing just prior to the launch of the new CX, it was decided that optimum fuel consumption would be the highest priority for the great majority of the car's potential customers. So no attempt was made to equip and present it as a high-performance sedan, equivalent to, and a worthy replacement for, the former *haut de gamme* or top-of-the-line Citroën model, the 141 bhp DS23IE, which was capable of 116 mph. Many buyers found this state of affairs disappointing, however, and to meet the widely voiced demand for greater power and speed, six months after the launch, in January 1975, the CX2000 was joined by a sister vehicle, the CX2200 sedan, powered by a larger, more lusty 2175cc engine (90mmx85mm) producing 112 bhp at 5,500 rpm, enough to give it a claimed top speed of 111 mph. This unit was also inherited from the D series range, having served, in its original guise, on the DS21 and D Super 5 models.

Like the CX2000, the CX2200 came in two distinct versions, the basic entry-level Confort and the more elaborately trimmed and equipped Super, the latter easily recognized internally by its electrically powered front windows and externally by its full-size stainless-steel wheel covers, which had a concave depression at their

The 2175 cc engined CX-2200, which arrived in January 1975, showing the huge concave rear window which required no windshield wiper to keep it clear of rain or slush. Like the GS, the CX sedan was a conventional three-box design with a separate trunk.

The CX Pallas, introduced in September 1975, had all the extra brightwork and other exterior details customarily found on Citroën's Pallas top-of-the-line models, including stainless steel sill covers, large dish-type stainless steel wheel covers and rubbing strips.

centers. The CX2000, of course, was equipped with small central hub caps only; these protected the wheel nuts but left the grey-painted surface of the road-wheels fully exposed. However, in September that year the range was extended by the addition of a third, luxury, version, the CX2200 Pallas, which provided a very high level of trim and equipment indeed, equivalent to that found previously on the DS Pallas models. From the outside, the CX2200 Pallas could be distinguished immediately by certain exclusive features, including the stainless steel cill covers running under its doors, the thin rubbing strips running along its flanks, the rubber overriders inserted in its bumpers, the metal beading strips that ran along its flanks beneath the windows and the Pallas badges on its steering wheel, trunk lid and rear quarter panel. The CX Pallas also boasted distinctive stainless-steel wheel embellishers; initially, these Pallas wheel trims were embossed with a six-pointed star design but, following the introduction of the CX2400, from the end of 1977 on, they took the simpler form of large, plain, unadorned dishes with just a small boss pressed into their centers; in fact, this second type of Pallas wheel trim was fitted to all three versions of the CX2400, including the Prestige.

The interior of the CX Pallas version also boasted other unique distinguishing features. Most noticeably, the seats were more elaborately upholstered than those of the standard CX models, covered with a superior quality of jersey nylon cloth, having a ribbed rather than a plain surface; leather was an option, of course. Initially, the CX Pallas was made available in a choice of seven colors, of which three metallic shades—grey, green and bronze—were exclusive to the Pallas. Obviously, the CX Pallas also benefited from the modification to the heating and ventilation system introduced on all models in July 1975, when two extra eye-ball vents were added to the center console, in the position previously occupied by the radio speaker grille; the speakers were repositioned in the front doors.

The original specification of the CX series offered conventional manual rack-and-pinion steering only, but in response to a demand for power assistance, in September 1975 the option of Citroën's unique DIRAVI (Direction Assistee a Rappel Asservi) self-centering hydraulic servo system was made available on the CX2200 Super and Pallas models. Always referred to in the U.K. as the VariPower system, this was an improved version of the device originally introduced on the Citroën-Maserati SM, modified so that the number of turns of the steering wheel required to change direction from lock to lock was increased from 2 to 2.5. In contrast to the constant and invariable level of assistance applied by a conventional power steering system, the VariPower device automatically adjusted the degree of self-centering action provided according to the actual road speed of the car. Thus, although the amount of hydraulic assistance provided to turn the road wheels was constant at all times, the artificially induced resistance provided by the Diravi system varied the effort required by the driver to turn the steering wheel. When the car was stationary the force required was virtually nil; but as its speed increased the resistance felt at the steering wheel became progressively greater, to eliminate all sensation of lightness or vagueness at high speed and impart an impression of absolute sensitivity, confidence and control at all times. Moreover, the automatic self-centering action allowed the road wheels to return to the straight-ahead position whenever grip on the steering wheel was released, so making parking maneuvers an effortless matter. The following month, air conditioning was also introduced as an option on the CX2200 Pallas.

December 1975 was a major milestone in the career of the CX range as it saw the arrival of the CX2200 Diesel sedan, the first diesel-engined Citroën passenger car to be produced since the late 1930s. This was powered by a 9CV 2175cc compression-ignition engine producing 66 bhp, developed in association with the British company Ricardo Consulting Engineers Ltd. and equipped with a cylinder head incorporating Ricardo Comet IV combustion chambers. With the Energy Crisis then at its height, the arrival of this outstandingly robust and economical diesel engine was timely indeed, and the CX2200 Diesel

Announced in September 1975, the CX Break (or station wagon) actually went on sale in France in January 1976, available with either the 1985 cc gas engine or the new 2175 diesel power plant which had been introduced earlier on the sedan, towards the end of 1975. Its wheelbase and overall length were 25cm longer than those of the sedan.

proved to be an immediate and substantial success. Over the next three years the annual sales of this sedan and the subsequent diesel-engined CX variants mounted annually until they came to represent no less than 48 percent of total CX production.

In January 1976 the long-awaited CX Break or station wagon version, announced the previous September, went on sale in France at last, available with a choice of two engines, either the 1985cc gas engine, or with the 2175cc diesel engine. However, this newcomer did not appear in the U.K. in right-hand drive form until April that year, marketed as the CX2000 Safari Estate, as was the case with the ID and DS breaks before them. Two derivatives of the CX Break duly followed within months; in September an ambulance version (specially constructed by Heuliez for the French market only) and, in October, an eight-seater Familiale. Although 4 inches shorter than the DS Break, the CX Break was a large and commodious vehicle nonetheless, nearly a foot longer than its sister vehicle the CX sedan; with its rear seats folded down, it offered an available floor length of 6ft 2in and a total 76.7 cu ft of fully usable load space. Uniquely, a payload of up to 1,650 lbs. (750 kg) could be carried in safety, thanks to the CX's self-leveling hydro-pneumatic suspension and braking system. At the very same time, but on the gas-engined CX2200 only, Citroën offered the option of its "C-Matic" semi-automatic transmission, introduced four years previously on the GS line.

Following its first appearance in July 1975, in February 1976 a new luxury limousine version of the CX entered series production, to fill the vacancy left by the demise of the DS23IE Prestige-Pallas two years earlier. Based on the floor pan of the CX Break, both wheelbase and body were extended by approximately nine inches over the ordinary CX sedan to offer greater legroom in the rear passenger compartment. Called the CX Prestige, and intended as appropriate transportation for the elite of France including the President of the Republic, this car was equipped with a new, more powerful 115 hp 2347cc engine combined with C-Matic transmission. Instantly recognizable by its noticeably wider rear doors (an extra seven inches) and broader rear quarter trim panel pressed from stainless steel and bearing a special inscription, the Prestige was also noted for a number of other special fittings and refinements, including footrests in the rear, air conditioning as standard, button-backed seats upholstered in jersey cloth (or leather as an option) black or metallic paintwork, additional beading around the front and tail lights, Pallas-style wheel-trims and an optional vinyl-covered roof. The CX Prestige did not arrive in RHD form until August 1976.

In July 1976, the new 2347cc engine from the CX Prestige was installed in the CX2200 sedan to present a new offering, the CX2400, available in both Super and Pallas form, with a choice of either four-speed manual or semi-automatic C-Matic transmission. The 2175cc engined CX2200 model was promptly deleted. The following year — in May 1977 to be exact — came the announcement of a new high-performance 128 bhp version of the CX sedan, capable of reaching 118 mph. This was the CX2400 GTi, equipped with the 2347cc engine now fitted with a Bosch Jetronic electronic fuel injection system and a new 5-speed gearbox. Curiously, both the DS21 and, later, the DS23 models had been available in fuel-injected form from 1969 on, but after their replacement by the CX a full two years had elapsed before an EFI system was reinstated beneath the hood of a Citroën. Marketed as an outright sporting sedan, well qualified to take on rivals from BMW or Jaguar, the CX2400 GTi was distinguished by a special GTi steering wheel and other badging, front

The arrival of the CX Break inspired the creation, in February 1976, of the luxurious CX Prestige, a stretched version of the CX Pallas built on the long-wheelbase floorpan of the Break, and thus 25cm longer than the standard sedan. It was powered by a 2347 cc engine (derived from the power-plant of the DS23), which was subsequently adopted for the new CX2400 line which replaced the CX-2200 in July 1976.

In May 1977, Citroën announced a new high-performance version of the CX-2400, the fuel-injected CXGTi, in which the output of the 2347 cc engine was boosted to 128 bhp, and top speed to 192 km/h (119 mph). Outwardly, the CXGTi was distinguished by its spoiler and alloy wheels. This example is the version sold during the 1980-1981 season. Note that the customary stainless-steel door handles, window frames and C-pillar panel have been replaced by a matt-black finish.

fog lights, alloy wheels with Michelin XVS tires and a matt-black finish on its window frames, although the door handles, c-pillar trim and other detailing conformed to the stainless steel finish seen on all other CX sedans until now. Appropriately, the car boasted an interior decor *tres sportif*, with black dashboard and carpets plus special sports seats incorporating integral headrests, which as an option could be upholstered in a flamboyant two-tone black and buff leather finish.

Little happened in the evolution of the CX range over the next twelve months, but then in July 1977 came an improved version of the CX2400 Prestige, equipped with the fuel-injected 2347cc engine from the CXGTi, similarly mated to the new 5-speed gearbox. Its roofline was raised by two inches, and consequently a model was immediately delivered to the Elysée Palace in Paris, for the use of President Giscard d'Estaing, a tall man who had requested that the Prestige be given extra headroom, to accommodate the *haut fonctionnaires* of France in appropriate comfort. This second edition of the CX Prestige featured a new style of wheel-cover—a plain and simple stainless steel dish unadorned by any pressed-in motif—which was soon adopted for all the other top-of-the-line CX models that were not fitted with alloy wheels. At the same time, the 5-speed gearbox also became available as an option on the CX2400 sedan; similarly an electric sunroof was offered as an extra on all CX models except the Prestige and the Break.

Next, in December 1977 another new CX variant arrived on the scene, the CX2400IE Pallas, which featured the fuel-injected 2347cc engine coupled with a C-Matic transmission, plus Diravi power steering as standard. Production of the CX that year exceeded 112,000 units for the second year running; the following year, 1978, it was to hit 132,000. Clearly, the car had reached the peak of its popularity. In 1978, 70,116 cars were sold in France and 53,374 exported, more than 16,000 to Germany as opposed to the 7,000 sent to the U.K. Despite the Energy Crisis, it had succeeded in establishing itself as one of the world's great cars—yet another formidable Grande Routiere in the French tradition, the ideal vehicle in which to exploit the advantages of the extensive network of new autoroutes and autobahns then being established across Europe.

It was surely this same demand for relaxed and economical high-speed motorway cruising that led to the arrival in February 1978 of two improved diesel-engine versions, the CX2500D sedan and station wagon, to replace the three-year-old CX2200D. With cubic capacity enlarged from 2175cc to 2.5 liters, power output was raised by more than 13 percent to 75 bhp, but more importantly, maximum torque was increased by 20 percent to 111 lb-ft, delivered at the much lower engine speed of 2,000 rpm. A four-speed gearbox with a higher final drive ratio was fitted, while Vari-Power steering was standard. Truly, the CX2500D represented the ultimate in diesel car development for that era; official EEC fuel consumption tests recorded 32.5 mpg at a constant 75 mph and 34.5 mpg on the urban cycle.

The following year further minor improvements were made to the interior of the CX, when in May 1978 a redesigned center console was introduced, equipped with new heating and ventilation arrangements. The earlier twin circular vents were replaced by a pair of adjustable grilles and a curious spherical ashtray was added, perched on top of the console unit, the radio having been relocated to a new horizontal position immediately beneath the ashtray. In July 1978, the five-speed gearbox was given wider employment throughout the CX range, initially as an option on the CX2500 Diesel sedan, but later that year on the CX2400 gas engine and CX2500 Diesel Breaks as well. By July 1979, Vari-Power steering had also become standard equipment on most models, as had the option of electric central locking, first seen on the CX Prestige. Later, this became standard on all models.

July 1979 marked a major turning point in the evolution of the CX range, in that it saw the introduction of two new models in the 2-Litre class, the CX Reflex and

The CX also proved to be a highly successful long-distance rally car, especially over rough terrain where its hydro-pneumatic suspension gave it an advantage. Its most notable outing occurred in 1977, when the British driver Paddy Hopkirk gained third prize in the second London-Sydney marathon in a CX2400.

The Douvrin engine was rated at 106 hp at 5,500 rpm and produced a maximum torque of 122 lb-ft at 3,250, enough to give both the Reflex and Athena a lively acceleration (0–60 mph in 11.7 secs) and top speed of 109 mph. However, because the Athena was equipped with a five-speed gear box while the Reflex had the standard four-speed box, its fuel consumption was slightly better when cruising; the official tests recorded 39.77 mpg at a constant 56 mph, but only 23.34 mpg for the urban cycle.

Even so, both cars were exceedingly well equipped and appointed by the standard of other economy models, having features normally associated with the more expensive CX2400. The Athena was trimmed to a higher standard internally, however, with ribbed, not plain, jersey cloth seats, tinted glass and electric front windows. Externally, each had special badging strips on their trunk lids, but the two cars could also be distinguished apart in side view, the Athena having Pallas-type stainless steel wheel covers and rubbing strips while the Reflex lacked such ornamentation, being outfitted with simple plastic wheel covers and, for the first time on a CX, matt-black window frames. Both had stainless steel door-handles and c-pillar trim panels, however. In August 1979 the U.K. price of the Reflex sedan was £5697, including car tax and VAT, while the Athena cost a total of £6,229. The Reflex was also available in a Safari version with virtually identical specifications, though not the Athena. The Reflex Safari was not seen in the U.K. until 1982.

Athena, which replaced the old CX2000 models. Specifically intended to appeal to the energy-conscious business motorist, these cars were equipped with a modern 1995cc all-light-alloy OHC engine, manufactured by the Societe Francaise de Mecanique at Douvrin and also employed on certain current Renault and Peugeot models. Clearly, the Reflex and Athena represented a positive attempt to widen the CX market downward; both were classed 10CV under the French *puissance fiscale* scale of motor duty, as opposed to 11CV for the old 1985cc CX-2000 model and 13CV for the 2347cc engined CX2400.

Three months later, another interesting innovation appeared in the CX catalog for the 1979–1980 season — the CX2500 Diesel Limousine which combined the long-wheelbase bodywork of the CX Prestige with the engine and five-speed manual transmission of the standard CX2500 diesel sedan. All the motoring commentators were agreed that this true luxury Grande Routiere diesel car (which had little real opposition in the catalogs of rival marques where use of the compression ignition en-

After five years of service, in July 1979 the CX-2000 base-model was replaced by two new 2-liter cars, the CX Athena and CX Reflex. Both were powered by a new 1995 cc 106 bhp all-alloy overhead camshaft engine, manufactured by the Société Francaise de Mecanique, a jointly owned Peugeot-Citroën-Renault facility located at Douvrin. Seen here side-by-side, the pair were distinguished by subtle differences in trim and equipment, and by badges on the trunk-lid. The cheaper of the two, the Reflex (right), had a simple unadorned appearance with no rubbing strips, while the Athena (left) was more elaborately finished, almost to Pallas standards.

gine was still largely confined to taxi models) was a testament to the very high levels of performance and refinement that Citroën had pioneered on its diesel-engined CX models in response to the challenges posed by the new economic circumstances then prevailing.

The passing of the 1970s marked a turning point in the history of the Citroën company. In 1979 production reached a post-war record of 815,173 units (375,395 exported) of which no less than 123,391 were CX models. Since reopening for business in 1946, after the Occupation, the company had managed to increase its output year after year, with only a slight faltering in 1974 and 1975 as a result of the first Energy Crisis, although its market share had actually peaked in 1964 when 30.7 percent of the French domestic market and 9.3 percent of the total European market were achieved. But in the new decade ahead, the 1980s, this continual regular upward progress would prove impossible to sustain. Already a second energy crisis (even more severe, being triggered by the Iranian revolution in 1979 and the subsequent war between Iran and Iraq) was having severe impact on Citroën's total sales, which fell by more than 150,000 units between 1979 and 1980. During 1980, for the first time since 1975, production of the CX fell below 80,000 units per annum; that year the firm built a total of 77,237 vehicles of all types, of which 42,578 had gas engines and 34,669 were diesel powered. In the French market, the CX range just managed to hold its own, but in the vital European export markets sales fell to 34,343 units, compared with 48,356 the previous year. The signs were that, if only temporarily, big cars like the CX were falling out of favor with private and corporate purchasers alike, and particularly in France due to the effects of the *puissance fiscale* motor taxation system which militated against engines of greater capacity than 1700–1800cc.

The process of improvement went on regardless, however, and in July 1980 a new paint-shop was installed at the Aulnay factory, designed to achieve a significant improvement in the corrosion resistance and overall durability of the CX's coachwork. The measures introduced at this time included injecting cavities with a rust inhibiting treatment, fitting rigid rubber sealing strips on the door bottoms and applying a final coat of clear lacquer to the paintwork. The first fruits of this major investment appeared in October 1980 and were immediately apparent; the cars produced for the 1980-1981 model year and thereafter could easily be distinguished from their predecessors by virtue of the far higher-build quality that they displayed.

The improvements were not confined to cosmetic details either. On all models, the front suspension was revised and the track widened by 40mm, while the handbrake lever was lengthened for reduced effort and the windshield washer-jets were incorporated into the single windshield wiper arm. At the same time, the spherical ashtray was replaced by a conventional sliding tray, positioned at the top of the console, above the radio. Lastly, all gas-engined models with manual gearboxes were equipped with Econoscope guide lights, placed in the instrument binnacle which indicated when the car was being driven with the optimum gear ratio and throttle setting for maximum fuel economy. Moreover, in response to a widely voiced demand for greater power and flexibility, the CX2400 gas engine received a number of modifications which raised its output from 115 bhp to 120 bhp. At the same time, the five-speed gearbox was made standard on the CX Pallas and CX2500 Diesel models.

That year also, the CX2400 GTi was given a substantial revamp. The changes included a new interior with improved seats, and the addition of a new airfoil spoiler mounted on the rear hatch. At the same time, the sporting attributes of the GTi were further emphasized by a switch from stainless steel to a matt-black finish for such exterior fittings as the window-frames, door-handles and C-pillar trim panel, which was also widened. Next, in September 1980, the CX2400 Pallas (both carburetor and fuel-injection versions) was equipped, as an option, with a fully automatic three-speed gearbox manufactured by the German ZF firm, and the C-Matic semi-automatic transmission, pioneered by Citroën, was discontinued on all models.

Lastly, at the Paris Motor Show in October 1980, a luxury version of the CX2400 Break appeared for the first time on the Citroën stand. Called the Evasion, this was available in a choice of either normally aspirated, fuel-injected or diesel-engined forms. Built by the specialist coachbuilder Heuliez, the Evasion was slightly longer (by 30cm) than the standard station wagon and could be recognized immediately by its vinyl roof and elaborate interior trim; this vehicle was never imported into the U.K.

The following year, in July 1981, the production of all CX2400 models having gas engines fitted with carburetors ceased (except for certain export markets), carburetion being replaced entirely by fuel-injection in the CX catalog. At the same time, cruise control was made available as an option on the CX Pallas (both 5-speed manual and automatic versions), the CX Prestige Automatic and the CX GTi. A far more visible change, however, was that the front wheel arches of all models were flared and enlarged to permit the fitting of the new Michelin TRX high-speed tires which were offered from then on as standard on the CX GTi and as an option on the fuel-injected CX2400 Pallas sedan and Prestige models; mud flaps were also fitted as standard from this point onwards, on all models. Similarly, all the sedans in the range received the new enlarged C-pillar trim panel introduced earlier on the GTI. In all cases except the CX Prestige, this new *panneau de custode* was made from matt-black plastic, instead of the polished stainless-steel used until this time.

Throughout the end of 1981 and beginning of 1982, the new range of CX Reflex Safari Estates and Familiales was introduced onto the U.K. market, based on the vehicles that had appeared in France two years earlier. These were the CX Reflex (1995cc gas engine), the CX Reflex D (2.5 liter diesel engine), the CX Reflex 2.4 Auto (2.4 carburetor engine) and the CX Reflex IE (2.4 liter fuel-injected engine). Competitively priced, these vehicles shared the same level of trim and equipment. Then, in the autumn of 1982, the entire CX range was reorganized and restructured, a process that involved the renaming of certain models. For example, the Reflex and Athena names disappeared, the CX Reflex becoming the CX20 and the CX Athena, the CX20TRE. Standing for Tres Riche Essence, the TR badge indicated the same very high level of interior appointments previously associated with the Pallas appellation, which was discontinued in France but retained in the U.K. in place of the TRE designation. The CX25D, CX20 and CXIE Breaks and Familiales also received an enhanced level of interior comfort and refinement, with central locking becoming standard on all models. Similarly, transistorized ignition was provided for the 1995cc Douvrin engine fitted to the CX20 and CX20TRE models.

April 1983 saw the introduction of a Garrett turbocharger on the 2500cc Citroën diesel engine, boosting its power output to 95 hp DIN at 3,700 rpm and torque to 159 ft lbs at 2,000 rpm. The result was the appearance

In July 1984 came three important additions to the CX diesel range — two sedans and a station wagon powered by a new turbo-charged version of the 2500 cc compression-ignition engine, first seen in 1977. The addition of the turbo-charger boosted power output by 30 percent to 95 bhp, so that the top speed of these diesel sedans was 108 mph. Yet when cruising at a constant 75 mph their fuel consumption was a mere 40 mpg. This is the cheaper of the two, the CX-25RD Turbo. Its sister-car, the CX-25TRD Turbo, had alloy wheels and stainless steel exterior trim.

of two new sedan models, known as the CX25RD Turbo and the CX25DTR Turbo, respectively, according to the level of trim provided, and also a turbo-diesel engined Break and Limousine; the non-turbocharged CX25D Berline (sedan), Break and Familiale all remained in the catalog, however, at least in France. The following July, all the vehicles equipped with the old 2347cc fuel-injected gas engine received a new uprated 2500cc fuel-injected power unit developing 138 hp DIN at 5,000 rpm. These CX2500 sedans and station wagons featured a computerized solid-state electronic ignition which dispensed with a distributor and thus avoided use of any moving parts subject to wear; this system replaced the transistorized magnetic-impulse ignition system fitted on the CX2400, which employed a distributor, though of the contact-breakerless type. That month also, two high-specification Break variants were announced, both featuring such refinements as central locking, electric windows all round, ribbed cloth upholstery and split folding rear seats. When introduced in the U.K. later that year, these were known as the CX25 TRi Safari, equipped with the 138 bhp fuel-injected 2500cc gas engine, and the CX25DTR Turbo Safari, fitted with the 95 bhp turbocharged 2500cc Diesel unit.

In March 1984 two new utility station wagon variants entered the line in France (but not the U.K.), the CX20 Entreprise (gas) and the CX25D Entreprise (diesel). As these were classed as strictly commercial vehicles, they were fitted with front seats only and had flat-load floors at the rear and thus qualified for a lower rate of excise duty under French road taxation regulations. Moreover, the following month the CX range was further augmented by the introduction of the budget-priced CX20 Leader limited edition, based on the CX20. Distinguished by its two-tone metallic grey paintwork, with a contrasting dark grey strip along its lower flanks and a decal on its front doors, it also boasted tinted glass, a rear spoiler and its own individual pattern of wheel embellishers. That year, only 700 examples of the CX Leader were produced, but as the model continued in production for the next five years at an average of 2,000 units per year, ultimately a total of 9,700 examples were manufactured.

In September 1984, heralded by a spectacular television advertising campaign featuring the American model Grace Jones (whose spiky hair was sculpted into a silhouette of the car) and bearing the slogan "C'est Demon! (It's Devilish!)," came the CX25GTi Turbo. Here, the performance of the standard fuel-injected 2500cc gas engine (mated to a five-speed manual gearbox) was boosted by the fitting of an exhaust-driven turbocharger, as on the earlier turbo-diesel cars. This improvement produced a substantial increase in the new car's performance, boosting power output by 22 percent and torque by 40 percent compared with its conventionally aspirated alternative, which remained in the catalog as the standard CX25GTi. Indeed, specific output was actually raised to 168 bhp DIN at 5,000 rpm and provided 217 ft lbs of torque at 3,250 rpm to lift its top speed from 125 to 138 mph. Acceleration from 0–60mph now took just 7.9 secs, making the CX25 GTi Turbo a true high-performance sedan and the fastest French car of its day. Appropriately, in addition to its unique new alloy wheels carrying a T symbol and fitted with ultra-low-profile Michelin TRX tires, the GTi Turbo was equipped with a large airfoil-shaped rear spoiler plus matt-black door handles and window frames. The Turbo T motif was also seen in the form of a badge mounted on the ventilation air-intake on the hood. At the same time, the CX25 GTi Turbo was also given an new all-black interior featuring special sports seats with integral head-rests, upholstered with an exclusive chevron-patterned velour fabric, plus a revised dashboard binnacle with round-dialed instruments. Fittingly also, the following March the availability of ABS braking was announced as an optional choice for this car, the first time that such a system had been offered on a French vehicle. In September

Until this point in time, station wagons or estate cars had generally been regarded both in France and on the Continent generally as semi-commercial vehicles. But this status was certainly changed in July 1984 when Citroën brought out a luxurious high-performance version of the CX Break. Powered by the new 2500 cc 138 bhp fuel-injected engine from the current CX GTi, the CX Break 25 TRi was equipped with alloy wheels as standard, as befitted its sporting character.

In October 1984 came the CXGTi Turbo, heralded by a notable publicity campaign (which doubtless would nowadays be considered the height of political incorrectness) proclaiming that it was devilishly fast. On this flagship model the fuel-injected 2500 gas engine was enhanced by the addition of a turbo-charger boosting power output to 138 hp and top speed to 121 mph. A true grand routiere, the CXGTi Turbo was the fastest French car of its era and the ultimate choice for rapid, long-distance motorway travel at that time.

1985, the CX25 GTi Turbo was priced at £12,572 including tax in the U.K. catalog, compared with £7,756 for the base model CX20, or £10,669 for the CX25 Pallas IE.

By the end of June 1985, eleven years after the commencement of production, no fewer than 912,500 examples of the CX had been produced, of which 42.3 percent had been exported, principally to Germany (90,610), Italy (63,433), Belgium (48,429) and Great Britain (39,848); 81 percent of this total had been sedans and 19 percent station wagons, 53 percent of them gas-engined and 47 percent diesel-powered. Even so, annual production — which had peaked at 132,675 vehicles in 1978 — was falling at an ever accelerating rate year by year, largely as a result of declining demand in France itself; indeed a total of only 41,949 CXs been built in 1984, of which a mere 17,847 found customers there. Clearly, the time had come to take drastic action to reverse these falling sales and revive the fortunes of the CX line.

Evolution — Series Two

Consequently, in July 1985, Automobiles Citroën announced what was claimed to be a complete transformation of its flagship model. This Second Generation of the CX family was presented as being entirely new throughout, inside and out, in an attempt to counter the attractions presented by more youthful rivals from Renault and Peugeot. In truth, however, the redesign was really only skin deep, a superficial and inexpensive revamp wrought by a team of designers at the company's new styling center at Velizy, led by Carl Olsen, a Danish designer previously associated with General Motors in Detroit. Beneath the CX's new bodywork, its engines and other mechanical elements were essentially unchanged.

Thus, of the grand total of 24 revised and improved Series Two CX sedans and station wagons revealed for the coming 1985-1986 season, only two, the CX25 Prestige Turbo sedan (a flagship model not offered in the U.K.) and the CX-22TRS sedan, were actually completely new offerings. The CX25 Prestige Turbo featured the turbocharged 2500cc fuel-injected engine previously available only in the CX25 GTi Turbo sedan, while the CX22TRS was equipped with an improved version of the Douvrin light-alloy OHC motor fitted to the earlier Reflex, Athena and CX20 models.

By July 1985, with more than a million sold, the CX had reached the grand old age of 11, and so a face-lift was considered appropriate, to rejuvenate its appeal. The result was the restyled Series Two CX range, in which the stainless steel bumpers were replaced by plastic moldings and the sharp kick-up angle of the rear wheel spats was reduced, to create a more beefy and aggressive look. Inside, the dashboard and console were completely redesigned, retaining the lunule binnacle, but with round-dialled instruments. This is the CX-25GTi Turbo, which was not changed mechanically from its Series One predecessor. In July 1986, however, came the intercooled CX-25GTi Turbo Two. With its power output now increased to 168 bhp, this car was capable of accelerating from 0 to 60 mph in 7.7 seconds and reaching a top speed of 138 mph.

This 2500 cc diesel-engined CX-25RD Break produced for the 1985-1986 season, shows how the Series Two look was applied to station wagons and familiales. For the following 1987-1988 season, the 2500 cc turbo-diesel engine on these models was also given an inter-cooler. This improvement increased power output to 120 bhp, providing 0–60 mph acceleration in just 11.5 seconds and a new top speed of 117 mph. Yet, traveling at a steady 56 mph, the Turbo Two diesel could return a frugal 52 mpg.

With its swept volume increased from 1995cc to 2165cc and its output boosted from 106 bhp to 115 bhp, this unit (matched to the five-speed gearbox, naturally) served to raise the car's top speed from 109 to 116 mph with little if any penalty in fuel consumption. Specifically designed to reduce the cost of luxury motoring, the 116 mph CX22TRS also boasted a particularly high level of trim and equipment, including grey herringbone tweed upholstery, tinted windows, rear seatbelts and head restraints and also a rear spoiler.

The remaining 22 CX models offered in Citroën's 1986/7 French market line (comprising three types of body, four types of trim and equipment level and no fewer than six different engines, ranging from 75 to 168 bhp) had all appeared earlier in Series One guise, with identical specifications. The most popular and widely produced of these new Series Two variants were the 1995cc gas engined CX20 sedan, the 2500cc gas engined CX25 Prestige limousine, the high performance CX25GTi and CX25Gti Turbo sedans, plus the 2500cc CXRD & CXDTR diesel or turbo-diesel sedans, together with the gas engined CX20 and CX25TRi breaks and familiales and the diesel or turbo-diesel engined CX25RD and CX25RD Turbo breaks and familiales.

In the U.K. that year, a reduced line of six sedans and three station wagons was offered, comprising the naturally aspirated 1995cc CX20RE and 2165cc CX22TRS sedans; the fuel-injected 2500cc CX25GTi Automatic sedan; the CX25GTi Turbocharged sedan (with five-speed manual transmission); the 2500cc CX25 Prestige Automatic limousine and the CX25DTR Turbo turbocharged diesel-engined sedan; plus the CX20RE Safari Estate and familiale, both powered by the naturally aspirated 1995cc engine; the CX25Ri familiale and the CX25TRi Safari Estate, powered by the 2500cc fuel-injected engine; and finally the CX25DTR Turbo Safari, powered by the 2,500 turbocharged diesel engine. That season also, the availability of the high-level Pallas specification of trim and equipment (offered since September 1977 on various Series One models) was at last abolished in the U.K., as had been the case in France since 1982, when the Pallas option had been replaced by the TRE designation.

Therefore, the essential differences between the Series One and Series Two CX ranges were purely cosmetic, arising from the various changes made to both the exterior styling and interior trim of the car. Actually, the work of revising the bodywork had fallen to an Englishman, Geoff Mathews, a graduate of the Royal College of Art's Automotive Design Group who was currently Chief Designer of Exteriors on Carl Olsen's team. From the outside, the Series Two models could be instantly distinguished from their predecessors by their revised frontal aspect, which now featured a large one-piece, wrapround structure incorporating both bumpers and underskirt, to replace the stainless steel bumpers fitted until then. Made from polypropylene, this molding was colored to match or tone with the bodywork color. Similarly, the radiator grille above it was also color-keyed on all but the cheapest models, instead of being plain black plastic as before. This theme was continued at the rear with a similar bumper molding that, on the sedans, curved round to meet the fender skirts, which were altered in shape, giving a lower line to the bottom edge of the rear fenders, so that the CX lost its characteristic kick-up rear aspect when viewed in profile. As well as the absence of the rubber seals that had been fitted to the bottom edge of the doors, on the Series One CX, the side view of the revamped version also revealed new protective polypropylene sill covers fitted beneath the doors together with a wide black PVC anti-rubbing strip running along the side of the car (and also across the base of the trunk lid), together with a new dome-shaped pattern of plastic wheelcover, although the same type of alloy wheels previously fitted to Series One cars remained an option. The traditional stainless steel wheel covers which had been such a notable feature of the earlier Series One cars were never fitted to any Series Two CX, however. Similarly, the other items of stainless steel bright work also disappeared on all Series Two models except the Prestige and the GTi, as the door handles, window frames and C-pillar trim panels were replaced by the matt-black fitments which had already appeared earlier on certain Series One cars such as the GTi. In addition, all the sedans except the CX20RE and CX25RD base models were given the matt black plastic spoiler, fitted to the trunk lid, that had previously been fitted to the Series One CXGTi; also, all but the cheapest base models were fitted with twin-optic halogen headlights incorporating long-range beams. The Series Two cars also featured a new and particularly aerodynamic type of rearview mirror (fitted to both the driver's and passenger's doors on RHD cars), adjustable either manually or electrically according to the model in question. These exterior changes served to improve the CX's aerodynamic efficiency—a decrease in its drag-coefficient from 0.30 to 0.35 was claimed.

From the inside, however, the changes and improvements were far more comprehensive. First, the dashboard and center console units were entirely redesigned so that the two elements were more closely integrated in a one-piece structure, housing an improved heating and ventilation system with relocated vents. This was the work of Michel Harmand, currently Chief Designer of Interiors, who had been responsible for the design of the original facia eleven years earlier. Fortunately, Harmand ensured that the unique and quite unmistakable feature of the CX, the original *lunule* driver's instrument binnacle was preserved, though it was now equipped with instruments having conventional round-faced dials. Many of the minor switches, controls and warning lights were also repositioned and, for the very first time, an electric servo-motor device was provided for ride-height adjustment, replacing the manual lever previously used. The ride itself was made firmer on most models by the incorporation of modified damper valves in the hydro-pneumatic suspension system, plus stiffer anti-roll bars, front and rear.

Second, the seating and trim of the CX were also given a complete makeover and the ribbed or plain jersey nylon cloth used previously was discarded in favor of a line of new fabrics. For the U.K. market, a choice of three coordinated interior color schemes—grey, blue or beige—was available, and each consisted of a variety of upholstery fabrics in these colors teamed with door panel moldings, dashboard and headlining in the same corresponding shades. Herringbone-patterned woolen tweed upholstery was fitted on the TR level models, such as the CX25 GTi and the new CX22 TRS, while jersey cloth with a red pin-stripe effect was seen on the RE sedans, station wagons and familiales, again in the same three basic color choices. The CX25 GTi Turbo retained its grey/black interior and special sports front seats with integral headrests, however, while black leather trim was an optional extra. This situation continued throughout the following 1987-1988 model year, except that the CX25GTi was given the same grey/black chevron-patterned velour upholstery and black dashboard previously exclusive to the CX25GTi Turbo. For the following, final, 1988–1989, model year, this velour fabric became standard for all the sedans then offered on the U.K. market, except the CX22TRS. As we shall see, this car was given a special-edition interior treatment, while the grey herringbone tweed cloth seats with which it had previously been fitted were adopted instead for all the CX station wagons and familiales currently available.

Last, in an attempt to add an ambiance of luxury and refinement to the Series Two cars, more in keeping with the style of interior furnishings adopted by other manufacturers of executive-class machines, the interior door panels (which had formerly been left bare of such adornment) were also clad with cloth. Remarkably, in restyling the avant-garde CX to appeal to the typical middle-brow business motorist, Citroën even went so far as to introduce synthetic wood door cappings on certain models (others had brushed alloy) as a concession to conventional taste.

The face-lift was indeed a visual transformation, rejuvenating the CX and giving it a more potent and aggressive appearance. This modernization did not win universal approval, however, and many commentators found the new Series Two styling somewhat less subtle and elegant than the original incarnation, and open to charges of ostentation and even vulgarity. Indeed, it is believed that Robert Opron viewed this revision of his work with a disappointment that verged on outright displeasure. Even so, it was claimed that these styling revisions and the wider use of tough, non-corrodible composite materials actually brought about tangible, practical benefits for CX owners, by improving the durability and longevity of the vehicle's bodywork as was reflected by the new six-year anti-corrosion warranty offered by Citroën.

The mechanical and structural changes introduced on the Series Two cars in 1985 were confined to the replacement of the manual ride-height adjustment lever by an electric servo motor and by a slight forward relocation of the headlight panel. This provided more space in which to locate the battery, so that it could be lifted in and out without the need to remove the left headlight. In July 1986, however, Citroën introduced the first and only major mechanical advance to be made on the Series Two CX, the incorporation of a new intercooler, or air-to-air heat exchanger, on the two top-of-the-line turbocharged fuel-injected gas-engined sedan versions, so that these became known as the CX25GTI Turbo 2 and the CX25 Prestige Turbo 2, respectively. The ABS braking system which had been introduced two years earlier as an option on the Series One 25GTi, in February 1985, was now made standard on both of these cars.

Nine months later, in April 1987 — the year in which the millionth CX rolled off the Aulnay production line — the Series Two CX25 Turbo-diesel sedan and station wagon were also modified by the introduction of an intercooler and renamed the CX25 Turbo 2. By increasing the density of the air which entered the combustion chambers, the intercooler served to boost power output by 26 percent to 120 bhp, making them simply the fastest diesel vehicles in the world. The sedan version, the CX-25DTR Turbo 2, had a top speed of 121 mph, a 0–60 mph acceleration time of just 10.4 secs and yet returned an average fuel consumption of 58 mpg. The new intercooled Turbo-2 diesel engine was substantially different from the earlier 2500cc turbo-charged compression-ignition unit introduced in 1983, in that its valve-gear was operated by a toothed belt rather than the pushrods that Citroën had employed on all its various other CX engines up till then.

To celebrate the arrival in England of this new addition to the CX diesel range, in August 1987 Citroën U.K. Ltd. staged two remarkable demonstration runs in conjunction with *Motor* magazine. In the first event, a standard production example of the CX25 DTR Turbo-2 sedan was driven non-stop for 24 hours around the Millbrook proving circuit, pausing only for refueling. During this time it traveled over 2,820 miles at an average speed of 117.64 mph. In the second feat, started just a few hours later, the same car proved that it was capable of traveling the length of Great Britain, from Lands End to John O'Groats, on one tank of gas, averaging no less than 63.9 mpg for the entire 861-mile journey. During these record-breaking runs, the car received no attention other than windshield cleaning; but not a single fault developed on either occasion, a remarkable testament to the economy and reliability of this outstandingly robust Citroën diesel engine.

Nevertheless, despite the very great success of these impressive turbo-diesel Series-2 models among high-mileage, long-distance motorists throughout Europe, the arrival of the Series Two CX failed to arrest the car's decline in popularity, and overall sales continued to fall; in 1984, the last year of the Series One versions, production was recorded as 41,849 units, but in 1985 it fell to 38,696 vehicles, in 1986 to 35,409, in 1987 to 35,630 and in 1988 to 23,979. Clearly, the imminent arrival of the new Citroën XM sedan, due to be launched in May 1989, was having a most discouraging effect on buyers, and the end of the road was now in sight for the CX line.

Therefore, for the final 1988-1989 season, the catalog was rationalized and reduced to just 15 vehicles— nine sedans and six breaks and familiales, of which a total of only nine cars were offered on the U.K. market, four sedans and five breaks. These were the CX22TRS, CX-25GTi Automatic, CX25DTR Turbo-2 and CX25GTi Turbo-2 sedans, plus the CX22RS Safari and Familiale, the CX25TRi Safari, the CX25DTR Turbo-2 Safari and the CX25Ri Familiale. However, as a final gesture towards the CX's British fans, in May 1988 the CX22TRS was offered in a special limited edition only available in the U.K., the Croisette. Fitted with ABS as standard and finished in Pearl Grey only, with grey side moldings instead of the normal black, this car also featured a unique pattern of sports seats upholstered in a special dark grey cloth unique to this model. The standard CX22TRS also continued in the catalog for the final 1989 model year, however, but enhanced by the so-called VIP interior pack (in effect, the sports seats and chevron patterned velour upholstery from the GTi) plus an electrically-operated sunroof, alloy wheels and ABS brakes as standard.

So it was that the last CX sedan left the Aulnay factory in May 1989, entirely without ceremony; exactly 1,041,560 had been built there since the first car had rolled off the production line in 1974, of which only 46,412 had found owners in the United Kingdom over those 18 years. Even so, its demise was viewed with great disappointment by many die-hard British enthusiasts who could see as many disadvantages as advantages in the replacement model, the XM. Particularly regretted was the decision to confine the fitting of the CX's Diravi steering system to the most expensive V6-engined version of the XM, and even then on left-hand-drive models only.

Although the sedans had vanished from the showrooms, however, the CX story was not completely over; in the absence of an immediate replacement in the XM range, the CX Breaks and Familiales continued in production for a another two years until the belated launch of the XM Break in June 1991. These 1990 and 1991 model year station wagons were built exclusively by Heuliez and marketed in France as the Evasion. Four versions were made available for the U.K. market, all to special order. These were badged as the CXTGE Safari (equipped with the 2.2 liter Douvrin engine); the CXTGI Safari and Familiale; which replaced the CX25TRI Safari and the CX25RI Familiale, and the CXTGD Turbo Safari, which superseded the CX25DTR Turbo 2 Break. Production of RHD vehicles for the U.K. market actually ceased in January 1991, although LHD assembly continued until later in the year. This swansong period also saw the continued assembly of the various types of CX ambulances by Heuliez and other specialist coachbuilders.

So it was that the lifespan of the CX — the last of the

The swansong of the CX was the limited range of CX Evasion station wagons and familiales produced under contract by Heuliez, following the replacement of the CX sedans by Citroën's new XM model in October 1989. Intended to bridge the gap in the line until the arrival of the XM station wagon two years later, in Autumn of 1991, five different versions of the Evasion were available, with either gas, diesel or turbo-diesel engines. A total of 2,081 examples were made in 1990, but only 563 in 1991.

real Citroëns—continued for no fewer than 17 years, a period throughout which, for all but the first few months at least, the company was controlled by Peugeot. After the withdrawal of François Rollier and the Michelin men in December 1974, responsibility for the affairs of Automobiles Citroën was entrusted to George Taylor, the first man from a Peugeot background to hold the position of its Chairman and Managing Director. But following the merger and reorganization of the Peugeot and Citroën car firms under the banner of the PSA Group in May 1976, Taylor headed a directorate or supervisory council of three which also included Raymond Ravenel and Jacques Lombard, and which reported to the current overall Peugeot supremo François Gautier (who had negotiated the purchase from Michelin) while day-to-day responsibility for the running of the firm was passed to another long-serving Peugeot executive, Xavier Karcher, who acted as Deputy Managing Director and Vice President. Karcher's influence at Citroën was to endure for more than 20 years, until he retired in 1997.

George Taylor retired on January 1, 1979. His successor, as Chairman or President-Directeur-General, was Jacques Lombard, who acted in an interim capacity until 1982, when Jean Baratte took over. Baratte's term of office also lasted barely a year, until he stood down in favor of Jacques Calvet, the new supremo of the PSA organization. As a former Minister of Finance in the cabinet of the Gaullist President of France, Valery Giscard d'Estaing, and subsequently as President of the Banque Nationale de Paris, Calvet had assisted the cash-strapped Peugeot firm by arranging for the sale of its Matra and Dodge Trucks subsidiaries (a relic of its 1978 acquisition of Chysler Europe) to the state-owned Renault company. With the election of François Mitterand's Socialist government in 1981, Calvet had joined PSA as its finance director; but eventually, in 1984, he replaced the out-of-favor Jean-Paul Parayre who had taken over from François Gautier as head of PSA in 1977. On his appointment as PDG of PSA, Calvet assumed simultaneously the role of Chairman and Managing Director of Automobiles Citroën S.A., with Xavier Karcher acting as his deputy.

Although he was a production engineer trained in the Peugeot tradition (he had joined the Lion company in 1941), George Taylor was quickly seduced by the special mystique or esprit de corps that radiated from the Quai de Javel. In fact, he was so committed to his delicate task as match-maker, uniting the two unlikely marriage partners while preserving the character and individuality of each, that he very soon adopted more of a Citroën than a Peugeot outlook in his attitudes and policies. Indeed, he eventually developed such an enthusiasm for all things Citroën that many old Double Chevron hands said he was the last of the true Citroënistes to rule the firm. Certainly, it is from the point of his departure at the end of 1978, some 27 years ago, that the development of the current, modern, era in the history of Automobiles Citroën can be traced and dated.

15

Conclusion: The PSA Cars, 1976–2000

Cynics might say that no auto manufacturer has ever prospered by giving its customers more than the bare essentials required by legislation and that the list of firms that failed by being overly generous is long indeed. Yet Automobiles Citroën provided an exception to this rule. Throughout the 20 years of rising post-war prosperity that elapsed between 1953 and the onset of the energy crisis in 1973, under Michelin rule, the company enjoyed a golden age of growth and success. Its output expanded six-fold over this period and by consistently producing vehicles that exceeded public expectations, it established an unassailable reputation for the creativity and intelligence of its designs.

Unfortunately, the good times could not last and, as we have seen, in 1976 it entered the third and present era in its history when, in another enforced change of ownership and management, it came under the control of its former rival Peugeot, a company with a very different corporate character and philosophy—cautious, conservative and above all money conscious, dominated not by ambitious engineering but by the disciplines of marketing and cost accountancy.

Previously, during the 1960s Citroën's current owner, Michelin, had entered into negotiations with a number of continental motor manufacturers, with the intention of establishing partnership or co-management arrangements for its car-constructing subsidiary or, alternatively, of divesting itself of its accidental automotive acquisition altogether, so as to concentrate its resources on the manufacture of tires and continue its rapid worldwide expansion, The most notable of these liaisons was the short-lived association with Fiat that occurred between 1968 and 1974.

However, the severe financial losses caused by the sudden, unexpected collapse in sales of both cars and tires that occurred throughout Europe in 1974 (as a consequence of the first oil crisis) made this policy of disengagement all the more pressing. Having invested heavily in the development of three new models—the GS, SM and CX—and faced with the task of recouping the costs of constructing brand new production facilities at Aulnay-sous-Bois and elsewhere, Citroën was more exposed than most other car firms to this recession, and once again drastic action was called for to prevent its collapse.

The consequent measures—a managerial reorganization and financial restructuring begun in 1974 and concluded in 1976—were radical indeed, and involved the sale by Michelin of an 89.95 percent stake in Citroën to its erstwhile French rival, Automobiles Peugeot, rather than to Fiat, as had earlier been envisaged. With French government backing and approval, the two ostensibly incompatible marques were immediately merged in a shotgun marriage, and combined within the framework of a new management structure known as the PSA group, entirely controlled by Peugeot interests. The intention was to create a truly global French automobile enterprise capable of competing on equal terms with the major American, German and Japanese multinationals. Although the former rivals would combine to provide mutual technical, financial and administrative support by sharing joint manufacturing facilities and pooling certain common components, such as engines and floor-pans, they would retain their own distinct character and identity—or so it was claimed—producing their own individual models, which would be sold by autonomous distribution networks competing in every sector of the market.

Thus the long-term survival of the Citroën marque was assured, albeit in the hands of a company whose management was entirely different in character and philosophy from the two regimes that had gone before. Cautious, conservative and bureaucratic, the Peugeot corporate ethos and philosophy was distinguished — not by adventurous, avant garde design — but by the rigorous disciplines of cost accountancy, product planning and marketing. Consequently, the center of gravity of the Citroën firm swung away from the Bureau d' Etudes, which had previously been the kernel of the organization and the source of its strengths. Not only was the Bureau responsible for the research and development work that upheld Citroën's enviable reputation for engineering expertise, but it was also deeply involved in the formulation of its product policies and commercial strategies. Not surprisingly, this clash of corporate cultures led to a number of departures among Citroën's key design and engineering staff, including that of Robert Opron who had created the exterior appearance of the SM, GS and CX and, thus, the current Citroën house style which was unmistakable in its individuality.

In August 1978 (again with French government encouragement and assistance) the PSA Group made a further important investment by acquiring Chrysler Europe's loss-making car and commercial vehicle operations, including the Simca firm in France, and Chrysler's major British business asset, the ex–Rootes Group factory at Ryton, Coventry. This plant was soon put to work assembling Peugeot models in RHD form, and a new marque, Peugeot-Talbot, was established to market and distribute these products. So it happened that, as a stop-gap measure, Citroën and Peugeot-Talbot dealers soon found themselves selling two cars that at first sight seemed identical. Badged by Citroën as the LN and LNA and by Peugeot-Talbot as the Samba, these shared the same three-door hatch-back body of the Peugeot 104 Coupe, but had different engines. The LN (built between 1976 and 1979) was powered by the 3CV 602cc air-cooled engine from the 2CV, while the LNA (built between 1978 and 1986) had either the larger 4CV 652cc air-cooled flat twin from the current Visa model or the 4CV 1124cc water-cooled engine from the Peugeot 104, mounted transversally. This was the version offered by Citroën in the U.K. between 1983 and 1986; very few were sold there, although a grand total of 281,206 examples of the LN/A were built.

It had been promised that the LN would be the first and last Citroën to be nothing more than a face-lifted Peugeot; but when, in October 1978, the replacement for the Ami-8 appeared, it turned out to be yet another hybrid, again combining a Citroën-designed body-shell with the floor-pan and suspension of the Peugeot 104. This car, the Visa, was a five-door hatch-back sedan available in two different forms: as the Special or Club when equipped with the Citroën air cooled twin-pot engine from the Ami-8 bored out to 652cc and rated as a 3CV, or as the Super when powered by a 1219cc water-cooled 4 cylinder Peugeot unit and rated as a 5CV.

The Visa had its origins in the Model Y, a design study begun well before the merger, back in the days of the liaison with Fiat when the use of an Italian floor-pan and other elements was proposed; but as actually produced by the new PSA regime, it was an entirely conventional car, a cross-breed that incorporated elements sourced from the inventories of both partners. For example, it had coil spring suspension rather than the torsion bar springing originally envisaged by Citroën. Its most advanced, original or innovative features were its unusual frontal aspect with integrated energy-absorbing polypropylene grille and bumpers and its extraordinary instrument panel with a single-spoke steering wheel and satellite-pod controls, the work of Michel Harmand, who had produced a similar arrangement for the GSA.

Although these idiosyncratic touches gave the Visa a strong claim to be considered a true Citroën, it was not well received in France and, initially at least, it failed to live up to the popularity of its predecessor. So after only

The first Mk 1 version of the Visa, introduced in October 1978 to replace the Ami-8, had its origins in design studies begun well before the marriage with Peugeot. The later reworked Mk 2 versions, sold from 1981 to 1988, were more conservatively styled.

three years in this form, it was re-launched in March 1981 as the Visa II with a completely re-designed front end. Sold in the U.K. from 1979 to 1989, the Visa range ultimately evolved into numerous different models, although the 952cc air-cooled Citroën twin-pot engine was soon dropped in favor of a 954cc Peugeot four, detuned for minimum fuel consumption. Eventually the line-up included (though not simultaneously) the Visa Super E with the original 1124cc 4-cylinder gas engine in modified form; the Visa Super X with a 1219cc engine; the Visa GT, powered by a high-performance 1360cc gas engine; the Visa GTi, using the 105 hp fuel-injected 1580cc engine from the Peugeot 205 GTi; the Visa Cabriolet which had the 1124cc engine; and the Visa 17-D, which was equipped with the outstandingly economical 1769cc Peugeot XUD diesel engine. The Visa was withdrawn in 1988 having sold 1,222,608 vehicles, though its front end and floor-pan continued in use on the Citroën C15 van, introduced in 1984. This vehicle arrived in the U.K. in the autumn of 1985 with a choice of either the 1124cc gas or 1769cc diesel engine and continues in the catalog to this day, with more than 750,000 having been sold to date.

Introduced at the 1982 Paris Motor Show, the BX was to prove a great success for Citroën, especially in its various diesel-engined variants. Ultimately more than 2,300,000 — of all types and descriptions — were sold by the time that production ended in 1994.

It is interesting to note that the Model Y/Visa design, as originally conceived back in 1973, ended up being built in Romania eight years later as the Oltcit, under a joint venture between Citroën and the Romanian government. Introduced there in 1981, the Oltcit was powered by a choice of three Citroën air-cooled engines— the 652cc air-cooled twin used in the Visas, or alternatively the 1129cc or 1299cc versions of the air-cooled four-cylinder unit from the GS/GSA, together with a GS transmission and running gear plus inboard front disc brakes. Later, between 1984 and 1988, this car was also marketed in France under the name Axel. Unfortunately, despite its superior engineering features (which included center Guild-point steering), its lamentable quality meant that only 13,175 vehicles found customers among French motorists.

The first true fruits of the Citroën-Peugeot merger, however, had appeared in September 1983 with the arrival of a new medium-class car, the BX — a five-seat, five-door hatchback that replaced the GSA. Launched in the U.K. with the advertising slogan "Loves Driving, Hates Garages," the BX was deliberately conceived and positioned to appeal to motorists who had never owned a Citroën before, and who were intimidated by the perceived complexity of hydro-pneumatic suspension, which was to be preserved as an essential Citroën feature and characteristic. As installed on the BX, this system was modified in a way that would have been unthinkable until now, by the use, on the front axles, of a hybrid MacPherson strut arrangement. This retained Citroën's oleo-pneumatic sphere-type springs, and thus also the self-leveling function of earlier cars, but the revised suspension geometry enforced by this simplification meant that the sacred principle of center-point steering was abandoned. Citroën's fully-powered all-disc braking system was also retained, but the power-steering system fitted was of the conventional hydraulic ram type when this feature was eventually introduced. Naturally, the use of front-wheel-drive transmission and transversely mounted engines was also preserved, though by now FWD had become virtually universal throughout the French motor industry, even at Peugeot!

Actually, it had originally been proposed at the planning stage that Citroën's hydro-pneumatic suspension would be discontinued in favor of conventional coil springs on the BX. But faced with the combined revolt of the Velizy design center and the entire dealer network, the PSA management relented and agreed that the hydropneumatics would be preserved as an essential Citroën distinguishing feature and sales advantage.

Based on the floor pan of the Peugeot 405, the BX also looked completely different from the Citroëns of the previous era, with boxy, angular lines that were entirely opposite to the fluid, curvaceous silhouette created earlier as a house-style by Robert Opron, who had left Citroën for Renault at the time of the merger. Instead, the new look came from the Carrozzeria Bertone, whose ideas

The angular styling of the BX, conceived by the Bertone design consultancy, was deliberately intended to look entirely different from previous Citroëns such as the GS and CX, produced under Robert Opron's direction.

were selected by PSA's senior management at the expense of Citroën's in-house proposals; Bertone had had a long relationship with Peugeot, but this was the first time that an outside styling consultancy had ever been employed by Citroën.

Moreover, the BX's body-shell was designed for extreme lightness, to maximize fuel economy, and for simplicity and economy of construction, to maximize the efficiency of assembly operations at the Rennes-la-Janais factory, which had been entirely robotized. Consequently, the body-shell comprised only 334 separate elements, instead of the 531 used on the GSA. It also employed a high proportion of plastic body parts, such as the hood, tailgate, bumpers and rear quarter panels.

Initially, three versions of the BX sedan were offered: the BX (62 bhp 1360cc engine and 4-speed gearbox), the BX14 (72 bhp 1360cc engine and 5-speed box) and the BX16 (90 bhp 1580cc engine and 5-speed box). These new all-alloy engines, which came from the recently established PSA "organ bank" as the design and manufacture of Citroën-only engines, were a thing of the past. This choice was soon augmented, early in 1984, by the advent of a diesel version, powered by a new 65 bhp 1905cc XUD series compression-ignition engine version; three years later, in September 1986, this sedan was joined by the BX17RD, powered by a 1769cc diesel engine. The previous year, in September 1985, the BX range had been augmented by a station wagon, available with the same choice of gas engines plus the 1905cc diesel, which from September 1988 on was also produced in turbocharged form, to power both the station wagon and sedan. The BX Diesel ultimately became the most popular diesel car ever sold in the U.K., revolutionizing public perception of the compression-ignition engine among British motorists. In due course, at the peak of its popularity in 1988, it held 13 percent of the market and outsold its nearest rival by 40 percent.

The BX was also marketed as a high-performance sporting sedan, in the form of the 105 hp 1905cc engined BX-GT introduced in July 1984. Next, in March 1985 came the BX Sport (not sold in the U.K.) powered by a specially prepared 126 bhp version of the 1905cc unit. This car was followed, in July 1986, by the 125 hp fuel-injected BX-Gti, which in turn was supplemented, in July 1987, by the 160 hp BX-GTi 16-Valve.

As each and all of these BX variants was offered in a minimum of two different levels of trim and finish (not counting the many Special Editions also sold, such as the BX Leader) at its zenith the total BX range offered no fewer than 23 different permutations—15 sedans and eight station wagons—to cover virtually every purpose and pocket. In 1986, the range was revamped, the most notable revision being a new, more conventional dashboard and instrument panel.

By the time that the BX was finally withdrawn from the market in 1993, 2,315,739 had been sold worldwide, of which 219,529 had found owners in the U.K. Like the GS/GSA before it, the BX was a commercial success that saved Citroën from extinction. Evidently, sophisticated marketing know-how had now been added to advanced engineering expertise, to complement the marque's traditional abilities and strengths and ensure its survival. Nevertheless, many commentators observed that in settling for a relatively conventional specification, the PSA bosses had missed an opportunity to take another great leap forward in technical achievement, as had occurred in the case of the GS under the Michelin regime some ten years earlier.

Similarly, when it arrived in July 1986, the replacement for the 2CV, the AX supermini, was widely regarded as a disappointment by Citroënistes who were still hoping for a radical go-anywhere, do-anything vehicle that would serve the needs of the third world as well as the consumer society of western Europe, Launched in France with the slogan "Revolutionaire," the AX was anything

The AX Supermini, available between 1986 and 1998, was entirely conventional in design and noted technically merely for its high power-to-weight ratio made possible by the use of lightweight thermo-plastic panels. More than 2,400,000 were built.

but revolutionary; in both conception and construction it was entirely conventional, down to self-canceling turn signals of the type that until now Citroën had refused to install. Plainly, PSA had aimed the AX squarely at the urban female drivers of France who in the customer clinics and focus groups, beloved by modern-day motor industry marketers, had expressed a marked lack of interest in owning anything more adventurous or unusual than Peugeot's own 205 model. With all traces of quirkiness having been eliminated, the most interesting technical feature of the AX—other than its impressive 0.31 cd—was its ultra low weight. Ranging between 1,411 and 1,534 pounds according to model, it was approximately 225 pounds lighter than the average for its class, a saving produced by a 30 percent reduction in the amount of steel used in its bodywork, compared to normal industrial levels. For example, the rear tailgate was a composite structure formed entirely of glass and molded thermoplastic. The intention, of course, was to be able to claim impressive fuel economy (72.4 mpg at a constant 56 mph for the AX 11) by virtue of a high power-to-weight ratio. But the strategy backfired and the AX was criticized for its flimsy construction. Its bland styling, banal interior and indifferent ergonomics were also panned by the critics—but at least it had an effective heating and ventilation system, a benefit not previously noted on a Citroën.

Available initially in three three-door versions (but with a further three five-door variants following a year later), the AX was powered by the familiar four-cylinder water-cooled engines also used in the Peugeot 205 series—an economical 45 bhp 954cc unit (AX 10), a 55 bhp 1124cc unit (AX11) and a more powerful 70 bhp 1360cc unit (AX14), the latter also being employed in uprated 85 bhp form in the 112 mph AX GT, introduced in July 1988. Earlier, in April 1987, the AX Sport (not sold in the U.K.) had joined the range, powered by a high-performance 95 bhp 1249cc engine. Weighing only 1,590 pounds it could reach 116 mph. The next arrival, in September 1988, was the AX Diesel, equipped with a 53 bhp 1360cc compression ignition engine. It offered one of the lowest fuel-consumption figures in Europe; a touring figure of close to 50 mpg was reported by *Autocar* magazine.

By January 1990 the AX was well established with over a million vehicles having been produced. For 1993, the model was given a light styling makeover with an improved interior and dashboard, though there were no significant mechanical modifications; at the same time the AX Sport was replaced by the AX GTi, equipped with a fuel-injected version of the 1360cc engine. Production of the AX ended in July 1998, by which time a total of 2,424,808 had been constructed.

When, in the late 1980s the time came to replace Citroën's flagship model, the CX, which was by then almost 15 years old, the PSA management chose to abandon all notions of continuity and evolution, to create an entirely new look that owed very little to the traditions of the past. Once again a contest was staged between the company's Velizy design center and the Bertone consultancy, judged by PSA's top bosses including Messrs. Calvet and Karcher. And once again, the in-house recommendations (which were a logical development of the fluid shape and subtle styling themes of the CX) were rejected in favor of the Bertone proposal, which shared no direct visual relationship or family resemblance with any previous Citroën design. The result, unveiled at the Frankfurt Motor Show in 1989, was the XM, an all-new luxury executive-class sedan that had nothing much in common with its predecessor save its gearbox. Despite the fact that it was voted European Car of the Year in 1990, the XM was less than a triumph both aesthetically and commercially, for Bertone's design was a curious compromise between the ancient and the modern, a confused and incoherent composition of contradictory themes that pleased neither the conservatives nor the progressives. To the regret of the die-hard Citroën fanatics, the XM also regressed to the use of quasi McPherson strut suspension geometry as used on the BX, and conventional power steering; only

Although the influence of its Bureau d'Etudes waned greatly following the Peugeot takeover, during the 1980s Citroën continued to produce a number of interesting experimental models, such as the ECO–2000 of 1981–1984, the Activa 1 and Activa 2 of 1988–1990 and the Eole of 1986, seen here.

the LHD vehicles of the top-of-the-line V-6 XM models briefly inherited the Diravi system from the CX.

The revisionist styling of the AX, BX and XM were not the only way in which the familiar Citroën identity or brand personality was debased. Throughout that era, the pedigree and heritage of the marque prior to the takeover was obscured and suppressed, to the extent that, in the U.K. at least, archives were destroyed and the discussion of such historical topics by staff with the press and public alike was forbidden, while dealers were prohibited from displaying Citroën's classic models in their showrooms on the grounds that they were old and obsolete. The company's advertising also ignored the achievements of the past. Certainly, no mention of its impressive pioneering pedigree was ever made, as in the slogan *Vorsprung durch Technik* (Progress through Technology) exploited so effectively by Audi, which by then had usurped Citroën's crown as the leader of Europe's automobile avant-garde.

The XM sedan first appeared in RHD form in the autumn of 1990, although it was to be a another year until a station wagon version was introduced. Notable for its adjustable, computer-controlled Hydractive oleo-pneumatic suspension—another Citroën innovation—the XM sedan was initially available in a choice of five versions—a 1998cc four-cylinder carburetor-engined model with manual transmission, a 1998cc fuel-injected model with either manual or automatic transmission, a 2088cc 2.1 turbo-diesel-engined model, a 2975cc 3.0 liter V6-engined model with either manual or automatic transmission, and finally a top-of-the-line high-performance variant equipped with a 200 hp 24-valve version of the fuel-injected V6 engine, capable of 146 mph but available with manual transmission only.

Designed by the Englishman Geoffrey Mathews and based on a CX platform, the Eole (first revealed at the 1986 Geneva Motor Show) pioneered Citroën's active suspension, eventually introduced on the XM and Xantia models in the 1990s. It achieved a Cd factor of 0.17—about half that of the CX—thanks to its fully enclosed wheels, front and rear. The front fairings opened and closed automatically by hydraulic power, at the appropriate steering angles.

In January 1996 the XM was relaunched as the Series II with, outside, a restyled grille and front end and, inside, a new dashboard. By this time three new engines were available — a 1998cc 16-valve fuel-injected gas engine, a 2138cc turbo-diesel, and a 2446cc turbo-diesel. Ultimately, the line consisted of seven sedan and four station wagon models, distinguishable by a combination of five different engines, four different trim and equipment levels and, of course, a variety of special editions too numerous to mention.

Alas, not even the most partisan of Citroën fanatics could claim that the XM was a success, either technically or commercially. Ultimately, by the time that it was discontinued 11 years later in 2000, the XM had sold only 333,775 units (100,000 in its first year, falling to 50,000 in 1991 and just 12,000 in 1996), having failed to capture its rightful share of the luxury market and re-establish Citroën's position as the doyen of high-quality engineering and the leader of the avant-garde, which by then had been relinquished to its German rivals, Audi and BMW. Early problems— especially with its complex electronics caused by inferior wiring connectors— gave the XM a reputation for poor reliability and excessive, indeed punitive, depreciation, from which it never recovered.

Although not exactly conventional, the XM sedan, produced between 1989 and 2000, was undoubtedly the most conservative (or least radical) of all the flagship Citroëns introduced since the Rosalie models of 1930. It failed entirely to equal the sales success of its predecessors, the DS and CX.

As we noted in the previous chapter, in 1997 the long-serving PSA supremo Jacques Calvet retired and was succeeded by Jean-Martin Folz, the current President-Directeur-General of the organization. Calvet's departure was followed by that of the then boss of Automobiles Citroën, Xavier Karcher (whose replacement was to be Claude Satinet, another *Polytechnicien)* so that, in effect, a new generation of top management took over the running of the Citroën-Peugeot organization, under the supervision of Robert Peugeot. Unlike Calvet, whose background was in banking and finance, Folz is an engineer and industrialist of wide experience who trained in the customary French tradition at the Ecole Polytechnique and the Ecole des Mines. He is, therefore, a bona fide member of the governing class of France, *les haute fonctionaires* (generally recruited from among *les enarques* and *les polytechniciens)*, the deeply patriotic elite of technocrats and administrators that directs both the private and public sectors of the economy to the greater good of the Republic. Motivated as much by a sense of public duty as a quest for profit or shareholder value they represent a modern aristocracy of talent that eschews personal gain and advancement, behaving in a tradition of *noblesse oblige,*

Described at best as classic and at worst as banal, the dashboard of the XM was criticized as marking a regression in Citroën's standards of interior design.

which contrasts deeply with the selfish short-sightedness or outright greed so often displayed by the business, banking and industrial leaders of the Anglo-Saxon world. Chauvinism or not, the surrender to a foreign rival of a famous Gallic motoring name and tradition, as happened in the U.K. recently in the case of the sale of Rolls-Royce and Bentley, would be quite unthinkable in France.

When taking over the Double Chevron marque in 1976, Peugeot expressed its intention to make Citroën more accessible to the ordinary motorist by eliminating its customary quirks and eccentricities. A strategy of standardization and uniformity was imposed, diluting the very essence of Citroën's distinctive brand personality and suppressing its innovative flair. Even the adventurous and flamboyant interior color schemes which had characterized the DS, GS and early CX models gave way to restrained and somber shades of grey and black (reputedly chosen by Messrs. Calvet and Karcher themselves), which gave an impression of conservatism if not downright banality. This policy of pandering to popularism and following rather than leading public taste (which today would perhaps be dismissed as crude opportunism and described as "dumbing down") contrasted markedly with the lofty idealism visible in the old days under the Michelin regime, when the use of marketing techniques such as customer clinics and focus groups was rejected. Just as a doctor diagnoses an illness and prescribes a remedy, Citroën drivers and dealers were given exactly what the engineers thought was good for them — and the medicine was lapped up with an appreciation and enthusiasm that bordered on the fanatical.

Undoubtedly, the move to center ground proved counter-productive, losing the marque more loyal supporters and devotees than it won. The opportunity to rebuild the company's customer base on the foundations of a design-led strategy similar to that pursued so successfully by Audi was lost, and between 1974 and 1998 its share of the French domestic market fell from 18.6 percent to 11.6 percent (and in the European market, from 7 percent to 4.7 percent) although the decline was masked in part by much-improved sales in other places, such as the U.K. The end result was that the reputation and prestige of the Double Chevron brand were gravely degraded. At the start it was acknowledged to be perhaps the most creative and inventive motor manufacturer in the history of the mass-produced automobile, commanding the interest and loyalty of devoted, quality-conscious clientele with high aspirations and expectations. But by the end of the process it had been relegated to a minority, niche-market brand, selling on price alone, and excluded, almost, from the mainstream sales arenas that its PSA partner chose to reserve for itself. What was the point, many observers asked, of continuing its existence, merely to produce cloned, duplicated or re-vamped Peugeots, albeit thinly disguised by "badge engineering"?

Fortunately, the new and enlightened policies adopted by M. Folz since his appointment have reversed the misguided trend to standardization and uniformity imposed throughout the 1980s and 1990s and have already begun to re-establish the Double Chevron marque's reputation for imagination and individuality, so that its popularity — and sales — are again on the rise among a new generation of European motorists—customers too young to know of its prestige during the 1960s and 1970s when it was at the height of its fame and fortune. Although it would be an exaggeration to speak of a return to radicalism, a succession of bold and original new products such as the C2, C3, C5 and C6 have already appeared to uphold the heritage of creativity and to exhibit once again the refreshing nonconformity that characterized Citroën products in the past. The latter car, the C6 sedan, introduced in 2006, marks a return to the luxury, high-performance sector of the market, a territory abandoned since the demise of the XM.

Plainly, the authentic Citroëns — such as the Traction Avant, the 2CV, the DS/ID, the GS/A and the CX, all of which form the subject matter of this book — have all survived the test of time to establish themselves as icons of automobile design. But what about the more recent cars that appeared in the 1980s and 1990s, such as the ZX, Xantia, Xsara and Saxo, which lie beyond the scope of this account? Will they also be recognized as true classics in their turn, generating as much interest, pride and affection among enthusiasts as their predecessors? The question is open to debate! Even so, those enthusiasts who hope and expect that the Folz renaissance may lead to the arrival of a modern-day 2CV or DS are perhaps overly optimistic. Those miraculous and visionary creations of the Michelin-Lefèbvre era came into being through an extraordinary confluence of events, circumstances, influences and talents that can never be repeated.

Appendix: Citroën Model Specifications

Note — This information and data relates to the first model of each of the nine principal post-war models produced by Citroën. It is impossible within the space available to catalog every subsequent variation or derivative introduced into these model lines.

1— The Post-War Four Cylinder Traction Avant Models

Model	Post-War Traction Avant 11CV
Currency	1945–1957
Engine	Four-cylinder water cooled
Capacity	1911cc
Bore and stroke	78mm × 100mm
Valve actuation	Pushrod
Compression ratio	6.2:1
Carburetors	Single choke Solex downdraught
Power output	56bhp SAE @ 3800rpm 60bhp SAE @ 4000rpm (11D version)
Torque	90.4 lb/ft @ 2200rpm
Transmission	Front wheel drive, 3 forward speeds. Second and top synchronised
Suspension	Front; independent with longitudinal torsion bars & telescopic dampers Rear; beam axle with transverse torsion bars & telescopic dampers.
Steering	Manual — rack & pinion
Brakes	Conventional drum hydraulically operated
Wheels & Tires	Michelin X radial 150×400
Bodywork	Four door steel monocoque
Styles available	Light Sedan (onze legere), Heavy Sedan (onze normale), Familiale, Commerciale

Dimensions (heavy sedan)

Length	4.65m
Wheelbase	3.09m
Track	1.46m
Width	1.79m
Height	1.54m
Weight	1100kg
Performance	Max speed 115 km/h — 71mph 0–50 mph 17.9 secs 0–60 mph 29.1 secs

Numbers built	620,455 (11 Legere & Normale combined)
UK price when new	£1,153 inc tax (March 1953)

Evolution

11CV Berline Legere 11BL	4cyl	1911cc	56bhp*	6/45–7/57
11CV Berline Normale 11B	4cyl	1911cc	56bhp*	3/47–7/57
11CV Familiale	4cyl	1911cc	56bhp*	7/53–7/57
11CV Commerciale	4cyl	1911cc	56bhp*	4/54–5/57

*60bhp from 5/55 (11D engine)

2— The Post-War Six Cylinder Traction Avant Models

Model	Post-War Traction Avant 15CV
Currency	1947–1957
Engine	Six-cylinder water cooled
Capacity	2867cc
Bore and stroke	78mm × 100mm
Valve actuation	Pushrod
Compression ratio	6.3:1
Carburetors	Single choke Solex downdraught
Power output	77bhp SAE @ 3800rpm
Torque	138 lb/ft @ 2000rpm
Transmission	Front wheel drive, manual gearbox with 3 forward speeds, second and top synchronised
Suspension	Front; independent with longitudinal torsion bars & telescopic dampers Rear; beam axle with transverse torsion bars & telescopic dampers
Steering	Manual rack & pinion, unassisted
Brakes	Drum, hydraulically operated
Wheels & Tires	Michelin X radial 185×400
Bodywork	Four-door monocoque
Styles available	Standard Heavy Sedan, Long wheelbase, Limousine & Familiale

Dimensions (heavy sedan)

Length	4.76m
Wheelbase	3.09m
Track	1.49m
Width	1.79m
Height	1.56m
Weight	1325kg
Performance	max speed 130 km/h — 81 mph
UK price when new	£1,333 inc tax (June 1953)
Numbers built	50,602

Evolution

15-Six D Berline	6cyl	2867cc	76bhp	3/47–7/56
15-Six D Familiale	6cyl	2867cc	76bhp	7/53–8/55
15-Six H Berline*	6cyl	2867cc	80bhp	4/54–7/57

*Hydro-pneumatic suspension on rear axle only

3—The Pre-War Traction Avant Models

7CV Berline	7A	4cyl	1303cc	32bhp	5/34–6/34
7CV Cabriolet	7A	4cyl	1303cc	32bhp	5/34–6/34
7CV Faux Cabriolet	7A	4cyl	1303cc	32bhp	5/34–6/34
9CV Berline	7B	4cyl	1529cc	35bhp	7/34–9/34
9CV Cabriolet	7B	4cyl	1529cc	35bhp	7/34–9/34
9CV Faux Cabriolet	7B	4cyl	1529cc	35bhp	7/34–9/34
9CV Berline	7C	4cyl	1628cc	36bhp	10/34–8/38
9CV Cabriolet	7C	4cyl	1628cc	36bhp	10/34–8/38
9CV Faux Cabriolet	7C	4cyl	1628cc	36bhp	10/34–8/38
11CV Berline	7S	4cyl	1911cc	46bhp	6/34–8/38
11CV Cabriolet	7S	4cyl	1911cc	46bhp	6/34–8/38
11CV Faux Cabriolet	7S	4cyl	1911cc	46bhp	6/34–8/38
11CV Berline Legere	11AL	4cyl	1911cc	46bhp	10/34–1/37
11CV Cabriolet Legere	11AL	4cyl	1911cc	46bhp	10/34–1/37
11CV Berline Normale	11A	4cyl	1911cc	46bhp	10/34–1/37
11CV Familiale	11A	4cyl	1911cc	46bhp	10/34–1/37
11CV Cabriolet Normale	11A	4cyl	1911cc	46bhp	10/34–1/37
11CV Berline Legere	11BL	4cyl	1911cc	56bhp	2/37–6/40
11CV Berline Normale	11B	4cyl	1911cc	56bhp	2/37–6/40
11CV Familiale	11B	4cyl	1911cc	56bhp	2/37–6/40
11CV Cabriolet	11B	4cyl	1911cc	56bhp	9/38–9/39
11CV Commerciale	11C	4cyl	1911cc	56bhp	1/38–6/40
15-Six Berline	15–6G	6cyl	2867cc	76bhp	2/39–2/40
15-Six Limousine	15–6G	6cyl	2867cc	76bhp	3/39–2/40
15-Six Familiale	15–6G	6cyl	2867cc	76bhp	4/39–2/40

3—The Type H Van

Model	Type H,HZ,HY
Currency	1948–1981
Engine	Four-cylinder in-line, water cooled
Capacity	1628/1911cc gas
Bore and stroke	72mm × 100 mm (9CV) & 78mm × 100mm (11CV)
Valve actuation	pushrod
Compression ratio	7.5:1
Carburetors	Single choke Zenith downdraft
Power output	43bhp SAE @ 4000 rpm (1628cc 9CV) 56bhp SAE @ 4100 rpm (1911cc 11CV)
Torque	N/A
Transmission	Front-wheel drive, 3 speeds, second & top synchronized
Suspension	Front, independent by longitudinal torsion bars with telescopic dampers Rear, independent with transverse torsion bars and telescopic dampers.
Steering	Manual rack & pinion
Brakes	Drum, hydraulically operated
Wheels & Tires	Michelin X radial, 400×17
Structure & Bodywork	Steel-panelled body on separate platform chassis
Styles available	Light van, pick-up truck and chassis/cab

Dimensions

Length	N/A
Wheelbase	2.33m (H — 1951)
Track	1.65m (H — 1951)
Width	N/A
Height	N/A
Weight	N/A
Performance	max speed 56mph / 63 mph
UK Price	Not available in UK
Number built	473,289

4—The Type A 2CV Models

Model	2CV Sedan & derivatives
Currency	1949–1990
Engine	Two-cylinder, horizontally opposed, air-cooled
Capacity	375cc / 425cc / 435cc / 602cc
Bore and stroke	62mm × 62mm / 66mm × 62mm / 68.5mm × 59mm / 74mm × 70 mm
Valve actuation	pushrod
Compression ratio	6.2:1 (375cc) 8.5:1 (602cc)
Carburetors	Single choke Solex downdraft
Power output	9hp SAE @ 3500rpm (375cc) 29bhp DIN @ 5750rpm (602cc)
Torque	16.6 lb ft @ 1800rpm (375cc) 29 lb ft @ 3500 rpm (602cc)
Transmission	Front wheel drive 4 speeds & reverse
Suspension	Fully independent by horizontal coil springs, interconnected front to rear
Steering	Manual rack & pinion
Brakes	Conventional hydraulic
Wheels & Tires	Michelin X radial, 125×400
Structure & Bodywork	Four-door cabriolet body on separate platform chassis
Styles available	Sedan & van

Dimensions (sedan)

Length	3.78m
Wheelbase	2.40m
Track	1.26m
Width	1.48cm
Height	1.60m
Weight	495kg
Performance	max speed 65 km/h — 39 mph (375cc)
Numbers built (sedans)	3,868,634

Evolution

2CV Berline	A	2cyl	375cc	9bhp	7/49–7/59
2CV	AZ	2cyl	425cc	12bhp	10/54–10/55

2CV	AZ	2cyl	425cc	12.5bhp	10/55–10/61
2CV	AZ	2cyl	425cc	13.5bhp	10/61–4/62
2CV	AZ	2cyl	425cc	15bhp	4/62–2/63
2CV	AZL & AZAM	2cyl	425cc	18bhp	3/63–2/70
2CV	2CV-4	2cyl	435cc	26bhp	2/70–9/78
2CV	2CV Special	2cyl	435cc	26bhp	9/78–7/79
3CV Berline	2CV-6	2cyl	602cc	32bhp	2/70–9/75
3CV	2CV-6	2cyl	602cc	30bhp	9/75–9/78
3CV	2CV-6	2cyl	602cc	33bhp	9/78–7/79
3CV	2CV-6 Special, Club, Special-E, Charleston	2cyl	602cc	33bhp	7/79–7/90
2CV 4×4 Sahara	AW	2×2cyl	425cc	13.5bhp	3/58–3/63
2CV 4×4 Sahara	AW	2×2cyl	425cc	18bhp	3/63–7/66

5—The 2CV & 3CV Fourgonnette Vans

2CV Fourgonnette	AU	2cyl	375cc	9bhp	3/51–10/54
2CV	AZU	2cyl	425cc	12bhp	10/54–12/55
2CV	AZU	2cyl	425cc	12.5bhp	12/55–11/61
2CV	AZU	2cyl	425cc	13.5bhp	11/61–2/62
2CV	AZU	2cyl	425cc	15bhp	2/62–3/63
2CV	AZU/A	2cyl	425cc	18bhp	3/63–8/67
2CV	AZU/A	2cyl	425cc	21bhp	8/67–8/72
2CV	AZU/B	2cyl	435cc	26bhp	8/72–2/78
3CV Fourgonnette	AK 350	2cyl	602cc	22bhp	4/63–5/68
3CV	AK 350	2cyl	602cc	32bhp	5/68–8/70
3CV	AK 400	2cyl	602cc	32bhp	8/70–9/75
3CV	AK 400	2cyl	602cc	30bhp	9/75–2/78
3CV	Acadiane	2cyl	602cc	33bhp	2/78–7/87

6—The Dyane Sedans

Dyane Berline	AYA	2cyl	425cc	21bhp	8/67–3/68
Dyane-4	AYA/2	2cyl	435cc	26bhp	3/68–9/75
Dyane-6	AYA/3	2cyl	602cc	32bhp	1/68–10/68
Dyane-6	AK/2	2cyl	602cc	32bhp	10/68–2/70
Dyane-6	AM/2	2cyl	602cc	35bhp	2/70–7/80
Dyane-6	AM/2	2cyl	602cc	33bhp	7/80–7/83

7—The Mehari Pick-ups

Mehari	AY	2cyl	602cc	32bhp	10/68–9/75
	AY	2cyl	602cc	30bhp	9/75–7/78
	AY	2cyl	602cc	33bhp	7/78–7/87
Mehari 4×4	AY	2cyl	602cc	33bhp	9/79–7/83

8—The DS Sedan Models

Model	DS19 and derivatives
Currency	1955–1975
Engine	Four-cylinder, water-cooled
Bore and stroke	78mm × 100mm
Capacity	1911cc (DS19)
Valve actuation	pushrod
Compression ratio	6.2:1
Carburetors	Double choke Solex 22ZACI
Power output	75 bhp SAE @ 3500rpm
Torque	101.3 lb ft @ 3000 rpm (DS19)
Transmission	Front wheel drive Semi-automatic gearbox, 4 speeds & reverse
Suspension	Fully independent hydro-pneumatic, self-leveling
Steering	Fully-powered rack & pinion
Brakes	Fully powered hydraulic, discs front, drums rear
Wheels & Tires	Michelin disc, initially single-screw fixing, later conventional studs Michelin X radial 165×400 front 155×400 rear
Structure & Bodywork	Four-door body on independent caisson chassis
Styles available	sedan only

Dimensions

Length	4.80m
Wheelbase	3.12m
Track, front	1.50m
Track, rear	1.30m
Width	1.79m
Height	1.47m
Weight	1125kg

Performance	max speed 140 km/h — 87 mph
Numbers built (DS&ID combined)	1,456,115

Evolution

DS19 Sedan	hyd	DS	4cyl	1911cc	75bhp	10/55–3/61
DS19	hyd	DS	4cyl	1911cc	83bhp	3/61–9/65
DS19 Prestige	hyd	DS	4cyl	1911cc	75bhp	10/58–3/63
DS19M	man	DW	4cyl	1911cc	83bhp	3/63–9/65
DS19A	hyd	DY	4cyl	1911cc	90bhp	10/65–9/68
DS19MA	man	DL	4cyl	1911cc	90bhp	10/65–9/68
DS21	hyd	DX	4cyl	2175cc	109bhp	10/65–9/68
DS21	hyd	DX	4cyl	2175cc	115bhp	10/68–9/71
DS21M	man	DJ	4cyl	2175cc	109bhp	10/65–9/68
DS21M	man	DJ	4cyl	2175cc	115bhp	10/68–9/72
DS21	auto	DX	4cyl	2175cc	115bhp	10/71–9/72
DS21 Prestige	hyd	DX	4cyl	2175cc	109bhp	10/65–9/68
DS21 Prestige	hyd	DX	4cyl	2175cc	115bhp	10/68–9/71
DS21 IE	hyd	DXI	4cyl	2175cc	139bhp	10/69–9/72
DS21M 1E	man	DJI	4cyl	2175cc	139bhp	10/69–9/72
DS21 IE	auto	DXI	4cyl	2175cc	139bhp	10/71–9/72
DS20	hyd	DY	4cyl	1985cc	103bhp	10/68–9/71
DS20	hyd	DY	4cyl	1985cc	108bhp	10/71–4/75
DS20 Prestige	hyd	DY	4cyl	1985cc	103bhp	10/68–9/71
DS23	hyd	FE	4cyl	2347cc	124bhp	10/72–4/75
DS23M	man-5	FE	4cyl	2347cc	124bhp	10/72–4/75
DS23	auto	FE	4cyl	2347cc	124bhp	10/72–4/75
DS23 IE	hyd	FG	4cyl	2347cc	141bhp	10/72–4/75
DS23M IE	man-5	FG	4cyl	2347cc	141bhp	10/72–4/75
DS23 IE	auto	FG	4cyl	2347cc	141bhp	10/72–4/75
DS23 Prestige	hyd	FE	4cyl	2347cc	141bhp	10/72–9/74

9—The ID Sedan Models

Model	ID19 and derivatives
Currency	1957–1975
Engine	Four-cylinder, water-cooled

Capacity	1911cc (ID19)
Bore and stroke	78 × 100mm
Valve actuation	pushrod
Compression ratio	6.2:1
Carburetors	Single choke Solex
Power output	66 bhp SAE @ 4000 rpm
Torque	97.6 lb ft @ 3000 rpm
Transmission	Front wheel drive — manual gearbox 4 speeds & reverse
Suspension	Fully independent hydro-pneumatic, self-leveling
Steering	Manual rack & pinion
Brakes	Initially conventional hydraulic, later fully powered
Wheels & Tires	Michelin disc — initially single-screw fixing, later conventional studs Michelin X
Structure & Bodywork	Four-door body on independent caisson chassis
Styles available	sedan, estate, familiale, commerciale & ambulance

Dimensions (sedan)

Length	4.80m
Wheelbase	3.12m
Track, front	1.50m
Track, rear	1.30m
Width	1.79m
Height	1.47m
Weight	1110kg

Performance	Max speed 135 km/h — 84 mph
UK price when new	
Numbers built (DS&ID combined)	1,456,115

Evolution

ID19 Normale	man	11D	4cyl	1911cc	62bhp	5/57–9/58
ID19 Luxe	man	DM	4cyl	1911cc	66bhp	5/57–9/64
ID19 Luxe	man	DM	4cyl	1911cc	75bhp	10/64–9/65
ID19 Confort	man	DM	4cyl	1911cc	66bhp	5/57–9/64
ID19 Confort	man	DM	4cyl	1911cc	75bhp	10/64–9/65
ID19 V.de M.	man	DM	4cyl	1911cc	66bhp	6/59–6/61
ID19A Luxe	man	DE	4cyl	1911cc	81bhp	10/65–9/66
ID19A Confort	man	DE	4cyl	1911cc	81bhp	10/65–9/66
ID19B Luxe	man	DV	4cyl	1985cc	84bhp	10/66–9/68
ID19B Luxe	man	DV	4cyl	1985cc	91bhp	10/68–9/69
ID19B Confort	man	DV	4cyl	1985cc	84bhp	10/66–9/68
ID19B Confort	man	DV	4cyl	1985cc	91bhp	10/68–9/69
ID20 Confort	man	DT	4cyl	1985cc	103bhp	10/68–9/69
D Special	man	DV	4cyl	1911cc	91bhp	10/69–4/75
D Super	man	DT	4cyl	1985cc	103bhp	10/69–9/71
D Super	man	DT	4cyl	1985cc	108bhp	10/71–4/75
D Super 5	man-5	DP	4cyl	2175cc	115bhp	10/72–1/75

10—The ID Breaks or Estates and Familiales (omitting other variants)

ID19 Break	DB	4cyl	1911cc	66bhp	10/59–3/63
ID19 Break	DB	4cyl	1911cc	83bhp	3/63–9/65
ID19 Familiale	DF	4cyl	1911cc	66bhp	10/59–3/63
ID19 Familiale	DF	4cyl	1911cc	83bhp	3/63–9/65
ID19 Break	DEF	4cyl	1911cc	81bhp	10/65–12/65
ID19F Break	DLF	4cyl	1985cc	90bhp	10/65–9/68
ID19F Familiale	DLF	4cyl	1985cc	90bhp	10/65–9/68
ID19FH Break	DYF	4cyl	1985cc	90bhp	10/65–9/68
ID19FH Familiale	DYF	4cyl	1985cc	90bhp	10/65–9/68
ID21F Break	DJF	4cyl	2175cc	109bhp	10/65–9/68
ID21F Break	DJF	4cyl	2175cc	115bhp	10/68–9/72
ID21F Familiale	DJF	4cyl	2175cc	109bhp	10/65–9/68
ID21F Familiale	DJF	4cyl	2175cc	115bhp	10/68–9/72
ID21FH Break	DXF	4cyl	2175cc	109bhp	10/65–9/68
ID21FH Break	DXF	4cyl	2175cc	115bhp	10/68–9/72
ID21FH Familiale	DXF	4cyl	2175cc	109bhp	10/65–9/68
ID21FH Familiale	DXF	4cyl	2175cc	115bhp	10/68–9/72
ID20F Break	DLF	4cyl	1985cc	103bhp	10/68–9/71
ID20F Break	DLF	4cyl	1985cc	108bhp	10/71–4/75
ID20F Familiale	DLF	4cyl	1985cc	103bhp	10/68–9/71
ID20F Familiale	DLF	4cyl	1985cc	108bhp	10/71–9/73
ID20FH Break	DYF	4cyl	1985cc	103bhp	10/68–9/71
ID20FH Break	DYF	4cyl	1985cc	108bhp	10/71–9/72
ID20FH Familiale	DYF	4cyl	1985cc	103bhp	10/68–9/71
ID20FH Familiale	DYF	4cyl	1885cc	108bhp	10/68–9/72
DS23F Break	FF	4cyl	2347cc	124bhp	10/72–4/75
DS23F Familiale	FF	4cyl	2347cc	124bhp	10/72–9/74
DS23FH Break	FF	4cyl	2347cc	124bhp	10/72–4/75
DS23FH Familiale	FF	4cyl	2347cc	124bhp	10/72–9/74

Note: For marketing purposes, from September 1973 on, all vehicles in the D series were referred to as DS models (i.e., DS23 & DS20 Break). All models had manual transmission except FH types which had semi-automatic transmission.

11—The DS/ID Cabriolet Decapotable Usine

DS19 Cabriolet	hyd	DS	4cyl	1911cc	75bhp	2/61–3/62
ID19 Cabriolet	man	DM	4cyl	1911cc	66bhp	7/61–3/62
DS19 Cabriolet	hyd	DS	4cyl	1911cc	83bhp	3/62–9/65
ID19 Cabriolet	man	DM	4cyl	1911cc	83bhp	3/62–9/65
DS21 Cabriolet	hyd	DX	4cyl	2175cc	109bhp	10/65–9/71
DS21 Cabriolet	man	DX	4cyl	2175cc	109bhp	10/65–9/71
DS21 EFI Cab.	hyd	FA	4cyl	2175cc	139bhp	10/69–9/71
DS21 EFI Cab.	man	FA	4cyl	2175cc	139bhp	10/69–9/71

12—The Ami 6 and Ami 8 Models

Model	Ami 6 & Ami 8
Currency	1961–1979
Engine	Two-cylinder, horizontally opposed, air-cooled
Capacity	602cc
Bore and stroke	74 × 70mm
Valve actuation	pushrod
Compression ratio	6.2:1
Carburetors	Single choke Solex 30 PBI
Power output	22 bhp SAE @ 4500rpm
Torque	4.0 mkg SAE @ 2500rpm
Transmission	Front wheel drive, 4 speeds & reverse
Suspension	Fully independent by horizontal coil springs, interconnected front to rear
Steering	Rack & pinion
Brakes	Conventional hydraulic drums all round
Wheels & Tires	Michelin disc 125×380 Michelin X radials
Structure & Bodywork	Four-door body on separate platform chassis
Styles available	Sedan, estate & van

Dimensions (sedan)

Length	3.87m
Wheelbase	2.40m

Track, front	1.26m
Track, rear	1.22m
Width	1.52m
Height	1.49m
Weight	620kg
Performance	Max speed 105 km/h — 65 mph
Numbers built Ami 6 & Ami 8 combined)	1,809,910

Evolution

Ami-6 Berline	AM	2cyl	602cc	22bhp	5/61–9/63
Ami-6 Berline	AM	2cyl	602cc	22.5bhp	9/63–9/67
Ami-6 Break	AMB	2cyl	602cc	28bhp	9/64–5/68
Ami-6 Berline	AM2	2cyl	602cc	35bhp	5/68–3/69
Ami-6 Break	AMB2	2cyl	602cc	35bhp	5/68–7/69
Ami-8 Berline	AM3	2cyl	602cc	35bhp	3/69–9/78
Ami-8 Break	AMB3	2cyl	602cc	35bhp	7/69–9/79
Also:					
Ami-Super Berline	AM/JF	4cyl	1015cc	61bhp	1/73–7/76
Ami-Super Break	AM/JG	4cyl	1015cc	61bhp	1/73–7/76

13—The GS and GSA Models

Model	GS & GSA and derivatives
Currency	1970–1987
Engine	Four-cylinder, horizontally opposed water-cooled
Capacity	1015cc / 1129cc (GS) 1220cc / 1299cc (GSA)
Bore and stroke	74 × 59mm, 74 × 65.6mm, 77 × 5.6mm, 79.4 × 65.6mm
Valve actuation	OHC, belt driven
Compression ratio	9.0:1 (1015cc & 1200cc) 8.7:1 (1299cc)
Carburetors	Twin choke Solex
Power output	55.5bhp DIN @ 6500 pm (1015cc) 60 bhp DIN @ 6750rpm (1220cc) 65 bhp DIN @ 5500rpm (1299cc)
Torque	52lb ft @ 3250rpm (1015cc) 72lb ft @ 3500rpm (1220cc)
Transmission	Front wheel drive — manual gearbox, 4 speeds & reverse C-Matic semi-auto optional
Suspension	Hydro-pneumatic, self-levelling
Steering	Manual rack & pinion
Brakes	Fully-powered, discs front and rear
Wheels & Tires	Michelin steel disc Michelin X and ZX radial 145×15
Structure & Bodywork	Four door monocoque
Styles available	sedan, estate, van

Dimensions (GS sedan)

Length	4.12m
Wheelbase	2.55m
Track, front	1.38m
Track, rear	1.33m
Width	1.61m
Height	1.35m
Weight	880kg
Performance	Max speed 147 km/h (GS) 91 mph Max speed 160 km/h (GSA) 100 mph
Numbers built	1,874,754 (GS) 565,009 (GSA)

Evolution

GS Berline	4cyl	1015cc	55.5bhp	10/70–8/72
GS Break	4cyl	1015cc	55.5bhp	9/71–8/77
GS-1220 Berline	4cyl	1222cc	60bhp	9/72–8/79
GS-1220 Break	4cyl	1222cc	60bhp	9/72–8/79
GS Berline Special	4cyl	1015cc	55bhp	9/73–8/77
GS-1220 Pallas	4cyl	1222cc	60bhp	10/73–8/79
GZ Birotor	–	1990cc	107bhp	10/73–1/75
GS-X1 Berline	4cyl	1015cc	55bhp	10/74–8/79
GS-X2 Berline	4cyl	1222cc	60bhp	10/74–8/78
GS-X3 Berline	4cyl	1299cc	65bhp	9/78–8/79
G-Special Berline	4cyl	1129cc	56bhp	9/78–8/82
G-Special Break	4cyl	1129cc	56bhp	9/78–8/82
GSA Berline Club	4cyl	1299cc	65bhp	9/79–8/82
GSA Break Club	4cyl	1299cc	65bhp	9/79–8/82
GSA Pallas	4cyl	1299cc	65bhp	9/79–8/86
GSA-X1 Berline	4cyl	1299cc	65bhp	9/82–8/86
GSA-X3 Berline	4cyl	1299cc	65bhp	9/79–8/86
GSA Berline Special	4cyl	1299cc	65bhp	9/82–8/86
GSA Break Special	4cyl	1299cc	65bhp	9/82–8/86

14—The SM Models

Model	Citroën Maserati SM
Currency	1970–1975
Engine	V-6 cylinder, water-cooled
Capacity	2670cc / 2965cc
Bore and stroke	87 × 85mm / 91.6mm 75mm
Valve actuation	Double OHC
Compression ratio	9.0:1
Carburetors	3 double-choke Weber carbs / Bosch fuel injection
Power output	170 bhp DIN @ 5500rpm (carb) 178 bhp DIN @ 5500rpm (efi) 180 bhp DIN @ 5500rpm (3-litre)
Torque	164lb ft @ 4000 rpm (2.7 litre)
Transmission	Front wheel drive — manual gearbox 5 speeds & reverse
Suspension	Fully independent. hydropneumatic, self-leveling
Steering	Fully powered rack & pinion with Varipower (DIRAVI) action
Brakes	Fully powered, discs all round
Wheels & Tires	Michelin steel disc or carbon fibre Michelin VRX radials 195/70×15
Structure & Bodywork	Two-door monocoque
Styles available	Four seater sports coupe only

Dimensions

Length	4.89m
Wheelbase	2.95m
Track, front	1.53m
Track, rear	1.33m
Width	1.84m
Height	1.32m
Weight	1450kg
Performance	Max speed 220 km/h — 137mph
Numbers built	12,920

Evolution

SM-SB (Manual/Carb)	6cyl	2670cc	180bhp	3/70–6/72
SM-SC (Manual/EFI)	6cyl	2670cc	178bhp	7/72–7/75
SM-SD (Auto/Carb)	6cyl	2965cc	180bhp	10/72–1/75

15—The CX Models

Models	CX2000 and derivatives
Currency	1957–1975
Engine	Four-cylinder, water-cooled
Capacity	1985cc (CX-2000)
Bore and stroke	86 × 85.5mm
Valve actuation	pushrod
Compression ratio	9.2:1
Carburetors	Double choke Weber
Power output	102bhp DIN @ 5500rpm
Torque	122 lb/ft @ 3250 rpm
Transmission	Front wheel drive—manual gearbox 4 speeds & reverse
Suspension	Fully independent, hydro-pneumatic, self-leveling
Steering	Manual rack & pinion, later fully-powered with Vari-power
Brakes	Fully-powered, discs all-round
Wheels & Tires	Michelin disc Michelin ZX 185SR-14 front Michelin ZX 175SR-14 rear
Structure & Bodywork	Four-door monocoque mounted on subframes linked by longerons
Styles available	sedan, estate, familiale, commerciale & ambulance

Dimensions (sedan)

Length	4.63m
Wheelbase	2.84.5m
Track, front	1.47m
Track, rear	1.36m
Width	1.73m
Height	1.36m
Weight	1265kg

Performance (CX 2000)	Max speed 179km/h 111 mph
Numbers built (sedans)	1,041,560

Evolution (sedans & estates)

CX 2000 Berline	4cyl	1985cc	102bhp	9/74–8/79
CX 2000 Break	4cyl	1985cc	102bhp	9/75–8/79
CX 2200 Berline	4cyl	2175cc	112bhp	9/75–8/78
CX 2200 Break	4cyl	2175cc	112bhp	9/75–8/78
CX 2200 Diesel Berline	4cyl	2175cc	66bhp	9/75–8/77
CX 2200 Diesel Break	4cyl	2175cc	66bhp	9/75–8/77
CX 2400 Berline	4cyl	2347cc	120bhp	9/76–6/82
CX 2400 Break	4cyl	2347cc	120bhp	9/76–6/81
CX 2400 GTI Berline	4cyl	2347cc	128bhp	9/76–6/83
CX 2500 Diesel Berline	4cyl	2500cc	75bhp	9/77–6/89
CX 2500 Diesel Break	4cyl	2500cc	75bhp	9/77–6/91
CX Reflex Berline	4cyl	1995cc	106bhp	7/79–6/82
CX Athena Berline	4cyl	1995cc	106bhp	7/79–6/82
CX Reflex Break	4cyl	1995cc	106bhp	7/80–6/82
CX-20 Berline	4cyl	1995cc	106bhp	7/82–6/89
CX-20 Break	4cyl	1995cc	106bhp	7/82–6/87
CX-25 Diesel Turbo Bn.	4cyl	2500cc	95bhp	7/83–6/86
CX-25 Diesel Turbo Bk.	4cyl	2500cc	95bhp	7/83–6/86
CX-25IE Berline	4cyl	2500cc	138bhp	7/83–6/87
CX-25IE Break	4cyl	2500cc	138bhp	7/83–6/87
CX-25 GTI Berline	4cyl	2500cc	138bhp	7/83–6/89
CX-25 GTI Turbo Berline	4cyl	2500cc	168bhp	7/84–6/86
CX-22 Berline	4cyl	2165cc	115bhp	7/85–6/89
CX-25 Diesel Turbo-2 Bn.	4cyl	2500cc	120bhp	7/86–6/89
CX-25 Diesel Turbo-2 Bk.	4cyl	2500cc	120bhp	7/86–6/91
CX-25 GTI Turbo-2 Bn.	4cyl	2500cc	168bhp	7/86–6/89

Bibliography

Bellu, Rene. *Toutes les Citroën*. Paris: Editions Delville, 1957.

Borge, Jacques, and Nicolas Viasnoff. *La Traction*. Paris: Balland, 1975.

_____, and _____. *La 2CV*. Paris: Balland, 1977.

_____, and _____. *L'Album de la DS*. Paris: EPA, 1983.

_____, and _____. *L'Album de la Traction*. Paris: EPA, 1983.

Brioult, Roger. *Citroën: l'Histoire et les Secrets de son Bureau d'Etudes*. Fontainebleau: Edifree, 1987.

Broustail, Joel, and Rudolphe Grigio. *Citroën: Essai sur 80 Ans d'Antistrategie*. Paris: Librairie Vuibert, 2000.

Citroën, Bernard. *La Conjuration de Javel*. Paris: Nouvelles Editions Latinees, 1996.

Colin, Marc-Antoine. *La Citroën CX de Mon Pére*. Paris: ETAI, 2000.

Collignon, Jerome. *Le Guide Traction Avant*. Paris: ETAI, 2001.

Daniels, Jeff. *Citroën SM*. London: Osprey, 1981.

_____, and Maurice Sauzay: *Citroën SM*. Paris: ETAI, 1982.

Darmon, Olivier. *Le Grand Siecle de Bibendum*. Paris: Hoebeke, 1997.

Demetz, Antoine: *La Citroën 2CV de Mon Pére*. Paris: ETAI, 1998.

_____. *La Traction Avant de Mon Pére*. Paris: ETAI, 2000.

Dumont, Pierre. *Quai de Javel, Quai André Citroën*. Paris: EPA, 1973.

Gregoire, Jean-Albert. *Cinquante Ans d'Automobile*. Paris: Flammarion, 1974.

Hemar, Christine. *André Citroën*. Paris: Hatier, 2002.

Jemain, Alain. *Michelin: Un Siècle de Secrets*. Paris: Calmann-Levy, 1982.

Lottman, Herbert. *The Michelin Men*. London: I.B. Tauris, 2003.

Norbye, Jan P. *Michelin Magic*. Tab Books, 1982.

Pressnell, Jon. *Citroën DS: The Complete Story*. Crowood Press, 1999.

Reiner, Sylvain. *La Tragedie de André Citroën*. Amiot Dumont, 1954.

Reynolds, John. *André Citroën: The Man and the Motorcars*. Sutton Publishing, 1996.

_____. *Citroën: Daring to Be Different*. Haynes Publishing, 2004.

_____. *The Citroën 2CV*. Sutton Publishing, 2001.

_____. *Eighty Years of Citroën in the UK*. Dalton Watson Fine Books, 2004.

_____, and Jan de Lange. *Original Citroën DS*. Bay View Books, 1996.

_____, and Paul Niblett. *Michelin Centenary 1905–2005*. Michelin Travel Publications, 2005.

Rocherand, Charles. *André Citroën: Souvenir d'une Collaboration*. Paris: Editions Lajeunesse, 1938.

Sabates, Fabien: *L'Album de la 2CV*. Paris: EPA, 1992.

_____. *Moi, Citroën*. Paris: Editions du Retroviseur, 1994.

_____, and Leonardo Bertoni. *Flaminio Bertoni: 30 Ans de Style Citroën*. Paris: ETAI, 1998.

_____, and Wouter Jansen. *Le Citroën Type H*. Editions Massin, 1992.

_____, and Wouter Jansen. *Le Citroën Type H de Mon Père*. Paris: ETAI, 2000.

_____, and Sylvie Schweizer. *André Citroën: Les Chevrons de la Gloire*. Paris: EPA, 1980.

de Serres, Olivier. *Citroën: Tous les Modeles*. Paris: EPA, 1988.

_____. *La Citroën SM*. Paris: ETAI, 1998.

_____. *Le Grand Livre Citroën DS*. Paris: EPA, 1992.

_____. *Le Grand Livre Traction Avant*. Paris: EPA, 1993.

Seguella, Jacques. *Quatre Vingt Ans de Publicitée Citroën*. Paris: Hoebeke, 1999.

Wolgensinger, Jacques. *André Citroën*. Paris: Flamarion, 1991.

_____. *La 2CV: Nous nous sommes tant aimées*. Paris: Gallimard, 1995.

Wood, Jonathan. *The Citroën*. Shire Publications, 2003.

Index